The System of Symbols

A new way to look at Tarot

By

Toni Allen

All material copyright Toni Allen ©

Toni Allen
The System of Symbols ©

All rights reserved. No part of this publication can be reproduced, stored in a retrieval system, or transmitted in any form or by any means, electronic, mechanical, photocopying, recording or otherwise, without the prior permission of the publishers and/or authors.

While every precaution has been taken in the preparation of this book, the publisher assumes no responsibilities for errors or omissions, or for damages resulting from the use of information contained herein.

Copyright © 2003 by Toni Allen. All rights reserved.

Toni Allen
The System of Symbols ©

Contents

Introduction	4
Numbers	5
Creating a Reading	16
The Cards	22
The Major Cards	24
The Minor Cards	169
Court Cards	356
The End	415

Toni Allen
The System of Symbols ©

Introduction

The method I use to explain the pure meaning of each card offers great insight into the laws of nature, and karma. These elements can be used and integrated in a reading, or employed for meditation. With each card I am explaining how one arrives at a pure, esoteric, meaning of the card through its number and symbolism, and then incorporating how this might be interpreted in practice.

In a reading it is impossible for a card to stand-alone. Each card is like a chameleon, influenced and coloured by the cards that surround it. Therefore, when interpreting a card for the purpose of divination, there is no absolute definition. The very art of card reading makes that a fallacy.

There is little or no value in a student of Tarot learning 78 interpretations by rote. Without a deeper understanding of the meaning of numbers and symbols there is no chance that anyone will be able to synthesise a reading and offer anything of substance to a client. However, the art of blending the interpretation of one card with the one next to it is easy when one comprehends the rhythms and cycles present in the universe. We are not separate but part of a much larger whole. Likewise, each card has its own individual identity, and yet is part of a greater system; thus reflecting us in all aspects.

I hope that this volume will add insight for all those who seek a greater understanding of why the Tarot Cards have the interpretations they do. By no means do I intend this to be a cook book of stock phrases to use off pat, but something more enduring, to be dipped into as a perpetual source of renewed inspiration and stimulation.

Toni Allen
The System of Symbols ©

Numbers

There are 78 Tarot Cards. The pack consists of 22 Major Cards, often referred to as Major Arcana, the word arcana meaning secret or mystery; 40 Minor Cards and 16 Court Cards. The Minor Cards and Court Cards are much the same as we find in contemporary playing cards being that they consist of pip cards and picture cards.

For 78 cards we have 78 interpretations. Upon being told this fact the first sound which usually emits from a new student's mouth is a great sigh of exhaustion, as if they're worn out before they've even started. 78 interpretations...wow, that's a lot to remember! Yes, there are 78 cards, but there are only 9 numbers to learn, from which the interpretations arise.

I use Vedic numerology, in which the limit of numbers is 9. All other numbers come from the numbers 1 to 9. So in truth the meaning of only 9 numbers has to be learnt. Once these meanings are grasped everything else is incredibly easy. The Tarot fits perfectly with Vedic numerology and the symbolism of the cards is an extra pictorial reference point to guide the divinator.

The 9 numbers are set around a circle, as illustrated in fig. 1, and throughout the following chapters I shall continue to refer to the meanings of both the numbers and their position on the circle.

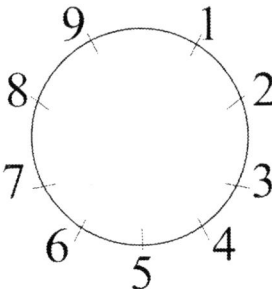

fig. 1

The Circles and Cycles of the Tarot

This Circle of 9 points runs from 1 to 9 and from 9 to 1, as illustrated in

Toni Allen
The System of Symbols ©

figures 2 and 3. The number 10 is created from the number 1 and the number 0. With the two directions of the circle we therefore have an outward movement from number 1 to 9 and a backward movement from number 9 to 1. When these numbers are related to specific cards we will be able to discern, during a reading, whether the questioner is moving forwards in a particular situation, or retracing their steps.

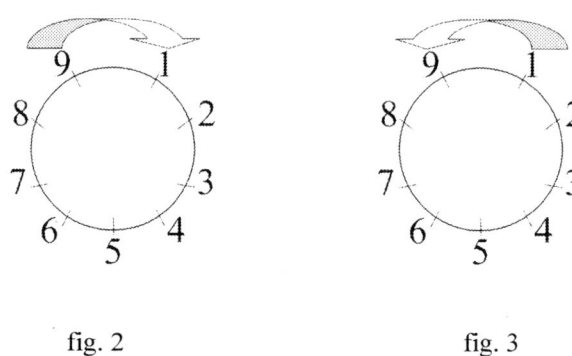

fig. 2   fig. 3

The Two Layers, or Cycles, of the Tarot

Using our circle of 9 points we find that in the Tarot there are two cycles from 1 to 10.
The first cycle runs through The Magician (1), The High Priestess (2), The Empress (3), The Emperor (4), The Pope, The Lovers (6), The Chariot (7), Justice (8), The Hermit (9) and The Wheel of Fortune (10).

As the limit of numbers is 9, on the first cycle the Wheel of Fortune connects with the number 0 and the number 1, symbolising the end of one cycle and the entry into another.

All of the cards on the first cycle symbolise pure, untainted action. They sit at the causal level. In a reading (when upright) they show that we have either overcome a problem, and therefore cleansed ourselves of Karma, or that this is an area of ourselves which does not require work to be done on it at the present time.

The second cycle from 11 to 20 runs through, Strength (11), The Hanged Man (12), Death (13), Temperance (14), The Devil (15), The Tower (16), The Star (17) The Moon (18), The Sun (19) and The Judgement (20).

This second cycle is in fact also running from 1 to 10, but on a different level. These cards symbolise tainted actions that bind us in karma. The seeds of past actions create doubt, fear and uncertainty, when life's lessons have not been learnt. We are always presented with an appropriate opportunity to deal with these inner sufferings, so that we may rise up and out of the bondage of karma. The cards on this second cycle reveal to us the areas where we need to do work on ourselves, and therefore help us deal with life's more difficult problems by offering insight. If we fail to learn their lessons then we easily fall into a grosser level of consciousness and experience our own Hell on Earth.

Card number 21, The Judgement, is not only unique but also quite wonderful. It comes after the end of the second cycle and symbolises the release from karma, the realisation of the truth and the ability to be free of long standing karmic influence.

In practice during a reading you will find that the questioner has cards from both cycles. This is perfectly natural. All of us have different areas of strengths and weakness, some of which change depending on circumstances or other outside influences e.g. A man may have the Emperor (4) symbolising himself as a good, hard working owner of a company, but also have the Moon (18) in connection with his home life, showing that he is uncertain of his role within the family and fearful of losing control when in his wife's domain at home.

We will continue to look at rhythms and cycles as we progress. This is a basic starting point, and as long as these fundamental truths are understood then everything else falls into place.

The Overturned Circle

Not only do we have the Tarot running on two interchangeable levels, but also on what I call the overturned circle.

Draw a circle on a piece of paper and place our 9 numbers on it. Then cut it out and fold it in half along a line drawn from top to bottom. You will find that 9 overlays 1, 8 overlays 2, 7 overlays 3 and 6 overlays 4. 5 sits on its own as a pivot point. This inter-relation between the numbers is what I call the overturned circle.

Toni Allen
The System of Symbols ©

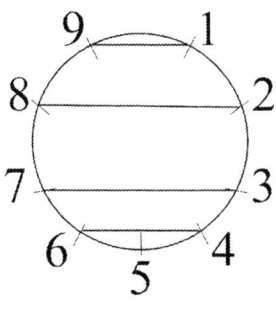

fig. 4

The numbers which overlay each other are linked in that 2 can become 8 and vice versa; and so on around the circle. As you continue to study the major cards this concept will become more apparent and easy to understand.

It is from this simple swinging backwards and forwards and round and round, that, using the deeper meanings of the cards, we can find the patterns of an individual's life. The minor cards show us daily occurrences, and with practice the trained eye will easily pick out the underlying rhythms. The reader can then accurately predict how the questioner will act and react to any given circumstance.

The Numbers

The following is a brief outline of the meaning of each number. Don't worry if you can't memorise every detail immediately. These concepts form the basis and structure of all of my interpretations and will be cross-referenced and expanded upon in greater detail throughout the following chapters.

The Number 1

Number 1 represents the absolute, the whole. Creation unfolds itself to 9 and then, when we have seen all 9 stages of manifestation, it reunites itself at 1. Everything is contained within 1. Everything ultimately returns there.

The Number 2

The number 2 symbolises duality. The absolute and the non absolute. The self and the ego. It is the opposite or compliment to 1. By itself it is passive, but becomes productive when fecundated by the active.

The number 2 is also the unmanifest. The unmanifest is the bank or store room where all things and forms lie hidden and manifest when the time calls. Just as one collects all things in a store and uses them when need arises, in the same way, all the multifarious forms of the universe lie stored in the unmanifest before creation breaks out; and are also absorbed in it when the creation is withdrawn.

The Number 3

3 is the number of first manifestation. What has come from the unity of 1 through the duality of 2 is manifest at 3.

3 represents nature. It is the matrix which sets the direction of the creation in a general way and the conduct or behaviour of the individual in a special way.

If the nature of a person is good then it leads him, (or her) towards the pleasures of heaven or advancement in a material way; and if it is bad, then one meets misery, pain and destruction.

Discrimination (The Lovers Card) takes one above nature and the individual is freed from the pleasures of heaven and the pains of hell.

Nature is divided into 3 parts. In Sanskrit these 3 parts are known as the 3 *gunas*. All nature is governed by them. The 3 gunas are sattva, rajas and tamas.

Sattva means:- Law, reality, purity...the highest of the 3 gunas. Sattvic nature allows growth of reason and discrimination, thus taking one over the duality of good and bad.

Rajas means:- passion, desire, energy...the second of the 3 gunas. In the rajasika nature we have the active world and the efficient activity which accounts for work of an artistic nature.

Tamas means:- darkness, ignorance, inertia...the lowest of the 3 gunas. Tamasika nature gets people into the habit of taking drugs and engaging in violent and deceitful activity.

The 3 gunas are very important. They govern all creation. As we proceed we will learn more about the different qualities of the gunas and how they can be observed in practice.

The Number 4

The number 4 relates to the feeling of I. Consciousness.

On our overturned circle the number 4 corresponds to the number 6. Later you will hear about the number 6 in more detail, but for now it is enough to know that the number 6 comes at the stage of air. It is air which holds all physical forms together, because once the vital air passes away from the body it starts to disintegrate.

In Sanskrit at the number 4 sits Mahat:- great soul; or ahamkara (*aham* I *kara* maker) ; meaning Self-will, the ego mask, the principle in man which makes him feel separate from others. Because these qualities sit at the number 6, as seen by our overturned circle, they also collect and hold everything that seems to belong to it in the feeling of I.

Thus the number 4 gives the impression of permanence, stability and a foundation quality. Here the 3 gunas are operating on a firm base. These 3 forces embodied at number 3 and the Empress have to be felt by something which is conscious. All the machines in the world are somewhere connected to a conscious being otherwise they cannot be regulated to proper use.

The Number 5

Number 5 relates to the Akasha. (sometimes referred to as the akashic records or etheric level)

On our overturned circle the number 5 falls in the middle from both sides. On the one side is the coarse physical world which can be subject to sense observation, and on the other side is the world of subtle and causal nature.

When the causal and subtle world is transformed into the coarse world, then it is done through the akasha, which connects both. It is like a transformer which changes one type of energy into another, or like an interpreter who makes obvious the ideas framed in an unknown language. It must have the qualities of both sides otherwise no communication would be possible.

Akasha gives way to all physical forms and it is only due to the akasha that the physical world has found manifestation. It stands as a bridge and joins the sensual world to the mental and causal world.

Anyone who practices meditation will recognise these qualities held within the akasha. When meditating we fall still, rest the mind and experience the deep silence of the akasha from which all creation is formed. This is how, after meditating, we find ourselves refreshed and given insight into current problems. Having connected with the causal level answers come which might not ordinarily have been seen.

The akasha carries sound, the most subtle of the 5 senses.

"In the beginning was the word."

The Number 6

Air sits at number 6. In Sanskrit the air is called prana:-breath of life, vital energy, capacity to desire and love.

Hand is the organ through which the force within can be expressed. Hand is also the seat of air which holds things, catches and throws them. The pranas are vital energy; they make or keep us alive, discharge polluted air, regulate the digestive process, keep the body in balance and also regulate involuntary movements within the body.

With air we therefore also have the sense of touch.

****

We begin to see how the numbers 3, 4 and 6 interrelate. The nature at 3 is given stability and a sense of being at 4. Once it has passed through the akasha at 5 it is given the breath of life at 6.

In terms of the Tarot, air is connected with the mind and reasoning.

We already know that 6 overlays with 4 and that at 4 sits the ahamkara, or self will. At 6 we therefore deal with the question of what an individual is going to do with that self-will, is he (or she) going to be wilful or willing. Hence the Lovers Card (6) talks of discrimination, and choice; not between one lover and another, but between the truth and the untruth; towards the repeated bondage of karma, or towards action which will break the cycle.

The Number 7

The number 7 comes in the realm of Tejas, the fire, light or glory which shines through the human being and makes up his stature, his brilliance, his light of knowledge and the heat which keeps everything moving.

On our overturned circle we will see that the number 7 relates to the number 3. At 3 we saw the Empress depicting the potential nature of a person, while at 7 we find the pattern of creation, or of the individual, fixed.

Nature is made up of the 3 gunas, sattva, rajas and Tamas. In Tejas we also find the 3 gunas manifesting as Sattvika, Rajasika and Tamasika.

Sattvika Tejas is the light of knowledge.

Rajasika Tejas is the celestial lights such as the light of the sun, moon, stars and lightning.

Tamasika Tejas is fire, lamp lights, etc. which we find on Earth.

The sattvika Tejas gives us knowledge.

The Rajasika Tejas gives us energy and the ability to perform practical works.

The Tamasika Tejas gives us bodily heat which keeps us going through days and nights.

The Number 8

Number 8 comes under the realm of water.

On our overturned circle the number 8 relates to the number 2 and the unmanifest. The cycle of creation and dissolution is started and merged in this state when under the realm of 8.

The number 8 is represented by water, which stands for bonds. This holds things together. In the realm of both atomic and other structures it is only the bonds which keep matter together. In both cases number 8 acts as the store which keeps all things together, and also as the bond which keeps them together on universal and individual levels.

Sugar is seen in crystal form, and when diluted in water it dissolves in such a way that nothing is seen of the crystal. The same substance, when heated, once again forms the bond and a crystal is created. Similarly the elemental particles of the universe come out of water and hold together. If there was no bond between the particles, the particles would disintegrate and disperse in space. The world of form is produced by particles only because the bonds of water hold them together.

This is also threefold. The store of the unmanifest, in which millions of universes are involved and out of which the substances are poured to form different universes, and in time these substances again return to it. The second store is that of the Brahma, who is the presiding deity of one single universe (God), and through which the multifarious forms of this world find their way in appointed time and go back to unity. The third is the store of the individual who manifests differently through the store of sanskaras*, and once again forms them for his next life.

[* Sanskara:- A deep mental impression produced by past experiences, a mental or behavioural pattern, latency.
Karma (*kri* to do) Action; former actions which lead to certain results in a cause and effect relationship.]

It is important to understand the full meaning of these Sanskrit words as I shall use them often. They are both pertinent to the number 8, which is why I mention them here in detail.

The mind (chitta) is likened to a blank cinema screen. As we project the film of life onto it we experience colours, pictures, etc.. When man is perfect there is no residue left on this screen after each action or experience. With imperfect men, such as ourselves, who have not yet obtained enlightenment, life's passage leaves the chitta, or mind, tainted, and it is these deep mental impressions and behavioural patterns which are known as Sanskara. Note how even the new born child has its own character right from birth, its own unique behavioural pattern. This is due to the individual's Sanskara which it has accumulated from life time to life time.

Karma, being action which will lead us to certain results in a cause and effect relationship, gives us the opportunity and right circumstances in which to deal with our personal Sanskara. In this way we can cleans the chitta and attain enlightenment.

Both Karma and Sanskara are binding, which is why they are pertinent to the number 8.

The element of water is the element of bond; and it is only the bonds which create limitation. Due to bonds all the shapes of the universe have their existence, and all shapes create a limit or boundary through which particular types of bond are working. With the end of the bond comes the end of the limit. The whole universe is thus distributed in different types of limit. Consciousness permeates and experiences the universe through these bonds and boundaries. The observer (watchman within each individual) looks at these, and when he associates himself with any of these big or small boundaries, he establishes duality. Thus bonds create duality (number 2).

The misery of our human race is only due to these different types of bonds with which he associates.

The first physical association of I is with the body, which is the smallest limit.

Duality creates separateness.

****

There are 3 states of water. The first is the universal water out of which the oceans are created. The water of the River Ganges is said to be Sattvika because it never gets polluted under any circumstances. The second is the water in the atmosphere which, stored as cloud, reaches us through rivers and rains, and is in daily use in drinking, irrigation, etc. The third is Tamasika water which is polluted and not fit for use.
From these last truths we might say that we live in the Tamasika age. We pollute our atmosphere and thus our rivers and life giving water to such a degree that often it is no longer fit for consumption.

The Number 9

Number 9 relates the the element earth.

On our overturned circle the number 9 relates to the number 1 and unity.

Earth is where physical phenomena has matured in full glory. This is the perfect physical form. The physical phenomena of the coarse world (as we see it) start from number 5 (ether). The ether is the transformer of the subtle energy into physical energy. It has the quality of both the subtle and the physical. The physical aspect of ether is sound. It comes from space and also manifests in space. Where there is no space there is no sound. Ether alone holds the sound.

Then comes air (6). Air gives the sensation of touch and can also carry sound. Thus it has two qualities. Third is Tejas (fire-7) which has 3 qualities within itself; the heat and light from its own form, touch of air and sound of ether. 4th is the realm of water, which has taste and bonds of its own, the heat and form of fire, touch of air and sound of ether. Thus it reflects 4 qualities. The last of the physical world is earth, which is the perfect medium to reflect all 5 qualities. It has the smell and crystalline form of its own, the taste and bond of water, heat and form of fire, touch of air and sound of ether.

In earth all these sensations are possible, but this does not mean that in ether there is no heat or touch. They are all there, but ether only manifests sound. They lie there unmanifest and only manifest according to the system described above.

Thus the element earth is the glorious end of 1 cycle, where the absolute (unity-1) stands as the glorious beginning on the other side. The element earth is glorious because it is only through earth that all things of the world are created. Man, birds, plants etc., are all created from earth.

The Number Naught (Zero)

The easiest way to relate to the number, or more exactly, the non number of zero, is to look at it as the circle on which all the other numbers sit.

Zero is the great unmanifest consciousness from which everything is created.

Zero is also the consciousness to which everything returns.

9 is the limit of numbers. At 10 we find the individual consciousness of 1 next to the unmanifest consciousness of the whole.

10 is 1 and 0.

Zero contains all of the other numbers, whether we are going out from 1 to 10 and reaching fulfilment, or returning from 10 to 1 to find the source.

As we look more closely at cycles we will learn how important the circle is. Life does not progress in a straight line. It is constantly made up of new beginnings, and endings, which overlap. All of these *new* beginnings and endings relate to zero.

Toni Allen
The System of Symbols ©

Creating a Reading

According to my dictionary a system is "anything formed of parts placed together, or adjusted, into a regular and connected whole...a set of things considered a connected whole".

The Tarot is a system in as much as it is an entire unit made up of 78 separate images, which make up a connected whole. We also have to consider the synthesis of the parts and how they work when placed together. For this we require a platform from which they can function, some kind of device that has consistency, yet is fluid and malleable enough to encompass ever changing possibilities. To this end a "spread" of cards is designed, each position representing a particular facet of operation, or situation in the questioner's life. The cards are subsequently interpreted in accordance with their respective positions.

Many traditional spreads have come down to us through history, such as the nine card spread or Celtic cross, the horseshoe, and the circle or astrological wheel, in which cards are placed in correspondence to the houses of the zodiac.

Personally I find all of these spreads limiting, simply because they have a set number of cards used for each and every reading. Life has many permutations and each individual who sits down in front of me for a reading is unique, with specific questions to ask and their own particular karma to address. For these reasons I devised a spread which has strong guidelines for use and yet holds infinite potential for personal growth and expansion. It is up to each student to explore the variations available and shape the spread to suit their client's requirements.

First the shuffle

There is much ritual written and expressed about the keeping of Tarot Cards and the shuffling and cutting of the cards in preparation for a reading. Although I have many packs, which I use for teaching purposes, I keep one pack especially for readings. Some people say that Tarot Cards should be wrapped in silk to protect them from negative vibrations, or perhaps kept safe and sacred in a wooden box. Each to their own, nothing is right and nothing is wrong. Mine are kept in the same cardboard box they came in, their protection....respect. They are only taken from their box to be used for a reading. They are kept shuffled in a mixture of upright and reversed, and *never* stacked in order for teaching purposes. I do not let students handle them for study; or take them to lectures or workshops, where they might become "sorted". I call them my "working pack".

I do not start a reading until my client and I are sitting comfortably, opposite each other across a low table. I take the cards and shuffle them while asking the client if there is any specific reason why they have felt the need for a reading. They do not have to give a specific answer, a simple "yes" they have a problem, or "no" they've never had a reading before and have come out of interest, will suffice. I then hand the client the cards and request they shuffle them. When they have finished I ask the client to place the cards on the table and cut them with their left hand. I then ask the client to place the bottom part of the pack on the top and hand them to me. The reason for asking the client to pass me the cards is that if they put them on the table and I pick them up then I am making a decision about which way round the pack is used. This crucial determination must remain with the client. It's useful to practice both disciplines initially to see what occurs. For example, let clients place the pack on the table and see just how many lay it sideways on, unable to make a decision about which should be its top or tail. Then investigate asking clients to pass you the pack, and watch just how many people unconsciously turn the pack around 180 degrees, so that the end initially facing you is now facing away.

The Initial Spread

Once the shuffle and cut are complete it is time to lay out the first six cards of the spread. I start by placing them face down, then explain the meaning of their positions before turning over only the first five cards to start with. See fig 5.

Positions 1 & 2

These cards sit in the centre of a downward axis representing the present time in the questioner's life. I call them "the central pivot point" of the current situation. Card number 2 crosses card number 1 and by its symbolism will indicate whether it is helping or hindering something at the core, or heart, of the situation.

Position 3

This card also sits on the axis of the present time and represents "the mind"; which includes thoughts, aspirations and desires. It quite simply suggests what is on the questioner's mind and might additionally indicate what they would like to happen, or intend to happen.

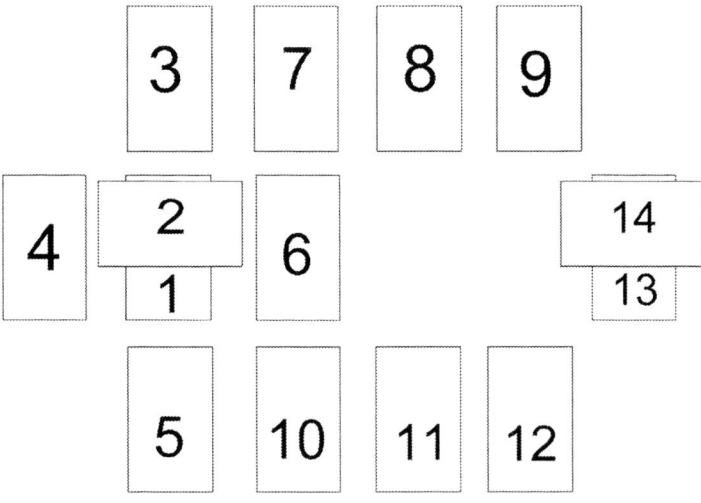

Fig 5

Position 5

Again on the line of the present time, but this time representing the "physical world", that which is manifest, or happening in the questioner's life.

Position 4

This card represents "the past", but it is that part of the past which has helped create today. We are working in the realms of cause and effect, where every action has a reaction somewhere in the future. This card of "the past", can therefore indicate the cause behind current circumstances, early conditioning or obstacles which have been overcome. On occasions it indicates residue from previous incarnations which has created present life karma.

Once the questioner has recognised that these initial five cards are relating to their life and personal circumstances I turn over card number 6.

Position 6

This card represents "the next step in the future".
I then take cards from the top of the pack and place them in positions 7 to 12.

Positions 7 to 9

These cards sit on the top line and continue to represent "the mind", and the clients thoughts and wishes on the problem as the future unfolds.

Positions 10 to 12

Likewise these cards sit on the bottom line and continue to represent "the physical world", and what happens as the reading unfolds in the future.

I then take cards 13 and 14 from the top of the pack.

Positions 13 and 14

Cards 13 and 14 continue to represent the future unfolding, the base card once again either being helped or hindered by the actions of the top card.

Once these cards are laid I spread the entire pack out, face down, and ask the questioner to take further cards, to either add information to what is already there or proceed into the future. At this point cards can be taken in response to questions, either concerning what has already been outlined or other issues.

This spread is fundamentally simple and very easy to use. Practice will bring confidence and show you endless possibilities. Each card will slightly change according to its position in the spread; for example a card depicting sorrow will symbolise hidden sorrow when appearing in the line of "the mind", and open grief when seen on the line of "the physical world". Continue to build upon this theme and you will find that a card showing sorrow in "the mind" might well be directly above a card on the physical level showing happiness. Thus you will be able to deduce that your client is inwardly very unhappy but puts on a smiling face to their family or friends, who probably don't know how unhappy the client really is.

Bach Flower Remedies

Before setting out on a career as a Tarot reader one needs to ask oneself why one is choosing such a path in life. Is it to predict the future? Is it so that one can say "Oh yes, I saw that for them, you know." Is it an unchosen path because one has always been a little psychic since birth? Is it to become mysterious and enigmatic? Or perhaps someone to be feared by others and held in awe? Or is it to help all those who sit in front of you?

People choose to consult a Tarot reader for many, many reasons, but 99% of them have something fundamental in common. They have a problem. Most of my clients consult me during a time of personal crisis, when life has taken a difficult turn and they need someone outside their own lives to talk to. Someone unbiased and willing to listen. For a lot of people the act of deciding to confide in someone else and air their problems is enough to bring about a positive change. Others need more help and support. For this reason I recommend the Bach Flower remedies, a set of Flower essences which work on the cause of a problem rather than they result. There are 39 remedies in the set which cover all known emotional problems from fear, feelings of rejection and anger.

I do not adhere to a specific card relating only to one particular remedy or to assigning each remedy to a card. However, I have found that particular cards suggest that one of the remedies would help my client. For this reason, when appropriate, I have included a note on which remedy suits the card, but this by no means excludes it from being correct with another selection of cards. I have found that suggesting Bach Remedies in connection with a reading offers the client immediate assistance in that they can start to take the remedy to alleviate their condition. Many people already use, or know about the Bach remedies, and so I also often find that to mention which remedy is appropriate offers my client a wealth of further information which they can instinctively relate to.

Offering the Bach remedies helps bring the client to a feeling of wholeness. With the correct remedy a healing can take place very quickly. However, if a serious medical condition is indicated it is appropriate to recommend suitable treatment alongside the remedies. As well as the client's G.P. being a first port of call, I also keep on file the names and telephone numbers of complementary therapists whom I either know or who come as highly recommended.

    A Tarot reading is a whole process. The cards themselves offer information, it is then up to the individual reader as to how they interpret that knowledge and how they choose to guide the client with it. The Bach remedies are one way of offering support and healing.

Toni Allen
The System of Symbols ©

The Cards

I do not intend to go into a lengthy dissertation on the history of the Tarot, or to intentionally endeavour to prove or disprove whether any one depiction of the Major Cards in the Tarot is "better" than another. Undoubtedly, and obviously, I have my own preferences as to which packs I favour, just the same as anyone else.

The Major Cards are archetypal symbols. They belong in the form we see them in the Tarot, and yet they appear in other guises throughout literature and art. Their starting point as images in the Tarot stems back to the Mantegna prints and to hand painted packs such as the Visconti Sforza pack. Their source lies in the symbol creating consciousness of mankind. In his first Encyclopaedia of Tarot Stuart Kaplan outlines a brief history of the Tarot and has pictorial references of most of the packs I refer to throughout my descriptions of the cards. It is valuable source material and a worthwhile addition to the library of any serious student of the Tarot.

I come from the basic stand-point that a "traditional" Tarot pack is a "Marseille" pack (circa 16th century). It's early woodcut images have continuously stood the test of time, and also done much to alter and put into question the exact pictorial rendering of the cards, due to printer error and the limitations of the method of wood cut engraving available at the time.

I also believe that their are only two modern major influences on the Tarot Card images, the Rider Waite pack as illustrated by Pamela Coleman-Smith and the Aleister Crowley pack as illustrated by Lady Freda Harris. These two packs changed the face of Tarot forever, in as much as they "transformed" the minor cards from ordinary pips to symbolic pictures of the cards' meaning. There is hardly a modern artist who has not cribbed their designs in one form or another. One only has to compare the Morgan Greer pack against Waite's to see that Greer has taken "close up" images of Waite's illustrations. I believe that Waite was a master occultist and that to pare down the image he considered symbolised the card's meaning is to omit a large part of the revealing illustration.

There are also the important fact that Waite's cards were initially

Toni Allen
The System of Symbols ©

bootlegged extensively, especially in America, and then the original lithographic plates of the pack were destroyed during the blitz. The cards were subsequently copied from existing packs. Reams and reams of words are written about Waite's symbolic meaning and the intricacies of the artwork. In consequence it's a shock to find that these "intricacies" are additions as perceived by artists copying from the vagaries of printed matter, or adding their own perception.

Crowley's images have survived reasonably intact, and any student who wishes to study them in depth will be well rewarded; although I do not profess to understand, or refer to, his cabalistic teaching, or to fully understand all of his imagery.

Thus, despite it's failings, the Marseille Tarot holds a depth of consistency suitable for study. It is useful to have minor card pictures for study, but during a reading the plethora of images can create confusion and bog down one's own intrinsic symbol making psyche. A Marseille pack has simple pip cards and the rhythm of the numbers alone allows for clear interpretation. Many modern copy packs of the Marseille Cards, such as Marixia Gula's, have been re-coloured to render interest with the addition of a different colour for each suit. This then allows for an easy overview of which suit is in abundance and how the suits are displaced throughout a reading.

Use as many packs as you like for study. After a while you will find that one gets used more frequently because the colours and images strike a chord within you. Do not be afraid to change packs, or feel obliged to use a pack simply because it cost you lots of money. Feel comfortable with whichever pack you choose and it will serve you well.

Toni Allen
The System of Symbols ©

The Major Cards

The Major Cards represent 22 archetypal truths.

Each symbol is perfect within itself. Its intrinsic meaning does not alter and cannot change. In their pure form the images are excellent as vehicles for meditation.

Within a reading the interpretation of the card is modified by the surrounding cards and judgement on the meaning of the card during a reading **must** take into account the cards placed around it.

The following chapters will give you an insight into the cards highest meaning and a taste of the variations apparent when used in divination.

Toni Allen
The System of Symbols ©

The Fool No. 0

The Image

The Fool is depicted walking along, often using a walking stick. He also has a bundle tied to a stick slung across his shoulder. Look closely and you will see that although his left hand holds this stick that it is leaning on his right shoulder. A sign of foolishness? or an anomaly of early card making? With the Fool it is possible that when stencilling the cards a stick originally going behind the head was coloured in a straight line, thus covering the neck, and was then later taken to be a stick held in this awkward manner. Later carvers then cut wood blocks with the design as they thought they saw it. The Jacques Vieville Tarot 1643-1664, made in Paris, has the Fool carrying his stick with its bundle quite sensibly over the

Toni Allen
The System of Symbols ©

same shoulder as the hand in which he holds it.

He is dressed supposedly as a fool, or court jester, although some designs make him look like a simple traveller, while others have him bedecked with baubles and bells.

There is a dog snapping at his heals, which in many cases has ripped his trousers and exposed one buttock.

The stick which carries his bag has a flat, rounded end, like a spoon. In medieval times this is what a shepherd's crosier looked like, before it was completely taken over by the Little Bo Peep type of hook, which we are now so familiar with. The shepherd would place a clod of earth onto the spoon end of the crosier and by lobbing the clod either just in front, or behind the sheep, frighten it into running back to the flock. With the dog at heel too, we arrive at a picture of the shepherd walking home.

Or do we?

In Vieville's pack the stick holding the Fool's bag is definitely a jester's bauble; a long stick with a humorous head carved at one end. It is an historical fact that medieval villagers set their dogs onto passing strangers to shoo them away. Add to this the fact that medieval hose, such as the Fool is wearing, were made as two separate legs and held up by latchets, (a sort of fore runner to braces), with underwear forming the centre part, or cod piece. Now we can see that perhaps the trousers are not ripped, but one side merely released from its latchet. In those days to drop one's trousers was a well known medieval "pooh pooh", probably the equivalent of gesticulating with one raised finger today.

So? is he a man ravaged by the villagers' guard dog, or a traveller saying "up yours"?

The enigma continues when we bear in mind the image of the court jester. His attitudes were open. He was the only man permitted to ridicule the king and was held in the highest favour; often sent to distribute alms to the poor and sharp words all in one breath. The Fool in Shakespeare's King Lear is an excellent example of how the fool proves to be the wisest of them all. By the end of the play one begins to wonder who is mad, the mad fool, or the supposedly rational king.

Even in one of the very earliest Tarot packs, the Visconti-Sforza Tarot, the Fool is depicted as a tattered man with a staff or cudgel. He is a loner, enigmatic; and whether we see him as jester, tramp, or traveller, his independent ways set him apart from the other Major Cards by standing him outside the accepted limitations of society.

Waite chose to depict the Fool in a far more definite manner. Pamela Coleman-Smith drew him as a dreamer, unaware or unperturbed by life's dangers and just about to stroll casually off the edge of a cliff.

In the Golden Dawn Tarot, illustrated by Robert Wang, the Fool is depicted in the throws of folly. Here the fool is a young child, innocent, yet eager to pick the flower from a tree while the wolf, or dog, looks on at his side. So far the wolf is tame, held firmly by a lead; but are the young fool's actions akin to those of Adam in the Garden of Eden? Will his desire unleash the wolf and bring about some dreadful repercussion?

The Number 0

The easiest way to relate to the number, or more exactly, the non number of 0 (zero), is to identify it as the circle on which all of the other 9 numbers sit.

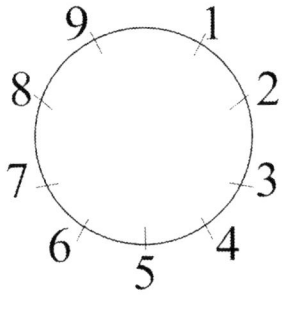

fig 6

0 is the great unmanifest consciousness from which everything is created.
0 is also the consciousness to which everything returns.
9 is the limit if numbers. At 10 we find the individual consciousness of 1 next to the unmanifest consciousness of the whole.
10 is 1 and 0.
0 contains all the other numbers, whether we are going from 1 to 10 and reaching fulfilment, or returning from 10 to 1 to find the source.

As we look more closely at cycles we will learn how important the circle is. Life does not progress in a straight line. It is constantly made up of new beginnings, and endings, which overlap. All of these new beginnings and endings relate to 0.

The symbolism of the Fool

The Fool is depicted walking, so he relates to action. Even in non-action there is action. Can we sleep without breathing? In Hindu mythology we hear of the dance of Siva, which represents the perpetual motion of the Earth, and everything within it and without it. It is believed that when Siva stops dancing, creation will end. So even in the apparent nothingness of 0 there is action.

There is a dog barking at the Fool's heels, but he pays no attention to this. The dog is symbolic of all worldly desires, and which, while we are in the free, liberated state of the Fool, we can easily disregard.

Over his shoulder he carries a bag, and in this he is said to carry all of his wisdom; all of that which he may manifest, and all of that which he has fulfilled. Some occultists say that this bag contains the four suits of the Tarot, representing the four elements, showing that he has them at his command and is capable of using these gifts, whenever he chooses to.

Interpretation and Divination

The Fool is the free spirit. He depicts a person full of self reliance, prepared to break free and start afresh, giving up outmoded ideas in favour of the new.

All of the cards may be read as moving outwards from 0 to 10, or inwards from 10 to 0. When the Fool is seen as moving from 0 to 10 his bag contains all of his intuitive knowledge which he is prepared to use; while from 10 to 0 the bag contains everything which he has learnt from a particular set of experiences, or life cycle, and may be called upon in the future.

The dog at his feet relates to worldly desires and our ability to ignore temptation. It is also the pull of the world. When we have the Fool in a reading it shows that we are willing and able to give up things which others might consider of great value, or importance. So here the dog represents gossip, the "advice" of others, and our own previous weaknesses trying to attract our attention and make us give up the new. Others will cry "you fool", but we know that we are making the right decision.

In a reading the Fool may mean impulsive action, the breaking free from bonds, perhaps walking away from inhibiting relationships. Look closely at surrounding cards to see whether the enquirer is acting rashly (foolishly) or not. If the enquirer appears to be breaking free from old attachments, as symbolised by the dog, look for cards which support this, or represent restrictive forces. e.g. the moon card, on which there are dogs trying to frighten the free spirit (as symbolised by the cray fish) back into the stagnant waters of stuck emotion.

It is also important to make assessments between the upright meaning of the card and the reversed meaning.

When **upright** the Fool shows:-
Freedom or folly depending on nearby cards.
A journey/traveller.
Easy going and full of forgiveness for others.
When **reversed** the fool shows:-
Easily persuaded by others.
Wishing to conform, against one's better judgement.
Considering worldly pleasures and possessions to be of more value than spiritual contentment.
Something from the past stops the enquirer moving forwards; "baggage" cannot be easily let go off.
Afraid to let go and tread a new path in life.

Key Words

Free spirit/Freedom/Adventure/Untainted
When reversed - Inhibited/Restricted/Pressurised

Toni Allen
The System of Symbols ©

The Magician No. 1

The Image

Traditionally the Magician is depicted standing behind a table set out with a variety of objects. In early packs these are cobbler's tools, a bag to put his goods in, and maybe trickster's dice or merely a selection of odds and ends. One must take into consideration the fact that early card makers copied traditional designs over and over again, each region having its own minor variations. Often card makers from one region stole a design idea from another area and thus evolved their own patterns. Very often the craftsmen were illiterate, which explains the spelling mistakes on early cards; and they also had to work in reverse on the wood block, which accounts for some early peculiarities. Add to this that a card they were copying may have been stencilled in dark colours which obliterated the original wood block out line, and we begin to understand how the carver could easily have become confused as to exactly what an object was supposed to be. This enables us to understand how small changes of detail have taken place, leaving some of the items illustrated seemingly unrecognisable today.

But what are these objects on the Magician's table? Tools of a skilled craft, or the craft of a skilled magician?

Waite stands his Magician behind a table on which lie the four Tarot suits of cups, batons, swords and coins, representing the four elements. In some respect Waite has sought to rationalise the dual nature of the Magician and elevate him to some high esoteric level of acceptability. He does the same with the Magician's wide brimmed hat, which is traditionally something akin to a sombrero, the brim twisted so that it appears to make a lemniscape over his head, an esoteric symbol for eternity. Pamela Coleman-Smith, under Waite's guidance, and many artists since, have taken off the Magician's hat and simply drawn the lemniscape hovering over his head.

The Magician usually holds a Baton or wand. In Marseille packs he tends to hold the wand in his left hand, the hand of the unconscious or feminine side to our nature, while Waite has moved it to the right hand, the hand of conscious action.

The Number 1

1 is the absolute, the whole. Creation unfolds itself from 1 to 9, and then, when we have seen all 9 stages of manifestation, it reunites itself at 1. Everything is contained within 1. Everything ultimately returns there.

The Symbolism of the Magician

The Magician represents the whole man (or woman), perfect in every way. He has his Baton, showing that he is master of his own nature, in control of his personality; and ready and willing to take part in the world; to experience whatever is presented to him. All the emotions are in perfect balance and he is adept at intuitively using the correct emotion in any given situation. He is also master of the physical world, capable with his hands and body. The Magician can often perform acts apparently impossible to others. He is the self realised man. This is his highest meaning.

In a traditional pack the objects on the Magician's table express his dexterity within the physical world. Manual agility is bred from calmness of mind. In Waite's pack, and therefore all those who have copied his imagery, the symbols of the four Tarot suits are laid on the table, ready for him to pick up and use whenever he desires. It shows that he has supremacy over these realms. The Sword of Air is his mental agility, the Baton (Wand) his fire energy, the Cup of Water his love, and the Coin (Pentacle) his prowess with wisdom or wealth.

Interpretation and Divination

As we learn more about numerology we will discover that number 3 is the first number of manifestation and that nothing happens in the physical realms until we have passed through the ether of number 5.
So who is the Magician?

He symbolises that perfect part within us all. The still, unmoveable, eternal part. Some may choose to recognise it as the spirit, or soul, which lives within the body. It is untouchable and impossible to damage.
Occasionally we have a glimpse of this side of our nature. We have one of those days when everything goes well and we feel as if we are in total control of our life. There is much to learn and we enjoy taking part in every activity which life offers us, whether it be great or small. There are no slip-ups, and we have an abundance of energy to perform even the most arduous tasks. During prayer or meditation we find that we have incredible insight into life's mysteries, as never experienced before. We are at one with life. Often we are only given a brief, fleeting glimpse, because staying there is difficult when we have not yet gained perfection.

The Magician's power is not a physical one, but an unconscious, spiritual one. We cannot touch it, yet we may use it. It is the inspiration to go ahead, the intuition which helps us make the correct decision, the force behind all actions.

The Magician's power comes from beyond the conscious mind, and the card can sometimes take on a similar meaning to the god Mercury. Any fleeting glimpse of inspiration, or higher knowledge, is brought to us by Mercury, the messenger of the gods, into our conscious mind from a place beyond and above human thought. The Magician can therefore be interpreted as "knowing that a particular action is right" even if logic appears to contradict. It is the ability to "hunch", to "know" the truth.

When **reversed** the Magician symbolises a disconnection between the enquirer and their higher self. Remember our two intrepid travellers the "ego" and the "self"? The "ego" is often afraid to let the "self" experience itself, because it is fearful of dissolution. The "ego" enjoys sense activities and relies on the physical realm for existence. To let go is to abandon oneself to something greater than the ego, and yet to refuse to relinquish one's ego identity is to deny oneself many useful, and wonderful experiences which help us to achieve our full potential.

Upright meaning

The enquirer is in good health, has much vitality and has the potential to do well in any forthcoming projects.

The enquirer's ability to see solutions clearly is very acute. Self confidence is high and the intellect sharp.

It is a good time to take on new ventures. (remember that the number 1 is always a new beginning)

If the card is taken to represent someone in the enquirer's life then this person is a good friend and useful colleague. (Beware of surrounding cards! If for example, the Page of Swords is close by then, although the Magician may be a wonderful person, they may also have the potential to be a devious and strong willed adversary, and turn all of the "magic" into "trickery".)

Reversed meaning

The enquirer is, for some reason or other, unable to use their full potential in life.

Possible failure due to circumstances. (Look for clues in surrounding cards)

Possible ill health. Perhaps the beginning of an illness due to something being out of balance in the psyche. All illness is caused by an imbalance within us. If we can establish the cause then we can deal with it and hopefully avert more serious consequences.

As the Magician is such a strong, benevolent card it is important to study surrounding cards when it is found reversed to place the cause of the imbalance.

e.g. Let us say it is a woman enquiring. She has a plan for a new business, and knows she is capable of achieving her goals. If the 3 Swords is close by, someone jealous, perhaps her husband or partner, does not wish to see her do better than him. The woman is therefore unwilling to go ahead for fear of losing her relationship.

Or:- Let us use the same woman and her business, but this time the 2 of Batons is close by, showing her oppressive upbringing. Her parents belittled her as a child, always telling her that she "could not", or "should not".

Another example would be is the reversed Magician was next to the 3 of Batons reversed and the 8 of Swords. Here we have a picture of someone who is troubled by stuck emotional experiences (8 Swords) and is therefore unable to achieve complete sexual fulfilment. The 3 of Batons reversed indicates their inability to express passion and the Reversed Magician indicates that they are unable to completely let go of their ego consciousness and become one with their partner. Sex may not sound like a very "spiritual" past time, yet many philosophies encompass the perfection of sexual union as a way towards self-realisation. It is impossible to unite fully with another until we have let go of the ego. In French it is called Le Petit Mort, The Little Death, when one dies as a me to become a we. It is only the ego which dies.

In all examples the reading can expand to explore potential ways of overcoming the problems and stand the Magician on his feet again.

Key Words

Unity/Oneness/The Human Spirit/New Beginnings/Potential
When reversed - Inability to let go of the ego/Unable to use a particular aspect of one's nature

Toni Allen
The System of Symbols ©

The High Priestess   No. 2

The Image

The High Priestess is also referred to as La Papesse, the Popess, or female Pope. By some historians this is thought to originate from the fact/myth that there was, on one occasion, a female Pope. There is some doubt as to whether or not she truly existed, but it is important to briefly outline the story, as some schools of thought give a lot of credence to this being the origination of the High Priestess. Joan, known as Pope John was alive in about the 9th Century and supposedly started pretending to be a man when she was forced into having to disguise herself as a young monk to flee from an invading army. She continued studying and practising as a monk, finding herself unable to give up the deception. Eventually she rose to be ordained Pope. Her downfall was when she fell in love. Foolishly they consummated their union, and Joan/John was ultimately discovered by the people when she suddenly started giving birth during a public ceremony. It is said that both her and her unborn child were brutally ripped to shreds by an irate, and confused, mob.

We also have to bear in mind that this story allegedly occurred during a time when both Christianity and Paganism existed, and that religious thought prior to Christianity gave much more emphasis to the powers of feminine creativity and the concept of "Earth Mother". Pagan religions ordained women as priests. It is therefore highly possible that the High Priestess is a depiction of a Pagan priestess and that the Pope John legend is a later overlay to excuse the appearance of a no longer valid concept in a predominantly Christian world. I often wonder if she was disguised with the myth of Pope John so that those who still sanctified the High Priestess did not have to openly admit to such a practice during times of inquisition and overt retribution.

The High Priestess is also referred to as the Veiled Lady.

In traditional packs she is depicted sitting with an open book on her lap. Her hair is covered and she wears a cloak around her shoulders, while a curling drape hangs behind her and sometimes a canopy sits above her head.

More recent packs place her sitting between two pillars, generally one dark and one light, representing the duality of two. On Waite's pack the "inner sanctum" which she guards is screened off by a drape patterned with pomegranates and palm leaves. The pomegranates symbolise fertility and regeneration due to their abundance of seeds; and the palm symbolises victory over death as Palm leaves were placed on the road before Christ on his entry into Jerusalem.

The book she holds is the book of wisdom. Not a written volume, but the knowledge of the truth which lies within us all.

The number 2

The number 2 symbolises duality. The absolute and the non-absolute. The self and the ego. The number 2 is the opposite or complement of the number 1. By itself it is passive, but becomes productive when fecundated by the active.

The number two is also the unmanifest. The unmanifest is the bank or store room where all things and forms lie hidden and come into creation when the time is right. Just as one collects all things in a store and uses them when need arises, in the same way, all the multifarious forms of the universe lie stored in the unmanifest before creation breaks out. They are also absorbed back into it when the creation is withdrawn.

The symbolism of The High Priestess

The High Priestess is the first step into creation, and yet still unmanifest. She holds her book of knowledge, those things which may come about if we go on to 3. She is the essence of our true self and yet at the same time the duality created by the ideas which we hold about ourself.

In the first chapter of the Bible, Genesis, we find the story of Adam and Eve. It says that when they ate from the tree of the knowledge of good and evil, that they became as God. This immediately rose Adam and Eve above the animal kingdom, because the animals have no concept of right and wrong, whereas, once they had eaten the fruit Adam and Eve had the ability to know good from evil. We may call it conscience. It is this dual nature of man that the High Priestess symbolises.

Interpretation and Divination

From 1 to 2 we are going out towards creation. From 2 to 1 we are working our way back. Already, unlike with the Magician, we have a choice of two ways in which to interpret the card. Is the questioner on a first step towards going out into creation, or on a final step towards seeking something within themself?

The High Priestess is like the sperm and the egg, holding the potential for life on her way out to 3, the desire to be born and experience the creation. Conversely if we see her as returning to 1, she is the questioner seeking for answers, the final step towards unity.

It is said of any question which we may ask, that the answer is already within us. The part of ourselves which we turn to is represented by the High Priestess. Her book is symbolic of our wisdom and the questions we might ask, while behind the drape is the store house of answers. We do know the answers, but to connect with them we must first contact our inner most intuitive part, the source from which the question first arose.

She is the link between the conscious and the unconscious.

In a reading the High Priestess is one of the most enigmatic cards, perhaps because of her almost unfathomable nature. She will often appear in a reading as a "block", an unknown obstacle which only the questioner can reveal for themselves. The questioner needs to ask the right questions, and it is the divinator's part to assist them by firstly suggesting that they look, and then, through gentle guidance, aid them in their search.

The High Priestess always speaks of the unknown. One way of trying to penetrate her meaning by laying more cards around her to see if there are clues at to which direction to "open her up". However, the High Priestess often refuses to speak, especially if the questioner is not supposed to know something at a particular time.

In my own experience I have had a case in which the questioner and I worked on four spreads, shuffling the cards between each time, to see if we could find out what the High Priestess was concealing. Each time she came up in exactly the same position! Eventually the questioner agreed that she must be patient, or privately meditate on her problem to gain insight.

Upright meaning

The most common meaning is the "block", where the questioner is not meant to know what will happen in a particular situation.

However, I have also see the High Priestess show that the questioner does not currently know what is happening in a certain predicament. For one man this came as him feeling "vibes" at work, and he instinctively knew that something was going on, yet he simply didn't know what. On another occasion it came up for a woman indicating that she did not have enough information about a given situation. "I know my sister is up to something", she said, "although I simply don't know what and therefore I can't do anything to help her. I think that my mum knows, and yet they both appear to be acting normally." When the same woman returned a few months later for another consultation she revealed that her sister had been in all sorts of trouble and that the family had excluded my client from "the inner sanctum" of family secrets because she had been taking exams at the time and no-one had wanted to upset her. "I knew something was up", the woman said "I just knew it."

The High Priestess often appears when the questioner has a major decision to make and can't decide which way to go. Such as "Shall I take this job offer, or that job offer?" The High Priestess symbolises that when the time is right, and more information has been gathered, that the questioner will find the answer for themselves.

If a woman is enquiring about a desired pregnancy then her **fertility** is assured by the High Priestess, as this is the card symbolising the mystery of conception. That which is to be born comes through the causal realm. However surrounding cards MUST be taken into consideration if the card is not taken as a one off in answer to a specific question. e.g. placed next to the Queen of Swords the High Priestess may indicate unseen, or unknown, gynaecological problems.

The Empress or the Ace of Batons the right way up would indicate possible conception.

The High Priestess assures fertility and conception, but does not necessarily indicate that the pregnancy will result in birth.

Remember to always read the card symbolically and to take into consideration all cards surrounding it. I once gave a man a reading in which the High Priestess was dominant in the opening spread. She was, however, surrounded by strong, potentially aggressive cards...the 3 of Swords (Anger/revenge), the King of Swords (A powerful leader) the Page of Swords (A tricky character, 'the spy') and the 6 of Swords (journey across water). When I told the man that it looked like he was to shortly work abroad, in a country where women wore veils, and that his work was military and probably top secret...he practically fell off his chair. The High Priestess indicated both veiled women and the top secret nature of his work. He informed me that he would be working for a powerful lady, who would not let her name be mentioned, but that in her country women wore veils. I recall doing this reading at a psychic fair and that as soon as his reading was over the man quickly disappeared into the crowds and I never saw him again. It was as if his "mysterious" work had to be kept secret at all costs and that he dare not tally to chat. I was left with the distinct impression that I already knew too much.

Reversed Meaning

The High Priestess reversed indicates that the questioner knows the answer to their problem, even though they may find it difficult to recognise the fact. Many people have the answers at their fingertips, yet presume that life has to be more complicated than they have made it out and that the simple solution they can see cannot possibly be correct.

Many people say, "Yes, I do know what to do. It's the doing of it that's the hard part."

Reversed the High Priestess also indicates that secrets have, are, or will be opened up, depending on her placement within the reading.

On some occasions the High Priestess reversed speaks of those rare, yet wonderful, flashes of deep insight we might refer to as a "peak experience". Duality disappears as we go behind her veil and unite with something greater than ourself.

Key Words

The unknown/Things we are not supposed to know yet/Hidden secrets
Reversed - Things we intrinsically know are right/The opening up of secrets/Peak experience

Toni Allen
The System of Symbols ©

The Empress No. 3

The Image

The Empress is traditionally pictured sitting on a throne with a crown on her head. In her left hand she holds a sceptre topped by an orb. In her right hand she holds a shield.

In Waite's pack her crown is wreathed in stars and the theme of abundance and fertility is alluded to throughout with pomegranates adorning her gown and a field of wheat growing in the foreground.

There have been many noble Empresses and Queens throughout history, however I don't feel that the Empress originally referred to any one in particular. Her stature is regal and she embodies the spirit of feminine nature. In medieval manuscripts Mother Nature was often depicted at her anvil, fashioning the animals and plants as if she were a blacksmith. So this is not a weak and flimsy slip of a girl, here is a mature woman, capable of continuous productivity.

The number 3

3 is the number of first manifestation. What has come from the unity of 1 through the duality of 2 is manifest at 3.

3 represents nature. It is the matrix which sets the direction of the creation in a general way and the conduct, or behaviour, of the individual in a special way.

If the nature of a person is good then it leads him (or her) towards the pleasures of heaven or advancement in a material way; and if it is bad, then one meets misery, pain and destruction.

Discrimination (the Lovers card) takes one above nature and the individual is freed from the pleasures of heaven and the pains of hell.

Nature is divided into three parts. In Sanskrit these three parts are known as the three gunas. All nature is governed by them. The three gunas are Sattva, Rajas and Tamas.

Sattva means:- Law, reality, purity-the highest of the three gunas. **Sattvic nature** allows growth of reason and discrimination, thus taking one over the duality of good and bad.

Rajas means:- passion, desire, energy-the second of the three gunas. In **Rajasika nature** we have the active world and the efficient activity which accounts for work of an artistic nature.

Tamas means:- darkness, ignorance, inertia:- the lowest of the three gunas. **Tamasika nature** gets people into the habit of taking drugs and engaging in violent and deceitful activity.

The three gunas are very important. They govern all creation. As we proceed we will learn more about the different qualities of the gunas and how they can be observed in practice.

The symbolism of the Empress

The Empress symbolises mother nature and all that can be born from the womb of life. She is both the Earth as mother and the individual as mother.

The Empress symbolises the nature of all things, whether they be animate or inanimate.

Interpretation and Divination

The Empress depicts the quality of the questioner's nature. Surrounding cards act like adjectives adding colour and description.

Near by cards will show the types of activities the questioner is best suited to. For example, let us assume that the Empress has already come up, which has triggered the question "what type of work would best suit me?". You, the divinator, may ask the questioner to take a card, and place it next to the Empress to find the answer. The Empress next to a Coin card would indicate a nature inclined towards business, planning, organisation etc. Next to Swords an intellectual nature suited to computers, investigation, the law etc. Next to Batons an artistic nature fitted to any of the creative arts; or nature's arts such as farming, gardening etc. Next to Cups an emotional nature suited to the caring professions, family, psychic work etc. Let your own intuition work around these concepts within the context of the rest of the reading.

During a reading the Empress means plans and projects; she is an indication that things are beginning to happen. The questioner, whether male or female, is about to give birth to something. e.g. a new business venture, creative projects, good health, femininity/masculinity.

Upright Meaning

If a female questioner asks if she is capable of having children the Empress would give a positive answer. However, be warned, the surrounding cards must be taken into consideration as fertility alone, or indeed the desire for children, does not conceive them. Other cards depicting the health of both the questioner and her partner must be carefully assessed.

I recall a man who came for a reading and asked if his wife would have any more children. He took two cards, which when turned over revealed the Empress and the 4 of Coins. Earlier in the reading he had come up as the King of Coins. By integrating the two coin cards it became apparent that although his wife was young and healthy he had chosen to stabilise the family, to give it a limit and take birth control into his own hands. I suggested that it was he who could not have any more children and he then openly admitted that several years earlier he had had a vasectomy. It was not a trick question, he simply wanted to know if she might ever "play away from home" and get pregnant.

Reversed Meaning

The Empress reversed indicates that the questioner's personal nature, or true personality, is inhibited. This can be for a variety of reasons and below are a few examples.

When someone is going against their true nature they may find it difficult to motivate themself. Projects are abandoned, dreams given up and a feeling of dullness pervades the personality. Self expression is lost.

The possible causes are:

In a situation where one partner, whether male or female, has been inhibited by their spouse. Their loved one wants them to follow their ideas, or way of life, and thus their own personality is left decaying. A common scenario is where the woman has had children and wishes to resume work. The man thinks of himself as breadwinner and does not want his partner to work, but stay at home and look after the house and children, even though they are of school age and making their own social life. The woman then becomes very dull because even some part time work would make her feel more fulfilled and worthwhile.

Additionally the Empress reversed can be seen in a situation where a very capable person is not allowed to express their talents at work.

For the artist it can mean creative inertia, such as writer's block.

In general terms it can mean the adult who was told not to do certain things by their parents, or not to pursue a particular career. This shows in adult life in frustration and feelings that they have "missed the boat" for their true vocation. I have seen this in someone as young as twenty four, who was still living with his parents and feeling that he had to continue with work that was acceptable to his parents, even though he hated it. He felt that life wasn't worth living and that he would never be able to express himself.

In connection with child birth the Empress reversed does not in itself indicate infertility, although it may, depending upon surrounding cards, indicate long labour or difficulty in conceiving. It can also indicate that it is not an appropriate time to have a child.

Key Words

A positive expression of one's talents/Plans and projects/Creativity/
Fertility and possibly birth
Reversed - Suppressed talents/True nature inhibited

Toni Allen
The System of Symbols ©

The Emperor No. 4

The Image

In many ways the picture of the Emperor is unexceptional. Traditionally we find an older man sitting on a throne, seated sideways rather than facing us directly. He is cross legged, wears a crown, and in his right hand holds a royal sceptre decorated with a cross and orb. Often a shield rests by the side of the throne bearing a coat of arms.

Unlike the Empress the Emperor has been both surreptitiously and openly designated to specific individuals of power and position throughout the Tarot's history. A pack dating from circa 1791 called the Carey French Revolution Tarot Cards, entitles the Emperor "Le Grand Pere" (the Grandfather), has given him a floppy sort of night-cap instead of a crown, and he holds a flower vaguely resembling a tulip instead of his sceptre.

Meanwhile his throne is almost too inadequate to sit on, and he ends up having to perch uncomfortably on it with his legs uncrossed. The consensus of opinion on this card is that it was created at a time when anti-royalist sentiment was running high and, for those who cared to note its overtones, a good chuckle could be had at the sly send up of the monarchy.

The Emperor has often been used as a characature type of figure in this way, and one of the more recent examples is painted by Dominique Balbi in his colourful pack. Here Balbi has Stuart R. Kaplan placed as the Emperor. "Who is he?" I here you ask. I would wager that 75% of readers can pick up their pack of Tarot Cards and read off the side of the box U.S. Games Systems, Inc. Stuart Kaplan is the President of U.S. Games Systems, Inc., has commissioned many modern Tarot Packs, has written three excellent Encyclopaedia on Tarot, and numerous other books and, at the last count owned one of the largest and most exclusive collections of Tarot Cards in the world, the rarest items of which he consents to have displayed in various museums. Oh yes, and I believe that he can read the cards too! A true modern day Emperor of the Tarot!

Whether we like it or not the Emperor is a figure of power and authority and even when we prod fun at him it is because we hold strong feelings about his position that we do so. We can despise, envy or lust after another man's power....especially when we are unable to find that sense of self worth within ourself. When we recognise and accept another individual's power without belittling our own, then we are able to ennoble the other, as Balbi has done with Kaplan.

The Number 4

The number 4 relates to the feeling of I. Consciousness.
On our overturned circle the number 4 corresponds to the number 6. Later you will hear about the number 6 in more detail, but for now it is enough to know that the number six comes at the stage of air. It is air which holds all physical forms together, because once the vital air passes away from the body it starts to disintegrate.

In Sanskrit at the number 4 sits Mahat:- great soul; or ahamkara [*aham* I *kara* maker]; meaning Self-will, the ego mask, the principle in man which makes him feel separate from others. Because these equally sit at the number 6, as seen by our overturned circle, they also collect and hold everything that seems to belong to it in the feeling of I.

Thus the number 4 gives the impression of permanence, stability and a foundation quality. Here the three gunas are operating on a firm base. These three forces embodied at number three and the Empress have to be felt by something which is conscious. All the machines in the world are somewhere connected to a conscious being, otherwise they cannot be regulated to proper use.

The Symbolism of the Emperor

We have already seen how Balbi has used the symbolism of the Emperor in a very modern manner. In "correct" traditional packs which do not hold any political sneer we find the Emperor is very sure footed and strong. He quite simply sits on a state throne and rules his empire. Yet in all empires there is the good ruler and the bad. So it is inside us all. The "good" Emperor inside us has a positive feeling of self worth and self value, and with this clear sense of "I Am" we are able to be kind and compassionate yet remain constant and strong. When the "bad" Emperor takes over we lose our feeling of self-worth and consequently rule others with a sharp tongue and harsh manner, demanding obedience rather than gaining it through respect. Due to the correlation between numbers 4 and 6 we find the sense of "I Am" intrinsically linked to the qualities of air and thinking. The Emperor is therefore also the lord of thought. Positive thought brings a positive sense of "I Am".

The Emperor's throne is usually square, and if you look at a square you will note that it has four sides and cannot be rolled around. When you three dimensionalise the square it becomes a cube...and cubes of stone don't move easily either! Thus the squareness of the Emperor's throne illustrates his fixed nature...his "I Am" is set. Although Waite's Emperor is seated so that he stares straight at us, his throne is so solid it would take a truck load of servants to move that ego-mask....he even has rocky mountains in the distance to emphasise his stature.

So the Emperor is Lord of "I Am". Consequently the Emperor's fine clothes can either be glorifying one's perfect consciousness, or embellishing the ego. One's sense of "I Am" rarely sits alone as pure consciousness and generally we all go around saying "I am this", or "I am that". The ego gains recognition through an outward display of somethingness. e.g. I am a teacher, I am a computer bod, I am tired, I am happy, I am rich etc. 4s connection with 6 ensures that the ego collects and holds everything that seems to belong to it in the feeling of I.

Consequently the Emperor also has his shield. Mostly the early emblems depicted are related to the patron or card maker who initially commissioned the pack. However I do not feel that the shield is merely a makers mark. The number 6 relates to air and at air sits discrimination (more explanation of this is given under The Lovers card). When we discriminate we make choices. The sword of air attacks and then the feeling of "I Am" which we have built up needs to parry the blow and defend itself....for this we need a shield. The Emperor has a shield yet he does not hold it, it rests quietly by his side, ready to be swung into action when required. Currently he clasps his sceptre and orb, another symbol of the wand or baton, his true nature. With this he directs his actions.

Interpretation and Divination

During a reading the Emperor represents the questioner or anyone else in their life who has a strong sense of self-worth.

Business acumen and leadership qualities are also shown. If the questioner is asking about their career then the Emperor shows that they are much better at being in charge than taking orders and that they would be far more suited to a managerial position or self employment than menial, mundane activity. Remember, the Emperor rules his empire, and therefore he needs to have something to take command of, otherwise his talents will be wasted and he will become frustrated. The seated pose of the Emperor shows that he is not a doer, but an administrator. All of his activity takes place in the realm of thought and ideas. Having said this, experience has shown that for many women who have this card representing their husband, the man often works in building or construction of some kind, and is generally self-employed. I feel this comes through from the solid structure of the number 4. Buildings are very much like our cube we discussed earlier and air holds all physical forms together.

When the Emperor relates to the husband he is a good provider and kind, yet strict when necessary with the children. Sometimes he over works, especially when in a high powered job relating to a large turnover.

When **reversed** the Emperor takes on a different note. He is fixed in his sense to the point of rigidity, and sometimes this manifests as physical symptoms such as stiff joints or general tension. Reversed the Emperor will not change his mind or alter his opinion on some matter or another however much he is outmoded in attitude or blatantly wrong. When reversed the ego is desperately trying to hold onto its mask, and its as if he holds the shield up to his face, refusing to glimpse an alternative view point. The shield becomes blinkers and its emblem a sign shouting "This is who I am, and don't you forget it!"

Key Words

The pure essence of I versus the ego/Businessman (or possibly woman)/ Positive sense of self worth/Good organiser/Father figure who is kind yet knows when to be strict
Reversed - Negative self image/Trying hard to hold on to outmoded ideas, or self image/Rigidity/Self-denial/Bully

Bach Flower Remedy

When the Emperor is reversed he shows the negative Bach remedy **Vine** traits of using great gifts to gain power and dominate, demanding obedience and has aggressive pride.

Toni Allen
The System of Symbols ©

The Pope No. 5

The Image

The Pope is traditionally depicted seated in front of two distant pillars, with an outstretched hand blessing two tonsured monks who kneel before him. He blesses them with the right hand while holding a three tiered cross, or orbed sceptre in his left. He is sometimes called the High Priest or the Hierophant.

He is the archetypal priest blessing his followers, the man they go to in times of trouble, or the master who has divine connection and is powerful enough to give them absolution. On one level he is the ruling power of external religion, the first portal towards the hidden secrets of the High Priestess.

Much has been suggested by some writers on the Tarot as to the importance of whether the Pope's head-dress has two tiers or three, and whether he holds a sceptre or a cross. Historians amongst you will, no doubt, enjoy the detective work involved in studying old packs and cross-referencing the Pope's costume with historical records. Certainly his attire did change slightly, but I feel that this was more to do with fashionable acceptability, or religious preference within a particular location, than any deep esoteric insight.

The only main adjustment of depiction which Waite has done is brought the two pillars closer and therefore made them larger, thus emphasising the similarity between the Pope and the High Priestess; that only once the dual nature of man is tamed can one go further towards self-realisation.

Crowley on the other hand has, for his own reasons, associated his Hierophant with the bull and the elephant. Masks of the four elements are placed in the four corners of the picture, bringing correlation between this and the World card. Crowley writes that the masks are "...the guardians of every mystery, culminating in the Grand Mystery of the uniting of microcosm and macrocosm." Although, unfortunately, the Hierophant's wand looks like a carpet beater, Crowley has included a very interesting female figure of Venus instead of the two monks. She holds a sword and he claims that she is "now armed and militant". What exactly he might mean by this is shrouded in mystery, but, once you have read the chapter on the Lovers (card no 6) you might like to give some contemplation to the parallelism of his figure of Venus and the Cherub with the flaming sword set up to protect the Garden of Eden after Adam and Eve's expulsion.

The number 5

Number 5 relates to the akasha. [Sometimes referred to as the akashic or etheric level]

On our overturned circle the number 5 falls in the middle from both sides. On the one side is the coarse physical world which can be subject to sense observation, and on the other side is the world of subtle and causal nature.

When the causal and subtle world is transformed into the coarse world, it is done through the akasha, which connects both. It is like a transformer which changes one type of energy into another, or like an interpreter who makes obvious the ideas framed in an unknown language. It must have the qualities of both sides, otherwise no communication would be possible.

Akasha gives way to all physical forms and it is only due to the akasha that the physical creation has found manifestation. It stands as a bridge and joins the sensual world to the mental and causal world.

Anyone who practices meditation will recognise these qualities held within the akasha. When meditating we fall still, rest the mind and experience the deep silence of the akasha from which all creation is formed. This is how, after meditating, we find ourselves refreshed and given insight into current problems. Having connected with the causal level answers come that ordinarily might be obscured from us.

The akasha carries sound, the most subtle of the five senses. "In the beginning was the word". All creation is made manifest through sound and the sound originates in the space of the ether. Without space there is no sound.

The Vesica Piscis

fig.1

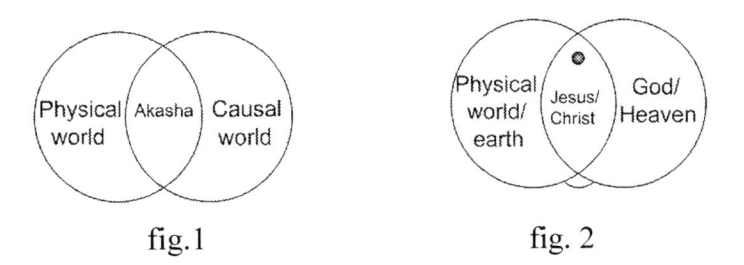

fig. 2

There are few symbols which carry so much meaning as the Vesica Piscis. This is by no way meant to be a definitive explanation, but merely an illustration in the context of our number 5 which we are presently looking at.

The two overlapping circles form a fish-shaped central area which is one source of the symbolic reference to Christ as a fish.

In fig.1 we see the circles illustrated as the physical world overlapping with the causal world, the central area being the akasha, which is the bridge between the two.

In fig. 2 we see the two circles representing the physical world (Earth) and God or Heaven, the central area being Jesus, or Christ, the channel by which the two levels of creator and creation are joined. In many branches of the Christian religion it is a strong belief that the only way to God is by praying to Jesus, the Christ. People who hold with this belief use Christ as their channel between Heaven and Earth.

In medieval art there are many illuminated manuscripts depicting both Christ, and the Virgin Mary and child, sitting within the Vesica Piscis.

In the Mantegna Prints, which are thought to be a fore-runner of the Tarot, Jupiter, the king of the gods, sits on a bridge within the same fish shape as at the centre of the Vesica Piscis. This is the same traditional pose that Christ has in medieval manuscripts. The shape is preserved within the Tarot on the World card as the wreath which the female figure dances out of into creation.

The symbolism of the Pope

The Pope symbolises our connection with the akashic level. In Christian terms he is the man who helps us link with the Christ and thus with the akashic level. In any other belief system he is the master who teaches us, and guides us to connect with the subtle world, via the akashic level of prayer and meditation.

The two pillars symbolise the two worlds. On one side the sensual world and on the other the mental and causal.

The two monks symbolise the two sides of every man's nature, his duality. Within all of us is the voice of truth competing with the voice of desire; one God given, the other based on physical desires and karma. One side of us is always prepared to listen to the truth and act accordingly; while the other rejects this higher influence and acts within the limits of habit.

Think for a moment on how many times, when a friend is offering some advice, that you've thought, or even said, "yes, I've heard all that before", without giving the other person space to have their say. We all do it at some time or another. We all switch off to the possibility of some fresh understanding or insight coming into a situation. And then how many times have we heard something only to say "Well why didn't you say that sooner?", for the other person to reply, "Well I tried to tell you the other day, only you wouldn't listen." This "other" voice, is also the voice within ourself, and our ability, or lack of it, to trust what our intuition says to us.

Interpretation and Divination

During one of my study groups I asked everyone to sit still for a few minutes and then tell me what they had experienced. Three of my four students shook their heads after the exercise and looked perplexed. The fourth looked shy and said "well, I experienced the space, a vast space around me in which there was the sound of silence. The silence was very loud."

This fourth student had connected with the akasha. She had experienced the space from which all sound arises, and, as she so accurately put it, the silence is very loud.

Some people talk about "getting messages from the other side". What "other side"? The other side they are referring to, whether they realise it or not, is simply the causal realm which lies on the other side of the akashic bridge of number 5. Some people have their own terminology and talk of "akashic records" when referring to the process of meditating and finding answers in the realms beyond the physical world. Some people even believe that it is only "special" or "enlightened" individuals who have the "power" to read the "akashic records". This is not so. Each and every one of us has the ability to cross through the akasha and receive information from the causal and subtle realms. My student connected very quickly with the akasha, and I have no doubt that had she continued for longer, that she would have been receiving relevant information within a very short period. Yet she was an every day sort of person, not a clairvoyant, or guru, or purporting to possess any special "power".

The Pope symbolises the connection with the realms beyond the physical world. In days gone past the Pope, or priest, was the person most people took their problems to. He was the person who gave them good counsel and sound advice. It was assumed that because he was a man of the church that he had higher insight into matters than the ordinary man and therefore his advice was well esteemed, as if coming from God.
These days fewer and fewer people affiliate themselves to a particular

church, and the role of the Pope is often taken over by counsellors and therapists. However, their role is slightly different in that their part is not to advise but to help the individual find their own answers through re-connection with their own inner voice. People seek therapy when they have a problem, and in some way or another have lost themself. Everyone wishes to feel whole, and the only way to wholeness is through a feeling of oneness and lack of separation. Many people come for a reading at these times, and then I act as the channel. Many clients say that they feel lost, lonely, isolated or pointless. It is my role as a channel across the akashic level to guide my client towards a greater sense of oneness rather than separateness. Sometimes the act of listening and offering the client space to be heard is all that it takes.

The Pope symbolises the truth and any channel through which we gain sound advice and good counsel. The highest interpretation is therefore meditation and our own ability to "speak with God" and understand life through right action. It is also prayer and the answers and comfort which come from the stillness of the mind. In some religions the Pope comes in the form of the Virgin Mary, or Jesus Christ, both of whom are used as mediators for the person to pray to and use as a channel to "God" on the other side. These deities are used as transformers. (see Vesica Piscis, above)

On more mundane levels it can mean, advice, spiritual teacher, friend....anyone who listens to us and offers solace. It can also indicate someone's solicitor as, in times of judgement by a higher authority at a mundane level, we need advice on the law of the land. At this level the country we live in and its judicial system become god, and we need the counsel of someone who is versed in its secrets to aid us.

Upright Meaning

Good or sound advice.

Some people have a really good friend, who listens sincerely and endeavours not to interfere, but acts as a sounding board so that the individual can work out different angles to look at their own problem. Here the Pope is that special friend.

With a good counsellor or therapist it is the space they give the client which aids the healing process.

Ability to trust one's own intuition.

Reversed Meaning

Reversed the Pope encompasses the "I've heard it all before" attitude. Incorrectly we believe that we know best, and do not wish, or need, to learn from the experience of others. An inability to change our attitude ultimately leads us to being chained to habitual ideas and actions as symbolised by the Devil at number 15.

Reversed the Pope can mean the "good friend" who we go to use as a sounding board, but they end up giving advice, and expect us to do every thing they suggest. It's the "I think you should do this or that." The word should sounds like a command and gives absolutely no space.

Remember that the Pope symbolises sound and we all have the ability to "hunch" when something sounds right or wrong.

Healthwise, when reversed the card can mean that the client's hearing is failing them, which often comes about through a desire not to listen, especially if there is strife and argument at home. One man had the Pope reversed at the "physical level", which threw a whole new meaning on the card for me. The man was deaf.

In legal matters the Pope reversed nearly always indicates bad counsel.

Key Words

Divine Wisdom/guided by one's higher self/Inspiration/
Good Counsel/Good advice
Reversed - Bad Counsel/bad advice/Isolated and disconnected from higher self

Bach Flower Remedy

The Pope card is relevant to the Bach Remedy Cerato. In the negative Cerato state we lack confidence in our own judgement and tend to constantly seek advice from others, which can make us easily influenced. Cerato can help strengthen one's intuition and connection with one's higher self.

Toni Allen
The System of Symbols ©

The Lovers No. 6

The Image

The Lovers card is traditionally depicted as a man positioned between two women. Above their heads is a sun burst and in front of this, covering the sun's light, is a putti, or cherub, who usually has a bow and arrow pointed towards one of the women. Sometimes the putti is blindfolded and sometimes not.

There are two stories which offer insight into the symbolism of the card, but these picture stories are best expanded upon when I cover the symbolism of the card.

Waite's depiction of the Lovers, with a flaming tree behind a naked man, and a tree with an entwined serpent behind a woman, is more in keeping with the story of Adam and Eve than any traditional mythology associated with the card, the relevance of which is explained later.

The number 6

Air sits at number 6. In Sanskrit the air is called Prana:- breath of life, vital energy, capacity to desire and love.

Hand is the organ through which the forces within can be expressed. Hand is also the seat of air which holds things, catches and throws them. The Pranas are vital energy; they make or keep us alive, discharge polluted air, regulate the digestive process, keep the body in balance and also regulate involuntary movements within the body.

******

We can begin to see now how the numbers 3, 4, and 6 interrelate. Nature, which we find at 3, is given stability and a sense of being at 4. Once it has passed through the ether at 5 it is given the breath of life at 6.

In terms of the Tarot air is connected with the mind and reasoning, due to its association with discrimination; and with the Lovers card it is particularly related with number 6's capacity to desire and love.

We already know that on our overturned circle that 6 overlays with 4, and that at 4 sits the ahamkara or self will. At 6 we therefore find a card which deals with the question of what an individual is going to do with that self will; is he (or she) going to act willfully or willingly. Hence the Lovers card talks of discrimination and choice; not necessarily between one lover and another, but between the truth and untruth; towards the bondage of repeated karma, or towards action which will break the cycle.

In the Bible, in Genesis, man ate of the tree of the knowledge of good and evil. The serpent beguiled Eve by saying "For God doth know that in the day ye eat thereof, then your eyes shall be opened; and ye shall be as gods, knowing good from evil." As we have seen in our discussion on the High Priestess it is this duality and knowledge of good and evil that has created the human dilemma. It is said that animals can only act within their nature and that they have no concept of good and evil and therefore do not possess the faculty of discrimination. At the end of chapter III in Genesis it says "So he drove out the man; and he placed at the east of the Garden of Eden cherubim, and a flaming sword, which turned every way, to keep the way of the tree of life." The sword placed at the entrance to the Garden of Eden is symbolically the sword of discrimination. In the Bible this sword is set alight with the flames of passion, to stop us entering the Garden and finding unity within ourselves once again, and the eternal inner peace which we once possessed. Conversely the flames are also symbolic of tejas, the inner light of knowledge which shines within us all. We can find our way back to the Garden, but not through passion and desire, only through the light of knowledge and correct action.

We can also see how the flaming sword and the cherubim are on a par with the veil draped behind the High Priestess: obstacles to us finding our true self within, and yet by the same token a guide to the tools available to us.

It is interesting to note that as soon as God came along to visit Adam and Eve that He knew they were hiding. He found them clothed, their genitals covered, because eating of the fruit made them realise that he was a man and she was a woman, a matter which previously hadn't bothered them at all. Suddenly they were creatures of duality, him and her. When God asked who had done the deed of eating the apple, Adam replied "She made me do it". Not only had they obtained duality but they had also learnt how to use the sword of discrimination to protect their own ego and blame another!

Waite's illustration of the Lovers encompasses many of the concepts alluded to in the story of Adam and Eve, having the theme of the serpent but then a flaming bush, rather than a flaming sword. However, in many Biblical stories God spoke through the brightness of a flaming bush, a symbol of the connection between humankind and a higher self.

The Symbolism of the Lovers

As I have said earlier there are two stories which are told in connection with the Lovers card. However I would like to start by outlining the philosophy behind a very famous painting, and soon you will see the relevance between this and the Lovers card.

The painting is La Primavera by Botticelli, c1478. It is said that the painting was commissioned as a philosophical piece by the Medicis to hang in the young Alfonso's chamber; and that it covered an entire wall. In the centre of the painting stands a young woman, apparently choosing between the activities taking place on either side of her. To the left of her

Toni Allen
The System of Symbols ©

(and the right of the viewer) is a trio, which although three figures I have always taken to represent only two people. There is Zephyr, the mighty west wind, either taking, or raping Chloris. He blows upon her and with this breath of life creates a union, a birth, and from Chloris' mouth spring flowers, which then turn into the third figure of Flora, or nature. This side of the painting symbolises base human nature, lust, passion, desire, and the fruits of these activities, which are all natural and can give birth to multifarious forms.

To the woman's right (and to the viewers left) are the three graces, beautifully poised, linking hands in a delicate dance. These symbolise calmer inner thoughts and reflection; an ability to rise above human desire.

Above the woman's head is a putti with a drawn bow and arrow, his eyes blindfolded, his arrow pointed towards the three graces. In fact the woman's hand is raised towards the three graces, maybe as if she has already chosen them. Or is she holding them back? Here the putti symbolises that playful part of our mind, direct in its choice as to where it shoots its arrow of desire, and yet blindfolded as if love of the truth comes naturally and without question.

The woman is given a choice between base desire, accompanied by the repeat karmic pattern of human nature, and the bliss of a higher truth. To her far right (the viewer's far left) is a young man, apparently Hermes Trismegestus (or Mercury), his caduceus raised high and piercing through clouds which might symbolically cloud his judgement. Hermes symbolises personal thought and he is the messenger of the gods, that part of us which connects to the higher self across the bridge of the akashic level. It is said that this Hermes is a direct portrait of Alfonso Medici, the young man in whose room the painting hung. Apparently his father had commissioned the piece to provide the young man with a constant reminder of correct discrimination, and hoped that his son would continue to reflect upon its meaning.

If we then look at the symbol of the Lovers in the Tarot we find an uncannily similar piece. A man between two women; and a putti above his head, covering the sun; which symbolises his clarity of mind.

The first story attached to the Lovers card is that the young man stands between his mother and his future wife. Here the story is simply that he must discriminate, or choose, between staying a child in which others make decisions for him or grow up and learn to make decisions for himself. In most Marseille packs the putti points his arrow towards the apparently younger woman, who is often depicted without a hat to indicate her youth. Occasionally the putti is blindfolded, but often not. The emphasis in this story is on growing up and taking charge of one's own life and all of the responsibility involved therein.

The second story is a little more saucy. For readings I use the Balbi pack, and he's depicted the Lovers beautifully. One of the women has her hand placed over the man's heart, undoubtedly saying words to the effect of "Come with me, I know that it will be a big commitment, but its a true love and worth the struggle to maintain.". The other woman has her hand just below his belt, definitely on his codpiece. She is undoubtedly saying words to the effect of "Come with me for the night, we can have a quick bonk, a bit of fun. There's no commitment, and maybe I'll see you again in a week or so." In Balbi's pack the putti is directed towards this second woman, no blindfold, and without any shadow of a doubt luring the man towards lustful living.

This is all very well, but what of the cards higher meaning? In this second story the lustful woman symbolises any repeat karma we may have. Time and time again we go down the same old road, through the same old pattern of behaviour and make the same old mistakes. Habit lures us there. We know it hurts us over and over again, but more often than not the pattern we are stuck in is comfortable, and we can predict the outcome, however tragic or traumatic, and yet by its very familiarity we feel okay. To strike out and change our behavioural pattern in order to break much larger karmic bonds is a far more difficult and daunting task. Often the man in the Lovers card is said to be the Magician on his path of enlightenment, and that the Lovers card shows his dilemma of constantly having to use right discrimination to rise above old habits and work through his karma.

We are all born with an individual, personal nature, as shown by the Empress at number 3. At 4 we acquire a sense of I and once through the ether of 5 we are given the breath of life through the air of 6. In many ways we are born twice during one lifetime. We are born to our mother, and in our formative years our nature (3) unfolds with all of its karma. As we grow away from mother we learn our separate sense of I and come to understand that we are no longer a part of our mother. At age 16 we are given the faculty of discrimination and become a young adult with an additional tool of reason. In this country we recognise this by 16 being the age of consent. It is also used in the legal system by an acknowledgement that a crime committed by a youth under the age of 16 cannot be judged in the same way as someone over 16. All of this comes under the realm of 6 and the Lovers card.

Interpretation and Divination

Within a reading the Lovers has many interpretations although all along the same theme.

Often the age of the client is very important. For younger people, maybe in their twenties, I often see the card in accordance with our first story above. They find that they have been thrust into an adult world and suddenly have big decisions to make for themselves. Some have parents who guide and help them, but even these reach a stage where they feel that they have to make moves, and consequently mistakes, for themselves.

When I refer to decision making with the Lovers card, I do not mean the every day trivia of deciding which clothes to wear, or which restaurant to eat out in. I pertain to the much more formidable decisions in life, in which the questioner's entire life may be changed, and subsequently the lives of those around them.

The most important question which every human being asks themself at some time or another is "What is my path in life?". This includes the all encompassing question of "What is my purpose on this planet" and goes on to other questions such as "If my life path is X, then how do I get from here to there?" Many, many clients come for a reading when they reach a cross-roads in life, a certain critical juncture where something has fundamentally changed within them and they know that how they lead their life requires adjustment. These people often have the Lovers card as the pivot point of their reading. Remember that the card symbolises discrimination, an inner search for the correct way forward, and does not suggest a resolution in itself, or that the questioner has made any decision what-so-ever. Ideas are available, but no step forward has been taken.

Another common scenario is when a relationship changes, for better or worse. Often I see the card when the client is deciding whether or not to leave their partner. Generally they have out grown each other and the client feels that their path lies elsewhere, although has not yet taken any steps to leave, or, in fact change the situation in any way at all. It also arises when the client is trying to decide whether the person they have met is right for them or not, which includes big issues such as "Will a committed relationship help or hinder me along my own path in life?"

The Lovers also comes up when the client is making a decision about their career, and may be wanting to break away from old patterns of work.

Many years ago when I first encountered the concept of the age of 16 bringing about a new faculty of mind I was sceptical. As with all things the absolute will provide. I had already decided not to take clients under the age of 16 because they legally come under parental jurisdiction, although I will see younger clients with a consenting parent or guardian present. Suddenly I had a spate of youngsters seeing me who were all between 17 and 19. Every one of them expressed a feeling that something had changed within them over recent months. "I now have to make my own decisions", one of them said, "and it's so frightening." "Everything in my life's up to me know", said one young man. "It's not that nobody's there for me any more, it's just...different."

How parents deal with their child's growing maturity varies enormously. What happens during this vital period affects everyone tremendously and the repercussions carry on for many years and negative effects can be seen in the 2 of Batons and other cards. There is really no such things as a "good" parent or a "bad" parent, as the parent always sincerely does their best within the limits of their own knowledge and karmic behaviour. What happens is that fear and failure creep in. For example, the parent is too frightened to let their daughter discriminate about what time she can home, or which boy she can have a relationship with. In consequence the girl grows up making choices for all the wrong reasons, such as 'posh' boys are okay and "you can only get pregnant after 10 o'clock at night.". Boys find they have a different scenario. Maybe it's "brave men don't cry", and "hard work gets you somewhere". Subsequently when such a man gets married he finds difficulty in expressing his deep emotions and the wife leaves him because he's always working. Some people have too much authority put upon them while others are given none and bluntly told, "You're an adult now, make your own mind up." These are simple examples, but take time to consider variations on how adults' lives are coloured by what happens at this age.

When reversed the card signifies that the questioner does not have any idea about how they might go forward and change a particular situation, or that they do not want to consider the alternatives, often because they cannot believe that they have ended up in such a dreadful situation in which huge decisions have to be made. I saw this recently for a client whose husband came home one day and informed her that he was having a homosexual relationship. The Lovers card reversed indicated that she had no idea whether she wanted to continue to live with him, or leave him, or even hated him. "I just don't want to consider the options", she said. "If I don't, then part of me hopes it will just go away."

When reversed the card may also indicate that the questioner constantly falls into karmic patterns and therefore always makes the same mistakes.

Key Words

Discrimination/Reaching a cross roads/Needing to choose or reassess one's life path/Opportunity to change karmic patterns/Patterns which have been created through upbringing/Having to make a big decision
Reversed - Cannot make a decision/Lack of discrimination/No idea what to do with one's life/One does not want to make a decision

Bach Flower Remedy

Wild Oat is especially useful when one needs to find one's path in life.

Toni Allen
The System of Symbols ©

The Chariot No. 7

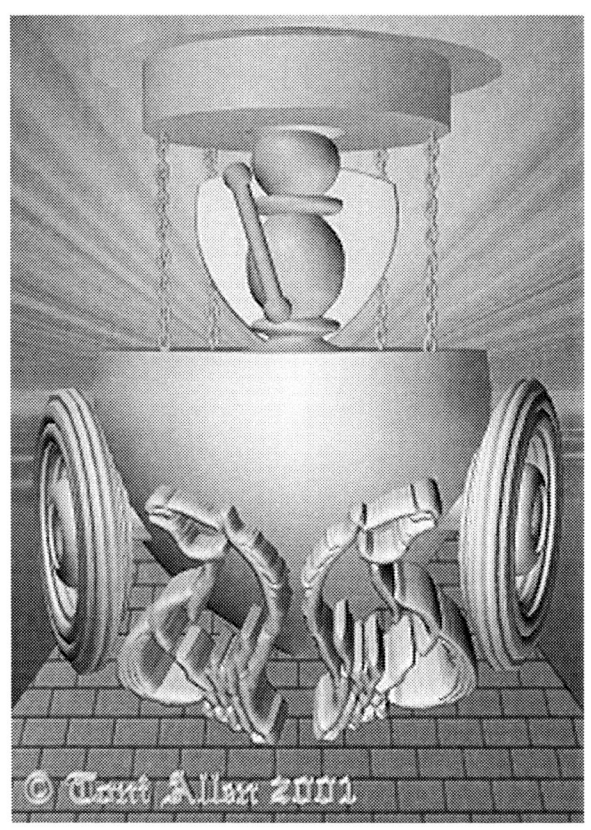

The Image

Traditionally the Chariot is depicted as a conventional charioteer, riding towards us. He stands in a canopied chariot, four posts holding the drape aloft, and two horses pulling the vehicle forwards. Sometimes the horses look in the same direction, but their gait is ungainly, often only their front legs being visible, the rear two merging into the front of the chariot. The wheels of the chariot are symbolised by two semicircles sticking out from the sides; more a limitation of the wood block and stencil print process used than anything more esoteric. The rider is dressed in full battle armour sporting a decorative breast-plate, complete with gargoyled epaulets, a fashion statement of the time, which also added extra protection as the enemies sword would get stuck in the indents of the design and make them lose control. These gargoyles were also supposed to make the wearer appear more fierce and frightening.

So, the Charioteer looks like a warrior; yet he wears a crown and holds an upright sceptre in his right hand. Is this then the King or Emperor, riding in his chariot of state, dressed in full battle regalia? There is an initialled shield shaped crest on the front of the chariot, but mostly these initials alluded to the card maker, and were probably nothing more than an advertising ploy.

When we look at Waite's Chariot we find Egyptian influence creeping in, the two horses here being exchanged for two sitting sphinxes, one black and one white. Waite's cards were initially published in 1910, a time when Egypt had become a craze, and excitement was reaching fever pitch as more and more rich tombs of treasure and religious artefacts were being uncovered. As far back as 1775 Court de Gebelin put forward the theory that Tarot originated from Egypt, although the pack accompanying his book published in 1781 entitled "Du Jeu des Tarots" is a traditional copy of a Marseille deck. In 1901 the Fatidic Egyptian Tarot was published in a book entitled Practical Astrology by Comte C. Saint-Germain. Although there were other all Egyptian style packs slowly creeping into circulation, most particularly the Papus Tarot in 1909, I feel that Saint-Germain's was probably most influential on Waite. Notably the Chariot is depicted as a Pharaoh riding in a chariot pulled by two resting sphinxes. Historically we know that Waite studied many packs at the British Museum and directed Pamela Coleman-Smith, the artist of the pack, towards designs derived from various sources. I therefore have no doubt that just as designers copy Waite these days, that Waite was heavily influenced by earlier designs.

Like Saint-Germain Waite has bedecked his canopy with stars. Likewise his black sphinx is on the left of the card (right of the charioteer) and his white one right of the card, therefore left of the charioteer. Here we find another parallel to the dark and light duality of man.

Crowley adds another dimension to the Chariot and depicts a cross legged, full armoured charioteer, presenting a pulsating circle to us, which is allegedly the centre of the Holy Grail. His Chariot is drawn by the bull, the lion, the eagle and man; the same four elements found around the World card.

The number 7

The number 7 comes in the realm of Tejas, the fire, light or glory which shines through the human being and makes up his stature, his brilliance, his light of knowledge and the heat which keeps everything moving.

On our overturned circle we can see that the number 7 relates to the number 3. At 3 we have the Empress depicting the potential nature of a person, while at 7 we find the patterns of creation, or the individual, fixed.

As we saw at number 3 and the Empress, nature is made up of the three gunas, Sattva, Rajas and Tamas. In Tejas we also find the three gunas manifesting as sattvika, rajasika and tamasika.

Sattvika Tejas is the light of knowledge.

Rajasika Tejas is the celestial lights such as the light of the sun, moon, stars and lightning.

Tamasika Tejas is fire, lamp lights, etc. which we find on Earth.

The Sattvika Tejas gives us knowledge.

The Rajasika Tejas gives us energy and ability to perform practical works.

The Tamasika Tejas gives us bodily heat which keeps us going through days and nights.

The Symbolism of the Chariot

Excerpt From the Essenes Book of Jesus

The Sevenfold Peace

And seeing the multitudes, Jesus went up into a mountain...he opened his mouth and taught them, saying:

> For, lo, I tell thee truly,
> The body and the heart and the mind
> Are as a chariot, and a horse, and a driver.
> The chariot is the body,
> Forged in strength to do the will

Of the Heavenly Father
And the Earthly Mother.
The heart is the fiery steed,
Glorious and courageous,
Who carries the chariot bravely,
Whether the road be smooth,
Or whether stones and fallen tress
Lie in its path.
And the driver is the mind,
Holding the reigns of wisdom,
Seeing from above what lieth
on the far horizon,
Charting the course of hoofs and wheels.

Excerpt From the Katha-Upanishad

The individual self and universal Self, living in the heart, like shade and light, though beyond enjoyment, enjoy the result of action. All say this, all who know Spirit, whether householder or ascetic.

Man can kindle Fire, that spirit, a bridge for all who sacrifice, a guide for all who pass beyond fear.

Self rides in the chariot of the body, intellect the firm footed charioteer, discursive reins the mind.

Senses are the horses, objects of desire the roads. When self is joined to body, mind, sense, none but He enjoys.

When man lacks steadiness, unable to control his mind, his senses are unmanageable horses.

But if he control his mind, a steady man, they are manageable horses.

The impure, self-willed, unsteady man misses the goal and is born again and again.

The self-controlled, steady, pure man goes to that goal from which he never returns.

He who call intellect to manage the reins of his mind reaches the end of his journey, finds there all pervading Spirit.

Above the senses are the objects of desire, above the objects of desire mind, above mind the intellect, above the intellect manifest nature.

Above manifest nature the unmanifest seed, above the unmanifest seed, God. God is the goal; beyond Him nothing.

The preceding two excerpts say all that is needed to be known about the charioteer. It is best to study the passages, and meditate with them.

Interpretation and Divination

The Chariot symbolises the individual on their path in life. Because it sits at number 7 it shows both the brilliance and energy of the individual.

Corresponding with the Empress at 3, we can tell from the Chariot's position during a reading how the person is using their talents and natural abilities.

The Chariot also symbolises beauty. However, the beauty it refers to is the beauty of the fire, or tejas, within the individual. The light that shines from within. "The glory which shines through the human being and makes up his stature, his brilliance, his light of knowledge...". To some people external beauty is of great importance, but, as we all know, this physical beauty quickly fades. The individual's tejas is of a different quality. Think for a moment on how many times you have heard someone who is feeling low say. "I'm not feeling that bright today", or a comment about an intelligent child, "He's a bright spark", or about a beautiful woman, "She's a dazzling beauty". We constantly use adjectives which in one way or another refer to the quality of light within another person. Glowing with health, fiery personality, brilliant scholar, dull so-and-so. But is it unconscious? Or are we simply recognising the tejas within another?

We can all experience the Chariot in our every day lives. On the days when we feel depressed, and walk around with a glum expression, people rarely smile as they hand over our change in a shop. Some shopkeepers might even pass comment and call out "Cheer up! It might never happen.". Yet on those days when we feel in control of our lives, as if we have the reigns of the Chariot between our fingers, over even the simplest project, then heads will turn and people around us strike up conversation. The tejas which we put out brings opportunity to us.

Due to the duality of human existence it is highly unlikely that many, if any of us, will manage to keep the Chariot up the right way all of the time. In readings the Chariot can give clear indications that a specific area of our life is constant if the card regularly comes up the right way round when asking about a specific subject, e.g. Work, marriage, hobbies.

Upright Meaning

Generally that life, or the specific aspect of life asked about, is going well, and that plans and activities are running smoothly.

If the Chariot is seen after cards such as the 8 of Swords, or the 4 of Swords, then it indicates that situations which were stagnant are now moving on in a more positive way and that a healing is taking place.

If seen after such cards as the 2 of Coins, the Page of Coins, or the Lovers, then it indicates that difficult decisions have been made and that matters will progress favourably. If, however, the Chariot is reversed after any of these cards then we could ask the questioner for more cards to find out why they have taken such a debilitating course of action. Have they sacrificed their own needs, or gone against their nature? Especially if seen after the Lovers, for then the Chariot indicates falling back into old habits and an unwillingness to change. Remember that this card falls after the decision making card of the Lovers, and that if one follows one's true path in life, that which suits one's individual nature, then one's own light and glory shines forth.

Reversed meaning

Simply, when the Chariot is reversed, we can say that life has run into a ditch. The reigns have been let go of and the horses have gone astray.

Most clients recognise this and offer me a wry smile. Their "umph" has gone, life has lost its lustre, and apathy holds them in the grip of dull resignation. Plans have gone drastically wrong, or merely halted, and they feel bedraggled and worn out. Somehow they have lost control. Surrounding cards will help offer hints as to what caused the situation. Look out for the strong influence of other people.

The Chariot can also, at a very mundane level, symbolise the motor car. After all it is Mankind's current most popular mode of transport and modern day Chariot. Once during a reading I saw that the questioner's husband would have an accident around the time of their holidays. The card she took to offer more information was the Chariot reversed, indicating that any accident would more than likely happen in a car. Extra cards said that no one would be hurt, but that it would cause delays. On their return from the holiday she telephoned to let me know that a lorry had gone into the back of their car while driving to the airport at the beginning of their vacation, and that fortunately nobody was hurt.

Key Words

Individual's brilliance/Correct path in life/Perfect control/Natural abilities correctly used/Colour (If appropriate use colours for healing e.g. Aura Soma)/Artists/Artwork/people who use colour
Reversed - Life has run into a ditch/Lethargy/Wrong path in life/No purpose in life/Lack of colour in one's life, again look to colour therapy for healing purposes

Bach Flower Remedy

Wild Oat for when the card is reversed, to help the questioner find their life path.
Wild Rose, again for the reversed card, when resignation and apathy are indicated.

Toni Allen
The System of Symbols ©

Justice No. 8

The Image

Justice is depicted as a woman seated on a high, curved backed throne. In one hand she holds an upright sword, in the other a pair of equally balanced scales. Traditionally she holds the sword in her right hand and the scales in her left. This is one card which has rarely been "rectified" over the years, although some artists have changed over the hands in which Justice holds her sword and scales, and Waite has moved her to number 11.

      The most noticeable variations to the design are those made to the drape behind the figure of Justice. In the 17th C Tarot of Jaques Vieville the drapes look remarkably like wings flanking her shoulders. This image has come down to us in a slightly altered form of what appears to be the high back of a throne. Due to the pillar like quality of the sides of the throne some occultists have elaborated upon this in their symbolism and defined two distinct pillars with a drape in between, which is reminiscent of the veil behind the High Priestess. Waite's pack is a clear example. This is, however, a natural progression and valid symbol, indicating that Justice sits in office between the duality of good and evil, past and future, etc. In medieval manuscripts there are illustrations of God's helpers weighing the souls of the dead on huge pairs of scales and balancing them against their sins, to judge if they are worthy enough to pass on to Heaven. The drape behind Justice holds the same meaning, in as much that if we overcome our karma then we can move forward to return to unity and self-realisation.

Once we have studied the meaning of the number 8 note its correlation with number 2 in connection to the symbolism depicted above.

Note also that the figure of Justice is feminine and this associated with the Empress and our individual nature.

The number 8

Number 8 comes under the realm of water.

On our overturned circle the number 8 relates to the number 2 and the unmanifest. The cycle of creation and dissolution is started and merged in this state when under the realm of 8.

The number 8 is represented by water, which stands for bonds. This holds things together. In the realm of both atomic and other structures it is only the bonds which keep matter together. In Sanskrit it is called Sneha. (Notice how similar Sneha is to our word snare, which means to trap or entangle.) Sneha is the bonds between things and people. It is the sort of love which keeps them together. In both cases number 8 acts as the store which keeps all things together, and also as the bond which keeps them together on universal and individual levels.

Sugar is seen in crystal form, and when diluted in water it dissolves in such a way that nothing is seen of the crystal. The same substance, when heated, once again forms the bond and a crystal is created. Similarly the elemental particles of the universe come out of water and hold together. If there was no bond between the particles, the particles would disintegrate and disperse in space. The world of form is produced by particles only because the bonds of water hold them together.

This is also threefold. The first store is that of the unmanifest, in which millions of universes are involved, and out of which the substances are poured to form different universes, and in time these substances again return to it. The second store is that of the Brahma, who is the presiding deity of one single universe (God, or whatever personal name you wish to use), and through which the multifarious forms of this world find their way in appointed time and go back to unity. The third is the store of the individual who manifests differently through the store of sanskaras*, and once again forms them for his next life.

[* Sanskara:- A deep mental impression produced by past experiences, a mental or behavioural pattern, latency.

Karma (*kri* to do) Action; former actions which will lead to certain results in a cause and effect relationship.]

It is important to understand the full meaning of these Sanskrit words as I shall use them often. They are both pertinent to the number 8, which is why I mention them in detail here.

The mind (chitta) is likened to a blank cinema screen. As we project the film of life onto it we experience colours, pictures etc. When man is perfect there is no residue left on this screen after each action, or experience. With imperfect men, such as ourselves, who have not yet attained enlightenment, life's passage leaves the chitta, or mind, tainted; and it is these deep mental impressions and behavioural patterns which are known as Sanskara. Note how even the newborn child has its own character right from birth, its own unique behavioural pattern. This is due to the individual's Sanskara which it has accumulated from life time to life time.

In Astrology, the natal, or birth chart, is representative of the pattern of Sanskara which an individual has been born with.

This is why it is so important for us all to follow a path through life which is correct for us, whether it be high or humble. Karma, being action which will lead us to certain results in a cause and effect relationship, gives us the opportunity and right circumstances in which to deal with our personal Sanskara. In this way we cleanse the chitta and obtain enlightenment.

Both Karma and Sanskara are binding which is why they are pertinent to number 8.

The element of water is the element of bond; and it is only the bonds which create limitation. Due to bonds all the shapes of the universe have their existence, and all shapes create a limit, or boundary through which particular types of bonds are working. With the end of the bond comes the end of the limit. Consciousness permeates and experiences the universe through these bonds and boundaries. The observer (watchman within each individual*) looks at these, and when he associates himself with any of these big or small boundaries, he establishes duality. Thus bonds create duality.

* The Observer, or watchman, is that part of each individual which consciously watches a situation. Raising our level of consciousness helps us to recognise the observer within.

The misery of our human race is only due to these different types of bonds with which we associate.

The first physical association of I is with the body, which is the smallest limit.

****

There are three states of water.

The first is the universal water out of which the oceans are created. The water of the River Ganges is said to be Sattvika because it never gets polluted under any circumstances.

The second is the water in the atmosphere which, stored as cloud, reaches us through rivers and rain. This is Rajasika water and the rain and rivers give us drinking water, irrigation etc.

The third is Tamasika water which is polluted and not fit for use.

The symbolism of Justice

Justice is depicted as a female figure, which symbolises the unconscious or the unknown. We have already seen how 8 relates to the High Priestess at 2, and here we find the external, or experienced influence of the expression of the High Priestess; that which has come through from the causal level.

In general we do not know what actions took place in a previous life which created a particular set of karmic circumstances. This is why, when we meditate, and seek to reach beyond the physical plane and enter the subtle and causal realms, answers come to us; not necessarily about what might have taken place, but how to deal with a situation. The techniques of Far Memory, or Past Life Regression, can help us to unravel the mysteries of karmic patterns. Tarot can also be used to gain insight into repeat patterns and cycles of karma.

The Sword

Justice holds the Sword of discrimination in her right hand. The right hand always indicates the conscious mind and the left the unconscious. Even psychologists and scientists alike have come to recognise that the left hand side of the brain controls the right hand side of the body, and reason and logic; while the right hand side of the brain controls the left hand side of the body, and creative and intuitive thought. Thus we see that it is the mind which discriminates, with knowledge, reason etc.

(You will find a fuller description of the symbolism of the sword under "The Ace of Swords")

The Scales

The scales fall under the realm of number 3. We have the two dishes, equally balanced, and the third point of the handle being held by Justice. The two dishes relate to everything which falls under the realm of 2:- the unmanifest, opposites, duality, etc. The third point relates to everything which falls under the realm of 3:- nature, manifestation, etc. Thus we see that all action comes from the unmanifest, and ultimately returns there. We also have the principle of Karma; right action which brings duality into balance, thus creating unity. Also it indicates that the three gunas are in balance.

The scales, being held in the left hand, indicate the unconscious nature of these forces. We often do not consciously recognise how our Karma is being dealt with, and that whatever happens, whether seemingly good or bad, it is meant to be, and that the individual has the power to learn and rise above any adverse conditions. The left hand also represents the creative energy which can be used to overcome our personal Sanskara.

The scales are, perhaps, more commonly associated with references as occur in the Bible. In Samuel (ii,3) Hannah prayed and said "for the Lord is a God of knowledge, and by Him actions are weighed". This type of quote very often gives the impression that "God", as spoken of in the Bible, is some kind of entity which is in control of us. This is not the case. "God" is within us all as the immovable, unchangeable self which stands beyond the ego. It is up to us to overcome our sanskara; we hold the answers in our hands; for we each have the sword of discrimination and knowledge within us. The absolute, of which we are all a part, provides the right circumstances and events in which to act. Which way we go is guided by our own free will.

Interpretation and Divination

The Justice card refers to all of the bonds which bind us to this life time. Some may feel positive and some may feel negative. To say to someone during a reading that "this is your karma" or simply "fate", sounds rather blase, yet this is the meaning of the card. Surrounding cards will help you gain insight into what part of the client's life is indicated and why current circumstances are so important in resolving karmic patterning. Often the Justice card will be surrounded by an abundance of Major Cards implying that this is a very significant phase for the client.

A very common question during a reading is for the client to ask "Why am I with this particular partner?" Frequently the Justice card is chosen from the face down pack in response, indicating that it is a karmic or "fated" relationship, and that the two people have had dealings with each other in a previous incarnation and have met again in order to work through particular issues. I recall one client who had the Justice card for such a question. She said, "It was such a strange meeting. I was at my brother's house, and when the doorbell rang I went and answered the front door. This man stood there and I just knew that I'd met him before, I knew him even though we'd never met in this lifetime. I also knew that he'd become my husband.". I have also known couples who have both felt that they have met each other in a previous life. As a test they have both secretly written on a piece of paper the type of relationship they had before or the kind of people they were. They have then exchanged pieces of paper and found uncanny similarities; such as "I rescued you" and "You saved me". It is the bonds between people which create this type of recognition. Once these bonds are realised the couples can go on to do fulfilling and meaningful work on their relationship or overall life path.
Sometimes these bonds can be examined during the course of a reading. For example, a woman may feel that she is in an unfulfilling karmic

relationship. When asked to take a card to represent her partner it comes up as the Emperor. This offers the image of a strong, dominant figure who treats her like a child or acts as a father figure. Further discussion may show that she was first attracted to him for these qualities and that she always felt that he had some authority over her; thus suggesting a father/daughter relationship in a previous life.

Some people talk about "owing" their partner something or another due to strong karmic bonds and do not realise when it is time to break from the relationship and stop creating further karma between the two of them. If this scenario is implied by a reading then it may be appropriate to suggest that the client considers going for Tie Cutting, a creative visualisation process, facilitated by a therapist, in which the ties which bind are symbolically observed and then severed. During this process the bonds manifest in many forms, and people have described their bonds to me as anything from gossamer spider's thread to a tree trunk. The cutting implement also changes from person to person and while some use a pair of scissors others choose a chain saw....and that's for the spider's thread! The benefit of this process is that it gives the individual space from the other person, allowing them to both move forward in life.

On a mundane level the Justice card can also mean the judicial system or legal matters. There is God's law and there is man's law. Whether we like it or not we are all bound by the law of the land in which we live. On this level the card pertains to judges, solicitors or legal issues in general.

When the card is **reversed** we experience resentment and feel that life is unjust and unfair. Yes, life often does appear unfair, but when resentment grips us we are unable to function efficiently and consequently we make ourselves ill with bitterness. At such times we also tend to alienate others and the whining whinge in our voice drives previously compassionate folk away.

The law of karma is very hard to fathom and it is extremely difficult not to feel bitter when life brings us tragedy and grief. To overcome the resentment is a way of breaking the bonds.

When the **reversed** Justice card is referring to legal matters then we might well feel justified in expressing our resentment, because here injustice, corruption and 'bad judgement' on the part of the authorities are indicated. We have only to watch programmes on television, or speak to people who have been falsely accused to realise how deeply wounding such issues are. Again we need to look to the karma of the individual to try and reveal why they have experienced something so traumatic. There are many possibilities. Some people find their life path through these injustices and go on to do a life-time's work, resolving to change certain aspects of the law and fight for justice. For others it is more personal and centred around their own sanskara.

Key Words

Karma/sanskara
Justice/Karmic bonds/Things which tie us to people, places or situations/
The Legal System/Judge/Legal representative/The Law
Reversed - Resentment/bitterness/Injustice/Feeling that life is unfair
Corrupt judiciary/solicitor or anyone who is supposed to uphold the law

Bach Flower Remedy

Willow - for feelings of resentment.
Walnut - to help break the ties which bind.

Toni Allen
The System of Symbols ©

The Hermit No. 9

The Image

The Hermit is pictured as an elderly, bearded man, walking along, bearing his weight on a wooden staff held in his left hand. He wears the cloak of a capuchin, the large hood pulled away from his head and down across his shoulders. In his right hand he holds a lamp, lifted to about eye level and slightly shrouded by his cloak, as if shielding the flame as he raises it to illuminate his path. Like the Emperor he faces the left of the card, as if going backwards rather than forwards, or perhaps he merely alludes to the secrets held at the causal and subtle realms rather than the external, physical world.

There is nothing specific to suggest that the Hermit is a religious man, except his habit like mantle...but wouldn't we all wrap up warm if walking when it's dark and maybe cold? Never the less he is often referred to as "the Seeker on the path".

Waite depicts the Hermit with only slight variations, the main one being that the cloak does not envelop the lamp. Waite himself likens the Hermit to "The Light of the World", which I believe refers to Christ as there is a painting of the same title by William Holman Hunt, painted between 1853-56. In Hunt's painting Christ stands knocking gently at a door (said to be that of the human soul) and holds a lamp in his left hand. In many respects Hunt's image and that of the Hermit are similar. Hunt's painting became highly popular and I have a copy of it on an old postcard on which is quoted, "I said to the man who stood at the gate of the year; 'Give me a light that I may tread safely into the unknown'. And he replied; 'Go out into the darkness and put your hand into the hand of God. That shall be to you better than light and safer than a known way.'". Here we find references to Tejas at all levels, and also to God, or the Absolute, being safer 'than a known way', which intimates connection with the Lovers card.

So, we begin to realise that the Hermit is on an unknown path, one he has never walked before. He uses his staff to steady himself, and in Crowley's version the entire design is encompassed by a spiral of corn, or wheat stems, portraying that however much he aspires towards self-realisation he inevitably takes his human nature with him, and uses it for support. Crowley has also added another dimension, bringing in subtle references to the Fool card by including a three headed dog leaping up towards the light, which, like in Holman-Hunt's painting is held down by the Hermit's heels. This symbol raises various questions. Is this dog the same worldly desire which we are able to ignore in the Fool card, or is it the human nature aspiring to reach the light?

The number 9

Number 9 represents the element Earth.

On our overturned circle the number 9 relates to the number 1 and unity.

Earth is where physical phenomena have matured in full glory. This is the perfect physical form.

The material phenomena of the coarse world (as we experience it) starts from number 5 (ether/akasha). The ether is the transformer of subtle energy into physical energy. It has the quality of both the subtle and the physical. The physical aspect of ether is sound. It comes from space and also manifests in space. Where there is no space there is no sound. Ether alone holds the sound. Then comes air (6). Air gives the sensation of touch and can also carry sound. Thus it has two qualities. Third is the Tejas (fire-7) which has three qualities within itself; the heat and light from its own form, touch of air and sound of ether. Fourth is the realm of water, which has taste and bonds of its own, the heat and form of fire, touch of air and sound of ether. Thus it reflects four qualities. The last of the physical world is earth. It has smell and crystalline form of its own, the taste and bond of water, heat and form of fire, touch of air and the sound of ether.

In earth all these sensations are possible, but this does not mean that in ether there is no heat or touch. They are all there, but ether only manifests sound. They lie there unmanifest and only manifest according to the system described above.

Thus the element Earth is the glorious end of one cycle, where the absolute (unity-1) stands as the glorious beginning on the other side. The element Earth is glorious because it is only through the earth that all things of the world are created. Man, birds, plants, etc., are all created from earth.

The number 9 cannot be broken in-as-much as one can multiply 9 with any number and yet the total of the digits will always be 9; for example, $9 \times 2 = 18, = 1 + 8 = 9$, and $9 \times 3 = 27, = 2 + 7 = 9$, and so on. The number 9 thus always remains the same.

The symbolism of the Hermit

The Hermit symbolises any person who is on the path of self-discovery. He is the earthly incarnation of the Magician at number 1.

There is a lovely story that fits the Hermit superbly. A guru, having finished teaching one of his students for the day, come night-time, sets him off on his way home. The guru gives his student a lamp and saying goodbye, leaves him at the doorway. The student stands in the dark and lifts the lamp up high, but cannot see the road ahead. Fearful, he knocks on the guru's door. "Master, master," he says, "I cannot see my way home!" The guru replies, "Look down and what do you see?" "I see the ground, master, and my feet, but no more." "Then you can get home," replies the guru. "Each step you take is illuminated. Each step you take is sure-footed. Take one step at a time, and you will get home safely."

This is the path of self-realisation. One step at a time, illuminated by the light within us. We have all been given a physical incarnation for the sole purpose of realising the self. There is no hurry, no rush, just a sure footed step.

The qualities of earth give us all the faculties we require to succeed on our journey. Connection with the causal realm through ether, and sound; intelligence and touch through air; many forms of fire through tejas; taste and bonds through water and lastly the physical body in which the soul can make its journey.

Interpretation and Divination

It is only through the use of the physical body that we can attain self-realisation in this lifetime. Thus the Hermit symbolises the body.

As a rule hermits are associated with isolation and loneliness, but the Hermit is not necessarily a lonely character. A hermit only appears lonely to those who look from the outside, and live in a world where constant chatter and companionship are deemed essential for the wellbeing of fragile souls who are often too afraid to be still and listen to their inner thoughts. A hermit chooses to be alone so that he may be at one with himself and his maker. Self-realisation is rarely found in the bustle of a disco or the continual noise of busy towns. We all require quiet times in which to reflect and be by ourselves.

Once on our spiritual path we gain knowledge and wisdom of secrets unknown to others. Whether we call these occult secrets, or religious secrets, or magical secrets is irrelevant. What is important is that they are known to us and maybe also to others who follow the same school of thought, but they are hidden from the world in general. As much as we might like everyone else to become as enlightened as we are, or follow the same philosophy because we find it to be true and exciting, there is little point in exposing ourselves to prejudice from ignorant people or ridicule from those who fear our presence.

I can recall a time when, shortly after having moved home, a

Toni Allen
The System of Symbols ©

neighbour called in to visit me. He was already aware that I was a Tarot reader and apparently had no problem with it. However, I had a large, hand painted Sri-Yantra hanging on my wall. Due to its triangular shapes he appeared to mistake it for another symbol and suddenly started flustering, saying, "Ah well, Devil worship, ha ha, yea, I'm okay with that. I've read Dennis Wheatley." I realised that there was no point in trying to explain that the Sri-Yantra has nothing what-so-ever to do with Hammer House of Horror films, and quickly decided that it might be more appropriate if I kept some of my more personal items upstairs, where ordinary folk were less likely to see them. The Hermit talks of this kind of action. Keeping one's religious or philosophical beliefs secret and hidden due to the reaction of others which arises through their lack of understanding.

Consequently the Hermit also talks of any situation in which it is wise to keep something secret, and thus he symbolises prudence. By no means is the Hermit a liar, or schemer, for sometimes it is wiser to keep things close to one's chest. I have seen the Hermit come up in many readings where the client agrees that they are keeping things to themself, often for reasons of personal safety or security, or to protect others. Once more we find a similarity with the Christ figure in that Jesus shared his secrets and taught others his beliefs. He held nothing back and was subsequently crucified due to other people's fear...they preferred to let a thief go free rather than hear the truth.

When the Hermit appears in a reading it not only shows the secrets but also advises that it is prudent to keep certain information concealed. When **reversed** the Hermit symbolises someone who is unable to open up to others at a close level and indicates lack of trust and over caution. We all have 'dark secrets' or 'skeletons in the closet' and somewhere in life there is always someone to share them with. It is when we refuse to speak to anyone, even those closest to us, that we become bound in fears of being found out or disclosed, and then it is difficult for us to shine our light in the physical world and ultimately the body becomes ill through disease.

I saw such a situation for one young woman. The reversed Hermit was centrally placed in the reading and crossed the Queen of Swords reversed. She was twenty three, still living at home with her parents and although she had a boyfriend was feeling that she should break off the relationship. Other cards made it obvious that because she held a 'dark secret' her parents were threatening to throw her out of home if she revealed it to anyone; yet they, who knew of it, were unwilling to discuss the issue. She desperately wanted to tell her boyfriend the secret as she felt that keeping it from him was stopping her from being able to get close to him and have an open, honest relationship. Whether he rejected her was not the issue, the most important aspect was to let go of the secret. Ultimately the secret was released into my hands, and as if by magic the young woman was transformed from looking old and exhausted into the bright youth that she was. This example illustrates how not only was the enforced keeping of the secret damaging the woman mentally, but also physically by inhibiting her fire energy and suppressing her from being who she truly was.

There is no striving in the Hermit, there is only being. We do not wake up every morning and order our body to do a particular task, such as breath, it simply happens. So it should be with life, one step at a time, without hurry or exertion. Yet we all chase and race around, fearing that we might miss a trick, or not achieve the goal we have set ourself. The Hermit is plodding and slow. Accordingly, if the Hermit card is taken when asking how long a matter might take we can see that it will be slow, and not ended quickly.

Key Words

The physical body/Prudence/Caution/The seeker on the path
Seclusion as a means to find oneself/Secrets/secretiveness
Reversed - Lack of trust/overcautious/Disease of the physical body, either through physical or mental inhibitions

Toni Allen
The System of Symbols ©

The Wheel of Fortune No. 10

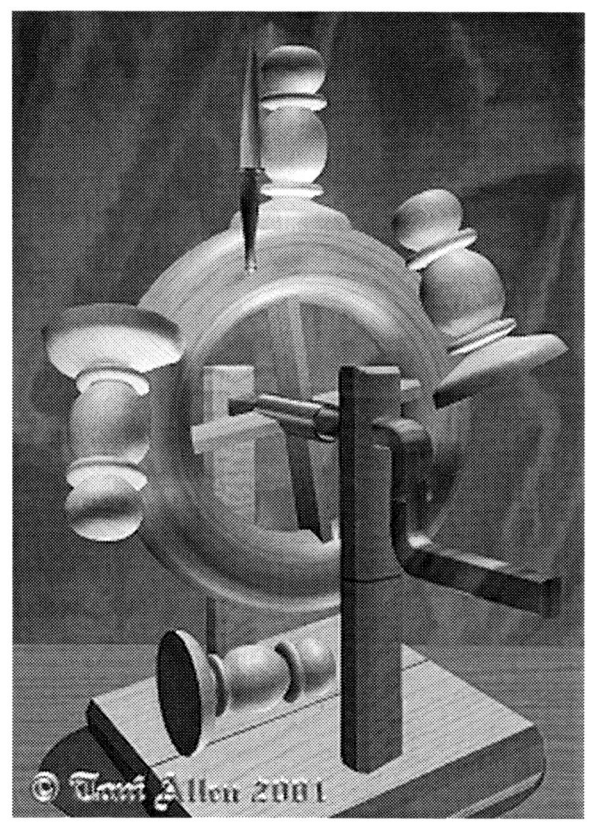

The Image

The Wheel of Fortune is a very ancient symbol, and in consequence there are variations on the theme and I personally feel that these alternatives are important as they can lead to very different interpretations of the card, especially as artists of the Tarot have incorporated most alternatives. These will be expanded upon under the symbolism of the card.

The Wheel is a circle, and there are many symbols of both.
1) A circle, or wheel has no beginning and no end, no corners or places to hide, no head of the table; hence King Arthur and the equality he dared to express through his round table.
2) Western astrology uses a wheel to map out the stars and the life pattern of an individual on a natal chart.

3) The Earth is round, and so are the planets.
4) The Yin-Yang symbol is circular. Male/female in equal proportion.
5) Then there are the wheels on the Chariot card, symbolising the cycles which progress the human spirit forward.
6) Clocks are circular...that is, non-digital ones. But have you noticed how non- user friendly digital clocks are? They tell us the time, but little else. A round clock gives us an immediate visual concept of how much time we have before the next hour, or how long we might have waited.
7) The trunks of trees and plants are cylindrical, their cross-section circular...and interestingly, so are flowerpots! Yet you can place far more square pots on a work bench than you can round ones. So why do we nearly always choose round ones? Is it that the shape is more sympathetic to some unconscious part of us?
And so on.....

The Number 10

The number 10 is literally 1 with 0 (zero) next to it. In Vedic numerology the limit of numbers is 9. 1 to 9 are the numbers of manifestation, and at 10 the same self which is 1 stands with unmanifest Prakriti by its side. The 1 at 10 embodies the 9 manifestations within it. The creation starts with 1 and at 10 it again stands as 1 with all 9 manifestations.

The absolute is 1 and with the start of creation it unfolds itself in 9 states and there it ends. In this 9 state creation we see all manifestation. When all the stages of creation have seen their fulfilment, it once again unites in the same absolute. The Vedas suggest that this universe is created by the absolute, the creation of manifested forms is sustained by it, and in the end the whole creation will once again merge into it.

Thus the number 10 is both the conclusion of one cycle and the beginning of another. It is the beginning and the end.

In Tarot the numbers 1 to 9 show a very pure line, a perfect unfoldment from 1 to 9. The numbers 11 to 19 depict a less pure line in which obstacles need to be overcome and we carry a burden of karma. The number 10 sits as a pivot point between these two unfoldments of manifestation, and by its very nature indicates that on our journey from 1 to 9 we have created karma. Everything we have done sits within the circle or zero of the wheel, and we can choose where and when to step off and take action.

The symbolism of The Wheel of Fortune

The traditional Marseille pack depicts the wheel of fortune as a large wheel set on a plinth, apparently on a piece of land and with a handle to turn it. Clinging to the right hand side of the wheel is an animal like figure rising to the top of the wheel, while on the left a similar figure riding down to the bottom of the wheel. Sometimes there is a figure directly at the bottom, but always a gremlin or lion type figure sitting at the top, on a little plinth, either cloaked or winged, often crowned and with an upright pointed sword in its left hand.

    The Marseille depiction is a positive one. The wheel symbolises the zero of number 10, the actions we have done and the actions we are yet to do. The wheel has a handle and we are free to turn it as we please. The figure rising up symbolises all of those times when we feel good and that "things are on the up", while the downward figure on the left symbolises all of those times when we feel that life has taken a downward spiral. Any figure directly at the base of the wheel shows us at rock bottom. The figure at the top, however, is different. It has the sword of discrimination in its hand and watches the events unfolding, unaffected by them. This symbolises the self within, that watchman side of us which is neither affected by the good, nor the bad. We all have the ability to rise above our emotions and watch events from a highly detached point of view.

    The whole of the Vedic scripture of the Geeta is about Arjuna's dilemma and the crisis within himself of how to perform certain actions. His main conflict is that he must go onto the battlefield and slay his relatives, without accruing more karma for his actions. One of the disciplines that Krishna teaches him is the way of non-attachment, which leaves no residue from an action. In the Wheel of Fortune card the topmost figure symbolises both our ability to stay non-attached, and our ability to create karma by becoming involved in the ups and downs that life throws at us. The sword in its hand has echoes of the Justice card, a reminder that whatever we involve ourselves in is either creating karma or dealing with it, thus we need discrimination to remain detached.

    The three figures also relate to the three gunas. The figure on the top is sattvik and filled with good judgement and discrimination, the upward figure rajasik and active in the world, while the downward figure is tamasik and inclined to negative behaviour.

In the Marseille pack we have a clear indication of the self within having some control over the events which unfold in a lifetime, while in the Swiss IJJ pack the story is different. Here the picture is similar, but with the inclusion of Fortuna, the goddess of good and bad luck vigorously turning the wheel. Here the wheel has tree like supports and grows on the top of a mountain. Fortuna is blindfolded, and looking away as she spins the wheel and rises some human occupants to the top of the wheel and revelry, and spins others over into the precipice of misery. The suggestion here is that life is indiscriminate and that no-one has any control over what happens to them as it is all in the hands of fate; her choice of lucky or unlucky people is not concerned with karma or right action, simply with fortune.

There is also the concept that the Wheel of Fortune symbolises man's cycle from birth to death to rebirth, as illustrated in a manuscript of 1461 entitled Losbuch from Augsburg. Around the wheel one individual's life is mapped out, the zenith of his career as a knight standing on top of the wheel, while his death, clutching a spade, slides down to a tomb at the bottom.

Waite's Wheel of Fortune pictures the four elements of the physical creation sitting in the corners of the design, bringing in parallels to the World card, and showing that cycles rely on, and include, these elements during their existence.

Interpretation and Divination

The Wheel of Fortune does not express fortune itself but the vicissitudes of life, its ups and downs. Upright the card shows one's ability to "stay on top" of a situation, like the watchman on the top of the wheel. Here one is not affected adversely and accepts that a situation simply is, and that whether one likes it or not one has to live with it. It also indicates that any predicament that is asked about during a reading will continue. It is on going. For some people this is good news, for others bad e.g. "Will my boyfriend and I stay together?" The upright Wheel of Fortune is a definite "yes" as it suggests continuation, but not without its ups and downs. (The ups and downs bit often brings a smile to the client's lips, due to its sexual connotations. Yet a good sex life is often instrumental in keeping a couple together. It also shows that sexual problems can be overcome, because after things have been down they go up again!) Conversely the same question answered with the **reverse** card indicates that the questioner is not in control of the situation. Perhaps the other person is in some way detrimentally influencing the overall pattern of the questioner's life, so more cards may be needed to find out exactly what is going on.

Due to the on-going nature of the card it also suggests time passing, and therefore often indicates delays. E.g. "Will my house sell soon?" The Wheel of Fortune indicates an ongoing need to market the house.

Due to its connection with 0, 1 and 10 the Wheel indicates the ending of one cycle in preparation for the next. Things culminate here while the groundwork is being done for the next phase or cycle of one's life. Take the above example of moving house. It may well be on the market, but just think of all the changes that have already taken place in readiness for the new home. The next house needs to be chosen. Perhaps the move is connected to major changes in life, such as marriage or divorce, or relocating for a better job, or needing more space so that a family can be established, or maybe even retirement. All of these show the individual at a specific stage somewhere on the wheel of life. Some people might equate retirement with the bottom of the wheel and death, while others will think positively, and see it as a release from the tomb of drudgery of continual work, and a time to be "on the up" and explore new hobbies and travel or play.

When the Wheel is upright one feels in control, as if one is turning the handle and can choose when to stop and jump off. However, when the Wheel is **reversed** we feel that others have taken control of our lives and that we are "out of control". Here we might have the feeling that our life is fated and unfair, or that it is time to change and rid ourselves of the circumstance, or person, who controls our life.

The **reversed** card brings speed because everything appears to be rushing past us, and things are changing too fast, and there is no time to think or judge the situation from a quiet standpoint. Bad luck might appear to take over here, but this is generally a result of not thinking straight due to being rushed or possibly being pushed into hasty decisions by others.

Key Words

The ups and downs of life/End of one cycle in preparation for the beginning of another/The beginning and the end/Change/Control/Continuing situation
Reversed - Out of control/Being rushed/Many changes

Toni Allen
The System of Symbols ©

The Strength Card No. 11

The Image

The Strength card is depicted as a woman opening the jaws of a lion. Like the Magician at number 1 she wears a wide brimmed sombrero which forms the sideways figure of eight of the lemniscape.

Waite does little to change the overall image of Strength, although the woman appears to have already tamed the lion and be stroking its nose as if it's a pussy cat. As with his Magician he has taken off her hat and the lemniscape floats above her head. He has also changed her number to 8, having transposed her with Justice who now sits at 11, but as he says, this is "For reasons which satisfy myself...." Meanwhile Crowley calls the card "Lust" and portrays a naked woman riding the lion like beast, as if in ecstasy. The lion is given seven heads and he describes them as "an angel, saint, poet, adultress, warrior, satyr and lion-serpent."

In the Mantegna prints Strength is named Forteza, or Fortitude, and shows a standing woman breaking a column with one hand, as if its an iced decoration off a wedding cake rather than the five foot high pillar made of stone in front of her. We can see the lion in the background behind her, and although in the sequence of the cards she is placed amongst what are described as the "Cosmic Principles" along with Faith, Hope and Charity; Fortitude is on the only one wearing an armoured breastplate over her flowing gown. The breast-plate echoes the shape of the lions head, and she appears to have a matching visor pushed to the back of her head, and she holds some sort of sceptre in her right hand. Here we have a cross between the Marseille image and a more war like quality of physical strength, courage and tenacity. A silent warrior.

The Number 11

Number 11 is the equivalent of number 1 on the second cycle.
The creation begins at one, and signifies the entry of the Atman into creation. The ultimate, or the Absolute (Brahman) is 1, and with the start of creation it unfolds itself in 9 states and there it ends. In this nine stage creation we can see all the manifestation. When all the stages of the creation have seen their fulfilment, it once again unites in the same absolute.

In the Tarot the unfoldment of 1 to 9 symbolises perfection, while numbers 11 to 19 depict our human struggles with imperfection, and the reaping and sowing of karma. One could say that 11 to 19 represent a parallel dimension to 1 to 19, exactly the same qualities but with a residue of karma attached. Here we can see how each stage from 1 to 9 manifests through our karma and the obstacles we must overcome in order to reach perfection.

It is not possible for any human being who has not attained self-realisation to constantly walk only the path of life from numbers 1 to 9. Our karma leads us from the line of perfection to the line of imperfection. By learning from the lessons of the numbers 11 to 19, and clearing our karma, we are able to attain wisdom through observing our personal samskara and thus it is possible for us to obtain release from the bondage of karma. Thus we can step back onto the line of 1 to 9 in certain areas of life, while the cyclical nature of life brings us new dilemmas in other areas. This can be observed in readings by the rhythm of the cards, patterns of numbers and placement of the Major Cards.

All the world of manifestation concludes into 0 (zero), which symbolises the unmanifest prakriti. With this unmanifest prakriti by its side, the 1, which is absolute, forms number 10. At number 11 we find all of this, plus the individuals sanskara which threatens to tie him to the physical alternation of constant death and rebirth.

The number 11 is therefore the absolute of 1 with the duality of its imperfect ego by its side.

The Symbolism of the Strength Card

In Shiva we find God in the aspect of the "destroyer", who brings about the destruction of the ego (ahamkara) and of death itself. Around his limbs he usually wears a tiger skin symbolising that the tiger of lust has been slain. It is this same "tiger of lust", although depicted by a lion, which the woman, equivalent of the magician or self, controls in the Strength card.

The lion personifies all of our desires and negative thoughts, which lead us away from perfection and attainment of union with the absolute. At number 1 the Magician has the potential to use any faculty he wishes, as set out on his table. At 11 he has the same inherent qualities, but can only realise them once he has tamed human desire in the form of the lion. Without controlling this desire nature one cannot obtain insight. It is only the ego which lusts after anything, even spiritual attainment. This may sound contradictory, yet in many "spiritual groups" it is not uncommon to find a master adept who "lusts" after power and is quickly prone to jealousy, especially when a new member joins, who, although apparently uninitiated, has greater inherent knowledge and understanding than the master. I have known of such people who consequently try and hold back the new pupil in an attempt to stay in the most powerful position.

In the Bible one of the most notable references to the principle symbolised by the strength card is the story of Samson. His strength lay in his purity. Samson slew the lion depicted in the Strength card with his hands. He overcame his animal, or base, nature. It is interesting to note that so long as Samson was pure in heart his strength was boundless.

Delilah was a harlot who enticed him to let off the lion of lust, which consequently lost him his strength, and his sight, which is symbolic of his spiritual insight.

If we review the cards already spoken of we can see a clear pattern emerging. The lion is a similar desire figure as the one depicted by the dog in the Fool. The Fool walks away, oblivious of the animal, unaffected and unperturbed by it chomping at his backside. In the Lovers card we find the Magician caught between two paths, that of truth and that of desire. One of the women might well be Delilah, seducing him towards a karmic path of repeat behaviour. Then at the Strength card we find the Magician, the seeker on the path, depicted in feminine form to show that no brute strength is needed to very calmly pacify the beast.

In the Visconti Sforza pack the Strength card is depicted by a man beating the lion into submission with a large cudgel. Perhaps this is Samson, or maybe it is how people of the time saw the taming of the beast within, something that could only be achieved with ferocious inner work. The Marseille depiction shows a much easier, calmer approach, suggesting that the less we do, as far as self degradation and wanting things to happen, the more we achieve. After all it is a physically weaker woman achieving control through simple self-mastery. The woman also symbolises the feminine, unconscious side of our nature, suggesting that self control may be achieved through silence and meditation, and that the power is intrinsic and cannot be sought in the logical world.

Interpretation and Divination

The strength card's main reference is to self control. On the highest level it is someone who mediates and quietly controls all of their inner thoughts and confusion. On a more usual daily level it is any situation in which we find that we require that we watch ourselves and master our actions or words.

How many times do we find ourselves in a situation in which someone has "pressed the wrong button" and we find ourself bristling inside, ready to jump down their throat if they say another word. We either let the lion off (reversed card) and allow our anger and irritation spew all over them; or we keep as outwardly calm as possible, deal with the situation in a composed manner, or perhaps remove ourselves from the situation all together. (upright card).

In a reading the Strength card depicts anything which we are consciously holding back. Quite often it comes up for people who are actively controlling their sexual desires. e.g. A married woman actively controlling her passion and not rushing head long into an affair. Or, a man controlling his desire for his wife because she is unwell. Neither of these situations are particularly comfortable, and the client is generally more than aware that a vital, passionate part of them is being held in check, yet they are consciously doing it because they feel that it is the wisest course of action in a given situation.

Anger and irritation are other common emotions that individuals hold back on, knowing that to lose their rag will only make matters worse and not resolve anything. For the **reversed** card a very common scenario is when a woman is suffering from PMT. I have had many a man sit in front of me and say that periodically their partner becomes irrationally irritable and crabby. When I propose that it's as if they've let the lion off and its going around snarling and biting people, they chuckle, and suggest that I must have seen their wife last week, because that's exactly what her change of character feels like. With PMT situations like the one described, the individual is thrown out of balance by a rush of hormones, which sometimes overwhelm them with such a torrent of emotions that everything appears exaggerated and difficult to deal with, so much so that their usual self control is gone.

Sometimes, however, the Strength card shows that the questioner is holding back something positive, rather than something negative. Here surrounding cards must be taken into consideration, but a simple example is the Empress card upright followed or crossed by the Strength card. Something vital which needs to be given birth to is being restrained. Following cards will suggest whether this is due to fear, fear of failure, fear of reprisals or disapproval etc. At times our karma is connected with things which we need to do, rather than things which we feel we shouldn't do. Life time after life time we may have censored ourselves, or had a rough ride and therefore become fearful of trying again. Relationships are relevant here too. So many people have difficult, or sad relationships, that they hold back on committing themselves again. Very often the Strength card comes up with the Ace of Cups reversed next to it, showing that someone has hardened their heart to full emotional and sexual expression.

Toni Allen
The System of Symbols ©

These people then start to experience sexual problems because they cannot let themselves go and once again enjoy the passionate side of life because something has happened which has made them cut off and suppress their natural urges.

There are also occasions when the **reversed** Strength card is very positive. The negative side of the reversed card is when desire, greed, anger, lust or jealousy control us to the point of us being out of control. The positive side is when hidden creativity emerges and is let loose in an unrestrained blaze of glory, or the person who has always worn a "hair shirt" and been incredibly "good" releases their grip and activates an unfamiliar, or remote, part of their nature. We have all been brought up not to do certain things, and although this may be sound advice to a child, it is not necessarily appropriate for the emerging adult. If we were never permitted to try paints because they were messy, or music because it was noisy, or gardening because it was dirty, then how are we ever to know if we might find creative self-expression through these media? Ironically, an all too frequent scenario with the Strength card reversed is when a woman hits middle age and decides to abandon "the dutiful wife" routine and pursue the career in art which her parents would not financially support her through when she was young, because it "wouldn't make money". Having reached an age of maturity and financial stability these women fund their own artistic courses, and I have seen several set up financially lucrative businesses.

It is when we have been inhibited in connection with drink, drugs, sex, or generally having a good time, that the reversed card shows the risk of us becoming overwhelmingly involved in licentious behaviour. Although it may sound like a contradiction in terms it is useful for any individual to get in touch with "negative" parts of themselves, such as anger, fear, sorrow etc. Sometimes drink, drugs or sex are a means of unlocking suppressed inner pain which normally would not be shown. A common example is when someone drinks heavily and then shouts at everyone and becomes aggressive. If, afterwards, they then consider what the experience has brought into the open and consider how to deal with it, then the manifested lion can be useful. However when this type of behaviour is used as a repeat pattern of self damage, and abuse to those around them, then it does nothing but highlight their lack of control.

Key Words

Self control/Holding back on passion and desire. This may have a positive or negative effect depending upon surrounding cards.
Fortitude/Strength/Courage
Reversed - Passion/desire/Irritability/Argumentativeness
Possibly violence/Expression of suppressed parts of one's nature

Toni Allen
The System of Symbols ©

The Hanged Man No. 12

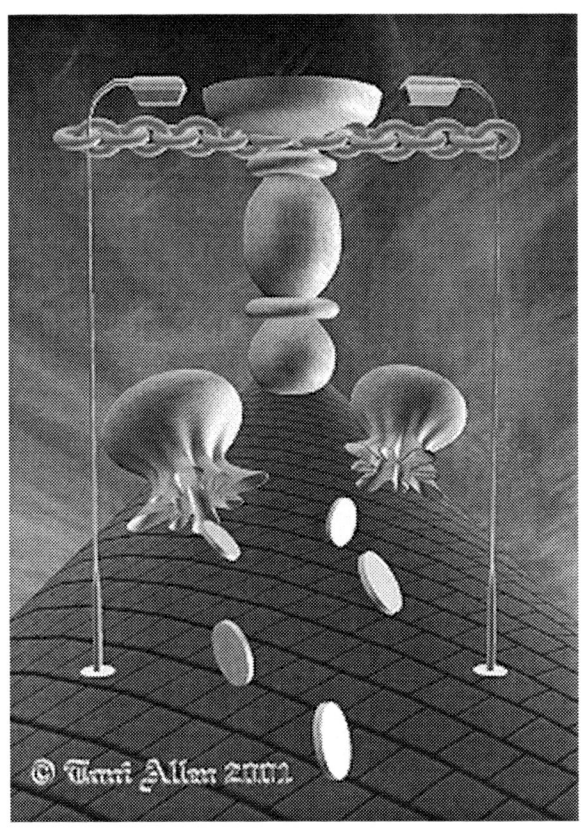

The Image

Recently, while running a lecture/workshop, I showed a series of slides of the Major cards, and when we came to the Hanged Man I was asked a very sensible question by one of the audience. "Why isn't he called the Hung Man?", I was asked. "Because he isn't hung", I replied. Or is he? Hanged and Hung do suggest much the same thing, except hanged is perhaps a more old fashioned way of saying it. The context in which we generally use the word hung today usually implies finality, such as "He was hung at dawn." In one sense he is not a Hanged Man at all, but a Hanging Man. So, maybe he should be called the Hanging Man? The answer is that somewhere the true title of the card has been lost in its translation from the French word Le Pendu. This derives from the French word pendre, to hang. Our word pendant comes from this origin and pendent means anything hanging. Of far greater interest is that pendency also derives from pendre; and means **undecided state**.

So what of this man who is hanging in an undecided state? He is not hung as at the gallows, but suspended by one foot from a crossbeam which is supported by two upright, chopped off at the top, trees. There is a fuller description of the image under the symbolism of the card.

Waite moved away from tradition a little by suspending the Hanged Man from a T shaped cross, which he calls a fylfot cross; while Crowley suspends him naked, tied with a serpent to an Ankh (symbol of life) rather than a tree, his other foot and hands nailed, as if in imitation of the crucified Christ._

The number 12

The number 12 is the second cycle of 2.

Number 2 represents the duality of the I and the non-I, or I and the rest of creation. This I is the ultimate unity of the absolute. Number 2 is where 1 stands as the consciousness looking around. Whatever comes into view forms another unit which is unmanifest Prakriti. (Nature)

Number 12, being on the second cycle, is where, rather than 1 "standing as consciousness looking all around", we have all of this, plus personal karma, as depicted by the number 11. This karma was created during previous cycles, thus showing that the number 12 holds both the duality of number 2 and the entire cycle of 10.

Thus the number 12 symbolises the duality before manifestation at 3, yet holds within it the potential for clearing one's karma; or carrying it forward.

The symbolism of the Hanged Man

Many people hold the preconception that the Hanged Man is a card of death and the gibbet, but a closer investigation of the picture will show that this is not the case. The Hanged Man is not hanging by his neck, but by his feet. Feet are a symbol of moving forward into the future and the Hanged Man (our Magician on his path) has consciously decided not to take any further steps at this point in time. In many respects he is in suspended animation. Simply hanging around contemplating his options. Undecided.

A crossbeam provides the support as the man is dangled by his foot between two poles. The two poles symbolise the duality of number 2, and we find echoes of the two pillars that the High Priestess sits between. The man is symbolic of one's nature and the samskara it has acquired. The man is no longer a free spirit, like the Fool, but weighed down by his past actions. In older Tarot's, such as the Grigonneur cards, he is often depicted holding moneybags. These moneybags, sometimes with coins spilling out, are indicative of many facets including his karma which weighs him down and the uselessness of worldly possessions; coins being not only characteristic of material wealth, but also his wealth of wisdom.

With the number 2's interrelation to number 8 we also have the binding quality of water. Are we tied to our karma, bound to it in just the same way as the Hanged Man is physically bound up between the poles of duality? But these poles are alive! They are not the same pillars of the temple of the soul that the High Priestess sits between. These poles have knobbly bits, like stripped branches, and sometimes they suggest the same shape as the Batons; as if they hold the qualities of nature. The self is caught up in the duality of its own human nature. Human nature creates samskara. The Batons the self is hung between are ruled by Tejas, fire, the light or glory which shines forth and makes up his nature. Here he only has himself to rely on, there is no High Priestess offering a book of truth. To indicate his self reliance the Hanged Man has his legs crossed in a most peculiar manner. Only one foot is tied, the other crosses this straightened leg at the back, thus making the number 4, expressing his sense of I AM.

In those traditional Marseille packs in which his hands are not holding money bags, but held as if clasped behind his back, they suggest a willingness to relinquish wisdom and gained wealth. As hands are the seat of air and the mental process, it also suggest that he is thinking about the situation.

Remember that the number 2 is also the unmanifest, the storehouse from which all things arise when the time is right. What we personally call from the store house depends upon what course of action we decide upon when in the realm of the Hanged Man. Anything can be made manifest when he steps forward to number 13, or backwards to number 11.

Forwards is the Death card, the repeated cycles of death and rebirth, while backwards lies self restraint and opportunities to control human desire and thus perfect one's nature.

The Hanged Man is suspended between duality, conscious of his past deeds, yet taking no action. His inertia is by no means a state of apathy; it's a state of contemplation. As yet he has not decided his right course of action.

Interpretation and Divination

The Hanged Man represents the action of non-action.

Taking no action in a given situation can sometimes be a much stronger statement than taking action. The Hanged Man symbolises those times when it is wiser to do nothing, and to wait and see what happens next. By doing this no further samskara is created. While one is doing nothing one has time to assimilate the consequences of one's actions and also assess one's role in the scenario which is unfolding.

The Hanged Man is also the state of non-action through indecision. Sometimes the High Priestess has a noticeable influence here, in that if the questioner does not have all the facts at their fingertips in connection with a particular problem, then it is difficult for them to make a well informed decision. Therefore it is wiser to do nothing until all aspects of the issue have come to light.

Alternatively the Hanged Man can also indicate that someone is biding their time and waiting for someone else to make the first move. One woman had the card in her reading crossed by the Ace of Batons, followed by the Devil reversed. We had already discussed the pending break-up of her marriage and the lack of sexual interest between herself and her husband. I suggested that the Ace of Batons (sexual awareness) covering the Hanged Man (waiting) indicated her being patient in finding a lover, but that she was not opposed to sleeping with someone else whilst still married (Devil reversed-lack of guilt). "Absolutely true", she answered. "Only I'm also waiting for my husband to sleep with someone else first. Once he's done that I won't feel guilty about doing it myself. I'm waiting for him to break the marriage vows first."

As always much of the interpretation of the card is related to other cards it is placed near.

E.g. The Hanged Man next to: - the Page of Swords - Someone is hanging around and loitering, perhaps up to no good.

Next to the Empress - waiting to give birth.

Next to the Justice card - waiting for a court hearing.

Next to the 4 of Swords - inactivity due to illness.

When the Hanged Man is **reversed** it suggests impatience and an inability to wait to see what happens next. Sometimes it's quite simply acting first and considering the consequences afterwards. On a more positive note it can also imply that the time of waiting is over, and that the questioner is now fully prepared to take action. "I can't wait any longer," one man said, "if I don't have all the facts now then I never will. I've sat on the fence for far too long."

One woman, who had been without word from her son for some considerable time, had the Hanged Man **reversed** placed some month or so in the future. "Thank God," she said. "He's travelling abroad and just to know that he's okay will be a blessing. This waiting without knowing how he is is driving me crazy." About five weeks after the reading she telephoned to let me know that her son had called her. "The waiting is over. The relief is incredible," she said. "It's as if I've been holding my breath these past months."

Key Words

Waiting/Patience/Indecision/Action in non-action/Hanging around.
Reversed - Impatience/The time for action is right/The waiting is over

Bach Flower Remedy

Impatiens - for those times when the reversed card suggests impatience.

Toni Allen
The System of Symbols ©

The Death Card No. 13

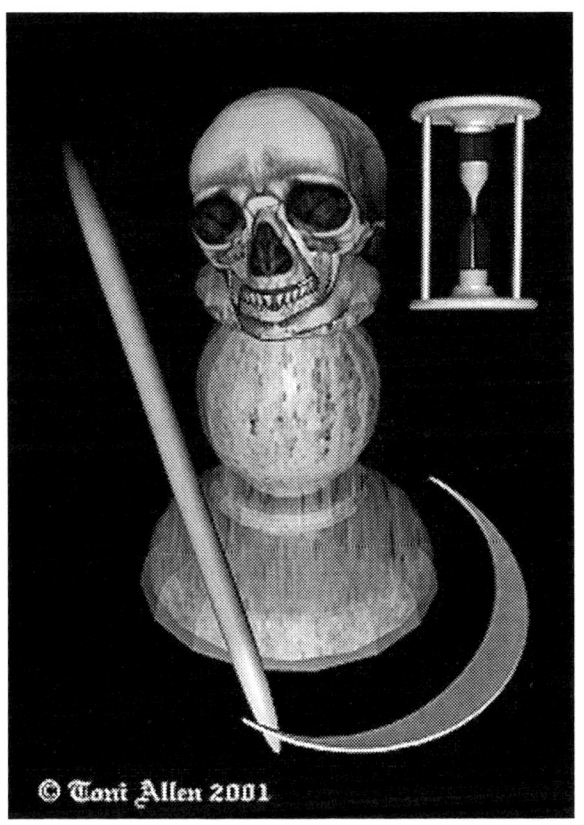

The Image

If you look at a selection of ancient Tarot packs you will find that all of the Major cards are titled...except Death. Mankind has always held its superstitions and many thought that to inscribe the name of Death was to invoke the spirit and call Death and consequent disaster upon oneself and one's family.

Historically there are many pictorial archetypes representing Death. Old Father Time with his hourglass, often seen sneaking up on children, kings or lesser mortals, has been a common theme in many artists' etchings. This represents a rather dark aspect of the deity, the hour glass reminding us of the transience of all things, that time is running out for all of us, and that when our time is up, Father Time will have what is

Toni Allen
The System of Symbols ©

lawfully his. Father Time also frequently carries a scythe, although once the scythe is in his hand he is more likely to be shown as a darkly cloaked, skull faced, figure...the grim reaper.

Today we do not hold these powerful images in such awe. Perhaps we do not accept Death, or understand it, or simply wish to mock it and shy away from our own mortality when we use the once mysterious and enigmatic figure of the Grim Reaper in comical television adverts to sell chocolates or insurance. This is a far cry from a society in which people were afraid to write the name of Death for fear of dark reprisals.

In a Marseille pack we find death represented as a skeleton, generally looking to our right, wielding a scythe through a landscape of human debris. There is nearly always a head or two amongst this carnage, one wearing a crown or a mitre to indicate that even the king or priest is not exempt from Death. No one is beyond the two things which intrinsically hold every human being in the race together, birth and death. They are equalisers. In between these two absolutes each individual can achieve a tremendous variety in social position, authority and wealth. During life men do not appear equal to each other, yet when Death comes along to reap his harvest no-one is privileged....or excluded.

In our two modern archetypes of Waite and Crowley we find them both naming Death...and there the similarity ends.

Crowley has the more traditional looking image, although his skeletal Death is positively hurtling along, his scythe sweeping onward in front of him, as if he's a man who really enjoys his work! We cannot see his face but I've always suspected that he's grinning with glee! At the feet of Crowley's Grim Reaper there is no human debris, but along with a selection of animals lurks a scorpion, linking the card with the star sign Scorpio, and consequently its ruler Pluto, the planet of death and regeneration.

Waite's Death card is a vastly different depiction. His skeletal Death is armour clad, rides slowly astride a white horse and sports a white rose emblazoned on a flag held in his left hand. This death holds connotations with one of the four riders from the Book of Revelation. Ch VI para 8 "And I looked, and behold a pale horse: and his name that sat on him was Death, and Hell followed him." Waite's picture is steeped in symbolism. At the horse's feet lies an ermine robed king, his crown in the mud next to where he lay, tossed aside in death. A woman and child respectively kneel and stupor, whilst a priest confronts Death, hands clasped together in prayer, as if begging for clemency. Beyond this scene is a river, a little boat sailing along it, conjuring up the river Styx with the ferryman sitting in his boat waiting to transport Death's victims to Hades. In the far distance, to the right, stand two towers, a bright sun rising between them. The two towers represent the dual nature of man, and endure like a portal to be stepped through, in order to attain what Waite describes as "...the sun of immortality".

The number 13

3 is the number of first manifestation. What has come from the unity of 1 through the duality of 2 is manifest at 3.

At 13 we are on the second cycle, in which 3 has been joined with 10, and therefore it carries everything acquired from the first cycle.

3 represents nature. It is the matrix which sets the direction of the creation in a general way, and the conduct or behaviour of the individual in a special way.

At 13 one's nature is no longer pure and untainted. It is influenced by past events and laden with samskara.

Nature is divided into three parts. In Sanskrit these three parts are known as the three gunas. All nature is governed by them. The three gunas are sattva, rajas and tamas.

Sattva:- Law, reality, purity.
Rajas:- passion, desire, energy.
Tamas:- darkness, ignorance, inertia.

Our actions and reactions to the three gunas- our interplay with them within the nature of the world and ourselves, go to clearing, or making, samskara. All nature lives by the three gunas. Everything which is born goes back to Tamas. It is the law of nature. Involvement in life brings with it karma, and karma brings with it the repeat cycle of birth and death.

During lectures and workshops students often shudder when they see the Death card. They gasp when I point out that it sits at number 13. Take a moment to consider the amount of superstition surrounding the number.

"13, unlucky for some".

13 people sat at the Last Supper which foreshadowed the death of Christ.

Toni Allen
The System of Symbols ©

Friday the 13th
Some city planners won't have the number 13 in a street.
All of these, and others, stem from our deep, inherent knowledge of the mystery of number 13.

Symbolism, Interpretation and Divination

Death is pictured cutting down people from every station in life with his scythe. It shows that everyone must die and that no one is so exceptional or special as to be passed over. Somewhere within us all we know, recognise and accept this, however much we may all secretly desire immortality. Nevertheless, the human race still fears death, for many reasons. For some it is the fear of the unknown, for some worry how family will cope without them, while for others it's simply a case of thinking they still have so much to do that they never feel ready, or prepared, for death. How often have we heard the phrases, "But they had so much more living to do" or "They had so much to live for."

Of all the cards the Death card is most likely to invoke fear in a client during a reading. They hold the preconception that someone is going to die, rather than something. More often than not the card refers to the latter. We only die once in each lifetime (excluding those who have near death experiences) yet many others things around us die. Living in England is an excellent location to describe the effect of the Death card because we have such distinct seasons here. Think of your favourite annual flower and contemplate its life cycle. In spring the world is born afresh each year. The flower's body pops up out of the ground as if by magic and gradually unfolds sweet fresh leaves. In summer everything is in full bloom, abundant, showy, fragrant and fulfilled. In Autumn nature transforms the flower's appearance to take on the semblance of old age and leaves turn brown and wrinkled, seeds are shed so that life may go on, and stems wither and fade. In winter it dies completely, and the gardener comes along and pulls up the dead carcass, perhaps giving its seed head a final shake across the border to ensure next years growth, and then throws it on the compost heap.

This is what happens to many facets of our life during each lifetime. Childhood dies to make way for adulthood and adulthood gives way to old age. Each one of these transformations entails letting go of who we were before. Society frowns upon an adult who acts as a child, or even the pensioner who dresses in youthful attire. Our skin wrinkles and our hair goes grey, and change is thrust upon us however much we fight against it. Hopefully at each stage we have sown abundant fertile seed to flourish in our next season of life, these seeds full of the abundance of our previous experience. Then we are able to grow old disgracefully, glowing in childish acts of fun and frivolity, but not yearning for the lost youth we once had.

For women one of the most pertinent physical changes is the menopause. It signifies an end to the feminine principle of birth as symbolised by the Empress. Who are they now that they can no longer physically produce a baby? Are they still female, and feminine? Many women find this transition, along with all of the physical changes taking place within the body, a major death in their lives. In women of appropriate age the Death card often suggests the struggle they are experiencing with this transformation.

But there are other emotional deaths which go beyond the physical stages of life. Education finishes, jobs come and go, relationships end. They die. The Death card can indicate any of these finalities and many more; although these are perhaps the most common major changes people have to deal with that bring them for a reading.

Of all these relationships are the most complex. Some people know that a relationship is over. The love has died, there is no warmth or tenderness left, and yet they persist in clinging on because to let go means to let it die and move on. Burying a relationship, regardless of how painful it has been, is nearly always very traumatic. Very often these people will have the Death card prominently placed in their spread. They know that it is over. Conversely others have the death card **reversed** showing that they realise it is dead, but they refuse to let go. Frequently this is the case when they are not the partner who has lost affection for the other, and therefore not voluntarily choosing the situation, after all, nothing emotional has died within them.

The Death card **reversed** symbolises the refusal to let something die. More often than not it highlights that an individual is unwilling to let go of a person, habit, place, job, or situation which is finished with.

It is important, however, to note than in some circumstances the exact opposite may be the case. The most poignant example I recall is of a young woman whose parents were determined to destroy the relationship she had with her boyfriend. The young woman was deeply in love, and everything in her reading indicated that an individual of lesser courage would have given up this painful love affair a long time ago. The Death card reversed showed her refusal to let go of the young man. Her lover was of a much lower social class than her parents wished her to be involved with, and they had tried everything to get rid of him. This included not speaking to their daughter for long periods and creating scenes around her boyfriend's place of work, in an attempt to make him lose his job, so that he could no longer afford the rent on the small flat they shared. With all of this they hoped the relationship would end and that she would be forced to return to the parental home. Not even her parents constant harassment could weaken her resolve, and it was most striking that the Death card reversed indicated how she refused to let others "kill off" a relationship which she truly enjoyed and benefited from. In the layout she was represented by the Queen of Coins showing that she knew what she was doing, and the Moon card coupled with the 8 of Swords showed the fear and restraint she felt from her parents attitude and physical conduct.

Crowley's illustration of the Death card incorporates the symbol for the zodiac sign Scorpio and attributes the card to it. Scorpio is ruled by Pluto and this planet is often referred to as the great destroyer; "that which breaks down to rebuild". The sign and planet cover sex, death and regeneration amongst other things. The deeper meaning in relation to Scorpio and the death card is associated with karmic attachments which we can break free of, but only by going deep within ourselves and working through painful emotions and experiences. This is what the young woman was going through, both with her boyfriend and her parents. On this level it is important to remember that whatever dies at an emotional level clears the way for something new; and hopefully better.

Death as Death?

In my now long career as a Tarot reader I have seldom seen the Death card representing an actual physical departure from the earthly plane of the client in front of me. Sometimes the card may warn of the possible death of a close relative, generally the parent of a much older person, where the parent would be in their eighties or over, and the prospect of death comes as no surprise to the questioner. On one occasion where my client did die some few months after the reading, ironically I was not the one to foresee the situation. His female friend who accompanied him saw the card as his death. She telephoned to inform me of the sad news and said that when the death card had shown in his reading she knew exactly what it had meant. I, on the other hand, had seen it as his good intent to give up the alcohol which was killing him. Apparently he had not been able to stop drinking and consequently died of liver failure. "Ah yes," the friend said to me, "you were right, he was always going to let it go, but never did. His intent was in the future, just like the Death card, only the drink killed him before he got to the future."

Key Words

Death/Letting go of something that is finished with e.g. Job, relationship, negative emotions.
Natural physical life changes, e.g. puberty, menopause.
Stages of life e.g. dying as a child to become an adult
Reversed - A refusal or inability to let something die/Finding letting go difficult or painful.

Bach Flower Remedy

Walnut - a remedy to help us through life changes.

Toni Allen
The System of Symbols ©

Temperance No. 14

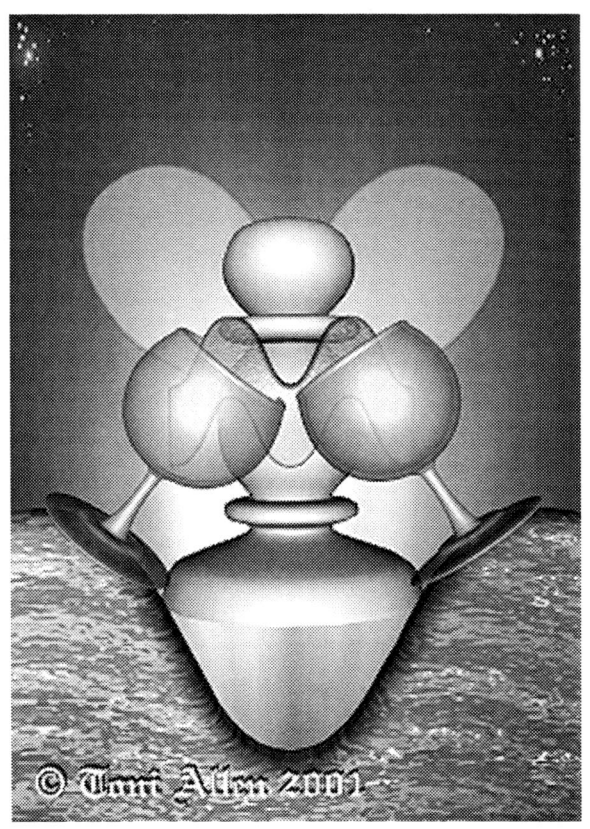

The Image

Temperance is depicted as a winged female holding an urn, cup or vessel in each hand and passing water from one to the other in a constant flow.

Amongst other things temperance means control, restraint, moderation, abstinence and humility. It derives from the word temper which means "to mix in due proportion" and "due mixture or balance of different or contrary qualities." The contrary qualities are symbolised by the two cups and their mixing by the water which flows between them. This then throws a different light on the use of the phrase "temper, temper", when someone has flown off the handle and hurled something across the room in our direction. We're not suggesting that they have a bad temper, but telling them to temper their emotions; bring the emotions, as ruled by water, back into equilibrium. When we are in a foul mood, yet know and understand that we need to restrain these overwhelming emotions, it takes all of our inner control to moderate our actions. We call upon our higher self; thus Temperance is depicted as an angelic deity. Temperance also means "moderation, especially in the indulgence of the natural appetites and passions," and it is these passions which we bring under control.

Temperance generally stands in an unspectacular landscape, but some artists have elaborated upon this. Waite stands his androgynous figure next to iris' at the end of a flowing stream which ends its journey at a small pool of water. The figure has one foot on land and the other dipped in the water, suggesting harmony between the psychic and material nature. Waite also includes a mountain range at the far end, or source, of his stream, above which rises a blazing sun. It looks as if the sun is rising between two mountains, and echoes the depiction of the sun between two towers on his Death card. However, this solar image is distant and behind the figure, at the end of an emotional journey back along the stream. Robert Wang, Illustrator of the Golden Dawn Tarot, has elaborated upon this symbol and altered it to an erupting volcano, which spits fire high into the air. Here is the passion. While all hell breaks loose inside her the angel of Temperance stays calm and undisturbed.

The number 14

14 is the second cycle of 4 and therefore relates to ahankara.

In Sanskrit at number 4 sits Mahat:- great soul, or ahankara (*aham* I *kara* maker) : meaning self-will, the ego mask, the principle in man which makes him feel separate from others. The ahankara holds everything that seems to belong to it in the feeling of I. This gives a feeling of stability.

At the Emperor this feeling of stability was expressed as the pure feeling of I AM.

On this second cycle at 14 we have the same feeling of I, but coloured by everything which has gone before. Here the human condition has acquired karma and is therefore holding on tighter to all that makes it feel stable. It represents a far more fragile state, in which, if that person, object or emotion which helped give the feeling of stability is taken away, then the individual will loss his or her sense of identity.

Symbolism, meaning and interpretation

The angel in the Temperance card represents our higher self, the watchman within, which is fully aware of the balancing act taking place. In her hand she holds two vessels or cups, and water is poured from one to the other. Very often the two cups are painted different colours indicating man's dual nature. The water represents all that comes under the realm of water and number 8, and thus also everything which comes under the realm of duality and 2.

She often reminds me of a game I used to play as a child, called uckey-uckey. It was a competitive game between two people. We each used to take two cups and fill one with water. The game was to then pour one into the other and then back again, as quickly as possible, for a set number of turns, say ten. The person with the most water left in one of their cups was the winner. As you can imagine it was a fun, wet sort of game, and usually neither party had more than an odd drop of water left by the end.

Perhaps Temperance is playing the same game? Her water represents all of her bondage to human emotions. She pours it from one part of her dual nature to the other, an apparently smooth balancing trick. She looks so calm and serene. But she only needs one person to sneak up behind her and go "BOO!" and she'll drop the whole lot. Or will she? Some occultists, such as Robert Wang, depict what looks like a volcano in the background, illustrating how serene and calm she is. Or are they trying to say that once it goes "Bang!" the game is over? Will she end up wet and miserable, or stay like this forever?

Temperance does not possess the same solid sense of I AM as the Emperor. Temperance's balance is inextricably connected with the flow of her bondage to her own personal karma, or sanskara. She is surrounded by demons, before her death at 13 and after her the Devil at 15. To step either way means suffering. Death offers freedom from the bondage and possible renunciation of human desire, while the Devil offers insight into that which binds her. Yet both of them beckon her to give up something which currently bolsters and maintains her sense of identity. It's the calm before the storm.

Toni Allen
The System of Symbols ©

On some occasions something has already died. An object, job or relationship which empowered the individual with a sense of I AM has been lost e.g. I am this marriage partner, I am this business man, I am this student, I am this home owner etc. has been taken away, and now the individual tries hard to maintain a sense of dignity and decorum. From the other side some people have come from the direction of the Devil and voluntarily given up something deemed to be a bad habit. Without our alcohol we are no longer a drinker. "I'm an alcoholic" gives a very positive condition to one's life. At least we know who we are. Then we give it up. First on the scene are withdrawal symptoms coupled with a need to keep the suffering body in harmony. Then the personal issues close in and our ego is under a constant barrage of questions from others such as "how/why did you give up?" Along with all of this is a lack of invitations to go out to the pub, lest we become a drudge, convert, or tempted back into bad habits. Suddenly we are no longer a social creature and our ahankara which holds everything that seems to belong to it in the feeling of I has lost a vital ingredient which gave it a feeling of stability.

Divorce is another example that brings with it the same supreme lack of I Am. "I am this man's wife" changes drastically to "now that I'm single I'm a threat to my female friends because they think I'm after their husbands, so they don't invite me over any more". Or "I am this woman's husband" changes to "now I'm single I'm in need of a girlfriend so that I can be invited to dinner parties again because it's awkward inviting a single bloke." Note how these are comments projected by both the individual and the society in which they live. These are real comments from real people.

Temperance is the supreme balancing trick. The emotions, and thus a sense of identity, appear to be well balanced, but it's a very precarious stance. To have a true sense of I AM is not to concern oneself with its machinations; to become constantly engrossed in its control is ultimately to be in trouble. In the illustration there is a sense of Temperance's great need to keep the water flowing from one cup to the other and never to spill a drop. Some people might say that she has balanced and harmonised the conflicts within her dual nature, and now has control over that which binds her. For a while maybe. It's a temporary balance. Her hands, and therefore her mind (air rules the sense of touch and hands) are not free to pursue other objectives. She does not have the same power as the Magician who is free to pick up his tools whenever he wishes, or the Emperor who sits in authority over himself. Her hands, and therefore her mind, hold onto the cups of binding karmic water.

Many contemporary alternative practitioners and spiritual healers use a highly definitive phrase when their client is unwell..."out of balance". When someone is well they say "Well balanced" or, when on the road to recovery "they appear more balanced". Nearly every time I hear these words the Temperance card springs to mind. What these practitioners are referring to is not only their client's physical condition but also how appropriately their client is dealing with current karmic issues that have surfaced and support their physical complaint.

Through time and experience I have learnt that the Temperance card does not speak of this calm personality which so many books refer to. I do not believe that we have reached a renewed state of calmness here as they suggest. A state of apparent calmness, yes, but the ego mask is fragile and here it is vulnerable and weakened by all which binds us to this earthly plane.

During readings people admit to feeling calm, or being "in balance" about a situation, but the catch is that there always is a "situation", often of horrendous proportions, which a client is dealing with; and in these circumstances the Temperance card illustrates their struggle to maintain a calm facade. More often than not Temperance comes up in the physical level, strongly symbolising the ego mask to its full extent and the wonderful show they put on for others. I had one client point to the Temperance card and say, "This is my happy theatre mask I put on for the sake of the children. They must believe that I cope and that I am happy to be with them, they must never think that I am angry at them...it would damage them too much." Meanwhile she continued to deal with the volcano like behaviour of her ex-husband who persisted in turning up drunk and violent.

Temperance symbolises anyone trying to maintain a balance in a situation. Some people do it at work when they do not get on very well with their colleagues. Some people do it home when friction is caused by a partner or children. Some people do it after a bereavement when they try to appear jolly, or maybe even cry for days on end to rebalance their feeling of grief. Everyone has their own bag of tricks, and Temperance does not always indicate what we might call angelic, harmonious or accepted "perfect" behaviour.

The balancing trick can be internal or external. Internally we try to come to terms with changes of mood and bring about a more positive outlook. It's the "fake it until you make it" syndrome. On an external level we might try to balance out work, play and family, struggling to make all of them fun and worthwhile, lest we have to give up something which makes us who we feel we are. The combinations are infinite.

Sometimes Temperance can indicate that although an individual is balanced and living a moderate, controlled life that they are in fact being too cool and restrained. Temperance is unemotional. She does not let others witness the exploding volcano inside. Consequently a character represented by this card does not permit themself the help of others, their pride keeping them aloof and in a state of saying "I'm okay", even at times when it is perfectly acceptable to say "I'm not okay, and that means I would like some help." With this cool type it can also denote a lack of sexual passion because they constantly hold their emotions in check and are therefore completely unable to let go and experience ardour even in their most intimate contact.

Temperance is also relevant to an individual's health. Upright the card signifies good health, or recovery, and **reversed** a lack of equilibrium. If health issues are in question then the reversed card may show signs of physical lack of balance such as dizziness, or disorientation.

When **reversed** Temperance suggests that the questioner's ego mask is crumbling. Not as earth shatteringly dynamic as with the Tower, but none the less a sense of "not feeling right" will pervade their life. The water they have juggled for so long has now spilt and suddenly they might find themselves in the midst of a karmic crisis. Often people will use the phrase "I feel out of balance". Irritability, loss of purpose and a frenzied scrambling around to pick up the water droplets and gather them together to make a whole once again ensue.

I can recall one client saying, "I've pretended for so long now. I kept making out to my family that everything was okay between my husband and I, but now I can't maintain the act." On another occasion I saw the card reversed in the line of the mind and the Tower reversed complimenting it at the physical level; both cards referring to the same qualities of ego consciousness. "I refuse to let them see how much they've upset me," said my client bitterly, "I may feel uptight and lost inside, but blowed if I'll let them think they've won."

Key Words

Forced calmness in the face of loss/Struggling to maintain a balance
Struggling to keep calm/Balanced, often seen in the "future" as a sign of improved health/Cool character
Reversed - Lack of balance/Disharmony/Inability to maintain a false sense of okayness within a difficult situation.

Bach Flower Remedy

Agrimony - for those who dislike conflict and prefer peace at all costs.
Scleranthus - for lack of inner equilibrium
Water Violet - for those whose pride does not let them seek help.

Toni Allen
The System of Symbols ©

The Devil   No. 15

The Image

Whenever we mention the Devil powerful images spring to mind. We all have some preconceived idea of who, or what, it or he, or maybe even she, is. I believe that everyone has heard the name in one context or another, and that every society has its equivalent evil, bad or anti-god image.

Our modern television based culture has done much to promote fantasy and fear around the Devil, perpetuating an age long tradition of learning to shudder at his name. Hammer horror films and Dennis Wheatley stories and films have idealised him into a deity who can only be evoked and appeased through the sacrifice of pretty young virgins, all taking place in a circle chalked with symbols and surrounded by burning candles. Even comedy has joined in with many a farcical tale built around

Toni Allen
The System of Symbols ©

some naive man selling his soul to the Devil in exchange for earthly status and wealth. All of this has, perhaps, made us a little blase, but there are still some people who have become locked into these images and truly believe that the Devil is a heebie-jeebie who creeps up at the window, jumps out of mirrors if we're too vain, or comes to take us away if we light a candle after midnight.

The Devil has always been spoken about, and repeatedly utilised throughout history by the Christian faith to obtain good behaviour and absolute obedience, thus keeping the minions in line through manipulating them with the threat of them taking up eternal residence in Hell, the Devil's domain. Powerful individuals, especially men, could easily get rid of troublesome women by denouncing them as a witch or Devil worshipper. These women had probably done nothing more sinister than fall prey to the wealthy man's sexual advances and needed to be despatched before the wife came home. Many were persecuted through ducking stools or supposedly purged by being burnt at the stake.

But who is the Devil, what does he look like? Throughout different cultures there are various images, and often he is depicted as a "shape-shifter", taking on a particular guise to suit the situation, or as an aid to trick an individual into falling from grace. In the Bible we first meet the Devil as early as Genesis when he changes his form into that of a serpent in order to beguile Eve into eating the fruit from the tree of knowledge. But what is his true image?

In early medieval manuscripts there are hundreds, if not thousands of depictions of the Devil. Often he is seen pitch forking the fallen into the burning mouth of hell. There are variations on a theme, but generally he is male with a lizard like tail, horned, club hoofed, winged and with a serpent-like penis. Frequently his head takes on the semblance of some imaginary beast and a strange enigma are faces on his abdomen, shoulders or knees, resembling the military armour worn during this period.

In early Tarot packs, such as Jacques Vieville's, made between 1643 and 1664, the Devil is depicted in the same way as in medieval manuscripts. He is a solitary, bird footed, bearded man, horns on his head and wings on his back. He has a tail and three extra heads, one on his shoulder, one on his abdomen and one on his knee. He has a little bit of everything. By the middle of the 18th Century the Devil has acquired two captives, chained to the raised plinth which he stands on. This is generally how he stays and how he is most commonly depicted throughout the Marseille Tarot.

Sometimes in modern packs the Devil appears a bit more, what I call Dennis Wheatleyish, with an inverted pentagram floating above his bearded, goat like head. Perhaps film makers favoured this image the most for its undeniable ability to make you go "aahh" when it pops up out of the dark accompanied by suitably dramatic music. Yet the person who undoubtedly took the image of the Devil to the most personal extreme was Aleister Crowley. I don't think that there is any doubt in anyone's mind that Crowley had the bulk of the Devil card painted as a giant phallus. A grinning goat, complete with spiralling horns and a third, all seeing eye, stands in front of the shaft of this grand penis, with what looks like a flowery bonnet tilted rakishly on its head. In front of the goat is a winged wand with two serpents, and the goat has its front hooves planted firmly on two testicles which are filled with what appear to be anguished souls. Crowley defines the Tarot using the Kabbalah, and has erudite affirmations to make about his symbol, not least that "behind the goat stands the tree of life...." And that "...the Goat represents the impulse to reckless creation without any regard for result." Is it sex as sin? Take a look at his image...then I leave you to draw your own conclusions.

The Number 15

The number 15 sits on the second cycle of 5. At 5 we have the ether, or akashic level; which acts as a bridge between the coarse physical world of sense observation and the world of subtle and causal nature.

At number 5 we have the Pope, a symbol of the vibration of truth being transformed through the etheric bridge. Everything which comes into creation is channelled through the ether, therefore it is not possible for anything to manifest at a physical level without passing through it. Ether carries sound, and space. We are all able to fall still and find great space within ourselves. Many of us meditate as a way of stilling the mind and contacting this vast silence which unites us with the whole of creation. But what happens when we start to meditate? Let us assume that we are following a traditional path and sitting still, eyes closed, reciting a mantra, designed to steady the mind. We bring our mantra to mind and intend to recite it continually for our dedicated half an hour. At first we're okay,

Toni Allen
The System of Symbols ©

but then thoughts start to intrude. We push them away. It happens again. Before we know it we're embroiled in thinking about whether or not we turned off the grill, or whether or not our boss really likes us after what they said earlier in the day. Meanwhile a multitude of other irrelevancies creep in like thieves in the night to steal our awareness, until ultimately our mind lacks clarity and space. It is very difficult for even the most minute element of high wisdom to come and enlighten us through this incoherent sheath of muddled thoughts. This is the number 15. This is the Devil.

I knew a woman once who said that the mind was like a naughty monkey which needed to be kept in control or it would get up to all sorts of mischief. Norse mythology recognises this in the figure of Loki. He is personal thought, the mischievous mind. He travels from Asgard, the home of the gods, along the rainbow bridge to Earth as a messenger. The rainbow bridge is the same etheric bridge of 5 as recognised by a different culture and used to symbolise the process by which the mind obtains information and insight from higher parts of ourselves in the causal level. Loki creates all sorts of problems for everyone and is thought to be evil, yet his counterparts in the guise of Hermes and Mercury are deemed positive, and are displayed with winged feet to show the speed at which the human mind can work. When we refer to people as having a mercurial nature it sounds rather clever and quick, but when we liken them to Loki we think of them as evil and up to no good. It all depends on what our personal thought process has run back and collected from the storehouse of the unmanifest at 2, in the causal level, and brought back to us.

At number 15 the number 5 holds impressions from previous life cycles, and earlier experiences in this life time. In Sanskrit these impressions are called samskara, "a deep mental impression produced by past experiences, a mental or behavioural pattern, a latency". Therefore the number 5 is no longer a clear channel; meaning that when an incident occurs rather than being able to connect with our higher self we draw on past sensations and feelings to gauge our reaction. Here the individual's first cycle up to 10 has collected personal debris and therefore the number 15 transformer quality brings results of past actions which have not yet become manifest into consciousness. Many people use the phrase "that pushed my buttons" when something reminds them of a previous experience, someone's attitude towards them, or an old problem. This is the Devil, and all that he binds us to.

Another important factor within the number 15 is its connection with sound. Of all sensations sound probably stirs our feelings the most, especially when it's a particularly pertinent piece of music to us. Perhaps it played when we fell in love, had our first child, opened a business, or split up with a lover. We have only to hear a few chords and we're swung into elation or dashed into misery; such is the power of sound.

Symbolism, Interpretation and Divination

The Devil stands on a plinth, or cubic form, which symbolises his rule over the ego consciousness as represented by the number 4. Our feelings of I AM are bound up in who we believe we are or who we want to be, and the Devil has the power to chain us to false identities created through past sensations and experiences locked in our Samskara.

The man and woman chained to his plinth symbolise the duality within us, our masculine/feminine nature. In the Bible it was the Devil who tempted Eve and thus bound us to this earthly existence and the cycle of birth and death. Thus they also symbolise Adam and Eve and the "original sin" which brought us to this human dilemma. The chain which binds them is simply that; our karmic link with this world, and all thoughts, feelings etc. which shackle us to it.

These are the same two parts of ourselves symbolised in the Pope, and yet they do not have the same free spirit. The Devil has dominion over them and they stand with bowed heads and clasped hands. The Devil is not a clear voice which guides us, but an inner reaction which tempts us back into old habits, obsessions and neurosis.

During a reading the Devil symbolises the questioner's inability to break from a habit, or habitual pattern of behaviour. Maybe one of the most common scenarios is the mentally or emotionally battered wife who continually returns to her partner. When this type of behaviour is indicated during a reading it is possible to guide the questioner back into their earlier life to try and establish the cause (coming from the causal level) of the behavioural pattern.

With one client I found that her creative nature was severely blocked. During the reading and open discussion we found that she was continually hooked into her parents financially and that they had perpetual control over her life, even though she was a grown woman with a child of her own. Her husband had left her, after what appeared to be a rather large parental push disguised as concern that he was "not the right man for her". The Devil was prominent in her spread, highlighting the importance of her need to break from the old habit of succumbing to her parents' wishes and a deep need to make herself financially independent. When we took cards to investigate her past the 2 of Batons was strong as well as the Lovers reversed, showing her parents dominance and her personal lack of discrimination, as they had always made decisions for her. All of her fire energy cards were weak, and the imposing figure of the King of Swords stood over them. "I was always supposed to be a good girl," she explained. She then tapped the King of Swords with her finger, "When I tried to rebel in my teens they sent me to a psychiatrist. I wasn't allowed to express myself at all. Now I don't know how to any more, and I feel guilty if I do, but then I also feel guilty if I don't."

Guilt is another important interpretation for the Devil. The above story is full of many aspects of the Devil and his work. My client was bound, both emotionally and financially to her parents. As a small child she was rewarded for being "good" and quiet and towing the family line. Her own nature was vibrant and bubbly, but this had been squashed beyond recognition, resulting in apathy and guilt. Much of her negative trauma probably went back to previous incarnations with her parents, but we worked primarily on this life. One of the most pertinent factors was that in her early teens, when she tried to break free from the Devil and the latent patterns she had built up around her parents expectations, she was sent to a psychiatrist which compounded her feelings that she was "bad" and therefore unacceptable.

The Devil symbolises our guilt about anything and everything. Guilt at being alive, guilt at not being right, guilt because we want something, guilt, guilt and more guilt. He is also habit. We are chained to his pillar of perpetual samskara and latent tendencies. The habit he inclines us to can be anything. Smoking, drinking, stealing, sex, being "good", victim, failure, giving, taking......etc.etc. In fact any course of behaviour which we perpetually rely on. In front of the Devil, on our first cycle of the Tarot, is number 6 and the Lovers card, suggesting that we have the ability to rise above these tendencies and discriminate as to whether or not to continue the habit. Ahead of the Devil is also the Tower at number 16 suggesting that if we do not break free from the chains of bondage to our personal way of acting and being that our world can be shattered and torn from beneath us. 6 is on the path of breaking the cycle through free will and raised consciousness, 16 is on the path of karma, as experienced through life forcing the change upon us.

The Devil **reversed** symbolises a lack of guilt or conscience, or the breaking of a habit. In most individuals this implies that they have changed a belief pattern or way of thinking or acting for the better. They no longer feel bullied by people or situations that previously made them experience guilt. They have smashed the chains of habit. For one woman this was when she put her elderly mother in a nursing home after several years of looking after her single handedly, even though the mother was incontinent and wheelchair bound. "I haven't had a life for years," the woman said. "I have two brothers and a sister, and they only ever came over maybe once or twice a year. They never helped. They used to make me feel so guilty if I phoned up and asked them to come and stay for a few days to give me a break. They called me demanding and selfish. But do you know what? I don't feel guilty about putting mum in a home. She enjoys it there. She loves being with people of her own age...and gets all of the care she needs...it's liberating, for both of us."

There is, however, a far more sinister side to the Devil **reversed**. Being free of guilt is one thing, but to never experience even the slightest twang of guilt, or remorse, leads to a total lack of conscience. Here the individual is driven entirely by latent behavioural patterns which leads to psychotic conduct in the form of criminal tendencies. It is rare for a truly criminal minded individual to come for a reading, and I have only ever seen one or two when they were trying to find out if I was able to suss them out. Needless to say I did not necessarily share with them all that I was able to see in the reading, having, I believe, a reasonably keen sense of self-preservation. However, I have often come across the type via other people's readings. For one woman it depicted her former husband's lack of conscience while taking her to court over joint finances. The Devil reversed was placed next to the 6 of Coins reversed and it was obvious that he wanted every penny from the former matrimonial home, even though she was looking after their children. "He's already re-married," she said. "They have a lovely home. He buys her children lots of things, and yet he wants more than his fare share of our house. I've already agreed to him having half of everything, but he wants more and more." It was evident that her former husband was being driven by compulsive behaviour stemming from early childhood experiences. He simply didn't care about anyone but himself.

Key words

Guilt/Habit/Compulsive behaviour/Being chained to repeat circumstances
Reversed - Free of guilt/Breaking negative habits/Lack of conscience

Bach Flower Remedy

Pine - for continued feelings of guilt

Toni Allen
The System of Symbols ©

The Tower No. 16

The Image

The Tower is traditionally depicted as a tall tower with three windows. We view this Tower at the moment in which the crown shaped roof is blown off by a bolt of lightning. With the blast two figures are thrown out of the building and they tumble, face down, towards the ground. The Tower is surrounded by many round objects, like huge hailstones, falling from the sky.

Sometimes the lightning bolt is depicted as fiery breath, or an olive branch, but always as some God given portent reaching down from heaven.

One brief interpretation for the Tower is "surprise", and in the Tarot of Jacques Vieville, and other similar earlier medieval based packs, we find this clearly depicted. A young, startled, herdsman looks up in wonder at the tree under which his flock grazes. His arms are spread wide as the clouds above the tree emanate a wondrous light, bringing strong connotations of the story of the burning bush and sudden messages from God. Again the surrounding sky is filled with strange droplets from heaven.

Lady Freda Harris' illustration for Crowley paints the entire Tower card blood reds and black. The Tower crumbles, spitting out what appears to be four people and a Hell's mouth roars fire in the bottom right hand corner, while an all seeing eye overlooks the horrific destruction. The dove of peace glides off to the top left of the picture, olive branch in its mouth and a serpent sits at the right. The card has a very violent, warlike quality; the Hell's mouth drawn in a style reminiscent of Picasso's Guernica. It is interesting to note that Lady Freda Harris designed the deck between 1938 and 1943 when war was raging across Europe and the blitz burnt, ravaged and crumbled many building in major cities throughout Britain. I do not believe that it was only the war that influenced how she chose to depict the symbol, even though Crowley wrote in connection to the card "the destruction of the old-established Aeon by lightning, flames and engines of war." It is known that occultists such as Crowley and Waite acquired ancient Tarot decks for personal contemplation, and spent time in the British Museum, and other institutions, studying their collections. In the Tarot de Paris, from the 17th Century, the Tower is entitled La Fouldre, and depicts a Hell's mouth spewing fire as the Devil beats a drum and human figures are thrust into the flames. In medieval manuscripts the Devil is often seen pitchforking human souls into the mouth of hell in just the same way.

The Tower has also been known as "Casa del Diablo" the Devil's House and "Maison de Feu" the House of Fire. There is much to suggest a belief that as the Devil sits at 15, the next stage on the path, at 16, is his home territory....Hell....if we are going in that direction.

The number 16

Sixteen is on the second cycle of 6, and on the overlaid cycle of 4.
At 6 we have air, the breath of life, and capacity to desire and love. Discrimination is depicted by the Lovers card at number 6. At 4 we have

The Emperor and at 14 Temperance, showing how the feeling of ahamkara, I AM, or self will, work within us.

At 16 we have everything which the individual has acquired on the first cycle from 1 to 10 influencing his expression of life and feelings of I AM. At 6 we are given the option of correct discrimination, to choose between new alternatives or karmic habits. At 16 the mind is so filled with past habits, emotions and traits (samskara) that it becomes overloaded. There literally isn't any room to breathe. This establishes a lack of feeling of I AM and oneself worth crumbles. Air, or the Pranas, keep all creatures going. The Pranas are vital energies; they make or keep us alive, discharge polluted air, regulate the digestive process, keep the body in balance, and also regulate involuntary movements in the body.

When people become incredibly stressed, their feeling of I AM, or self worth, is under threat, and it is not uncommon to find such individuals fidgety, trembling, or in extreme cases suffering panic attacks. All of these bodily functions are regulated by air. In Chinese medicine, especially acupuncture, it is said that when one evacuates one's bowels that one is letting go of all waste within the psyche as well as the body; and it is not uncommon when having treatment to embarrassingly start expelling air from various parts of the body. This is part of the healing process of balancing the air within the body so that "dis-ease" can be eliminated. Anyone who has gobbled up a meal too fast will recognise the experience of trapped wind and heartburn. This is the physical side of number 16...further beyond is the subtle realm of causal nature and the thoughts associated with air which induce the suffering. Number 16 is all to do with what we think about ourself, and how these illusions are easily shattered.

Symbolism, Interpretation, and Divination

The Tower itself represents the false ego. An untrue sense of personal identity. At number 4, which is overlayed with 6 on our circle, we have the feeling of I AM. When we overlay this feeling of I AM with I am plus something else, e.g. I am a teacher, I am useless etc., then we move into the realm of ahamkara which means, Self-will, the ego mask, and the principle in man which makes him feel separate from others. This is what sits at 16 with the Tower. Only here we have a depiction of that point in time when the individual's discrimination discovers that they have been living by a false ego identity. Thus the Tower is blown to pieces. One's illusion of who one is is destroyed.

The two figures falling from the tower are the same two qualities echoed throughout the Tarot, the dual nature of man.

The crown, which is being toppled from the top of the Tower, represents the crown chakra. It is said that the crown chakra is the seat of spiritual experience, and that if one meditates and aligns oneself with this energy that a state of non-duality manifests. "I AM" consciousness, without any addition, is eternal and changeless; and to reach this state we have to be centred in a point of non-duality. Thus in the Tower the lighting bolt is heaven sent and spiritual awakening occurs resulting in the figures representing duality being expelled from the building. No-one has ever yet given a completely adequate explanation for the round snowflakes falling all around, but the one I have most empathy with is that they symbolise sattvic consciousness all around, like manna from heaven.

This all sounds very grand, for here is a picture of the hardened heart opening up to new possibilities, and releasing negative ideas which have bound us up in eternal cycles of karma, and personal samskara. However, we are human, and the human state is one of holding on to habits, and fixed ideas. Thus the Tower is a card of immense pain and suffering. Sudden change is a shock to our system, however enlightening the experience might ultimately be. The here and now feeling is one of pain and turmoil, not one of illumination and relief, for our ego is destroyed and that means the possibility of breakdown and loss of self worth. Temporarily we lose connection with who we are.

So how do these concepts manifest themselves in daily life? There are several ways. One is shock. Suddenly we find out something which changes our perception of who we are. It can happen in a fleeting moment, take many years to come to terms with, and consequently we'll never be the same again. I recall a female client who was unexpectedly having problems in her relationship with her boyfriend. He was pictured by the Tower covering the 9 of Swords. It appeared that the shock, to his ego identity, was extreme. "Last week his brother turned up on the doorstep," she said. "He didn't know he had a brother, let alone an identical twin. He didn't even know that he was adopted!" A week ago he had been somebody, today he was somebody else. Another client had the Tower after the sudden death of his young wife. She had been snatched away from him some three years before he came to me for guidance, yet his entire reading revolved around the issue of how he re-established who he was without her in his life. "My whole identity was built around being her husband and provider," he said. "I now feel as if I'm a nobody in my own right."

The sudden shock of the Tower is not only associated with personal relationships. Many people have it come up in connection with work, especially when they are suddenly, or even not so suddenly, made redundant. The computer has taken over many manual skills, and I have seen lots of people who find that their craft is no longer needed, much the same as in the industrial revolution.... Only now it's a computer revolution. People heading for retirement are also liable to have the Tower come up, especially if they have lived their entire life through their work. They are not prepared for a time when no one looks up to them, or they are no longer able to say "I'm so-and-so, I'm a job description."

All of the above are examples of when life itself deals us a blow for which we are unprepared. Perhaps something greater than ourselves causes these adverse conditions, these trials to overcome. Yet there is another side to the card, the human factor, when one person undermines another and takes the role of "god" into their own hands. This manifests when one individual wants to destroy someone else's personality, due to differences in ideas, jealousy, revenge etc. Or they go chip-chipping away at someone else's personality structure, in order to dominate and have control. The person having the Tower in their reading will have the same feelings of ego destruction, lack of confidence and identity crisis, but coupled with a real person on whom to direct their hostility at the sudden, or prolonged, changes in how they perceive themselves and the world around them.

The Tower symbolises a false rigidity attached to the heart and thus a fixed personality filled with karmic habits. When the lightning bolt comes from "god" then it is a time for us to learn some powerful life lessons. However, when it is someone else who is attacking the personality, it is their idea and perception that something is wrong with somebody else's personality. The person who is under attack may have been feeling just fine. Firstly the victim will try to strengthen their sense of I AM, and hold onto it despite the verbal, or physical onslaught, (the

Tower reversed), then, if they cannot maintain this, the Tower will crumble.

The Tower is very common in readings where the woman is suffering verbal or mental abuse in a relationship. (It does happen to men as well, but is less common) There are thousands of different scenarios, but all result in the woman losing self-confidence and self-esteem and ultimately feeling worthless. Here are just a few examples: -

1) A woman has worked until the birth of the couple's first child. She then takes time off to look after the family. Suddenly she is 'stupid' and no longer an intellectual equal...or...as she is no longer bringing home a wage she is 'sponging' off her partner and he punishes her by giving her no personal spending power.

2) A couple of equal intelligence meet when they both have reasonable jobs. She goes on to better her position and gain a higher wage packet. Suddenly she is 'money grabbing' or has become 'tough'. This is a situation in which the male partner feels threatened, or jealous, and therefore projects his own identity crisis onto his partner. Initially she felt good about her new job, but by the time he has finished insulting her, week in week out, she feels small and inferior, as if there is something wrong with a woman doing well, and that in some way she is abnormal. Along with the insults he has also probably removed sex from their relationship as a type of punishment. All of these factors bring into question who she is and what she is doing with her life.

3) Another classic example is where the man is having an affair and lying to his partner. The woman has questioned him about certain issues and suddenly he claims that she is 'mad', 'needs to see a shrink', or is paranoid. Every time she confronts him about being late home, not being at the office when she phoned or "but Fred phoned home saying you weren't working late, and you weren't there", he says she is ill, overly suspicious, or "...well, if you don't trust me...". Slowly but surely the woman starts to believe that she is going insane and her Tower starts to crumble. When the affair eventually comes out into the open the lightning blow is doubly painful because her husband's denial has already damaged her self- esteem.

The old black and white film "Gaslight" is a fine example of a husband doing this to a wife. In the story the husband keeps taking the wife's valuables and hiding them, then accuses her of being ill because she has forgotten where they are. All of this is a clever ruse to certify her insane so that he can take her fortune. Ah, but that's fiction, I hear you say, people don't really act like that. But they do.

One client came to me after she split up with her live in lover of some three years standing. She was an older woman, with property, and had taken the lover some time after her husband's death. The Tower was heavily placed in her reading, not simply because he had just left her, but because he had returned to his wife, whom he had never really left. Now he was demanding half the value of my client's property, which he had never paid into. "I've been used," she said as she wept. "They've done this to me deliberately, haven't they? I always suspected that he spent time with his wife when he went away for the weekend...and he would never divorce her." There are many issues in this scenario which add to the feelings of "cracking up" associated with the Tower. She was left in a position where she might lose half of her property, her trust had been shattered and her sense of humiliation was overwhelming.

When the Tower is **reversed** it indicates that the questioner is trying very hard not to 'crack up' or fall to pieces after a crisis. Sometimes it is necessary to hold onto one's sense of identity, so that one can continue to cope in a crisis; while on other occasions the opposite is valid and it is necessary to let go of outmoded ideas and move on.

One client came to me shortly after her husband had walked out and left her with two small children to look after. She had the Tower reversed. "I just haven't got the time to feel sorry for myself," she said. "I'd love to cry, and be all emotional about it, but I have to stay strong for the children. If they see me falling to pieces then it'll effect them badly, and I won't have him do that to them. I have my tears at bedtime, or when they're out, but that's it. I put on a brave face, I know that."

Often the Tower **reversed** is a sign that the individual will not let someone get close to them for fear of letting down barriers. It indicates that they have not dealt with past hurts and that to become emotionally involved would be to open the floodgates of bottled up feelings. It's as if they have bricked themself into a castle's keep of self defence, and others often refer to them as "cold", "uptight", "hard to get to know" and "unfeeling". Here we lock ourselves in Hell, preferring the pain rather than to let anyone else witness our suffering.

Key Words

Personality breakdown/Shock/Sudden events
Loss of self confidence/self worth/sense of who one is
Suddenly finding that one has based one's life on false ideas about oneself
Reversed - Refusing to crack up/Holding onto old hurts

Bach Flower Remedy

Star of Bethlehem - for shock

Toni Allen
The System of Symbols ©

The Star No. 17

The Image

The Tarocchi of Mantegna Cards, dated from 1470, are an early sequence of printed images similar to the Tarot. There is some dispute as to whether or not all of the series are actually attributable to the hand of Mantegna, but their relevance here is not the artist, but the content. They are one of the first printed sequences that can truly be named as a forefather to the cards we now know as the Tarot. They have no minor cards as we recognise them and include "The conditions of man", "Apollo and the Muses", "Liberal Arts", "Cosmic Principles" and "Firmaments of the Universe". Under this last section are included all of the major planets in our solar system, as known in their day. The Sun, the Moon, Mercury, Venus, Mars, Jupiter and Saturn. Following on from this, again dated from

Toni Allen
The System of Symbols ©

the 15th Century, we have the D'Este cards, which has a paired down delineation of the solar system, and incorporates the recognisable sequence of The Star, The Moon and the Sun, running in the same order by which we now know them.

It may be the same arrangement as today, but the renditions are significantly different. In the D'Este pack the Star card appears to be a depiction of two scholarly men looking up, writing tools and measuring instruments in hand, mapping the heavens as they gaze up at a star. A little later, in the Rothschild Tarot or Minchiate cards (Minchiate was an extended version of the Tarot which included astrological images) we find a clear illustration of the Star card as the three wise men apparently dancing under the star which guided them to the baby Jesus. In this context the Star would be synonymous with Jupiter, which is, *allegedly, the star which the wise men followed, and also symbolic of joy and of kings. This last rendition then, brings us back to attributions found in the Mantegna cards where all of the planets were named.

These types of images continue until around the mid-1600's when we then encounter the picture of the Star which we are now familiar with. How and why it changed I do not know; or from whence the image originated. It's as if the symbol sprung into consciousness from some secret source, and has been refined ever since.

The Marseille Star card pictures a naked woman, kneeling on the ground, tipping out two urns of water. Mainly there is a small pool of water in front of her and she either empties both urns into the water or tips the contents of one urn into the water and the other onto the soil. Her hair is long and flowing and she appears to be tranquil and at peace with the world. To the left, and behind her in the distance, is a tree, often full of fruits and mostly with a bird sitting in it. Above her head, in the firmaments of the sky, hangs one large star surrounded by a cluster of smaller stars, making up to maybe eight in all. It is useful to remember that for many centuries only the seven planets named earlier were known to mankind, as these could be seen with the naked eye. As telescopes improved astronomers discovered more of the qualities of each planet and in time detected hitherto unknown planets: Uranus, Neptune and Pluto.

Of our two contemporary masters, Waite stays with this traditional approach, doing little more than placing the bird in the tree to the right of the picture in preference to the left. Crowley on the other hand, as so often in his representations, breaks completely with convention. All art is subjective, and our liking or disliking for a particular image is based solely on personal taste, however, Lady Frieda Harris's painting has always struck me as one of the most beautiful of modern Tarot symbols. The colours used are incredibly emotive, blue, purple and magenta. Every part of the structure appears to be based on the spiral, and as the woman empties her vessels she is alive and filled with vigour. The Star spirals like a Catherine Wheel in the top left hand corner and in the mid distance a large magenta orb fills the heavens. Maybe it's our world we live on, maybe somewhere else...who knows. It's a fully integrated image, allowing our intuition to connect with the fact that all of these forces interplay with each other, making up the vibration of the Universe in which we live.

The Number 17

The number 17 sits on the second cycle of 7 after it has collected karma on the first cycle up to 10. It also relates to 3 and 13.

At 7 we find the symbol of the Charioteer in relation to the number, and a personal, individual, treatment of Tejas. Tejas is the force which governs all the movements of the world. On a personal level Tejas is the energy by which one sees, moves and does all sorts of work; and a man is valued by the Tejas he possesses. The same applies to the physical world. Tejas is heat and light. If there were not enough heat in the body of a human being, or in the world, it would all freeze down to immobility. Tejas also relates to the celestial bodies like the sun, moon and stars, which govern the life and movement on the planet earth.

It is this latter description of Tejas which is illustrated by the Star card, we find the movement of the heavenly bodies and our interplay with them. Due to 7's connection with 3 we also find that 17 is a reference to the human nature, or personality. At 3 we have the Empress symbolising the forces of nature. At 17 we have the suggestion that this nature is in some way governed by the planets and the stars above us. As above, so below.

Toni Allen
The System of Symbols ©

Symbolism, Interpretation and Divination

If we commence by looking at the early symbols for the Star card we can see that initially it was the card of the astrologer. This implies a sentence of destiny, or fate, upon the individual. In Shakespeare there are many references to how the stars influenced the individual and in King Lear the specific question is put forward as to whether the stars govern our destiny, and if so, what point free will? Early astrologers took a very fatalistic view of the birthchart and it is only with modern ideas over the last century that psychological astrology has been born. These days a study of one's Natal Chart, does not simply imply a "this will happen" attitude, it also gives profound knowledge and insight into the human persona and thus can be used as a tool to overcome problems by shining light into otherwise darkened corners of the psyche. Hence the Star card can be called a card of hope.

The image of the three magi again echoes an astrological note. Many modern day scholars believe that the magi must have had a certain amount of astronomical, and astrological, knowledge in order to follow the star for some two years. Many people have long believed that the magi were following the planet associated with kings, Jupiter, and recent astronomical data has backed up this theory; as well as astrological research. Again we have connotations of hope, and even rebirth, due to them following the star to find a king and a new regime in life.

Jupiter is also the planet of good luck, abundance and joy; recurring signs of hope for a better future. This might all sound like phooee, but science is fast proving these points, as in a television documentary on Jupiter, when the scientists were analysing the phenomena of the string of meteors which collided with the planet in 1994. It was an astronomically based programme and the overview was that Jupiter acts like a sort of cosmic dustbin, its huge size and gravitational pull continuously sucking in universal debris and thus protecting Earth, as it did with the meteors. A theory was presented that the meteor that wiped out the dinosaurs missed Jupiter and crashed into Earth destroying the entire species. The presenter rounded off by saying that if it wasn't for Jupiter that this type of catastrophe might happen to Earth every few hundred years and that the human race would never secure the opportunity to progress. He ended by saying that Jupiter was a truly lucky planet for us and that we should rejoice in it being there to protect us.....perhaps the early astronomers and astrologers knew far more than we credit them with.

So, what about our traditional Marseille symbol? Who is this naked woman and why does she empty out two vessels? If we reflect back on the image of the Tower we can see that it's a symbol for the breaking down of the ego structure and false ideas about who we are. As a storyboard the Star comes next and here the woman is naked to symbolise that she has been stripped of all false ideas. There is nothing left for other people to find out about her, or try to upset in her; everything is laid bare. Clothes would make her a somebody, give us a clue to her identity, but here she has none, she simply is.

The two urns are the same two cups which Temperance was juggling at 14. Here the pretence of coping, or being someone she isn't, are let go of. However, they are not dropped so that the water spills, or thrown in temper. Their contents is consciously tipped out, one upon the ground, the other into the water. With the Tower at 16 the false ideas were ejected from the ego, while here the false attachments and bonds are deliberately let go of, so that one's true nature can be revealed. Often these days the two cups are painted different colours so that a picture emerges of opposite aspects of ourselves being given back from whence they came, the emotions to the water and the physical attachments to the earth. Once the two cups are empty a sense of unity pervades and one's heart (the cup) can be filled up again, hopefully with a truer sense of who we are.

The bird pecking its fruits in the distant tree is symbolic of the multifarious opportunities in life which can aid an individual along their path. When the woman has finished her meditation she can turn around and see the many possibilities open to her. She will also look up at the stars, and contemplate where she fits in with the larger scheme of things. As this is a card of nature it is also thought that the star is not a star at all, but a planet; the planet which rules our nature as depicted in our natal birth chart, and the surrounding stars refer to the constellation we were born under. In astrology our birth chart indicates our personality during this lifetime, past karma and personal samskara we are carrying through from other lifetimes. We are all born under one of the twelve signs of the zodiac and an astrological concept is that our life path is to perfect attributes associated with our birth sign. Sometimes we may have been living according to our birth sign, but on one side of it, and then a particular transit evokes situations that force us into emerging as the other side of our sign. e.g. Pisces is associated with Victim/Saviour. Someone who has spent the first part of their life taking drugs and being a victim may later change through rehabilitation and then become the saviour by counselling others in similar crisis.

During a reading the Star card always appears as a card of hope. The questioner nearly always feels that the worst is over and that they have been through the wringer. Now it's a time of self-assessment and meditation on what happened and how their own personality held a key part in the play that unfolded.

Depending on the individual reading I find it useful to advise the client that this is a good time to have a birth chart drawn up. Due to the very nature of the card people are often highly receptive to further self analysis and finding out more about who they are and how they fit in with life and others around them.

I did one reading in which my client immediately hooked into the image on the Star card. "Look she's naked", she said. "That's me all right. Everybody's seen everything. They've seen my tears, they've seen me cry, they've seen me shout, holler and scream, they even saw me in the street in my nightie the night my husband threw me out. I have nothing left to hide." This last display had left her with a strong feeling that nothing could be worse than the public humiliation she had experienced, and had subsequently given her hope that the only way was up.

Another client said that she had been through so much suffering and emotional turmoil that she felt empty of all passion and pain. "I feel like a blank sheet," she said, "Ready to be written on again."

When the card is **reversed** the opposite effect is in play and the individual feels hopeless. They find themselves stuck in the feelings of humiliation, degradation and loss. They genuinely cannot see how to rebuild for the future, and believe that opportunities are only out there for other people.

I often see the Star **reversed** when a client is going through a marital breakdown which is not of their choosing. Whether they are male or female is irrelevant, they still come forward with the same feelings of hurt and rejection. They cannot empty their heart of the mixed emotions left over from the past, or come to terms with the fact that someone whom they are in love with no longer feels the same about them.

Key Words
Hope
A recognition of inner emptiness so that one can start afresh
A good time to have an astrological reading to find more out about one's self and one's place within the larger scheme of things
Luck and good fortune
Reversed - Hopeless/Feeling that there are no opportunities left in life

Bach Flower Remedy
Gorse - for feelings of hopelessness

Toni Allen
The System of Symbols ©

The Moon No. 18

The Image

As with the Star, the image of the Moon originates from a pre-Tarot de Marseille tradition of much earlier sacred icons based on the Mantegna prints, in which the Moon was represented as the deity presiding over the planet. Thus we find the goddess Diana holding up the crescent Moon, sometimes riding in a chariot over a mountainous landscape which harbours a deep pool, or inlet of the sea, on which sea faring boats move around. A little later, as in the D'Este cards, we find the card depicted as a scholar, or scholars, measuring the phases of the Moon with astronomical instruments.

These images then gave way to the picture we have come to recognise today as the Moon card. A crayfish sits in the foreground, about to leave some watery haven. A path stretches out before it. Along the path, one on either side, it first encounter two dogs, and then two towers; beyond these the moon hangs high in the sky, sporting a fiery corona, as if it eclipses the sun. All around fall drops of consciousness, as in the Tower card. There is no doubt that it is night, a time of fear and mystery, the dogs howling up at the Moon, the towers looming threateningly in the distance, the road winding on forever.

The number 18

18 sits at the second cycle of 8. It relates the element of water; and to the number 2 and duality.

At 8 we had the Justice card and its relation to karmic bonds. At 18 we have an image of samskara, the personal karma which binds an individual after it has been through the first cycle of 1 to 10. In some respects it is the making, or indeed, the breaking of personal karma.

Samskara is a deep mental impression produced by past experiences, a mental or behavioural pattern, a latency. This is a limitation which binds us to old habits and can lead us back into repeat situations, which then creates misery, pain and fear.

Symbolism, Interpretation and Divination

In the foreground of the card we see the crayfish, or crab, about to climb out of the water. The crayfish symbolises the human being, a soft centre covered by a hard outer shell of protection. The shell is the ego, a tough armour of personality, which we believe has to be maintained at all costs, so that we are not easy prey to those who would wish to harm us emotionally, physically, or even psychically.

The crayfish exemplifies the duality within us all. The ego and the self. The self, or soul, can never be damaged, yet we continually live under the illusion that someone else can harm it, or even "capture our soul"; hence the protective shell of the ego. This is not to say that the ego is bad, or even undesirable; nor for that matter incredibly good if we make it thicker and tougher. Like all of our faculties and attributes the ego is an instrument for us to use, but only when it is honed to perfection can it permit the self within to function perfectly and reach its full potential. All of the time that the ego continually deludes, stifles and intimidates us, it restricts the free flow of our true nature and then it gains control rather than the self within.

The water in the picture symbolises the bonds which restrict us. This is tamasika water, stagnant and stale, clogging up our emotions and restricting the free flow of our life. This water cannot support life. It is filled with outmoded attachments, emotional ties, financial worries, inner turmoil...it is time to move on. In the natural world it has been found that crayfish leave the river they inhabit as soon as there is any sign of pollution in it. Natural historians witnessed a mass exodus of crayfish from a river, and filmed it, believing it to be some strange migration ritual. On further study of the river they found it to be filled with minor traces of toxic substances and that the super sensitive crayfish had recognised this and left their habitat long before the river authorities had picked up any signs of the trace elements. I believe that the originators of the Moon card design knew this fact and therefore used the crayfish to symbolise human sensitivity to underlying negative emotions in their private world.

Ahead of the crayfish is the path along which it needs to travel. It is our life path. Overhead is the moon, beyond it the halo of the sun. Day always follows night, light always follows darkness. Perhaps it is not the night, but an eclipse, a temporary darkness, which we did not expect. Whichever, it is dark and we need to get to the light way up ahead. First the crayfish encounters two barking dogs, symbolising potential attack along the road. Hazards abound, but the ego cannot be physically torn. It experiences danger from emotional and mental hurt in the form of gossip, bad feeling and exposure through loss of reputation and other status imposed limitations. Further ahead are two towers, one sometimes depicted as broken and already blasted as in the Tower card. These two towers represent false egos in which we might try to hide. If we cannot make it to the perfection of the light then we'll choose another image, just as false as the last one, but safe for the time being until it comes tumbling down like the Tower at 16 and we tread the same route again. These are dual images, reflecting the duality within man, the two towers looming up like the two great pillars in the High Priestess....another gateway to the realisation of our unity.

I'm sure that we all hold some ideas about what the moon means as a symbol. In astrology it refers to the feminine principal, caring for others and our emotional needs. With its placement within our solar system it orbits the Earth and has a recognised force upon our tides, and a more secret force upon our plant life. Almanacs often give Moon planting guides and many gardeners follow these principles with amazing success, finding that to follow these natural rhythms means that seeds germinate well under the feminine quality of the Moon. Then we have lunatics (from the French La Luna, meaning the Moon), those who go mad at the time of the full Moon, and various tales such as men changing into werewolves under its influence. Many women find that their menstrual cycle is stirred by the Moon, some feeling out of balance, while others feel they are more in rhythm with the world.

    The Moon card can be interpreted to include any of the above connections....although I must admit I haven't seen any werewolves recently! However, there are those who become disturbed under the influence of the Moon. The card is depicted as happening at night, and although this is a journey of rebirth and of finding our true self, it is difficult to see our way clearly under the Moon's silvery light. Events are shrouded in the illusion of uncertainty. Many years ago I took a walk around Virginia Waters under the bright light of a full Moon. I was with a friend, and although we could see dark shapes and clear shadows cast by the piercing light, it looked like a television on which the colour had been turned down so that there was only black and white. Trees became dark forbidding shapes, my companion a sinister form rustling by my side. Everything was something else. It reminds me of the story of the man who was travelling home in the moonlight and found a sleeping snake curled up blocking his path. The man became fearful and found that he could neither pass by the snake nor sleep due to his anxiety. He stood rigid all night long, eyes on the snake, anticipating that it would uncurl and leap up at him. The man was simply rooted to the spot with fear. When the dawn broke and sunlight fell upon the snake the man was astonished to find that it was nothing more than a piece of old string. This is Maya. Illusion.

    Maya is the cosmic illusion of duality, appearance (as opposed to reality). Maya is said to have two functions: avarana "covering" and vikshepa "throwing out". The first hides the inner reality from us, and the second deceives us into believing that fulfilment lies without. Hence the Moon card is also a symbol of fear. We all create our own fears through

Toni Allen
The System of Symbols ©

illusions that we put upon the world. We may hold fear of the dark, fear of the unknown, fear of change, in fact people can be frightened of almost anything.

When we have reached the stage of the Moon card on our journey, the knowledge is already within us that the situation we find ourself in is not a healthy one. The restrictions, whether inner, or outer, stifle us. The love for a person or situation, which was once so exciting and bonding, has now gone stale and become the negative side of water and is binding. If things do not change then we will literally fester in a limiting set of circumstances, which is akin to a living death. However, the path ahead of us is not an easy one and fraught with dangers, whether real or imagined. Feelings of separation might overwhelm us, bringing a turmoil of impressions such as "us and them", me in my protective shell and all of those who would wish to harm me. We feel that we have to protect ourselves at all costs. It's like having to run the gauntlet of gossip, or authority, any minute having to succumb to what others might say or what they might try and make us do. Opinions of others become a source of self-doubt, robbing us of our discrimination, and making us want to run back to the familiar dark waters. Suddenly even something like a painful marriage we know and hate, appears better and safer than the great "unknown" out there.

During a reading the significance of the Moon card will be seen from surrounding cards. Often the questioner feels trapped, or fearful of a huge change they are just about to make. A very common example of the Moon card is when one partner feels that a relationship has turned sour and wishes to break free from it. Here the dogs symbolise everyone else putting in their pennyworth of advice. "Why do you want to leave when you have everything? A house, a car, lots of money. When he's nice he is so nice, can't you live for the good times? Perhaps a better job would make you feel more fulfilled. And what about the children? etc., etc.". All of these suggestions are based on either physical/emotional desires, or appearance; they are what the commentator thinks they see, rather than a true experience of the situation as felt by the individual who is going through it. Unless the questioner has strength of character and determination they will easily be persuaded back into their bleak set of circumstances, or maybe get that 'better job' and hide in a false tower for a while, only to return to the same dilemma in six months time.

Toni Allen
The System of Symbols ©

There are many situations in which people choose to leave a stale environment e.g. growing up and needing to leave home. Changing job. Moving house. Retirement.

Old attachments need to be let go of. The path may be unknown and frightening, but there is light at the end of the tunnel. The Sun shines behind the Moon and with the Sun comes colour, warmth and contentment.

When the card is **reversed** it indicates that the questioner realises that changes need to be made but is either too fearful or not prepared to make them. This is not necessarily a negative interpretation. Often individuals have something suddenly occur and they require time in which to assimilate the circumstances before going forward. However, the reversed card can also indicate someone being literally rooted to the spot with fear, and consequently are unable to cope with the concept of changing anything.

On some occasions other people and extreme circumstances are actually preventing the individual from moving forward...on the path they were on. I saw this once for a career woman who was intending to resume work shortly after the birth of her second child. Sadly her child was born with a very rare condition which meant continued hospital treatment and round the clock attention. The woman was both fearful of resuming work for dread of others thinking she was unfeeling or selfish, but also deeply confused about how to change herself into a full time nurse/mother and thus become somebody she had never been before. "I'm frightened every time she comes home from hospital for a few days. I'm never sure that I'll cope...and yet I'm used to running a business! I'm sorry, I just want everything back as it was before." There was no easy answer for my client, except for her to assimilate the changes gradually and not to expect too much of herself too soon. Not only had she had her life path abruptly changed, but also the extreme suddenness and unexpectedness of the situation had thrown her into turmoil and fear. If she resumed work then others might bark that she was a "bad mother", and yet if she stayed at home she knew that in time she would become deeply resentful and feel that she had little of her true nature to share with her child. The stagnant water in the Moon card represented both her staying at home with frightening emotions, and her job, for this was the binding attachment she wanted to stay with.

Key Words

Fear of the unknown, yet willing to try something new
Moving away from limiting situations
Illusion/Influences of the Moon
Reversed - Inability to walk into the fear of change
Living with stagnant, binding emotions because they are familiar

Bach Flower Remedy

There are several Bach Remedies for different types of fear
Aspen - for vague, unknown fears e.g. general apprehension, anxiety
Mimulus - for known fears e.g. fear of going to the dentist
Rock Rose - Terror e.g. after an accident
Red Chestnut - fear for the safety of others
The Moon is a highly complex card and other remedies will be relevant depending upon surrounding cards e.g. Walnut - for helping break bonds between people who influence us
Wild Oat - for establishing one's life path.

Toni Allen
The System of Symbols ©

The Sun No. 19

The Image

Traditionally the Sun is depicted as a jolly card. Two children dance or hold hands in the safety of a walled garden. Sometimes they are completely naked, more often a sash covers their modesty. The sun shines over head, droplets falling down upon them. It's a simple, peaceful image, occasionally embellished with a few flowers.

Older Tarots depict the sun held high by a putti, while others have the representation of scholars charting the heavens as in the Moon card. Waite breaks from the norm by having a single, naked child, gleefully riding a white horse. It holds a fluttering flag and a row of radiant sunflowers grow behind the wall, while the sun fills the sky. Although apparently original in design there is at least one earlier example of this child rider in the Vandenborre pack from the 18th Century, and possibly other packs in the British Museum, where Waite was known to study.

Crowley expands upon the theme and has the rays of the sun spiralling like a wonderful Catherine Wheel across the entire card. Between the rays sit the twelve signs of the zodiac and there are two winged children in the foreground who dance with glee, arms raised in praise. Their merriment takes place on the green leafy mound of a small hill, said to represent the fertile earth, and its summit is crowned by the wall. It is suggested that "The twin children are represented as dancing outside the wall, because they typify the new stage in human history, the stage of complete freedom from the restrictions imposed by such ideas as sin and death." Personally, although I like the image, I fail to accept the new concept offered. If, at this stage in the process depicted by the Tarot, we were at a level of "complete freedom", then we would have reached the end of the cycle and therefore not need any further cards of instruction. Two more cards come after the Sun, and my explanations which follow support my dismissal of Crowley's symbolism. It's then up to you to decide whether Crowley's ideas stand fast or not.

The Number 19

19 falls on the second cycle of 9. It also relates to 1 and 11. The element earth sits at 9. All sensations are possible at earth as it holds within it all five qualities of the physical world. It has smell and crystalline form of its own, the taste and bond of water, heat and form of fire, touch of air and the sound of ether.

The element earth is the glorious end of one cycle, where the Absolute stands as the glorious beginning on the other side. Earth is glorious because it is only through earth that all things of the world are created. Take anything from man to birds to vegetables, they are all formed of it. Houses, clothes, PC's, cars etc., everything is shaped from it. This earth is the basis for all physical expansion and it provides everything where all the multifarious forms and creatures find their abode. The fish in the water, birds in the air and men on land all depend on the element earth, even though they differ in the quantity of different elements in their constitution. For instance, fish have more of the element water than man, and birds more of the element air than fish or man, but they all owe their origin to the earth.

Number 9 is thus the base of all physical phenomena on one side, and the basis of all phenomena from the other. There are, of course some phenomena like sun and stars which are not directly connected to the earth, because if they were, their extra tejas would disrupt all bonds and the particles would disperse in space. Yet their movements are directly related to earth, which is a relationship which is not obvious as to be readily seen.

Symbolism, Interpretation and Divination

We know that the planet Earth orbits the Sun, and that the Sun's gravitational pull keeps us circling it. Thus the cycle of the earth is dependent on the sun, and without it we would have no natural heat or light. Consequently many civilisations throughout history have worshipped the sun, and lived in awe of its power.

In the Tarot the Sun is depicted as a benevolent deity, something which makes us feel happy and inclined to rejoice. It's warm, hence no need for much in the way of clothing. It always reminds me of the phenomena of summer. When the sun shines everyone seems to lose their inhibitions. People who are usually conservative strip off down to bare essentials and drape themselves on a beach without any sign of shame. Men walk down the high street in shorts and no shirt, and women wear miniskirts and bra tops. It's all perfectly acceptable.....after all, it's summer. But come winter it's a different story. Knock on someone's door and catch them coming out of the bathroom half dressed and they'll hide behind the door, or say, "One moment, I'll get a robe". Under the influence of the sun we're like the little children playing on the card, innocent and back in the Garden of Eden, sexless and indiscreet. Without the sun's influence we once again become separate and different enough to want to cover our bodies, even semi-nakedness being suddenly unacceptable.

Thus we begin to get a picture that these children playing in the garden are once again symbolic of the duality of our nature, yet here reconciled and united, if only temporarily. The children always touch each other, there is no gaping chasm between them as with the two towers in the Moon card, or the two pillars in the High Priestess. The number 1 is unity, and at the Sun we see this reflection of the number through 9. It is truly glorious; all things are possible when we start from a point of unity rather than duality.

The rest of the image is simple. A couple of happy children cavort under the Sun's sattvic rays in the protection of a walled garden. Or is it really that simple? There is no doubt that the Sun represents happiness, joy, abundance and harmony; but why is the garden limited by a wall? Are the children held prisoner here, or merely protected? Or, as Crowley's image suggests, are they outside the wall and not contained by it at all?

At 9 we are working on an earthly plane. Earth is full of glorious manifestations, and we are able to enjoy the pleasures and delights of this earthly realm. Yet it is said that God made man in order to experience himself at a physical level, and if we are on a spiritual path then our main objective is not to stay tied to the earthly world but to rise above it and join "God in Heaven" rather than coming back to this world time and time again. Thus the wall serves both purposes. It helps protect us from negative influences, but at the same time it can also stop us from progressing. If we like where we are then there is no desire to aspire beyond it. The wall is any boundary we erect to stop ourselves from going forward, and in time it may become the wall of another false tower. When we are truly happy, maybe having just fallen in love, we sit back and wish that the world could stop and that we could stay in this state of bliss forever. "I don't want anything to change", we say. "I want this moment to last forever" Yet it does not, and if we rely on this other person, object or circumstance for all of our contentment, when things do change it's a shock and the protective tower around us crumbles. Happiness is fleeting and ephemeral. We must learn when to let it go so that it can come back to us time and time again.

If we are already outside the wall, as Crowley implied, we must be free of sin and rebirth, because we are no longer attached to the physical level. Yet the number 9 and earth are all about the physical world and the joy we can obtain from our incarnation. We need a physical body in which to experience the self, and when that body is in good health, and life is filled with harmony, then bliss pervades our lives. We feel at one with others...but that unity must take place at a physical level before we can hope to attain it at a higher level. Note how every time you, or someone you know, believes that they have obtained or attained something perfect it changes, and leaves a feeling of disappointment and separation. Even the happiest, most glorious marriages on the planet end when one partner dies and leaves the other alone to weep. On extremely rare occasions happily married couples die together through exceptional circumstances...but even then we have to question the strong bond between them and how this will affect them in the next lifetime, because bonds bring karma. No-one on the earthly level of 9 escapes death, and even though it may feel as if innocence and complete freedom abound we are not free until we have heard the sound of the trumpet in the Judgement card.

During a reading the Sun card usually depicts that the questioner is of a positive disposition, content within themselves and having an inner sense of unity and oneness with the world. They are of a harmonious disposition and able to see the good even in difficult circumstances.

The Sun card's position within a reading is ultimately very important. If the questioner has the card in the line of the mind then this is a true reflection of their inner state, but if it appears at a physical level, then the questioner is putting on a happy, jolly, face to the world and may feel quite different inside.

There are two main alternatives for the **reversed** card. One is quite simply happiness tinged with sadness. We all live and we all go through stressful karmic situations. Here the Sun card accepts these and shows that although life is not perfect, we can bounce back, smile and extend our hearts to the world again. I recall a client who had this card saying, "Yes, I have some regrets and some sadness, but nothing that overwhelms me any more. I don't dwell on these things, but then again I don't deny their existence either....to say that I am completely immune to the tragedies in my life would be a lie, but I do believe that they have made me the, perhaps more positive, person I am today."

The alternative interpretation for the **reversed** card is when somebody is so exceedingly happy that they do not want a situation to change and grow, and thus they are in danger of killing the life in it. A common example is when one of a couple is due to move away, perhaps to study or work. It doesn't matter whether it is the one going or the one left behind, either party can feel a resistance to change for fear of losing the happiness they have found. The one left behind may not want the other to go, believing they will forget them or find someone else, and vice-versa. If the one who is due to leave does not take the opportunity then they risk stagnation, regret and living an unfulfilled life blaming the other party.

9 reflects 1. 9 is the glorious end of one cycle, but also the glorious beginning of another. The knack of the Sun card is not of staying put, but of dancing and enjoying the continuous play of life, without fear of what "might happen". Relationships go stale if they are not filled with variety and freedom of expression. The same goes for jobs or modes of creative expression. Artists never originate new work by being "happy" with what they produce, they push themselves further along the path of self expression and that is the source of their contentment.

In astrology it is said that our life path is to perfect our Sun sign qualities, so a Gemini is fulfilled through communication, a Sagittarian through teaching, travel or philosophy, and so on. The Sun card speaks of this perfection of the quality we are bound by our nature to achieve in this lifetime.

Key Words

Harmony/Contentment/Bliss/Happiness/Joy
Reversed - Happiness tinged with sadness/Inability to feel joy in life
Holding on too tight to relationships etc. for fear that the happiness it gives will go.

Toni Allen
The System of Symbols ©

Judgement No. 20

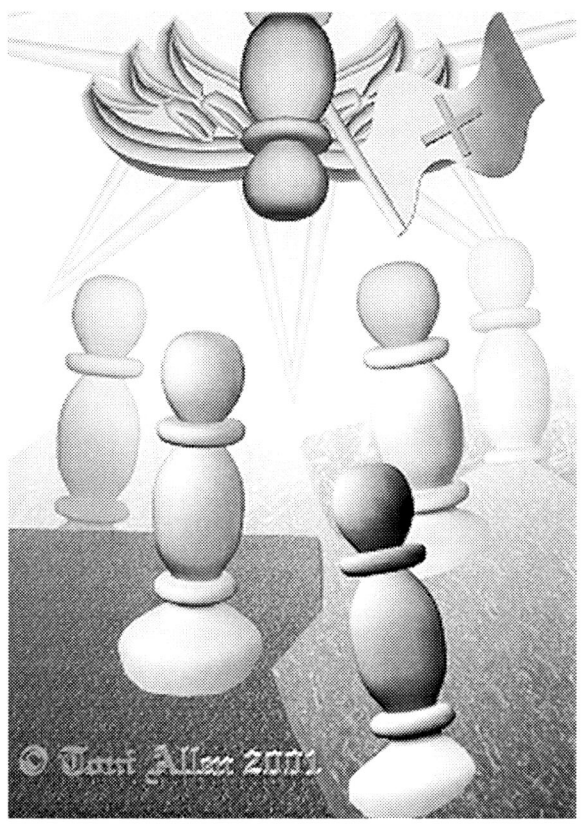

The Image

The symbolic themes on the Judgement card have been used throughout Christian art for centuries. If you look through a selection of Medieval Books of Hours you will find that many of them have a depiction of the resurrection of Christ. The Bible tells us that Christ was laid to rest in a tomb with a large stone closing its mouth and that the stone was rolled away by angels. Yet in medieval manuscripts Christ's resurrection is depicted from a sarcophagus-like tomb, the lid cast aside so that the risen Christ can step out. He often holds a banner with the cross of St. George emblazoned on it, and is accompanied by angels trumpeting, merely an angel or two in attendance, along with Mary Magdalene or the occasional sleeping guard. Another archetype of the time was The Last Judgement.

Toni Allen
The System of Symbols ©

In Rogier Van der Weyden's painting of the subject from 1446 we find naked human figures rising up out of the earth, the ground cracked and split where they have clawed their way out of the tomb of the barren land. Now they clasp hands in prayer as an assortment of clergy and saints, led by the Virgin Mary who floats on a sea of fiery clouds above their heads.
The image on the Judgement card is a merger of these two emotive scenes. A winged angel fills the sky, blasting on a trumpet pointed down towards the earth. A flag with a cross on it streams out from the trumpet and as the sound cracks the air naked figures rise up from the ground, sometimes from black pits, sometimes from more tomb-like structures. Like the figures in Van der Weyden's painting they clasp hands in praise as they stretch up, reaching ever higher towards the sound, as if awoken by its vibration.

This archetype remains nearly unaltered throughout the Tarot and Waite holds fast with tradition. Crowley on the other hand entitles the card the Aeon and changes the image completely, assigning it heavily to Egyptian mythology, the meanings of which are too diverse to go into here.

The Number 20

The number 20 is made up of 2 and 0. 2 is the unmanifest and duality, and 0 is the great unmanifest consciousness and the consciousness to which everything returns.

20 is also the second cycle of 10, and on the overturned circle relates to 5 and 15, the ether. 2 is also related to 8 and the binding qualities of water.

9 is the limit of numbers and as we progress into the multiplicity of numbers the variations of interpretation become more vast and complex.

In the Tarot 20 represents the end of the second cycle. An individual who has travelled from 10 to 19, the cycle of working through one's personal samskara, finds themself enlightened by the journey and thus answers come through the ether (5) from the unmanifest level (2). At 10 one was not entirely in control of one's destiny, but at 20 past issues have been resolved and enlightenment takes place. Duality becomes wholeness through the power of 0 and the individual is freed from karmic bonds and ties.

Toni Allen
The System of Symbols ©

Symbolism, Interpretation and Divination

The angel's trumpet channels the sound from the ether. At 19 with the Sun card there appeared to be the dilemma of wishing to stay in such an idyllic place and go no further, the wall offering seclusion and security. Here, however, the vibration from the trumpet is so fine that it's as if one has passed through a sound barrier and shattered the wall, like bringing down the walls of Jericho. This unique sound makes the earth split and the lids of the tombs vibrate until they slide off, enabling the naked people to rise up towards the angelic figure.

The dark pits or tombs that the people rise up from are symbolic of their individual samskara. The black spaces are all their emotional attachments built up over a lifetime, or lifetimes. This attachment, comes from the bonding process of water which sits at 8, 2's counterpart on our circle, which binds us to this earthly existence of repeat cycles. The same dark stagnation sits at the bottom of the Moon card in the form of the water which the crayfish needs to move out of, only here, in the Judgement card, there is redemption in the vibration set up by the trumpet whose sound resonates from deep within the causal level of the unmanifest and the storehouse of number 2, bringing with it previously secret knowledge. Everything in the universe lies stored in the unmanifest before creation breaks out, and here the sound from the ether makes it manifest and the people rise from the earth, like flowers in spring. Thus they become free of spirit, like the Fool at 0.

So, what does this mean to us in our every day lives? The tombs represent our samskara, and here we are pictured rising up out of it. Once again we are naked, cleansed of all inhibition and re-united to a feeling of oneness, as we were in the Garden of Eden before eating the apple. There is no need to hide ourself here. The sound of the trumpet has made this evident and in our daily life we recognise this as something ringing true or sounding right. Have you ever had that awe inspiring experience when you gain a tiny piece of information about a situation you've been struggling with for ages, and that one little piece of extra knowledge makes you gasp and say "Yes, that's it!"? Suddenly everything falls into place and the mind is overwhelmed with clarity. Hitting the right spot makes all the difference. It's a true Eureka moment!

As with all cards there are multiple levels. In its highest sense this is a card of triumphant breakthrough over life patterns which threaten to clog our progress and stifle our existence. It's not so much a card of seeing what others do to us, but of seeing what we do to ourselves. Like, for example, a woman who continually gets involved with men who hit her. Yes, the men do physically abuse her, but something in her nature lures her towards this type, partly so that she can experience the situation and break her personal samskara. So, we have a scenario of a woman repeatedly being physically abused, until one day she recalls that her father was a very busy man and that the only way to gain his attention was to be naughty. This invariably resulted in her being smacked because she'd interrupted him. When she recalls this early experience, insight is offered into the situation, and this is the Judgement card at work. From this memory she comes to realise that in her adult life she is not being naughty, but that a smack is the only type of display of affection she was ever programmed to expect from a man; thus she perpetuates it. From this starting point of profound self-knowledge she is then able to work through situations at a physical level and start to consciously make choices and decisions based on the changes she knows she needs to make, first in her consciousness and then in her actions.

Remember that Samskara is "a deep mental impression produced by past experiences". Samskara acts like a coloured piece of glass through which we view the world, each episode of experiences setting up a different colour. Perfection is about making each piece of class crystal clear so that actions are taken which leave no residue. Thus we find phrases in use such as "they were coloured by that experience", or "they're viewing that through rose tinted glasses". Hence the Judgement card offers opportunity to gain insight into what shades of colour we have been living under and thus work towards eradicating them.

On another level the Judgement card refers to breaking away from life situations which have bound us to a particular path, or course of events. The breaking away, however, only comes through the knowledge which the card offers us. I recall one woman who came to me for a reading when she was severely tormented by jealousy because she felt that her husband was having an affair. The Judgement card was placed a couple of months in the future, crossed by the Ace of Coins, which symbolises both wisdom and documents. It appeared that she would find out the truth through something written down, and even though the reading implied that her husband was being furtive there was nothing specifically relating his actions to another woman. When my client returned for another reading a few months later the Judgement card came up as the card for the past, suggesting that she now knew what it was all about. She appeared a lot happier in herself. "I found those documents you mentioned", she said. "His business is going down the drain. That's what he didn't want to tell me about....and he really was working late at the office." This knowledge had brought relief from her black hole of jealousy and depression, and freed her from the bondage of deep, confused emotion. She was very practical about the business issues and consequently doing all she could to help him, now that it was out in the open.

A very interesting combination of cards one client had was the Judgement card on the line of the mind, crossed by the Moon card and followed on the physical line by the 4 of Coins and 3 of Batons. My client had come to me during a very stressful time when his physical well being was being overtaxed and stretched by apprehension and worry. The Moon card crossing the Judgement card indicated that the only course of action was for him to recognise and accept his fear and do what needed to be done anyway. To know and understand what made him anxious would bring him relief, as indicated by the 4 of Coins, a positive sense of I Am, and the 3 of Batons, a positive sense of one's true nature. This he understood and saw clearly. "Fear is making me ill," he stated. "No doubt once I've been through everything I'll look back and ask myself 'what was all that about?' Every time I'm frightened it's a challenge, and I look inside myself to try and find the root cause of the fear." The whole process he was going through, although unpleasant, gave him loads of opportunity to process and clear personal patterning, e.g. it was not until his wife left him that he recalled how his mother had left him for the first time when he started school. "I'd spent every day of my life with my mother, never left her side", he said. "And suddenly she wasn't there. I was desperately grief stricken." The current situation had triggered off the same feelings, and he realised that he had never come to terms with this fear of being suddenly cast out from a feeling of oneness which he had initially had with his mother. In consequence he had chosen a wife who was unable to give him this unique bond and the relationship had collapsed. His wife's departure had offered him insight into early

Toni Allen
The System of Symbols ©

patterning which had coloured his perspective and trapped him in a particular mode of action and re-action.

Another particularly important interpretation for the Judgement card is release from illness. All illness has its root in the causal level. Illness comes in many forms ranging from the common cold to life threatening diseases. Each time we are unwell there is an opportunity for growth as we learn to observe the repeat cycles of our dis-ease and discover the originating cause. Do we always become ill as soon as we get a break from work? Do we get a sore throat directly before a job interview? Does it rain and we get a snuffly nose, or is it the sun shining that makes our hay fever immediately bring on a sneeze before we've even experienced the pollen count? All of these symptoms, and more, lie in the black tombs of the Judgement card. The trumpeter's fanfare rises us up from these traps and makes us well again. Sometimes the card can signify release from extreme patterns of illness, e.g. no longer suffering from hay fever and finding that for the first time one can enjoy summer. Often individuals consciously do work on themselves before experiencing this type of breakthrough. Along with complementary therapies there are many self-help books, tapes and essences on the market which can help facilitate change. One of the most popular self-help books is Louise Hay's Little Blue Book which gives a highly comprehensive list of the root causes underlying illness. If you have any doubt then read her suggestions for a particular illness which you know someone suffers from. You'll be amazed at how accurate the correspondences are. Louise Hay's ideas can be readily incorporated with the Bach Flower Essences, and when using these in practice I have seen many a client experience the Judgement card as an expression of their release from the bondage of repeat suffering and debilitation, e.g. freedom from stress headaches/ release from anxiety.

The Judgement card also symbolises clear communication, the type that brings truths to the surface and clarifies a situation. Often relationships flounder due to poor communication, often based on preconceptions such as it not being appropriate to bother or burden the other person with one's problems. This sets up all sorts of negative reactions from the person who is on the receiving end because they simply do not, and cannot, comprehend where the other person is coming from without being told. Thus the Judgement card signifies bringing these issues to light and literally raising the relationship to a higher level of trust

Toni Allen
The System of Symbols ©

and self- awareness in both parties.

When the Judgement card is **reversed** it indicates an inability to free one's self from a characteristic manner of self-expression due to lack of knowledge. This encompasses both personal self-knowledge and knowledge of what others are doing to manipulate the circumstances. For one woman the card came up in connection with her young son and his repeated bad behaviour at school. It appeared that whatever exploratory measures she and the school took to try and discover why he was acting so negatively they always drew a blank. He appeared to be happy at home and in a stable background. He showed no signs of a learning difficulty, yet his attention span was incredibly short and this made him fidgety and disruptive. With the Judgement card reversed, and the Pope reversed further on in the reading, I asked whether she had taken her son for a hearing test, as it appeared that for some reason messages were not getting through to him. Until this point everyone's emphasis had been on emotional difficulties. "We haven't really looked at the physical," she said. "He speaks perfectly well, but at this point anything's worth a go." Some months later my client reported back that she had taken her son for a full medical and they had found his hearing to be below par, which was the cause of the trouble. "If only we'd known sooner," she said. "We simply couldn't see the problem for looking."

In other situations it is the individual's own manner which keeps them trapped. Often people will say such things as "I'm too old to change" or "tried that and it didn't work". Samskara does not go away overnight and it is not uncommon for people to become easily discouraged when trying to shake off old habits. However, there is also a warning note to be made here. No-one can make a change which they are not ready and willing to make. However much a therapist may see the need for change within a client it is highly dangerous to push a client towards a path for which they are, as yet, unprepared. In some cases the Judgement card reversed can show that it is okay to stay where one is and that the time for break through and change will come later. To force a change at the wrong time can make people unwell because it brings up painful material far too quickly....only the Fool can walk off a precipice without a care in the world.

Key Words

Release from Samskara/New insight into a situation
When something "sounds right", "rings true", "the penny drops"
A Eureka moment/Release from repeat pattern illness
Reversed
Inability to change/Refusal to change/Inappropriate time for change

Bach Flower Remedy

Gentian - for the reversed card - when one is easily discouraged while working through samskara.

Toni Allen
The System of Symbols ©

The World No. 21

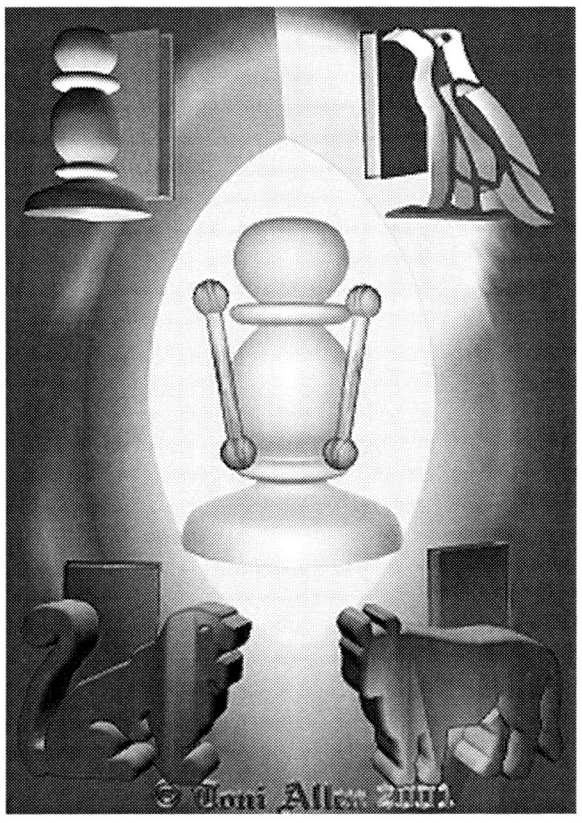

The Image

In early hand painted Tarot packs of the mid-15th century the image on the World card was quite different to the one we have come to associate with it now. In the Pierpont Morgan-Bergamo-Visconti-Sforza pack we find a circle, raised high by two putti, encapsulating a city surrounded by the sea. This idea persists throughout several packs and the central theme of a castellated city endures in other areas, such as on the Ace of Coins in the Fournier Visconti-Sforza pack and on what is believed to be the Empress from the enigmatic Goldschmidt cards. In the D'Este cards the world is depicted slightly differently with a putti sitting on top of the circled city while more commonly, as in the Grigonneur Cards, a regal looking woman holding a sceptre and orb, stands on top of the circular window-like motif which opens onto the world. This type of portrayal continued into several early printed packs and we find it as late as the 17th century in the Tarot de Paris, where a naked figure holds a large drape behind him while standing on top of the globe.

When we compare these images to contemporary illuminated manuscripts we find that the circle in which the world sits is very similar to the way in which Christ, or the Virgin Mary, are pictured in the Vesica Pisces, sometimes sitting on an arc with the world at their feet. Likewise, Jupiter in the Tarocchi of Mantegna cards is also pictured sitting in the Vesica, and here we have an even greater synthesis of images because Christ was born when Jupiter, the King of planets was high in the heavens.

Once the depiction of the World changed to how we have come to recognise it now the middlemost shape of the elliptical laurel wreath is even more easily distinguishable as the central section of the Vesica Pisces. Instead of Christ sitting in the centre we find a naked woman dancing, a sash often covering her modesty, as she places one foot on the rim of the wreath while taking her first step into the world. In the four corners of the card are the four images of the elements, as recognised in the gospels, the system of the humours, the Tarot and astrology.

Man-air-intellect.
Lion-fire-passion.
Eagle-water-emotions.
Bull-earth-substance.

In astrology we find correspondence with the fixed signs of the zodiac, Aquarius for air, Leo for fire, Scorpio (which was previously known as the eagle) for water and Taurus for earth. The fixed signs denote exactly that, a fixity of purpose, self-reliance, will power and a high degree of determination in overcoming problems.

Waite does little to transgress the traditional image of the card, except the addition of a baton in each of the woman's hands. Crowley entitles the World The Universe and consequently appears to have a much larger vision of the symbol. The four traditional elements are placed in each corner, surrounding the same ellipse, but the central woman appears to grapple with a giant snake, as if she is untangling the ouroboros, one hand holding a dark moon, the other stretched up towards the all-seeing eye which shines down upon the scene. At the bottom of the painting sits a building resembling Crystal Palace, which Crowley calls "the skeleton plan of the building of the house of Matter", which brings us full circle back to our earlier images with a central theme of a city.

One other depiction which is worth mentioning here is that of Robert Wang for the Golden Dawn Tarot deck. He again entitles the card the Universe and has the entire scene set against the starry heavens. Instead of the woman stepping onto a plain ellipse or laurel wreath he has a string of twelve rainbow coloured circles strung together with smaller white circles, like gems strung on a beautiful necklace. It is a very powerful image and the woman gives the impression that she is running towards us, eager to step out into the world across the rainbow bridge of the ether.

The Number 21

The number 21 is made up of 2 and 1.
It also holds the qualities of 10, 5, 8 and 0.
3 x 7 = 21
2 + 1 = 3
As you can see, when we go beyond 9, we end up with multiplicity in terms of number relationships.

The most important point here is that once the two cycles from 1 to 10 and 11 to 20 have been completed we step out another new cycle at 21.

Having travelled through a cycle of perfection and a cycle of karma, we are then invited to start all over again. The 2 indicates that there is still more duality to overcome and the 1 shows that having returned to unity we are ready to begin again. There is always more in the storehouse of number 2 for us to experience through the power of 5 and the etheric level.

Symbolism, Interpretation and Divination

The central woman is symbolic of the eternal dance of Shiva. It is said that all the while Shiva dances the world continues to rotate....she therefore gives us life. The naked woman is also the free spirit, ready to step out and participate in the world. Here the ellipse takes on the form of the yoni, or vagina, and suggests birth and physical incarnation. It is said that we choose our parents and our time of birth in order to experience a

Toni Allen
The System of Symbols ©

particular set of circumstances that will give us suitable events to overcome our karma and samskara. Thus we see our birth into the world of physical matter. The four elements sit in each corner, inviting us to choose our temperament for this lifetime.

In our day to day lives the female stepping out into the world symbolises the choice we make when we start any new activity. Like the Magician she has the four elements to select from. Would we like to do something fiery or earthy, watery or airy? Here the world is our oyster, filled with abundant opportunities. We have the ability to do anything we would like to, everything is on offer. There are no limits here, only possibilities.

The World card is a card of great freedom and also expectation. The ties of the past have been released at 20 with the Judgement card and now we are able to start something fresh. We always expect the new to be better, and perhaps, greater than the old. It is not until we start a new relationship, or another job, that we find out whether we have, indeed, cleared our samskara. If we have then things will go well, and our problems will arise elsewhere in our lives, allowing us scope to clear even more space within our hearts.

In many respects the World is a very simple card. It signifies efforts made on ourselves and freedom to enjoy life's bounty. In practice it relates to anything which opens us up to further growth. One interpretation is opportunity, another, many more possibilities than one has had for a while. The storehouse which sits at number 2 is released into creation, and many people simply don't know where the opportunity came from, it appears as if luck is on their side. There is also freedom to explore here and for lots of people the world indicates their holiday, or some other travel, where they will go off and have fun, experience other cultures and come back refreshed and vibrant. Seeing the world and finding out who else shares the planet with us can be both enlightening and educational. Some people go and never return, finding their path lies in another country, or at the other end of this one.

For many people to World card is the light at the end of the tunnel experienced in the Moon card. Struggles are over and it's time for new beginnings and fun. Struggles come in many forms. I have seen the World card come up for people who have recently moved, their house at last straightened and now it's time to go off and explore their new surroundings. For others it's the end of exams and a bright step into a new career, while for others it's the end of grief or sorrow.

One quite exceptional interpretation for the World card is when a homosexual or lesbian decides to "come out" and show the world who they really are. On the one hand that first step is like the Fool ignoring the dog biting his buttocks, society saying 'we must not do that' and yet it's also a terrific sense of relief to be able to stand up and be who one is.

When the World card is **reversed** we find the opposite at play. We find individuals whose lives are very small, with no opportunity for change or personal growth. For one woman it came up shortly after the birth of her first child. "Everyone was so keen to support me to start with," she said. "But their ardour's worn off and I'm the one left with this appendage all day and night. I'm often too tired to go out and there's no chance of an evening out at all. My whole world's changed."

For others the trap has been of longer standing, such as with a difficult marriage or an unrewarding job. "I don't like my job," one man said. "I'm due for early retirement in two years time, and I'll be fifty five then. If I stick with it I'll get a good pension and, who knows, maybe do something else career-wise; meanwhile there's no opportunity for advancement, so I'm stuck." Here he really was between the Devil and the deep blue sea. Risking leaving now and losing his pension, or staying put and festering. The side of his life which, until this point, he had completely ignored, was his personal life. He had a wife and grown up family, and regularly involved himself with their activities in a kind and generous fatherly role, however, he never pursued any type of hobby which gave him any personal satisfaction. "I don't have time for a hobby" he responded. With this comment alone he was limiting his own life. Meanwhile he undoubtedly gave it some thought and when he next came for a reading he said that he had taken up picture framing as his wife liked to paint. "I'm really enjoying myself," he said. "Some of her art club members have asked me to frame their work too. Who knows, by the time I retire I could have a thriving little business of my own already up and running". Through his own efforts my client had turned his World card up the right way and created opportunity where before there appeared to be none.

Key Words

Birth
Travel/the world/holiday
Opportunity/Abundance
"Coming Out"
Reversed
Trapped/Lack of opportunity
Small world, maybe through confinement or other circumstances.

Toni Allen
The System of Symbols ©

The Minor Cards

There is no accurately dated evidence as to when the first interpretations were assigned to the minor cards. Methods of divination were originally passed down through an oral tradition in the same way as story telling, with an elder teaching the pupil their art, so that they could continue the practice. In this way much of the initiation and craft was kept secret and only handed on to the chosen few. It was undoubtedly a very different world to the one we inhabit today. Now we have books, magazines, radio, television and computers which all bombard us with information so that everyone can get a slice of the action. There are no mysteries any more. There is no "secret information" or "trade secrets" as there used to be, maybe even as little as twenty years ago. Once upon a time people would adhere rigidly to their own trade and teach this to their children and their children's children. Names arose out of one's occupation and we find people called Smith, Fletcher, and Butcher. The introduction of reading, writing and general education for the masses slowly eroded this system and took the mysteries of life away from oral tradition and onto the written page.

The truth of the origination of interpretations is an enigma locked in this oral tradition. Some fortune tellers claim to be of Gypsy decent and therefore hold the secrets passed down through the generations, for it has long been claimed that it was travelling people, or more especially people of Romany decent, who started using the Tarot cards for telling fortunes. Again there is no evidence to substantiate this as fact, and several interesting books have sprung up alleging to be long lost manuscripts. One such publication is "Cartomancia Suprema" a Spanish publication reprinting a work of 1621 allegedly written by one "Benita La Bruja" (Benita the Witch), the original manuscript of which was not available for reference, or inspection in a museum, when requested for my research.

Examination of early Tarot packs will show that they have simple pip cards, with no illustrations or words labelling them, only the number of the card, generally written in Roman numerals. After all, few individuals could read, so anything written would simply have meant more hard work for the wood carver to little advantage. The first cards to assign specific interpretations to each card appeared near the end of the eighteenth century and were created by a man named Etteilla, who

Toni Allen
The System of Symbols ©

followed the beliefs of Court de Gebelin. For the first time ever words were written at the top and bottom of each card to allow for easier interpretation. His minor cards, although adhering to a basic depiction of the suits, included a rectangle at the bottom, some third the size of the entire frame, which added symbols and simple illustrations to aid the reader. Although unique, the overall format of Etteilla's cards is a cross between the Mantegna prints and a type of fortune telling card which was evolving around this time, examples of which can be found in the Parlour Sybille and Madame Lenormand cards. These generally maintain the use of simple words and phrases for each card, while modern occultists dispense with them. Crowley is the exception to the rule in that his minor cards have a one word description, although his Court Cards do not.

It was not until Waite, in conjunction with the artist Pamela Coleman-Smith created the Rider Waite pack that every single minor card was illustrated with a detailed pictorial scene, or episode, as if telling a story; a concept which has been repeated ever since. It's interesting to note that a popular Victorian parlour past-time for a rainy day was for the ladies to sit with an ordinary pack of playing cards and transform the pip cards into pictures. Some full packs of these still exist and it's possible to buy replicas. The suits take on a life of their own, alternatives being as limited as the boundaries of the individuals imagination, with the spades becoming gentlemen's coats, hearts butterflies, and so on. Waite's pack is often described as a transformation pack after this Victorian trend, but the difference that Waite and Coleman-Smith made was that they were inspired to have figures pick up and use the elements of the suits, as if they were a total part of the picture; thus we find men wielding Batons, carving Coins, running away with Swords or raising their Cups.

A few of the Waite/Coleman-Smith images still retain a more symmetrical layout, with the picture placed in the background. The Crowley/Freda Harris designs use a more elaborate method of incorporating a pattern picture of the number of the element along with symbols and ideas to aid interpretation. Again this concept has been continued by others, such as Balbi and Maritxu Guler.

None of these ideas are better or worse, right or wrong, it is simply a matter of taste as to which pack one prefers to use. I often advise students to have a copy of Waite's pack so that they have a pictorial reference with which to associate the card, but then use a Marseille pack, or other pack with plainer Minor Cards for readings. Reading cards is all about synthesis and pattern building, watching the ebb and flow of an individuals life cycles, so I, personally, find having lots of little pictures laid out far too distracting. Plain Minor Cards allow for a rhythm to be built up, along with instant recognition of how many of a particular suit have been drawn and how many cards of the same number, or of numbers close to each other. Packs such as Balbi's and Maritxu Guler's re-coloured version of the Marseille Tarot are very easy to use because, once laid out, they offer the added dimension of blocks of colour giving another visual tool to allow both reader and client to see what the bulk of cards are. e.g. with Balbi's pack Swords are dark blue and the Coins yellow, a mixture of which might suggest that stress is being caused by money problems.

So, what are these Minor Cards and why do we need them? The Major Cards illustrate 22 archetypal truths. As we have seen, their concepts are encompassed by many religions and belief systems, and there is no doubt that they are able to stand alone as a system for revealing man's cycle of existence in the world. Life, death, nature and rebirth, fear, change, insight and discrimination are all indicated. Yet these are very meaningful and deep mysteries, which we can all spend time pondering on and working with during periods of major change and upset, but might not wish to concern ourselves with every day unless we are following a spiritual path as the totality of our life's journey. Mostly we work and play, having little concern for these high notions until something goes adrift. This is where the Minor Cards find their place, in the every day routine and ritual of daily life. They illustrate happenings in our lives, things which have caused us pain or created karma, how we feel about these great changes which occur to us, or, quite simply, how much the wife upset us this morning because she didn't kiss us goodbye when we left for work.

Each Minor Card comes under the rulership of one or more of the Major Cards. They too sit on our circle of nine numbers. All of the 1s associate with the Magician, the Hermit, Strength, the Sun and Judgement; the 2s with the High Priestess, Justice, the Hanged Man, the Moon Card, and the World, the 3s with the Empress, the Chariot, Death, or the Star...and so on around the circle.

The Minor Cards are also split into four suits.

Swords come under the realm of air.
Batons come under the realm of fire.
Cups come under the realm of water.
Coins come under the realm of Earth.

Swords therefore also come under the realm of the Major Cards associated with air:-

The Emperor-I AM
The Lovers-Discrimination
Temperance-I AM okay
The Tower-I AM not okay

Batons come under the realm of the Major Cards associated with fire:-

The Empress-Nature
The Chariot-Personal Tejas
Death-Endings
The Star-Our Divine Nature

Cups come under the realm of the Major Cards associated with water:-

The High Priestess-Duality
Justice-Karma
The Hanged Man-Patience
The Moon-Samskara

Coins come under the realm of the cards associated with Earth:-

The Magician-Knowledge
The Hermit-Prudence
Strength-Restraint
The Sun-Bliss
Judgement-Enlightenment

The Minor Cards are of a lower vibration than the Major Cards and can therefore indicate which major influence is affecting an individual at a particular time e.g. a group of 1s would indicate new beginnings or personal breakthroughs.

During the following chapters I will show you how to merge and blend each number, suit and major card to find the interpretation of the minor card. As with the Major Cards the Minor Cards have a unique meaning, and yet we hardly ever see this as they are constantly influenced by surrounding cards. In many books on the Tarot the writer gives a whole string of interpretations, which the student is expected to swallow, without any realisation or understanding as to why the cards might mean what is proposed. These words or phrases are often contradictory, and as human beings we end up scratching our heads and wondering how on earth a card could possibly mean both things at the same time. I certainly did! I created a notebook in which I laboriously wrote out a word or two under each card from every book I could find. Confusion reigned....until I realised the problem. No one was giving a definitive meaning, merely how they had seen the card in practice, when next to another card and therefore coloured by it.

Once you have the nuts and bolts it's easy to build something lasting. Hopefully the following chapters will also give you a spanner and screwdriver too, along with some solid pieces of metal, so that you too can build a system and drive this wonderful vehicle called the Tarot. I hope that by the end you will have enough power to switch on its headlights and see the road ahead for yourself.

Toni Allen
The System of Symbols ©

The Ace of Swords

The Sword relates to the element of air and therefore to the number 6.

The symbol of the Sword is a very powerful one. In all Tarot packs you find the Swords depicted clearly as having a light side and a dark side, or with a line running up the centre of the blade which splits it in two. Here we immediately see that the sword relates to duality. It has the ability to be light and dark, which can equate to good and bad, right and wrong, true and untrue, and so on through all opposites. There are always two edges to the sword. If we relate this to its physical attributes in battle a sword is designed to attack or defend. Who cast the first blow? Who raised their sword first? Are we swinging our blade up to crash it down and cleave someone's head in two, or are we bringing it up to parry the blow and protect ourself? Hopefully our sword is a finely honed blade, razor sharp and weighted perfectly in our hand. Like this it cuts through opposition, but if its blunt and unbalanced then we find it difficult to control and we lose the fight, not through lack of skill, but by having an unsuitable weapon.

In the Major Cards we first come across the Sword placed on the Magician's table as one of his attributes. It symbolises his faculty of discrimination and the mind. Next we find the Sword held erect in the hand of Justice. Here it is the discriminatory power of truth. At a mundane level the legal system uses it to represent a judge's ability to discriminate between the rights and wrongs of a situation in order to make a judgement. This suggests that once all of the evidence is laid before him that he is able, in his role as a servant of God, to discriminate between good and evil. On the Wheel of Fortune a sword is often found in the hand of the figure sitting on top of the wheel. This figure is the observer within us all who sees the situation with an objective eye and chooses right action to aid our progress away from the repeat cycles of life and death.

We have already seen how the number 4 relates to the feeling of "I AM" and across the circle to 6 and the element air. With the feeling of "I AM" comes the ego; symbolised by the Emperor at 4. The ego creates separateness, and when we experience the pain of our association with the ego at 16 and the Tower we find that at 6 with the Lovers we lacked discrimination. Thus the sword not only represents our discriminatory faculty but also the mind itself. Clarity of mind brings clarity of judgement, but when the mind is clouded we experience torment because the ego expects us to be a somebody and therefore get it right at every turn. The self within is perfect; it is only ever the ego that fails.

Air is the very life force within us all, the pranas. When we think of this in practical terms we can see that air creates wind, breath and the life force. When all of the air in the body is dispelled a man dies. We are all affected by air every moment of our lives and the gunas play a large part in the quality of our experiences. We talk of the day being 'airless' and find it difficult to concentrate. This is tamasika air. We become sluggish and grumpy, hot and bothered. I recall on one such day feeling very tired by about 6 o'clock and then bumping into someone who was full of beans. He was enjoying the stifling heat and thought it was great. "Yes," he said. "I did look out of the window of my air conditioned office at about lunch time and thought it looked hot outside." During the day his office had regulated the air quality to maintain a sattvic environment in which the staff were able to work efficiently, keep mental agility and therefore have maximum output. Consequently the day's heat had not affected him at all and he was still feeling lively when the rest of us wish we'd had a siesta! The third quality of air comes with the wind and is rajasika. Leaves on the trees rattle, the wind howls around and everyone appears to be agitated and unsettled, sort of busy without purpose. All of these examples show the external force of the air upon us, yet we all have our own inner air system too, and this can be affected by the gunas without any influence from the weather. Each of us has the ability to have excess wind and feel bloated by it, or unable to concentrate without knowing why. Air is vitally important to us, without it we die. Under extreme circumstances it is our breathing which shows the first signs of stress, such as having a panic attack after a shock (the Tower). During a panic attack people hyperventilate and believe that there is not enough air for them to breath, and therefore gulp in more than required and overload the system.

Thus we begin to see how air, the mind and the ego are intrinsically linked. If you asked several people to choose between having an operation to cure an illness or receive hypnotherapy to effect the same cure, many more would willingly opt for surgery and have their bodies interfered with than have their minds tampered with. Mankind so closely associates himself with his mind that he is often deluded into believing that this is his soul. We may become possessed by the body, trouble ourselves over our physical health or beauty; yet still class our mind as the last sanctuary, something private, something personal, that bit which is me. To have it touched and tampered with is to lose something fundamentally so precious as to be a human outrage. Likewise with our thoughts. People fight each other all the time, not because they hate each other, but because the opposition has questioned their belief system, or suggested that the way their culture thinks is wrong, or denied their god, or attacked how they run their family, or country. Someone has said that someone else's ideas, what comes from their thoughts, is wrong, and this creates the desire to stand up and defend one's personal truth.

When someone comes for a reading, even if they have never had a reading before, they generally react with abhorrence when a sword card is turned over. Of all the suits the sword is the only one to evoke such instant dislike and fear, a sense of danger. It is due to the very nature of the symbol that its meaning reaches the inner man so rapidly; for the sword speaks of conflict, fighting and struggle, whether inward or outward. On a sword we find a hand guard, and hand is the seat of air and the mind, something which we seek to protect at all times, especially when in battle.

The Ace of Swords encompasses all of these facts. In a reading it is interpreted as truth. The upright card suggests that the questioner is seeking the truth, or knows the truth, or will not be moved from the truth. Honesty and integrity are prevalent here. It shows that one is discriminating well and has a clear, sound mind. A life changing decision might also have just been made depending upon the position of the card within the spread. Intelligence is also suggested.

When the card is **reversed** it indicates the opposite in that someone has lied, or is lying. Dishonesty and untruthfulness are suggested as well as an inability to decide what to do about a situation because judgement is over shadowed by ego desire. A wrong decision is also likely.

Here I feel it is appropriate to mention the superstition set up around the Ace of Spades and its confusion with the Ace of Swords. In true cartomancy one uses an every day pack of playing cards which consists of spades, clubs, hearts and diamonds. These suits are often cross referenced with the Tarot suits in which spades become swords, clubs-batons, hearts-cups and diamonds-coins. In general superstition and cartomancy the Ace of Spades is often referred to as a 'bad' card and a card of death, but this is due to the history of the card. Early packs of playing cards originally had a very simple stencilled Ace of Spades. With the introduction of cheap printed cards gambling soon became a social problem of epidemic proportion and the government decided that something drastic had to be done about it. In consequence they devised what has become known as the 'Frizzle' ace, an Ace of Spades ornately etched, much like a bank note is today. Each card manufacturer created their own pack and then had to buy their Ace of Spades from the government at a premium rate, thus putting a heavy tax on playing cards and taking them out of reach of the common man's meagre pay packet. A stop to gambling? Not at all. No one wanted to pay nearly five times the price for their pack of playing cards, so forgers sprung up in abundance. As a result of the ensuing mayhem the government made forgery of the

Ace of Spades a crime punishable by death, and many a man was sent to the gallows, right up until the end of the 19th century. Hence the Ace of Spades came to be known as a card of intrigue and death. A bad card to draw. However, although this superstition has crept into cartomancy, I do not feel that it has any relevance to the Tarot, except maybe within the Ace of Swords reversed interpretation of deceit and lying. However, I do not believe that this meaning for the Ace of Swords has its roots in the same historical acts which brought about the fear associated with the Ace of spades.

As with all of the aces the Ace of Swords represents new beginnings as in truth it is a number 1. Every reading has its own rhythm and cycle, but it is not uncommon to find similar patterns. In an ideal world 10s turn into 1s and it is not uncommon to find the Ace of Swords following a 10 of any suit, indicating that one cycle has finished and a new one beginning, this time with greater understanding. The Ace of Swords on the line of the mind indicates that the questioner knows the truth of the situation, even if they are unable to do anything about it at a physical level, while the Ace of Swords following, or crossing, the Judgement card indicates a unique breakthrough in mental patterning.

Key Words

Truth/Honesty/Discrimination/The mind
Defence/attack, depending upon surrounding cards
Reversed
Untruth/lies
Dishonesty/deceit
Lack of discrimination
Inability to accept the truth of a matter

Toni Allen
The System of Symbols ©

The 2 of Swords

The 2 of Swords relates to air at duality or the unmanifest.

It is the air which holds all physical forms. Air sits at number 6, while its counterpart 4, relates to the feeling of "I AM".

Number 2 represents the duality of the I and the non I, or I and the rest of creation. This I is the ultimate unity of the absolute, represented as the Atman. Whatever is not Atman, or whatever is not being felt as Atman, is the universe. Thus number 2 is the stage where one stands as the consciousness looking around. Whatever comes into view forms another unit, which is unmanifest Prakriti (Nature).

In Sanskrit language, the I stands for Aham, and the non-I stands for Idam. Aham is for the Atman, and Idam is for everything else.

Thus at the 2 of Swords we have knowledge of ourself through the feeling of "I AM" combined with a sense of duality. This gives rise to a feeling of self consciousness, and an awareness of being different to someone else. The water, number 2s counterpart at number 8, binds these to us. This difference is generally experienced with the mind alone rather than via any physical deformity; unless other cards indicate that the latter has created the former.

Generally the 2 of Swords indicates that the questioner holds a different, or conflicting opinion, to someone else, and that neither side is willing to change their outlook. This gives rise to a feeling of "Us and them", or "Him and me". However, as the 2 of Swords sits at the unmanifest, nothing happens outwardly; any outburst occurs at the 3 of Swords.

Consequently the 2 of swords symbolises "keeping the peace". Tension is in the air, but neither party is willing to verbalise their opinion and start the fight. Knowing that these differences are present creates great tension. It also heightens anticipation because we know that unless a fine line is trodden to maintain this rather precarious balance then an outburst will ensue.

As the Swords symbolise truth, both sides in this dilemma believe that their side of the dispute is true. "I am right and you are wrong". In truth there is no "right and wrong", that is if we go from 2 back to the unity of 1. However, in the physical world, we all hold a subjective outlook on situations, backed up by colouring from our past personal experiences, which all join to create a feeling of separation from one another.

I say "another" because the 2 of swords usually indicates a conflict between two people, or possibly two factions. It is the two opposing sides in any particular situation, argument, conflict or dispute.

We all hold our own truth on any given situation because we saw what occurred on a given day, and we were physically there, acting in our body and our mind. However, the other person's subjective viewpoint considers what they think we were up to, or just about to do, or even what they think we were thinking at the time. This can be a remarkably different truth from our own, regardless of how much we assure them that we not thinking or acting in the way that they perceived it. e.g. "You were about to steal my cat". "No I just picked it up to stroke it." They attack, therefore we defend. Hopefully we keep the peace.

In readings I have seen the 2 of Swords show itself in the

Toni Allen
The System of Symbols ©

following ways.

The 2 of Swords symbolises both before and after "the fight". In marital situations it is both the tension before the argument, and the truce which is silently called afterwards. The truce is generally fragile and neither side wishes to say anything further. This is not to say that there are not a thousand remarks that both partners would like to come out with. As in any situation of truce, each side continues to believe that they are right and that it is therefore up to the other side to make the first move back into battle. After all, if the other side brings the subject up first, then we can always throw the blame back onto them for any further consequences.

The same goes for work situations in which we have consciously decided "not to say anything", so as not to "rock the boat". As with all the 2s this cuts both ways. Peace is maintained, but at the same time nothing happens to create a change for the better. We prefer to live in tense silence rather than suffer the pain of argument.

Here we can see the influence of water at 2, reflected from 8. Bonds are created which unless dealt with, go on to create further suffering. As with all bonds we have attracted these situations to ourselves and only surrounding cards in a reading can indicate precisely whether or not it is better to maintain a stiff truce or to take action. Sometimes it is indicated that the opposition will take action first.

When the questioner asks "what should I do about the situation?" the 2 of Swords being turned up as an answer simply says "for the time being it is wiser to do nothing." Remember the Hanged Man at 12 and that there is often action in non-action.

When **reversed** the card symbolises an inability to maintain the truce and that enmity will ensue as soon a single word is said out of place. It can even be that the questioner has consciously decided to face their adversary and is now merely waiting for an opportune moment in which to strike. I saw this clearly for one woman who, over many years, had struggled to keep matters on an even keel with her husband. The situation concerned the interference of her husband's mother in their private affairs. "The next time we go and see her I'm going to have it out," she told me, "I've kept quiet for too long now."

If the 2 of swords appears to indicate a solution, or conclusion, to a problem during a reading, then it's always wise to take the reading further as this card rarely signifies a final outcome due to the very tentative nature of the harmony it describes.

Keywords

Calm before the storm.
Keeping the peace.
Truth through personal perception.
Tension between two opposing people or factions
Reversed
The next time the opponent is on hand the peace will be broken, yet no action has yet been taken.

Bach Flower Remedy

Agrimony-for those who like to maintain peace at all costs

Toni Allen
The System of Symbols ©

The 3 of Swords

With the 3 of swords we find air at prakriti (nature).

Air is related to the numbers 6 and 4, 16 and 14, hence we know from our study of the Major Cards that all of these cards relate to the feeling of "I AM", and that the Swords therefore rule mental powers and ideas we hold about ourselves.

Prakriti sets the nature of an individual in a special way.
Hence at the 3 of Swords the individual believes that he, or she, *is* their strong thought or emotion. The number 3 also relates to tejas through the number 7 and so the passion of fire is felt as well.
In the Geeta it says:-
"When a man dwells on the objects of sense, he creates an attraction for them; attraction develops into desire, and desire breeds anger,
Anger induces delusion; delusion loss of memory, through loss of

memory, reason is shattered; and loss of reason leads to destruction."

The "loss of memory" referred to is the "forgetting who we truly are".

All of this is symbolised by the 3 of swords.

The 3 of Swords has a lot to do with karma and samskara. It highlights the areas we have to deal with by showing us age-old traits and habits, which we have brought with us from previous incarnations.

The 3 of swords inter relates with the 7 of Swords and I will describe the importance of the inter-connection between these two cards when interpreting the 7.

The air holds the prakriti tight creating anger, jealousy, hatred and thoughts of revenge. We come to believe that these things are our true nature; that we are a "bad person" or simply unkind.

How I have seen the 3 of swords in practice:-

In a reading very simple words can describe the 3 of Swords; anger, jealousy, hatred. In fact anything which is not love. When the card is **reversed** then the questioner is holding back on expressing such powerful emotions.

The card in itself by no means expresses physical violence, unless surrounding cards suggest this to be a contributing factor. e.g. The Page of Swords, the 9 of Swords. I say "suggest" due to the complexity of the Swords suit. The 3 of Swords crossed by the 9 of Swords often does indicate a physical attack. I saw this clearly in a reading for one young man whose temper had, on occasion, become so fiercely wound up by his girlfriend, as depicted by the Queen of Swords, that he was terrified he might severely injure her one-day. He had come for a reading because of his sudden "red haze" outbursts, which he admitted were mainly alcohol induced. He was signified by the Page of Swords. His dilemma was whether to leave her, for both of their safety, even though he held great positive emotion for her as well. The entire reading was taken into account before I even suggested that he had violent thoughts towards her; and only then when the reason why was clearly seen. She, being older than him, was more worldly wise and capable of holding down a job and handling finances. It was his own feelings of inadequacy in these areas, and his desire to prove himself that fired his anger every time he felt that he had failed.

Another reading in which the 3 of Swords was crossed by the 9 of

Toni Allen
The System of Symbols ©

Swords told a different story, again because of the entire spread. In this case a woman harboured feelings of anger after her husband was killed in a car crash and suddenly taken from her when still young. She often felt suicidal, and had suffered a breakdown after his death. (9 of Swords) She also had great thoughts of revenge on the other driver in the fatal collision. (3 of Swords)

These are two extreme cases in which individuals had suffered deep mental affliction and turned their anger either inwards or outwards.

In most cases the 3 of Swords shows itself in much simpler terms. The need for 'a good row', to 'clear the air', to 'get something off one's chest'. All of these suggest letting it out. If we are angry at an appropriate time, when the situation creating the feelings is in front of us, then the 3 of Swords does little more damage than a paper cut. It is short and swift. We quarrel, shout, 'have a go', hear the opposition's point of view, then lay our Swords to rest. Finished.

Sometimes it is even appropriate not to be angry, but simply to say 'that makes me angry', or 'that makes me jealous', to the person who stirs these feelings up in us. The other party then has the opportunity to allay our fears and clear the air.

Sometimes it is not possible to speak directly to the person who has made us feel like this, but other steps can be taken to 'disarm' the powder keg inside. The 3 of Swords followed by the Pope indicates that the questioner may be able to seek appropriate counselling from a priest, close friend or professional therapist. On one occasion where I saw this need, my female client had recently lost her husband. Within weeks of his death her three daughters, now all adults, had told her that their father had systematically abused them all as children. My client's anger was phenomenal. She was angry with her daughters for not having told her before. She was angry with her husband for doing it. She was angry at herself for being a "bad mother". She was angry because he was dead and that he had no chance to defend himself against these dreadful allegations. She was angry that her daughters had even chosen to tell her at all. "Why?" she asked, "Why tell me now? What on earth am I suppose to do with this information?" Most of all, she was angry that the happy memory of some forty years of marriage had been taken away from her. She came to me looking for a way forward and out of the 3 of Swords. The answer came in the form of the Pope, suggesting that her and her daughter's would benefit from some type of counselling therapy, in which they could openly discuss the situation.

If, however, we hang on to these negative feelings then they fester inside us. As children a lot of us were taught that anger was naughty, an absolute no-no. It was not a 'nice' thing to have in one's personality. So, to be loved and liked we stopped showing our rage, or having our temper tantrums, and learnt to suppress this "nasty" demon inside us. As adults we all continue to do this until something presses the trigger and like Vesuvius it erupts, totally uncontrollable, spewing over everything and everyone in its path, directed at the world. However, all of this generally means that the person who instigated the anger in the first place is nowhere in sight. But what happens if we bottle up these feelings? Or think it's wrong to let them out on an unsuspecting world?

The 3 of Swords **reversed** shows us burning up inside, tight and stressed due to these corked feelings of hatred, jealousy and so on. A very simple prediction, in any reading, is that if the 3 of swords is shown **reversed** that somewhere in the future there MUST be a reaction. Nine times out of ten the reaction comes as the 7 of Swords (detailed later), but other forces are possible depending on how the individual is dealing with these strong emotions. Human nature has many coping mechanisms, and surrounding cards may indicate running away, working hard, excessive drinking or any other method of denial. These all show signs that the problem is being buried deeper rather than being resolved.

If left unresolved the 3 of Swords can lead to physical, as well as emotional, ill health. e.g. depression is unexpressed anger.

Key Words

Anger, jealousy, hatred, revenge/Anything which is not love/Suspicion
Reversed - Suppressed anger, jealousy etc./Inability to express one's negative emotions, possibly due to childhood "programming"

Bach Flower Remedy

Holly-for those who suffer from hatred, envy, jealousy suspicion, aggressiveness, greed etc. Holly is also able to protect us from the effect of these conditions in others.

Toni Allen
The System of Symbols ©

4 of Swords

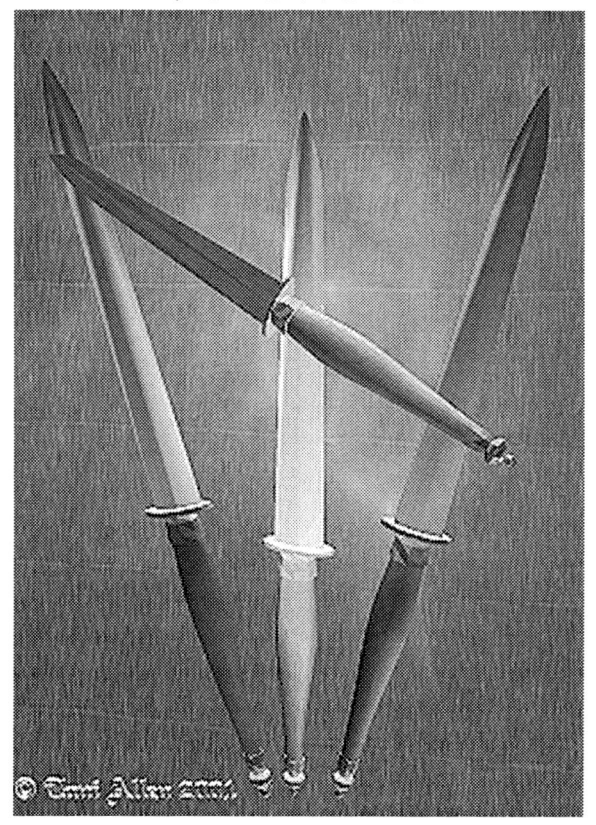

The 4 of Swords relates to air at Ahamkara, or "I AM".

Everything is held by air, the body is regulated by air and also held together, because once the vital air passes away from the body, it starts to disintegrate. This falls at number 6, but as the numbers 6 and 4 are interchangeable on the circle then we find an overlap with Ahamkara which also connects and holds everything that seems to belong to it in the feeling of I.

Consequently the 4 of Swords symbolises an almost desperate holding on to the feeling of who "I am".

This relates to the Major Cards through the Tower (16) and then Temperance (14). One's ego is damaged at the Tower and apparent harmony re-established at Temperance.

The ego, and physical body, are a covering, and tool, for the true self within. What so many people forget is that striving for perfection, or self-realisation, does not mean solely refining the self within; but also bringing it into harmony with the physical world via the ego, the body and the work we do. If one's ego, or personality, is fragile, damaged, lacking in identity or direction, then disharmony is set up which separates us from the true self, and consequently the rest of mankind.

At the 4 of Swords this is experienced as such feelings and ideas as "I am hurt", "I want to be on my own", "That person has destroyed me", "I am ill", and so on. The conflict between the self and the ego is so strong that a total separation comes about in which the individual finds it increasingly more difficult to participate in the world around them.

In practice the 4 of Swords can be interpreted in the following ways.

One of the most common situations in which the 4 of Swords is seen is where one person within the home has been so constantly emotionally and mentally battered by another that they feel that their own personality has been destroyed. They can no longer face up to the constant arguments, friction or long silences. They need to retreat and be on their own to rebuild their ideas about who they are. This may be done by:- Leaving the room in the middle of, or straight after, an argument. Going for long walks to be by themselves, so that they have space to think. Going to a favourite "sanctuary" such as their bedroom, a church, or even driving the car.

Because the ego is so fragile during these times this is never a card of turning to one's friends for comfort. The individual has to heal themselves from within before they are ready to accept help from others. At this crucial time the opinions of others could easily do more harm than good by making the insecure personality even less sure of themselves when confronted by someone who apparently "knows who they are".

It is therefore hardly ever appropriate to suggest counselling when the 4 of Swords comes up. In practice I saw this for one man whose wife had been badgering him, for some considerable time, to go for counselling. He had recently discovered that he had been adopted and had consequently lost his sense of identity, especially in relation to the rest of his "family". The 4 of Swords described how he was feeling, and that he needed to be alone with his feelings. When I suggested that he needed time to himself, he was relieved. "I'm so glad you said that," he said to me. "I don't know who I am any more, and I'm so frightened of somebody else, like a counsellor, influencing the process I'm going through at the moment. I'm frightened of somebody making me into someone they think I ought to be, or might be, or could be. At the moment I'm nobody, I've lost who I was and I have to find out who I am on my own, then perhaps my wife and I will go and see a counsellor together, but not yet, it's too soon." The 4 of Swords had also given him 'permission' to feel as he did, and to know that in his circumstances it was okay to feel the need for isolated contemplation.

The 4 of swords symbolises withdrawal from the world in every way. Sometimes people go on a spiritual retreat as part of a healing or self-awareness process. At these times the seclusion is socially structured in that others at least know where they are and have some kind of label to attach to the activity, even if they do not fully comprehend what the need for solitude is all about. Others do it in their own way, as with a man who came for a reading shortly after the breakdown of his relationship. He had the 4 of Swords prominently placed and even though friends kept phoning up asking him out, he continually declined all invitations. "It's my way of dealing with it," he said. "I hide and lick my wounds. I'm not ready for parties, or pubs, or well meant set ups of a date for the night." He needed his own company to find out who he was again, in his new role as an individual rather than part of a couple. He recognised this fact, and knew that in time he would be ready to face the world again on a social level.

All physical illness starts within the causal realm, therefore the 4 of Swords is also a significator of possible ill health. The card appears at those times when the body and mind have been so overtaxed that an "illness" such as flu, takes control of the body to ensure that it rests and recovers from the much larger symptoms of stress. Unconsciously we do this to ourselves all the time. A headache, stomach upset, or other malady comes over us and we go and lie down, quietly, on our own.

Solitude and isolation are expressed, therefore the card also refers to hospitalisation, imprisonment, sanctuary and exile.

With the interpretation of hospitals be wary when seeing the 4 of swords next to the Page of Cups. It might appear that the questioner is going to go into hospital and be nursed, however, I have more often seen it as the Page of Cups referring to the questioner as a nurse and therefore the hospital is her place of work.

With the 4 of Swords surrounding cards will suggest the context of the isolation and to whom it refers. One must use caution here. e.g. next to the Queen of Swords a lonely isolated woman with few friends. Next to the 10 of Batons, family and friends putting pressure on the questioner to do favours, thus creating exhaustion and a desire to be alone to the point of maybe even deliberately ignoring the phone or doorbell.

The **reversed** card suggests that this period of separation from the world may be coming to an end and that recovery is taking place.

In one reading a woman had the 4 of Swords **reversed** close to the Moon reversed and the 2 of Coins. It became clear that she was often afraid to leave the safety of her own home due to past experiences, yet at the same time disliked the self-created isolation. The 2 of Coins showed how strongly she was pulled this way and that between her desire to "shut herself off" and her desire to "get out of the house". The 4 of Swords reversed also emphasised how unwell the situation had been making her. The cards suggested an answer in having a close friend to stay to help relieve her sense of separateness and wean her back into the living world. No sooner was this mentioned than she knew exactly the friend to invite.

The 4 of Swords can also be indicative of physical pain, especially to do with breathing problems.

Keywords

Isolation.
A need to be alone
Retreat from the world to aid recovery from emotional and physical problems.
Solitude
Hospitals/imprisonment/sanctuary and exile
Reversed
Recovery from illness
Wishing to go out into the world again
Release from solitude

Toni Allen
The System of Symbols ©

The 5 of Swords

The 5 of swords relates to air at ether.

As number 5 falls in the middle of the circle from both sides it acts as a transformer, or bridge between the two worlds. The physical world is on one side and the world of subtle and causal nature on the other.

The etheric level is exceptional in that it cannot be touched or seen, only heard. It is space. It carries sound. With the Major Cards it is symbolised by the Pope and the Devil. Both represent what is carried, or coming through, from the causal level; the Pope symbolising a true listening to our inner self while the Devil symbolises habitual karmic traits of behaviour.

Air, or the Pranas, are the vital energy which make or keep us alive and in balance; on the other side of our circle at 4 is Ahamkara, the feeling of "I AM". With these forces working in the etheric level the 5 of Swords symbolises one's deepest beliefs. The space holds what we "believe we

Toni Allen
The System of Symbols ©

are", those ideas which keep us in balance. For some people this means a deeply rooted religious belief, while for others it means principles and ethics, but overall the air of swords at the ether of number 5 holds those ideas which make us who we are.

In practice the card generally shows itself when either the individual, or someone else, is attempting to change how they think, act or behave; and therefore the individuals concept of "who they are" is challenged.

For the individual who is working on themself it is a voluntary, yet very soul searching change. I saw this very clearly for a friend of mine who came to me for a reading. I knew her to be an intensely religious person, who kept her faith to church and Sunday school and never thrust her beliefs down my throat when she visited. At the time of the reading I had not seen her for many months. On turning over the 5 of Swords crossing the Pope I was truly astonished. "You've changed your religion," I said. She was equally astonished that I knew via the cards. "I've been thinking on it for months," she admitted, "But only decided for sure on the bus over here!" Her previous vicar had done things, which to her, went totally against her belief in how vicars should conduct themselves. He'd had an affair with one of the congregation. This she could not condone and for several weeks she had struggled with the idea of changing to a different church. Immediately prior to the reading with me that day she had visited the woman with whom the vicar had had the affair. "She's in a mental hospital," she told me. "That bastard put her there." The bus journey had given my friend enough time to think, and she was now absolutely certain that she could no longer continue attending his church, or follow that particular religious order if its advocates acted in such a manner.

Religion is one's deepest belief; yet there are many thousands of equally strong beliefs which people hold, e.g. whether or not to allow abortions; political views; "the starving thousands"; the atomic bomb; the judicial system; and so on. All highly emotive issues, which make one raise one's sword to make a stand. Just think for a moment of the suffragette movement. Those women believed so fiercely in their right to vote that they chained themselves to railings, threw themselves under race horses, and generally fought in whatever way they could to make men change their mind. Yet the women could not actively make the men change their mind, they had to do it through reason, argument and persuasion. What they did, in fact, was to make them see their point of view.

Sometimes emotive circumstances make us do this to ourselves. Close to cards of loneliness, such as the 9, 10 or 4 of swords, the 5 of swords indicates that the questioner is on the verge of breaking with "their God". They are questioning whether or not there really is a "god" due to the severity, cruelty or apparent injustice in their own situation. For example; the woman whose child has died; the man who has lost his job and then his wife walked out; or the couple who lose everything when their house catches fire.

The Knight of Swords next to the 5 of Swords shows that the questioner is fighting for what they believe in. These two cards came up for a woman who worked in a branch of a nation-wide chain store. She was appalled by the lack of staff to serve customers properly; believing that each individual required sufficient time and courtesy. This inadequacy made everyone short tempered and grumpy, so in her role as departmental manager she constantly battled on with her superiors, for the customer's right to decent service.

When the 5 of Swords represents someone other than the questioner in a reading it symbolises a battle of wills, in that the questioner is being persuaded to change their mind against their will. It indicates a very persuasive person, who has the mental agility to talk others into doing, saying or acting how they wish. This creates conflict and tension, and may even make the one being pressurised question the validity of their own standpoint on the issue.

In close relationships this is where one partner expects the other to think and act like them, and therefore coerces the other into doing so. It is not the same subtle domination as the 2 of Batons in which an idea is drip fed over the years, this is much more of the "agree with me or be a social outcast" routine. This is an active force in which if one does not agree then one is "mad", "not thinking straight", or maybe "influenced by those awful people". It is never a physical onslaught, but an attack on one's mind, the suggestion being that if you dare think any differently to the aggressor that you are in some way mentally unwell or deficient. e.g. Husband to wife, "Those friends of yours are really cranky, you'll end up warped if you continue to go around with them," or boyfriend to

Toni Allen
The System of Symbols ©

girlfriend, "We're over sixteen, you're a grown woman, you're not going to let your parents dictate how you think now, are you?"

Both statements are designed to make someone feel inadequate, as if they don't know their own mind and that others are somehow influencing them. To keep the peace it is often easier to go against one's own judgement (the Pope) and bend to the voice of this other person, who apparently can see the situation more clearly than us, even though in truth they are influencing us just as much, if not more, than anyone else.

These examples are every day persuasions, apparently quite normal and part of life; yet the consequences of changing what one believes in can be devastating. People are persuaded into affairs, to hand money over to 'con-men', to steal so that they are seen to 'keep up with the lads', to study science in preference to the arts because "they're young, and don't know their own mind yet" etc. All of these activities might never be undertaken by the individual without the influence of someone else persuading them into it. In other words they have gone against their 'better judgement'. These more sinister interpretations are influenced by the Devil, and in a reading might symbolise being karmically drawn back into old habits from a previous incarnation (or from earlier in this life if cards suggest it). Alternatively it may suggest that rather than listening to one's own inner voice, one is being mesmerised by someone into believing they know best.

For one woman who had the 5 of Swords it depicted the persuasive argument of her husband and his family. The marriage was over and she was being told to leave the family home with their two young children. She had been told that as the house was financially tied up in the business that there was no money for her to have and that she should leave with nothing. "I must be due something after seventeen years," she said. "But if they say there's nothing, then I suppose there isn't." Having been told "the facts" often enough, she had become convinced of the genuineness of their argument, and at the point of seeing me had no intention of making any stand against her husband to try and have him maintain her and the children. However, the 5 of Swords also indicated her need to seek legal advice from a solicitor. (See later paragraph as to why the card implies the judicial system)

There are, of course, very positive and useful forms of "persuasion", and we find this in hypnosis. The hypnotist actively, and with the individual's consent, endeavours to unlock the gateway and cross the bridge into the causal realm to bring about a healing via a new and healthier attitude to life.

As the 5 of swords is influenced by the Devil, which symbolises guilt, and reversed no guilt, the card also refers to any matter which is taken to a court of law. Ether carries sound and in court the matter is "heard", listened to by a judge, who then becomes the equivalent of the Pope with his two alternatives in front of him. A court hearing is that time when witnesses are asked to take the stand and pledge an oath before God that what they say they believe to be true. Court cases are also a battle of wits, in which both parties try to persuade the judge, and often a jury, that they are right.

The 5 of swords in itself will not show which side will win, although the upright card is stronger. However, upright it means that the case will go to court, reversed that it will not. If the matter is to be taken to court then the following examples apply:- next to the King of Swords reversed a very dogmatic judge, next to the Page of Swords various tricks will be played, next to the Ace of Coins there is a very important document, and next to the Chariot reversed the case will be adjourned. Of course, all other cards must be taken into account.

I have often seen the Judgement card reversed next to the 5 of Swords implying that the case will not be heard. It does not get as far as the court room but is resolved in chambers or through mediation, or adjourned.

Keywords

The individual's belief system
Legal matters and court cases
Being persuaded that you are what you are not.
Being persuaded to do something against one's better judgement.
Reversed
Not wishing to change one's beliefs, even against strong opposition
Unwillingness to change mental attitudes.

Toni Allen
The System of Symbols ©

The 6 of Swords

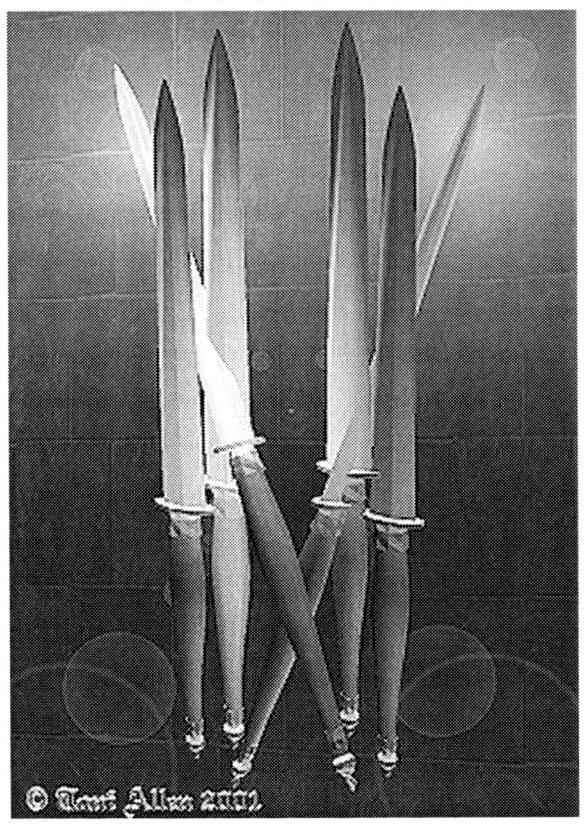

The 6 of Swords relates to air at air.

The Pranas, air, are vital energies; they make or keep us alive, discharge polluted air, regulate the digestive process, keep the body in balance and also regulate involuntary movements in the body. Hand is the organ through which the forces within can be expressed. Hand is also the seat of air which holds things, catches and throws them.

On the one side air regulates the forces, and on the other Ahamkara, at 4, appreciates these forces.

Air bestows thought and movement, discrimination and intelligence. Coupled with Ahamkara it bestows a belief in our ideas and movements, making us think we are these things. By comparison with the 4 of Swords, being air at Ahamkara, which makes us feel very introverted and isolated, the 6 of Swords being air at air, holds similar qualities

Toni Allen
The System of Symbols ©

because it encompasses Ahamkara, nevertheless it acts differently by showing itself as rational thinking about who we are. Logic and analysis are key words here.

At the 6 of Swords a lot of thought goes on about who we are, how we think and what we want. In many ways it is a struggle with ourself, sometimes like trying to navigate through thick fog, knowing that our goal is somewhere ahead, yet not being able to see the way.

All computers, regardless of however apparently complicated, work on the binary system. Yes-No, Plus-Minus. They are man made minds working on the simple truth of duality. This is how our mind is working at the 6 of Swords. It is not the same quandary of "should I do this or that?" as depicted by the 2 of Coins, but a logical stage required when working out any problem. Imagine the mind as being full of small pigeonholes, the type one puts letters in. Next put into the mind lots of information connected with one of your problems. Logic makes us put these random segments of information neatly into these pigeonholes. These pigeon holes can be labelled anything we like from love to fear, work to play. At first the pieces do not make sense, so we rearrange them until eventually something clearer takes shape. A matrix is formed and an answer comes up. The finished picture is like placing the final piece to complete a jigsaw puzzle. The 6 of Swords illustrates this sifting and sorting process.

In a reading the speed with which someone can achieve a finished 'answer' to any problem is emphasised by surrounding cards. The 6 of Swords by itself represents the struggle to work out the problem. Struggle being the main issue, because intuition is no where in sight with this card! It's all about thinking, thinking and more thinking.

Mathematicians, scientists, accountants, computer programmers and all people associated with problem solving would be depicted by this card. It represents the "thinking man", who bases life more on what he can logically deduct, than what his inner voice might urge. It is a card of cleverness, and intelligence, but not a card of genius. All geniuses throughout history have been recorded as having their quirks, or flashes of inspiration, their lateral thinking. After all Einstein was reported to be dyslexic!

Coupled with the Lovers at number 6 we can relate the 6 of Swords to the Magician standing between his two desires. Without a knowledge of who we are the Cupid's arrow of desire will continually lead us back to the same karmic path, time and time again. Hence the 6 of Swords is our struggle to resolve one karmic situation and move on to tread a truer path in life.

In practice I have seen the 6 of Swords as follows:-

In a difficult situation the 6 of Swords will appear to show that the questioner is trying to rationally work out the best stand point to take. How will they tackle the situation? It shows them gathering all the information they need to come to a conclusion. Very often they will feel that life is taking them one step forwards and two steps back as new information is gathered which subtly changes the facts of a situation.

An appropriate phrase for the 6 of Swords when **reversed**, might well be "It's not logical, Captain", as so often spoken by Mr Spock from Star Trek. This is a good expression for The Tower at 16 shows the individual's vulnerability when the personality is under attack. Often this attack is very subtle and unseen by others, creating set backs and a continuous struggle to stay ahead. This I saw for a man whose business was under attack from some very evil people. Initially it appeared that they had no motive, but over a period of several readings the 6 of Swords reversed kept suggesting that if he analysed the situation enough that the answer would come to him. Money was obviously involved but it was difficult to see exactly how. These people did everything imaginable to destroy his business, including contacting his suppliers and telling them that he was a bad creditor. They also took legal action over products they claimed were damaged when purchased, claiming he'd refused to exchange them. He continued to be unable to see the situation clearly, as it was apparently illogical.

Many of the claims made against him were incredibly petty, yet slowly they created a web of deceit and his business went down hill. The 6 of Swords reversed continued to symbolise his determination to outwit their attack and find the most rational way of dealing with their lies. After many months he came to me again, this time triumphant. He had discovered that his landlords had been offered a large sum of money for the land his business premises were on, and with suitable planning permission it could be used for redevelopment. "Without that one fact," he said, "I've been struggling in the dark. My landlords have contrived this whole fiasco." This last time his 6 of Swords was upright because eventually his problem had a logical reason behind it.

For one woman this card came up in 'the present', crossed by the Queen of Coins, with the 8 of Swords in the 'physical world'. It showed that she continually found life to be a struggle. The 8 emphasised a particularly stagnant phase she was presently labouring through, and she agreed that the trapped circumstances had come about because she analysed everything before making a decision. Although she was clever and intelligent, she never let her 'irrational' intuition take over. She was actually very frightened of this 'irrational' side. She liked the control of 'thinking things through'. Consequently she had missed several very good opportunities by not being spontaneous enough.

Alternatively I have seen this card in the readings of highly artistic and psychically gifted people. It goes against their nature to ponder too much on the problems of life, and yet there are times when facts must be taken into account. Without the strength of this card helping them through they run into the possibility of their fire energy overwhelming the situation and making it very difficult for others to grasp what is happening, hence they might appear eccentric or 'airy fairy'.

As air relates to movement we also have the 6 of swords symbolising physical movement; and this can quite simply be interpreted as any journey. Because we have 'double' air here, the duality of 2 is experienced as bonds and water, making the journey highly likely to be 'across the water'...but not necessarily by boat as 'planes and trains also cross water. When I lived on The Isle of Wight about 90% of my clients had this card at some point in their reading, because they all needed to "cross the water" to the mainland for either business or pleasure!

Related to health the card can indicate a struggle to recover from illness. If looking for where a questioner's ill health may lie it indicates digestive problems, lack of balance, shock, excess air in the body, stiffness and stress.

Key words

Struggle to make sense out of a problem.
The logical thinker.
Analysis
Journey across water

Reversed
Delays through a lack of understanding of what is going on in a particular situation.
Illogical actions, motives or circumstances.

Bach Flower Remedy

Vervain-for extremes of mental energy-over effort and stress

Toni Allen
The System of Symbols ©

The 7 Swords

The 7 of Swords relates to air at fire (Tejas)
    Tejas can be divided into three parts as governed by the three gunas, Sattvika Tejas, Rajasika Tejas and Tamasika Tejas.
    Against these three forms of Tejas one can see three obstacles.
Sattvika Tejas is the light of knowledge and its obstacle is **Avarna**, Ignorance.
Rajasika Tejas is the celestial lights, such as the light of the sun, moon, stars and lightening and its obstacle is **Vikshepa**, which comes as Interference, like clouds interfering with the sun's rays falling on earth.
Tamasika Tejas is fire, lamp lights, etc. which one finds on Earth and its obstacle is **Mala**, which is like a thick or hard covering which does not allow the light to show, as when a lamp is shielded.
    These obstacles, if they are allowed to take hold and become part

of one's nature, create samskara.

At the 7 of swords the individual is mentally endeavouring to sort out, through reason and understanding, where problems arose and how to overcome them.

The 7 of swords is what arises out of the 3 of swords, generally reversed. The two cards are inseparable.

With the 3 of swords we saw the expression of anger, hatred, jealousy etc. If these negative emotions are not resolved then they cling to us, like an unseen thorn which festers or irritates. The 'thorn' may have been lodged yesterday, many years ago, or in a previous incarnation. In the same way that we see skin grow over a lodged thorn, burying it deeper with each fresh layer and making it increasingly difficult to prise out, the hard covering of Mala, the Interference of Vikshepa and the Ignorance of Avarna continue to create a barrier between the personality and its higher self. From events which arise solely from any particular 'thorn', there is much to be learnt about the present karmic patterns in an individual's life.

The 'thorn' will continue to suppurate, creating inner pain and suffering until it is removed forever. The very fact that it repeatedly flares up is positive, in that each time the problem arises we are given another chance to deal with it and remove the ideas, feelings etc. that produce the pain.

People often say "that's a sore point" about matters that they would much rather not discuss, then they retreat and become unapproachable. We speak of "that hurts", "don't open old wounds" and "mental scars". The 7 of Swords is the realisation of what caused these "scars" and potentially the first move towards healing them.

At the number 3 we saw the Empress depicting the potential nature of a person, while at 7 we find the pattern of creation or of the individual FIXED.

Therefore that which was not expressed at the 3 of Swords becomes FIXED in the nature of an individual at the 7 of Swords. The individual believes that "I AM" this ignorance, this darkness, this shadow over my light.

In practice the 7 of Swords shows itself in the following ways:-
When the 3 of Swords **reversed** is seen in 'the present' then the 7 of Swords will nearly always arise in 'the future'. If the 3 is not turned then groups of other cards will imply the meaning.

Toni Allen
The System of Symbols ©

The unresolved angers, jealousies and hatreds experienced at 3 sit within the individual like a time bomb, ready to explode as soon as somebody presses the right button...or implode into dis-ease. At the 3 reversed the individual, for one reason or another, could not, or did not, communicate the problem to the person who had upset them. Now they need to talk the problem over, yet know that as soon as they approach the other person they will be greeted with something along the lines of, "but that was years ago, what are you bringing all that stuff up again for now?" or "That's dead and buried, I don't want to open that up again." An impossible situation is created because one side sees it as "old stuff", long since forgotten, or maybe as a potential battle of words which they might lose. Neither of these help the aggrieved party to let go of the old pain, which needs to be expressed before they can move on.

Communication is a key word here. Very often the best way to communicate is via a neutral third party, who may be able to defuse the situation and liase in an unbiased manner. This third person can be a friend or relative the individual asks to speak on their behalf. Sometimes the intervention needs to be of an official nature, and someone such as a solicitor, who acts on behalf of the individual, may be employed. People require solicitors when they have become so incensed by someone else's actions that they are too angry, or damaged, to continue the argument without help. This appears most pertinently in divorce matters. More often than not one party is attacking while the other defends. These days couples are encouraged to go for mediation, in which a solicitor helps them thrash out a divorce settlement without the need to go to court. Thus the mediator becomes the third person indicated by the 7 of Swords.

There are also rare occasion when the 7 of Swords indicates times when someone wishing to express a problem tells a friend and the friend then unwittingly goes on to tell someone associated with the other party. There is absolutely no malice involved here, and often this kind of accident works out very well. I saw this last scenario in practice, concerning a woman who still retained a lot of anger after her boyfriend had suddenly left her some years earlier. "He never explained why he just upped and left. Now I continually fear rejection," she said. My session with her awoke her need to discuss this problem with her friends and when she next came to see me she told me that one of these friends had passed on her story to someone else who just happened to be her ex-boyfriend!

Toni Allen
The System of Symbols ©

"He came round to see me," she explained. "He was so apologetic, so sorry for the pain he'd caused. Apparently his previous girlfriend had contacted him and said she had a child that was his. He didn't know how to tell me, so just upped and left to live with her and support the child." Even though she was hurt by his original inability to explain the situation she felt relieved to have some understanding of what had gone on. "My anger isn't so acute now," she said. "To have him face to face, to talk to, and find out that he hadn't left me because I was bad, or horrible, or unlovable was such a relief."

In some cases the 7 of Swords is also an appropriate indication of counsellors who work for Relate, where both parties attend and the professional helps to unravel why the relationship has broken down. A simple scenario is the husband and wife. "He never helped when the children were babies," she says, "And that made me angry." "I thought you were happy with the extra money coming in from my overtime," he replies, astonished. "We discussed that I'd be away from home a lot, and you didn't seem to mind." The wife, having never expressed what she really felt all those years ago, for fear of creating a scene (3 Swords reversed) built up misunderstandings, which led to bitterness that possessed her like a ghost for many years.

Remember to differentiate between the Pope who gives counsel to the individual and the 7 of Swords which represents a negotiator between two parties. However, for one man I repeatedly saw the 7 of Swords in his readings in relation to his partners' therapist. His ex-wife had gone for counselling and when he requested to be a party the therapist had declined. Now his new girlfriend was also going to a counsellor and he wanted to be included. He felt he needed a mediator, but was unable to instigate any appropriate couple counselling, yet continually wanted to ride piggyback on his partners' sessions as if he was outside the process and not a party to it. "I want to help her with her anger", he said, and always denied having any such negative emotions himself, as if it was always the woman's fault that things had gone wrong between them.

Direct confrontation never comes out of the 7 of Swords and therefore it also symbolises acting very carefully with information that we might have. The fight, which takes place at 3, can be avoided by 'disarming the enemy' at 7. One's 'middle man' may well come back with information that shows new ways to handle difficulties. In physical terms this can literally mean employing a spy, or private investigator, especially if the Page of Swords is close by.

In highly personal readings where the questioner has some deep rooted problem which they cannot resolve the 7 of Swords signifies 'using a thorn to take out a thorn'. Often the problem is karmic and the questioner may never discover its actual source; only see how it manifests in this lifetime. They appear to be treading the same ground repeatedly e.g. all relationships end the same way; or, they are constantly suspicious of the motives of others but don't know why.

For one woman in her mid twenties it came up as repeatedly choosing men to live with who ended up treating her badly, both emotionally and physically. Her 3 of Swords reversed indicated that she was not very good at standing up to these bullies, thus allowing situations to self perpetuate and grow out of proportion. The King of Swords symbolised that she had a very exacting father whom she had never dared answer back to for fear of punishment; and that she had learnt from a very young age to 'swallow her anger'. Consequently she harboured many negative ideas about herself due to his influence, and had come to believe that all men would punish her if she dared show her anger. Her belief about herself had invited this punishment to herself for many years. The 7 of Swords indicated that either she could communicate with her mother about various issues concerning her father, or tackle the problem via her boyfriend and one of his friends. The 7 stressed that each time she stood up to men then she was taking another step towards removing the layer of samskara she had built up over many life times.

If the 7 is in the same spread as the 5 of Swords then legal action is often specifically indicated.

The 7 upright generally indicates the need to find a third party to help resolve the issue and **reversed** that the process is already underway. However the **reversed** 7 of Swords can also indicate that one is denying one's negative emotion even more and pushing it further into the recesses of one's psyche. At this point one is often too afraid to consider a mediator, or to try and remedy the situation.

Key words

'Disarming the enemy'

Toni Allen
The System of Symbols ©

The need to resolve old hurts.
Liaison, negotiation, mediator.
Solicitor.
Karmic 'thorn'.
Repressed emotions that need expression.
Reversed
Extreme denial of old wounds
Refusing to even contemplate dealing with 'old issues'.

Toni Allen
The System of Symbols ©

The 8 of Swords

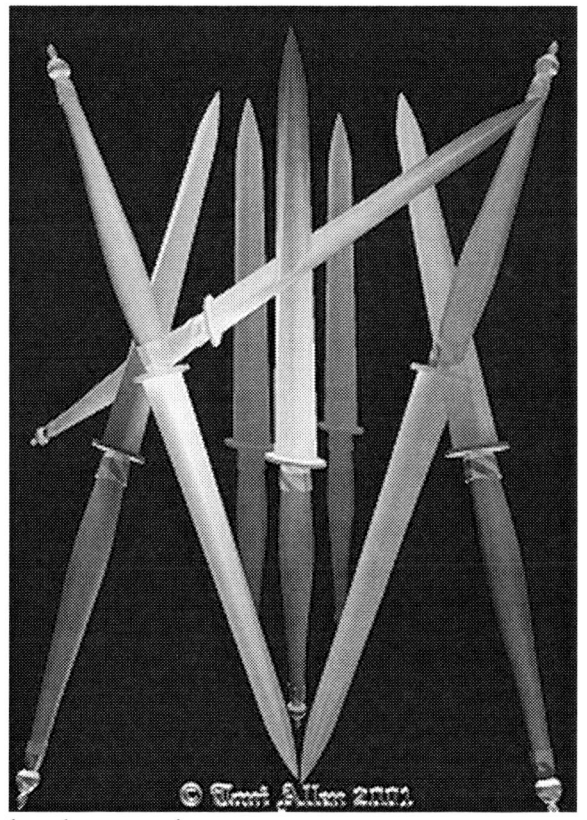

The 8 of Swords relates to air at water.

Water is the element of bond. It is only the bond that creates the limitation. Due to bonds all the shapes of the universe have their existence, and all shapes create a limit or boundary through which particular types of bond are working.

At the 8 of Swords the Pranas are bound up, therefore one's own mind becomes the limit of one's existence. Mental stagnation, inner torture and fear of breaking away from the negative pattern take hold. The mind is trapped.

There is also, with relation to the number 2, the feeling of separation, in that "nobody else could ever understand how I feel".

For an individual this card symbolises great inner torture and anguish. The prisoner of war would have this card. Although physical circumstances can add very much to the quality of the 8 of Swords it is not necessarily the circumstances themselves that create it.

Giving limits to what is limitless creates the inner pain. The 8 of swords is the stagnant water at the bottom of the Moon card (18). It is love turned stale. It is Justice (8), in that it is the karma we have created for ourselves; our Samskara. If we continually react to the same type of negative situation in the same way, then the bonds are strengthened; but, if like the crayfish in the Moon card, we start to navigate a new path and face up to our fears, then we can achieve success.

Sometimes we do not understand how we ever managed to get ourselves into a particular situation; yet there we are living it, as if it's a script from somebody else's life. This couldn't possibly belong to me! The way to clear samskara is to act in the moment and thus set up a new pattern that is more harmonious, until ultimately perfection is achieved. Easy isn't it? The answer is most definitely not...even for those of us who tread a spiritual path. Most of us mere mortals go through 'terrible experiences' at various levels, which shake the foundations of our existence until life itself forces us to change. Each individual's perception of a 'terrible experience' is totally different depending upon their personal karma. One person's bliss may be another person's trap. e.g. two women are pregnant. One is elated, while the other finds it a disturbing force to be reckoned with. The woman who enjoys her condition glows and feels accepted; while the other bottles up her anxieties and feels separate from the rest of the world. The woman who hates being pregnant is experiencing the 8 of Swords, but there is no suggestion that she does not want the child. It may be that she is afraid of child-birth, or suffers continued morning sickness, or finds the child inside her a strange invasion of her body.

Samskara is a latent mental or behavioural pattern, thus the 8 of swords shows that the questioner's experience is on a repeat cycle. Many clients will accept that they have been through something very similar before, e.g. "This is my third husband and every one has hit me. I really thought this one was different and I don't know why I keep going for the same type," or "I'm a slave to my boss. I let the last one walk all over me and yet I've let it happen again." Those who do not recognise the repetition are reaping karma from a previous lifetime, or have created a new karmic trait in this.

The difference between the isolation of the 4 of swords compared to that of the 8 is as follows. At the 4 of Swords one wishes to be alone, while at the 8 the root cause of suffering goes very deep and very often people appear quite cheerful on the surface. They will still experience their agony even in good company, and cry inside, often unknown and unnoticed by those closest to them. In fact they often seek companionship as a way of trying to forget their sadness, and yet always appear to be the life and soul of the party.

The following are examples of how the 8 of Swords has appeared in readings.

1) A woman who came for a reading had the 8 of Swords prominently placed in 'the mind' at the beginning of her reading. In 'the centre' was the Page of Batons crossed by the 4 of Swords. The 9 of Batons reversed was at 'the physical' level. The 4 and Page indicated a child who was ill, the 9 her depletion at constantly having to nurse him, while the 8 showed her feelings of being trapped by the situation. Notice that the 8 of swords is placed at the level of 'the mind', thus adding emphasis to her mental anguish.

Although her son had been handicapped since birth it was the fact that she had been coping on her own for so long which was running her down. She felt that none of her friends fully understood her situation and she therefore stopped talking to them about it. "He wets the bed every night," she said. "It's part of his condition, so I never get a full nights sleep, and sometimes he cries as he wakes up all wet. It breaks my heart to hear him upset, but there's nothing I can do. I have to stay cheerful for his sake."

This woman's reading showed the negative side of bonds, which is bondage. Even though she loved her son his constant demands had turned her devoted mother's love into a kind of slavery. She did not feel resentful or bitter towards him, but mentally confined by his handicap. She said that some days his wheelchair felt so heavy to push that at night she cried about it. All she desired was the freedom to walk on her own for a while with nothing to push, lift, carry clean up after or feed. It seemed like an impossible dream.

The cards suggested gaining advice through a professional counsellor who specialised in talking to people in her situation. She returned six months later saying that she already felt much better in herself. Social services had started to organise respite care for her. "I never thought I'd be entitled", she said. "I've had to let go as a mother, understand that he might need other people apart from me, give him some variety in life too!" Ultimately her 'letting go' was re-establishing the bond in a positive way, rather than as bondage.

2) I cannot remember all of the cards my next client had, but I do remember the 2 of Cups being reversed, the 3 of Swords being reversed and the 8 of Swords being upright at a 'physical' level. One day this woman's husband had "gone out to post a letter" and never returned. She had no idea where he was. She had no idea why he had left her. The 3 of swords reversed represented her bottled up anger; after all how could she possibly shout and yell at him for having left her when she had no idea where he was? The 2 represented her broken heart, while the 8 depicted her tortured mind. Her grief was beyond belief. She was trapped in the past with no way of stepping forward because she could not manage to sever the ties that bound her to him. Yet outwardly she lived a busy, active life, was the jolly one at parties, and would do anything for her friends.

3) Another, very common, example of the 8 of Swords is the trapped housewife, whose husband subtly keeps her tied to the kitchen sink and denies her the opportunity of a career.

In connection with health stagnation is the keyword, and stagnant, or 'bad' blood is relevant because all of the joy has been squeezed out. Stuckness and slowness, sluggishness. Wounds which refuse to heal. Female clients often have menstrual problems.

The 8 of Swords **reversed** shows the first step taken towards changing the situation, like the crayfish moving towards the sun. It is not a conclusion in itself.

Key words

Feeling trapped, or being trapped/Stagnation/Inner torture/
When bonds have turned to bondage/Anguish.
Reversed - Initial steps towards releasing oneself from the bondage.

Bach Flower Remedy

Agrimony:- for inner torture
Walnut:- to help break the ties that bind

Toni Allen
The System of Symbols ©

The 9 of Swords

The 9 of swords relates to air at earth.

The air, or Pranas, are vital energies which regulate the body. They are the breath of life and the capacity to love.

Earth is the glorious end of one cycle, where the absolute stands as the glorious beginning on the other side.

Very few of us take death to be "the glorious end of one cycle" but this is what happens when the vital air passes from the body. First the body crumbles to dust, then physical matter gives way to the absolute, allowing rebirth to take place. Thus physical death is one aspect of the symbolism of the 9 of Swords.

Air, relating through the number 4 is also symbolic of the intellect, our ability to "know who we are". At earth the vital air is trapped, immovable. On the one hand this quality may be very useful to know about if we're gardeners wishing to put the air of life into the soil to feed the plants, but it is not so positive for a human being to be trapped in the soil. We cannot breath under the earth because there is so little air. As explained earlier each element holds within it a quantity of the other elements. Imagine yourself potholing, or caving, travelling on a journey deeper and deeper into the earth. There is no light of fire, yet me might experience the fire element through stifling heat if we're under a desert, or find an extreme lack of the fire element if we're under a more succulent landscape. Ironically even the deepest caves hold water, and we find this phenomena in the formation of stalactites and stalagmites, as well as underground pools or damp rock faces. As we go deeper we find less and less air to breath, so the hardened caver takes breathing apparatus in order to explore further. Now imagine that this cave is our physical body, the deepest recesses of it lacking in the air of intellect. We would come across dark, stagnant places where thoughts and memories are buried deep within our psyche, which then reflect within the physical body. There is no clear thought in this dark place because one's mind is filled with old images of pain, grief and horror; thus the 9 of Swords is the physical, earthly manifestation of Samskara.

It's interesting to study various complementary therapies, such as Rolfing and Bodytherapy®, which come from the premise that trauma and emotional life patterns stay within the muscles of the body as disease. Deep manipulation of the muscles therefore releases the cause of the trauma and allows a healing to take place. One Bodytherapist I spoke to said that with many clients once the root cause is reached that the effect is highly cathartic, with the patient often bursting into tears and re-connecting, and thus releasing, the old emotions which they have been so bound by. Interestingly he also mentioned an improvement in the patient's breathing and an increased ability to enjoy life. A psychotherapist works on the same problem via communication, but we can see how working with the residue hidden deep within the body, that the same change can take place. Our mind and physical body are intrinsically linked and always mirror one another.

The 9 of swords is multi faceted and although on the one hand it illustrates physical death, this is rarely the case during a reading. More often the card describes how the individual is mentally suffering, but without the jovial facade of the 8 of Swords. This is the type of mental anguish which makes one believe that one is going mad, or will crack up, or has reached the end of one's tether. Images suddenly rush up from the psyche in the form of nightmares and flashbacks, or the body gives way to panic attacks and extremes of mental illness. There are many ways of dealing with this type of deep mental stress and each individual is unique. Some people contemplate suicide as a way of escaping the anguish, while others take to alcohol or drugs in order to mask the pain. Conversely some people become violent, hitting out at those around them as a way of venting their agony. However none of these methods deal with the cause of the problem, only with the effect.

The 9 of swords is an active card due to it association with the Magician, Hermit, and Strength card, so although it describes a type of depression, it is a very dynamic force. People who experience the 9 of Swords want to do something about the dark energy around them, so this is not the same type of feeling as with the 4 of Swords where someone is prepared to hide away and sit it out. People who draw the 4 of Swords might say they are depressed, but someone with the 9 of Swords will actively try to relieve themself of the extreme pain by attempting suicide, taking anti-depressants etc. In fact anything to bring about a physical death to the mental pain.

In all respects the 9 of Swords is a card to be judged with extreme caution during a reading. If the card appears near the beginning of a reading I often gloss over the intensity of its meaning until I have gauged the mental state of my client and also whether it is referring to my client or someone else in their life. I can then come back to the card later. These are extremely sensitive issues and it is the card reader's responsibility to ensure that their client is looked after and not caused further pain by rashly suggesting that they are an alcoholic, drug addict, or depressive, suicidal personality type. I often find that the person who has come for the reading is fine and that they have concerns over a partner who is involved with drugs, or drinking to excess. However, I have also seen many clients who have either already attempted suicide or had extreme feelings that this would be their only way of stopping the deep mental pain.

Here are a few examples of how I have seen the 9 of swords in practice.

One elderly woman who came to me for a reading had the 9 of Swords in 'the mind', under it the 5 of Batons crossed by The King of

Cups. Other cards showed her to be a reasonably happy person, who went about her daily affairs with efficiency. When I suggested that the death of a man she loved kept playing on her mind, she looked at me with astonishment. "But that was eight years ago", she said. As the 9 of Swords also relates to the night and great fears that the mind will give way, I went on to suggest that he had died in his sleep next to her. She agreed that this had been the case and that on waking she had been terrified, and never yet been able to put the image out of her mind, so much so that she was afraid to go to sleep at night. The image had literally become stuck in her Chitta (or heart) and created Samskara.

"I can't tell anyone," she said. "I sleep so badly, if at all." We took cards to see how she might best deal with the problem, and they suggested that she did simple things such as change to a different bedroom, redecorate the house, or sleep with the light on. Sadly she said that she had tried all of these obvious changes and that nothing had worked. It was not until the 7 of swords reversed and the 4 of Cups came up that I realised that in eight years she had not yet shed one tear for him. The shock and grief had affected her so deeply that her own vital energies had been blocked and now emotion was beyond her. Gently I explained this to her and quite unexpectedly she burst into tears. The reading had affected a healing. "I never thought I would cry again", she said. "Never. I thought my mind would give way first." We both knew that these tears were only the first and that many more would have to flow while she went through the process of shedding her grief, and fears. For her it was a new beginning. This was backed up when, some months later, her daughter telephoned me to say that her mother was much brighter than she had been for years. I was told that when she had returned home after her reading she had spoken at length with her daughter and had done a lot of crying. Neither of these things had she ever shared before, with anyone, and now, very gradually, her sleep pattern was improving.

The woman in this example mentioned fear that 'her mind would give way' and again this comes under the realm of the 9 of Swords. There is a fear that one cannot suffer the content of one's thoughts or emotions any more. When referring to physical death the card does not always include the emotional suffering, although the two go hand in glove if it is a loved one we have lost.

One young man had the 9 of Swords as his card representing the past. When he came to me his aura was grey and I had the impression that he was surrounded by death. He wanted to embark on a spiritual path and learn the Tarot, yet everything suggested that this would not be possible until he had resolved issues concerning these many deaths in his past. However, he repeatedly insisted that no one he knew had died and that he was okay. Then we went on to discuss his work and he mentioned that he had recently changed jobs. "I used to work in an abattoir," he said. I pointed out that the animals he killed every day were his many deaths from the past. "I stopped seeing it like that," he said. "I only saw it as a job and never considered how it might have been affecting me."

For one woman the 9 of Swords next to the Page of Swords represented the man she had been having a relationship with. She had been seeing him for some time but was unable to deal with his violent mood swings. When I suggested the influence of alcohol or drugs she nodded sagely. "He takes drugs," she said. "Speed mainly, but it doesn't seem to matter whether he's on or off it, both are equally as bad now." She explained that he was already taking drugs when they met, and that his addiction appeared to stem back from traumas in his early life.

For another client who was going through heavy divorce proceedings I saw the 9 of Swords in relation to drinking. "I have been drinking much more over the last two years," he agreed. "I used to be an occasional drinker and now I'm a regular drinker. It helps me forget."

Key Words

Death/Extreme inner anguish where one feels that the mind will give way. Feelings of suicide/Drug or alcohol addiction/Physical violence Nightmares/flashbacks/symptoms of post traumatic stress
Reversed
The same as the upright card, often more acute

Bach Flower Remedy

Cherry Plum - to help the mind stay calm despite mental or physical anguish. An excellent remedy for those times when one feels that one will do something awful to oneself or others.

Toni Allen
The System of Symbols ©

The 10 of Swords

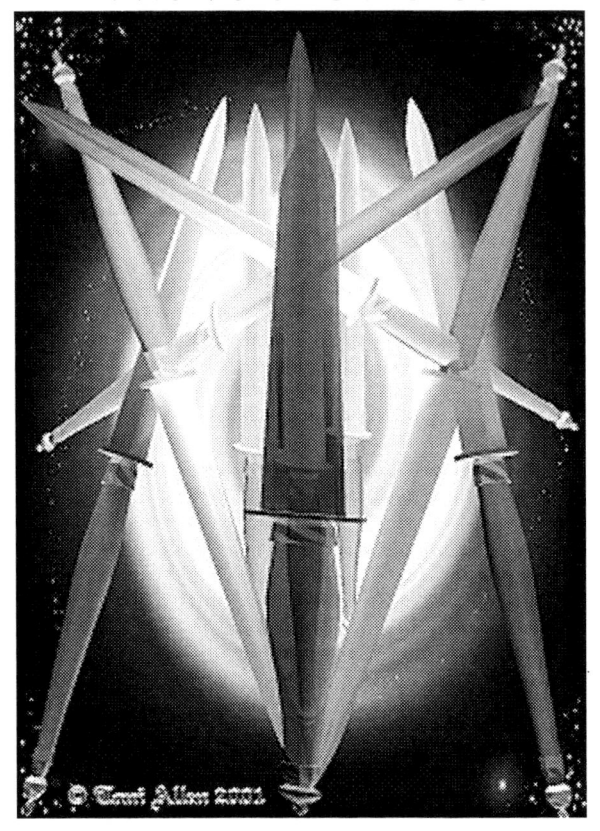

The 10 of Swords relates to air at ether.

At the 5 of Swords we saw how the air of Swords was influenced through the ether by the qualities of the Pope and the Devil in the form of mental influence from others. 10 is everything and nothing, the Magician at 1 and the Fool at 0. Thus we see, with the 1 of 10, that the any mental latencies created on our journey from 1 to 9, are now able to start another cycle.

At the 10 of Swords we once again find a type of depression due to the mental patterning which comes through the ether from the causal level. 10 being an equal number is influenced by duality and we find that the root cause of any mental patterning is hidden in the realm of 2 and the unmanifest. However, ether is the bridge between the unmanifest and manifest worlds and thus we experience the 10 of Swords as anxieties and depressions coming from an unknown cause.

In practice the 10 of Swords is experienced as bouts of depression which come and go. They are nowhere as extreme as the 9 of Swords because one always realises that the depression will pass, just as easily as it came. It came from nowhere and will return there. This in turn means that anyone who draws the 10 of swords will not experience the same traumatic feelings of suicide, or desperation, as with the 9 of Swords. This is because they recognise that the feelings will pass, like a dark cloud over the sun which in time moves on to let the light shine down again.

Many people experience the 10 of Swords and in general they cope well with these feelings and take them as the highs and lows of life, in much the same was as they are depicted in the Wheel of Fortune at 10. Mostly they do not know the root cause of their sadness and many people do not even bother to question where it originated. These depressive phases can last any period of time, from a day to a week, to a month or more.

Some people recognise that the depressive cycles started after a particular event, and in these cases work can be done to explore what happened during that time. Episodes such as divorce, birth, death, separation, failure, and moving home can all leave their mark.

With others the cause is well hidden and I have seen the card symbolise deep-rooted mental expectations and traumas affecting the individual from a previous life. For one woman it was a dislike of summer time. Every year she fell into the same depressive phase as soon as the sun started to shine. "I just don't like summer," she said with a shrug. "It's too hot, too busy, too everything. I become a sort of mental vegetable during summer and my concentration is lousy. I find it difficult to comprehend everyone else's joy when I feel so down and locked into myself. I get on with life, but feel much more alive during the cooler months." She decided to go for a far life regression, more out of interest than any belief that she would find answers. After the regression she came to see me again and explained that she had been taken back to a previous life in Egyptian times, during which all of her family had died of famine during a very hot, dry summer. "I felt this incredible sense of loss," she said. "And what amazes me so much is that it's the same type of feeling I get every time it's hot and sunny." She continued to work on her feelings in connection with this and in time started to feel much better during the summer months. Through the far life regression she had constructively used the etheric level as a gateway to her past memories, and thus opened up answers for herself. She ended up having the **reversed** 10 of Swords in her readings, showing that she had connected with the Judgement card at 20 and risen out of her darkness.

Key Words

Bouts of depression which come and go for no apparent reason.
Sadness
Melancholy
Reversed
Finding the root cause of these depressive phases.

Bach Flower Remedy

Mustard - for descending gloom and melancholia, which comes suddenly and lifts just as suddenly without apparent reason.

Toni Allen
The System of Symbols ©

Ace of Batons

Batons relate to the element of fire and therefore to the number 7.

On a traditional Marseille pack you will find the Ace of Batons depicted as a club or cudgel, sometimes sprouting fresh leaves. Here we find an immediate correlation with the Empress and nature at number 3, 7s counterpart on our circle. At 7 and the realm of Tejas we find the fire, light or glory which shines through the human being and makes up his stature, his brilliance, his light of knowledge, and the heat within the individual which keeps everything moving. At 3 and Prakriti we find the matrix which sets the direction of the creation in a general way and the conduct or behaviour of the individual in a special way.

Animals act on their nature alone, while human beings, who are able to discriminate, have the ability to rise above their nature. Discrimination takes one above nature and the person is freed from the pleasure of heaven and the pain of hell. Number 7 is the state which fixes the pattern of the individual. With the Major Cards we find this symbolised by the Chariot. Here the individual is in perfect balance, one's mind, body and spirit finely attuned to each other, thus offering a clear-sighted vision of one's life path and purpose. Conversely, at Major Card number 17 we find the Star Card, which, although it offers hope, also suggests that we are governed by the stars above, and that in some way our lot in life is fatalistically influenced by the configuration of the planets at the moment of our birth. An accurate astrological birth chart will show an individual's personality, with all of its strengths, weaknesses and pitfalls; yet it will also guide the individual towards a greater understanding of their own nature, their life path and the karmic influences which have brought them to a birth which includes all of these anomalies. Thus we see the side of nature which is fixed by karmic patterning. Such is the power of Tejas and the Baton. In a perfect world we would all have wonderful Tejas, like the Charioteer. However, most of us experience but brief times of such excellent control, and live mostly on what appears to be a fated path of struggling to surmount one hurdle after another.

The Ace of Batons symbolises the Tejas with which we were born, that initial spark, our personal charisma. The Tejas within us gives us warmth, light, and energy. Whether we realise it or not we all instantly recognise someone else's Tejas. Often people refer to someone as "A warm character", or "A bright personality". People are admired for their Tejas and we hear this in terms of "Boundless energy", "Bright spark" or maybe even "Fiery temper". Conversely when someone's tejas is diminished we describe them as "dull" or "lifeless".

Not everyone is made of the same stuff, and if we return to the principles governing the elements on our circle, you will note that every element contains a quantity of the others, even though it is a smaller amount. Earth, water and air, all contain a proportion of fire. People governed by these characteristics may not be so overtly fiery as someone ruled by fire, but they can be equally warm and enthusiastic. Modern day computer buffs are ruled by air and the intellect, but just watch how passionate and heated they become when engrossed in conversation about their pet subject. Likewise a businessman who is earthy and level headed, can become impassioned by the complexities of finalising the deal of a lifetime. Within their specific fields of expertise both are admired for their Tejas and personal brilliance.

Thus we can appreciate the Ace of Batons as a symbol of the individual's true nature, as fixed by karmic patterning and appertaining to this lifetime. It represents the appropriate Tejas for the individual. As we go through and study the Baton cards you will see how one's Tejas can be inhibited and quashed by those who are our keepers in early life. A studious child born into a family of sporty types is told to "get out into the fresh air" or "leave the books alone for a while" and slowly, or sometimes forcibly, led away from their true nature. The converse can also occur, when a sporty type is born into a family of bookworms. They are banished from the playing fields, and made to study hard, lest their vocation be missed. And so it goes on.

The Ace of Batons is a wonderful card because it shows that the individual is connecting with a part of themselves which is natural and alive. For many it takes numerous years of inner work to find their true light and glory, and come to terms with who they really are, having been brought up to deny their own exceptional talents. For this reason the Ace of Batons symbolises rebirth, regardless of one's age. One is born again true, and able to throw off the attitudes and expectations of others, who have moulded and shaped one to be the person whom they would like them to be.

The Ace of Batons also symbolises intuition and one's ability to connect to and follow one's inner light of knowledge.

Due to the Ace of Batons relationship to nature it also symbolises fertility. Often the card is drawn when the questioner asks if they will have children (or more children). However, as the Ace of Batons also symbolises sex, procreation and passion, the answer to such a question is never as clear-cut as it might first appear. Whether the questioner will fall pregnant or not is only made obvious by surrounding cards...but the Ace alone does suggest that whether they are successful or not, they'll certainly have a jolly good time trying! The Ace of Batons symbolises the erect penis, passion, lust and hot love. The act of sex is a complex part of our nature, and unless we are leading the path of the celibate aesthetic then it is a vital component of our adult existence. Many people come for a reading when their marriage, or permanent relationship is flagging. I recall one woman, who's partner appeared to show more interest in propping up a bar than being with her, complaining that in recent months he had gone off sex. The Ace of Batons came up some three months in the future and I suggested that their sex life would improve. About six months later she returned for another reading and told me that exactly three moths after the previous reading her partner had started to make love to her again on a regular basis. She positively glowed compared to how I had seen her before, showing that his renewed sexual interest had relit her own fire energy in a very positive manner.

The Baton as an image has been used throughout history as a symbol of growth and fertility. Often we see it in grander form as a tree. There is the Tree of Life, the Tree of the Knowledge of Good and Evil, and the Tree that grows on Glastonbury Tor, which stories tell us grew from the staff of Joseph of Aramathea. Nature has always been revered as a deity, and close to our hearts in England is the image of the Green Man, often seen carved as decoration on churches from times when the old ways entwined with the new.

Thus in the Tarot we find the Hanged Man suspended between two wooden pillars or sprouting branches. Whether notably in leaf or not these two columns are always made of wood, never metal, stone or any other substance. He hangs between the duality of life, and life is symbolised by nature and that which comes into creation to die and be reborn. During readings I have, on several occasions, seen the Ace of Batons close to the Hanged Man when the questioner is in doubt about their sexuality. Are they heterosexual, or gay? It's a dilemma which many people face and the two cards together show them undecided about whether their nature is this or that.

When **reversed** the Ace of Batons indicates that the questioner's vital energy is low and that they are lacking an intrinsic desire to live every moment to the full. In some cases the Ace of Batons reversed is triggered by exhaustion, overwork, or maybe illness. In others the lack of spark in their life is due to bereavement, loss or shock; all of which can make one feel numb, and as if life has lost its purpose and joy. Reversed the card can also symbolise impotance or lack of sexual desire.

Key Words

Inner light
Joy

Intuition
Sexual desire, lust and passion
One's true nature
New beginnings/rebirth
Birth
Fertility
Reversed
The card indicates the opposite of all of the above e.g. Hiding one's true nature.

Bach Flower Remedy

When the Ace is reversed, Cerato – for those who tend to imitate others without realising it, due to doubting one's own judgement and intuition.
Centaury – for those who follow the dictates of others rather than their own nature.

Toni Allen
The System of Symbols ©

The 2 of Batons

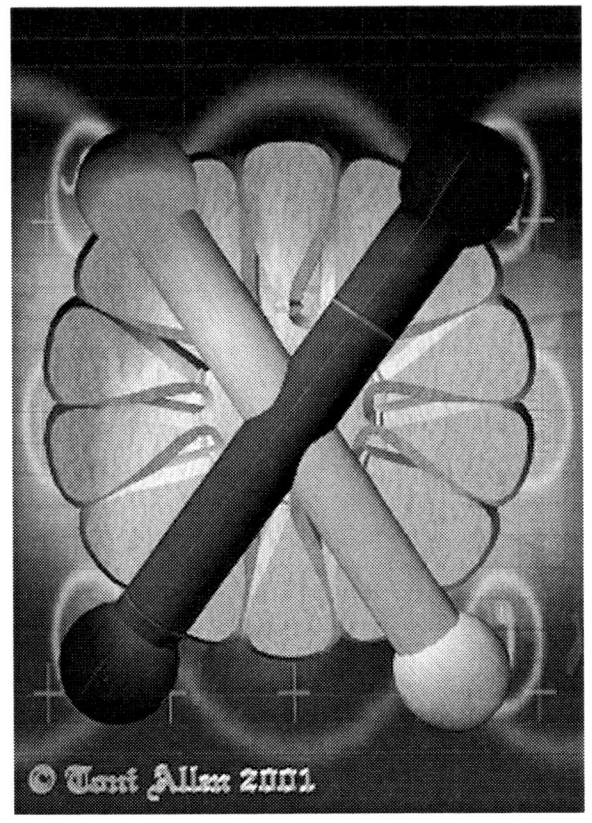

With the 2 of Batons we have fire at the unmanifest and water.

Fire, or Tejas, which sits at number 7, is the force which governs all movement in the world. With Tejas one sees, moves and does all sorts of work. Prakriti, which sits at number 7's reflection at 3, sets the direction of the creation in a general way, and the conduct or behaviour of the individual in a special way.

In physical terms fire is doused by water. However, if the fire is created by electricity then the water has the opposite effect and conducts the current, acts as a channel, and can spread the energy.

The 2 of Batons depicts a conflict of energies. The behaviour of the individual, which is obliged to be set in a specific way by their own Prakriti, is caught in the bondage of water. The bondage is either that of another individual, and the emotional bonds between the two, or their own samskara. What then occurs is that the individual cannot live out their own true nature, and it is left unmanifest.

The two Batons are like two personalities, two types of nature, rivalling for superiority within the one individual. These are either two sides of ourself, or oneself in conflict with someone else; but at an unconscious level. Our unique character is suppressed by someone else's conception of who we are, or who we ought to be. Due to the very nature of fire energy, when immersed in the bondage of water, one of these energies has ensnared the other. The dominant one holds the other back.

In a reading this domination of one energy by another, as symbolised by the 2 of Batons, can be interpreted in the following ways, depending upon surrounding cards.

When young our parent, or other mentor, has constantly told us we are 'something negative', i.e. useless, worthless, undeserving, ugly, fat and so on. Such phrases as "You'll never get anywhere", "You're so easily led", "Who'd want to marry you?", "You're mad", "You're pathetic", "You're weak", have been repeated so many times, and at exactly the right growth point to achieve maximum damage. These phrases then become 'stuck', or bound up in our unconscious, and by the time we reach maturity we have come to believe that these statements about ourself are true.

As we grow up we find that we cannot attain our goals in life due to some unseen barrier surrounding our personality. Our true nature is bound up in untruth. We do not understand why we find it so hard to feel attractive, even when our friends affirm that we are pretty, or handsome. Eventually something unties the illusion and we recall a dim memory of a jealous mother cruelly insulting our curly hair or slim legs. Our self confidence may well have been broken in the cradle. As an adult we may find it incredibly hard at work to approach the boss and ask for that much deserved raise. Our feet won't do the walking and our tongue trips up and we ask if he would like a coffee instead. When taking his coffee in, feeling flushed and embarrassed, it's probably the furthest thing from our mind that when young our Dad kept drumming it into us that "He who asks doesn't get. I told you to wait." Consequently we stopped asking for things a long time ago, and started expecting to be refused anyway.

Not everyone will take on board the same words in the same way. It's all an element of degree, and dependent on the clash between various types of personality. Sometimes there are no words and the dominion is based on feeling. Accordingly there is a lot of emotional blackmail symbolised in this card, which is often evoked just as easily by a sharp look from a mother who does not want her child to go out and play. If the child goes out then the mother will feel lonely. Guilt pulls the child back, and consequently, when older, he or she always feels guilty about "doing their own thing", yet never relates to why they should feel like this, even if they are living alone and beholden to no-one else.

Sometimes no one has put this invisible barrier around ourselves apart from us; and then we find a strong karmic influence. Even when we can attribute the control over our nature to someone else's influence, then we must look closely at why we have chosen to have a relationship with the individual in question, and what lessons there are to be learnt in our quest to break away from their influence.

Surrounding cards will highlight what has created the barrier, and the depth of the questioner's ability to deal with it in a positive manner. In simplistic terms the following associations can be made when the 2 of Batons is next to:-

Swords-mental affliction-mental cruelty.

Batons-lack of libido-physical ailments.

Cups-emotional distress-husband/wife dominant.

Coins-lack of self worth, especially in work/career-financial worries.

The 2 of Batons always refers to the specific time when our mind first wakes up to what the cause of the problem is. It takes us back to the causal level and the unmanifest, which opens up a channel to deal with the issue. It is like discovering the seed from which the plant has grown.

The 2 of Batons is often seen when a parent is directing, or even forcing, a youngster towards the wrong career. The parent is not allowing the child to follow their bliss and achieve their true vocation. I saw this clearly when a 17 year old, studying in his final year for A levels, came to me in a deep suicidal depression. In fact he was advised to come for a reading by his mother, who had seen me the week before, desperately worried about her son, and the dreadful atmosphere everyone was experiencing at home. With only three months to go the teenager was studying around the clock to achieve good grades, and his parents gave him total support. However, he told me that he did not understand what

Toni Allen
The System of Symbols ©

was wrong inside himself, as he loved his parents dearly, got on well with them, and would never wish to do anything against them. The 2 of Batons lay over the 3 of Batons, showing that his natural artistic talents were being suppressed. His father had directed him over the years towards sitting A levels in science and mathematics. There was no doubt about his ability to pass the exams, everything showed that he was an intelligent, articulate young man. It appeared that his feelings of depression arose from his lack of love for the sciences, and he despaired of his future vision of having to spend the next forty years working in an area in which he felt uncomfortable.

When I explained the 2 of Batons he saw the situation clearly and affirmed that he felt that he had to live up to his father's expectations. "I want to study music," he said, "but I wasn't allowed to take it even as far as A level". With further cards we found a way for him to both please his father and himself. He could take an A level in music at evening class once he had finished this academic year. We resolved the situation by him agreeing to speak with his father about taking a year or two off before going on to university. He agreed to finish his A levels, but on the understanding that if he passed he passed, and that if he failed he failed, the outcome was neither here nor there. "You mean it's okay if I fail", he gasped. "Of course," I replied. "As long as you do your best, what more can be asked. And it's only three months to go in these subjects, not forty years." With the pressure of "having to pass" taken away, he left feeling as if a huge burden had been lifted. A couple of weeks later his mother telephoned to say that she didn't know exactly what I had said to her son, but that he and his father had had a long chat, and that her son was so much better in himself that he was like a different person. Perhaps he wasn't a "different person". Perhaps he was simply more himself, his true nature.

This young man was very fortunate in that he combated the 2 of Batons early on, in a seedling stage. A much later realisation came to another questioner who, at forty-seven, felt that he'd wasted his life by continuing his father's trade, which he was thoroughly unsuited to. In his teens it had been expected that he would apprentice to his father, and this he had done, never once fighting back against the domination of 'the family business'. When he came to me he was at the point of wishing to sell this business, much to the absolute horror of every relative in sight.

Toni Allen
The System of Symbols ©

The 2 of Batons showed that he knew his father had influenced him, and even though it had taken him thirty years to understand this, he was willing to break the bondage and defy his father; who was still alive, retired from the business, but a minor share-holder.

Another relevant, and very common situation to find the 2 of Batons highlighting is that one partner in a relationship has been persistently 'brainwashed' by the other into believing that they are no longer capable of 'thinking for themselves', 'holding down a job', 'being a good lover' etc. In such readings the brow beaten partner has usually reached breaking point and is on the verge of leaving the marriage, because they have come to realise that they no longer have a life of their own, even in small matters. Here you might find the Lovers close by indicating that there is a major decision to make. If the 3 of Swords is close it symbolises the partners jealousy and fears that the dominated partner might be 'better than them' if not suppressed.

More commonly this situation relates to a woman being put down by her husband, but this does not mean that women never subjugate men with this sort of behaviour. More often women control the men in childhood by various manipulative methods of motherhood. In the husband/wife situation the 2 of Batons appears when the wife wakes up to the fact that she is not 'stupid' because she has stayed at home and raised three children instead of going out to work; or 'neurotic' because she is concerned over the children's safety; or 'hard' because she has chosen to work and not start a family yet. In such relationships the controlling male figure, King of Swords or another King reversed, is nearly always suffering within themselves but trying to disguise it.

In general terms the 2 of Batons up the right way indicates that someone realises that another individual has a particular influence over them, while the 2 of Batons **reversed** indicates that the specific cause behind the way they are being treated is uncovered.

A simple example of this is a when a woman finds herself in a physically abusive relationship. With the 2 of Batons up the right way she realises that she does not have to put up with being hit whenever she does something deemed to be wrong, and that it is not her birth-right to be someone else's punch bag. With the 2 of Batons **reversed** she goes deeper and recalls occasions when her father hit her, the cause of her seeking abusive relationships, which she has come to associate as love from a man. This example is very simplistic, and very often there is far more complex and subtle programming towards loss of personality.

It must never be ignored that the 2 of Batons can show that it is the questioner who is dominating someone else. Here extreme tact and caution must be used when raising such a suggestion with the questioner, because although when someone is dominated the card signifies that they have become aware of this hard fact, it does not indicate within itself that someone who is manipulating someone else necessarily realises the damage, whether intended or unconscious, that they are doing to another.

In purely physical terms the 2 of Batons symbolises anything which dominates or suppresses, e.g. a property which cannot be sold, a tree overshadowing the house, debt which makes the individual feel poor in spirit, a job which can go no further etc.

Key Words

Domination/suppression/manipulation
Conflict between two personalities
Barriers
Reversed
Discovering the causes behind limiting behavioural patterns.

Toni Allen
The System of Symbols ©

The 3 of Batons

The 3 of Batons relates to fire at Prakriti.

Fire, or Tejas, is the force which governs all the movements of the world. With Tejas one sees and does all sorts of works. Prakriti sets the direction of the creation in a general way and the conduct or behaviour of the individual in a special way.
At the 3 of Batons Prakriti sets the nature of an individual towards creative works of all description.

Ideally it is the card of the artist. Creative ability, which is only captured in dreams and visions at the 7 of Cups, can be directed by the fire energy of the 3 of Batons. For the artist is the practical act of 'doing'.

The 3 of Batons is a dynamic card, full of energy. Here the three gunas of nature are in perfect balance and we find Sattvika Tejas which gives the light of knowledge, thus the energy is never dissipated. Due to its connection with the Empress at 3, who still sits in the causal level, it is the card of having 'intent' to make something happen, and therefore symbolises making plans for the future and drawing up plans, as in blueprints.

Any type of creative activity falls under the realm of the 3 of Batons. Graceful movement, as in dance, is very important. Colour, light, brightness and beauty are all shown here, hence it symbolises a nature which creates beautiful objects and positive thoughts. It is not, however, the same methodical precision depicted by the 3 of Coins, its natural fire energy making it far more flamboyant. Here I feel it necessary to draw a comparison between the two cards as they both depict artists and craftsmen. The craftsmen of the 3 of Batons are more interested in a rush of colour and movement, while the craftsmen of the 3 of Coins deal more with physical matter such as in pottery, sculpture, or architecture. Imagine the difference between two artists, Vincent Van-Gogh and Leanardo Da-Vinci. I always consider Van-Gogh to be ruled by the passion of the 3 of Batons with his fantastically vivid colours, broad brush strokes and enthusiastic temperament. He studied, and slogged away at 'conventional' art theory without success, until ultimately he let his own personality rush out and break the rules, thus discovering new and uncharted ground. On the other hand Da-Vinci produced delicate artwork, had a futuristic knowledge of engineering, and a fascination with perspective and human anatomy. I consider him to be far more 3 of Coins orientated, as his enthusiasm lay with gaining an ever greater knowledge of how things worked and the structure of nature. They had different modes of expression, yet both equally valid.

In a reading the 3 of Batons may be seen as follows:-

A desire to express oneself positively. Surrounding cards will show in which particular direction the questioner's talents lay.

Related to the Empress, which rules the number 3, the card depicts a desire to 'give birth' to some idea or project, and as an interpreter you need to assess whether it is in fact a desire to literally 'give birth' to a child. If the questioner is pregnant and the 3 of Batons is seen in the 'future' part of the reading then it depicts the time of birth. Surrounding cards may indicate how the birth will go:-
Next to the 2 of Batons-possible obstructions and delays.
Next to the 4 of swords-the birth takes place in hospital.

Toni Allen
The System of Symbols ©

Next to the King of Swords-the need for a consultant or surgeon to be close at hand as well as a midwife
Next to the 8 of Batons-a quick delivery

With such a delicate subject tact and diplomacy must be used. Most clients who ask about the forthcoming birth of an expected child say words to the effect of "I want to know everything...I can take the good with the bad". This does not necessarily mean that they can take everything you might see in their stride. If you see adverse conditions then work towards them diplomatically. You, as the reader, have a duty to ensure your client's wellbeing, and fear can cause irreparable damage. A good reader will always assess throughout a reading 'how much' a client can take; and if need be avoid over sensitive issues until the questioner is more comfortable about what is being said. Impressionable areas can always be gone back to, if appropriate.

On the subject of childbirth and pregnancy most women will acknowledge problems which they already know about. Even if it is the woman's first child she may well say words to the effect of, "Oh yes, my mother had extremely high blood pressure throughout her pregnancies as well. She had a hard time having us, so there's nothing new there really."

I have found through experience that at times the guiding light of the absolute takes over in very strange ways. Some years ago I did a reading for a young woman who was nearly eight months pregnant. She was bright and cheerful, and had brought a friend to sit in on the reading. When the young woman asked about how the birth would go she drew the 3 of Batons, the King of Swords reversed, and the 4 of Swords; followed by the 10 of Batons. I asked if she had a good gynaecologist and suggested that she should get the best, and have him present at the birth. She said that she thought her consultant was all right, but didn't expect him to be at the birth. "I feel fine", she said. "I've only got four weeks to go." "It's further away than that", I said. "You're baby won't be born in four weeks, it's much further away than that." Her friend laughed and pointed to the young woman's bulging tummy. "Haven't you noticed this?" she asked jokingly. "No, " I replied. "When the time comes you need to be in hospital and get the best surgeon you can. I think the baby will need immediate help. Get the best, you must ask for the best."

They went home from the reading and I heard nothing more until over two years later. It was the day before I was to move house, the telephone was disconnected and everything packed in boxes except the kettle, and my pack of Tarot cards. There was a knock at the door and a woman stood there. She had tried to 'phone, but come round on the off chance that I still lived at the same address. She introduced herself as the older friend of the young pregnant woman. I invited her in, and she asked if her friend could come in and have another reading. We sat and drank tea while the young woman said, "You were so right. My first baby, the one I was pregnant with, was fine. What you were talking about in the reading was the birth of my second child." "It was the way you kept insisting that she needed the best consultant much further away than four weeks," said her friend. "I never forgot your words. I was with her at the second birth and when problems arose I pushed for the best consultant possible, I just knew that she had to have someone special."

I have no explanation as to how such a phenomena comes about. Call it divine intervention, if you like. However, I do know that the woman's second child was born with a very rare condition, and that from the first seconds of her birth the child needed expert assistance. Thanks to her friend remembering the reading she managed to push for the best and gain immediate support for both mother and child.

The 3 of Batons also symbolises one's sex drive. It shows a good, healthy approach to sexual intercourse. When placed next to various cards the emphasis changes. Here are a few examples:-
With the 2 of Cups, sex in a loving relationship.
With the Strength cards reversed, unbridled passion.
With the Page of Swords, sexual deceit, or perversion. Transvestites often have this combination because they enjoy cross dressing, as signified by the Page of Swords ability to become someone he isn't.
With the 4 of Cups, sexual boredom, or frustration that a partner has lost interest in sex.
When **reversed** the 3 of Batons symbolises frustrations of many kinds due to unfulfilled creative urges.

When an individual's energy is blocked they can become depressed, irritable and listless. Surrounding cards will show who, or what, is affecting the questioner so that they are unable to fulfil their potential.

Key Words

The artist
Passion
Birth
Creativity
Plans
Colour
Reversed
Blocked creativity
Lack of energy
Dullness

Toni Allen
The System of Symbols ©

The 4 of Batons

The 4 of Batons relates to fire at Ahamkara, or 'I am'.

At the 4 of Batons the Tejas, or fire, is beautifully balanced in one's feeling of 'I am', as it relates to the harmony of the Temperance card at 14, joined by the strong feeling of self worth depicted by the Emperor. It gives the individual a solid sense of 'who they are', and what they want, but in a comfortable and relaxed way. Because the individual is doing what comes naturally to them their Tejas shines out and they are friendly and popular.

The harmony and peace within the 4 of Batons makes it lack any great complexity.

In a reading it may be interpreted as follows:-

When this card comes up for an individual it shows that they are comfortable with themself, maintain an easy going manner with others,

Toni Allen
The System of Symbols ©

and generally have good health. A respect for nature, in all its forms, is usually prevalent, and, depending upon surrounding cards, they might well enjoy gardening, long country walks or generally communing with nature.

Due to the 4 of Baton's association with feelings of 'I am' and beauty, the card often symbolises the home, the place where most people place efforts to guard their personality's security in the physical world. At home we feel safe from the outside world, at home we can relax and can be ourselves, at home we can shine and be equal to others, without having to bow and scrape to a boss.

The type of home depicted by the 4 of Batons is what I have come to refer to as 'the young home', in which friends are free to drop in for coffee without notice, children have their friends popping in and out, or to stay the weekend, and everyone 'mucks in' together. I call it 'the young home' regardless of the age of the questioner, because it portrays a home established away from the traditional hierarchical traditions of the 10 of Coins. It is whatever is different for the questioner than how they were brought up, their own ideas and values, their parent's life style seeming outmoded, or unsuitable.

As I get older my clients somehow appear to get younger. For many years the above interpretation of the 4 of Batons fitted in with clients that I saw. They had been brought up in the forties and fifties. This was a time when rules applied and children were told what time to come in at night, when they could have their friends round, and to do as they were told without question. This attitude was their version of the 10 of Coins, and a hence a very lackadaisical life style was the youngsters' way of rebelling and being themselves. A few years ago I had a young female client with the 4 of Batons prominently placed next to the 10 of Coins. I suggested that she was wishing to break away from the strict rules set out by her parents and live a more easy going life style. "Oh no," she replied. "It's the other way round. My parents were hippies. I was born in the sixties. I don't want my home full of 'free love' and drop outs crashing on the floor every night. I want structure and form, friends to phone up before they come round, arranged dinner parties and a complete dinner service!" Yes, this was her version of the 4 of Batons. She felt that she could not be herself with all these people hanging around, and that her idea of relaxation and bliss, in order to be herself, was a much more ordered household. It's a salient reminder that the world moves on, and with it our interpretations must expand and modify. Now I make sure that I assess the age and cultural background of my client before interpreting the card, and often include a brief explanation of the differences I have found within the card, so that my client can grasp how each generation has it's own sense of "I am" and personal identity.

Often the 4 of Batons comes up as a contrast between what the questioner has and what they would like. I see it in readings of many women who lead a dull life. They find themselves trapped in an unhappy marriage, in which the husband creates tension and a bad atmosphere; shown by such cards as the 5 of Cups or 3 of Swords, and possibly a Court Card depicting the husband close to the 4 of Batons. However, when the husband is at work, or away on business, the home atmosphere changes completely, and the woman feels able to have her friends in for coffee or other children over to play with her own. These people (husbands do it to wives too!) are caught in the dilemma between the physical security offered by their partner and the desire for a more unconstrained attitude within the home. Note also that the 4 of Batons relationship to Temperance can indicate that the harmony is temporary or in some way false. After all, when the husband returns home, the balance is broken and the friction returns.

The 4 of Batons is also indicative of a youth reaching an age when he, or she, desire to 'flee the nest'. For one young woman the 9 of Coins depicted the 'past', representing a firm, established lifestyle full of safety and financial security; while the 4 of Batons came up within the reading to represent some four months in the future. She was in the process of moving in with her boyfriend, who already owned a property. The 4 of Batons depicted the new, fresh home she was to make for herself, in which she could exhibit her own personality through choice of decoration etc. The 9 of Coins showed two aspects of the past. Firstly that her parental home was always there as a place of safety and recovery, should the relationship fail, and secondly, that her boyfriend had already purchased the property, and was therefore financially sound, but as yet had done nothing to make it any more than an economic investment.

The 4 of Batons **reversed** shows that the harmony and balance within one's sense of "I Am" have temporarily broken down. In connection with where one lives it is likely to illustrate that something is affecting the 'happy home'. e.g. close to the 5 of Coins might show that the questioner has no personal support within the home; or that financial problems entail having to give up the home, or struggle to keep it.

In many respects the 4 of Batons sounds like perfection itself, but as a Tarot reader you must always remember to place the card in perspective with the rest of the reading. For one man it came up to reveal he had created a very warm atmosphere for his wife and children, and worked hard to maintain it. However, his wife yearned for bright lights, foreign travel and excitement. His wife's attitude was throwing the home into disharmony and he was struggling with the dilemma of how to maintain two conflicting lifestyles; his T.V. and gardening routine, versus his wife's need for expensive nights out.

Hence we can see how to some people the 4 of Batons might represent a very 'stodgy' lifestyle. Certain personality types find stress and achievement the nectar of life; home purely somewhere to lay their head. So, a woman depicted as a strong Queen of Coins, seen surrounded by lots of active cards, showing that she's busy climbing the career ladder, will not necessarily be impressed if you see that her new boyfriend is looking to settle down.

Key Words

A home which represents the individual's personality, and is not simply a reflection of what their parents achieved, or wanted.
The new, or young, home.
Good health.
Popularity.
Minor social events that take place within the home.
Reversed
Minor upsets within the home.

Toni Allen
The System of Symbols ©

The 5 of Batons

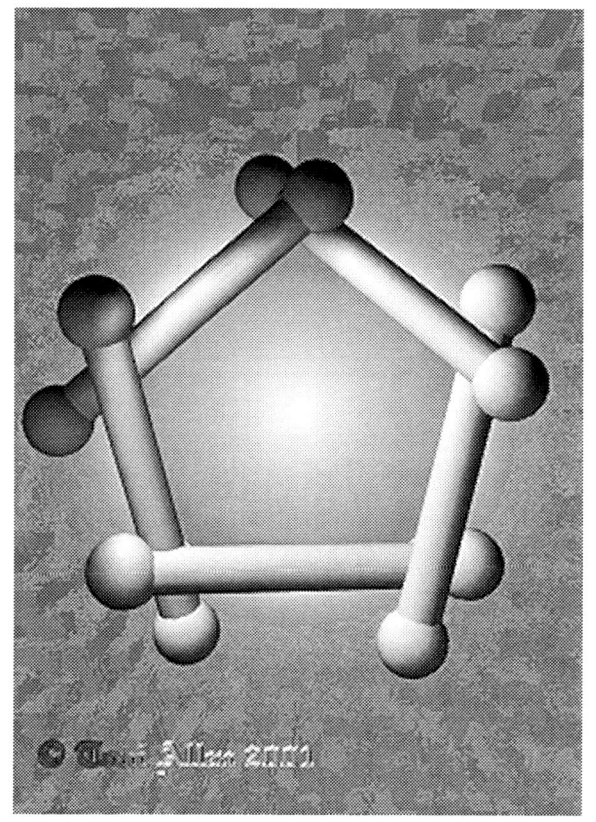

The 5 of Batons relates to fire at ether.

Tejas (fire) governs all the movements of the world; it is also the light or glory which shines through a human being and makes up his stature. Ether is the bridge between the physical world and the world of mental, subtle and causal nature.

As 7 and 3 are interchangeable, fire also relates to prakriti (nature).

Ether works as a transformer, changing one type of energy into another. The physical aspect of ether is sound; it comes form space and manifests in space.

The 5 of Batons may be interpreted in two distinct ways, yet one does not exist without the other.

Primarily the 5 of Batons symbolises energy and nature transforming themselves through the ether. In practice this can be observed as bodily changes; which are connected with changes in ideas, thinking etc. All action in the physical world starts in the causal and subtle realms, therefore physical changes and mental changes are inseparable.

In a reading the most common way to see the physical side of the 5 of Batons is in a change of metabolism. For women this is very clearly observed by their natural menstrual cycle. Menstruation is a natural phenomenon, and when the balance of nature is upset, for whatever reason, then a woman's characteristic cycle will be affected. Many women suffer from Pre Menstrual Tension, and this is an excellent example of the type of effect indicated. Depending upon surrounding cards, the 5 of Batons may indicate for a woman:- irregular or painful periods, a sudden worrying change in their normal cycle, hormonal imbalance which affects them psychologically as well as other physical symptoms, or the onset of the menopause. As I mentioned earlier, all action in the physical world starts in the causal and subtle realms. Along with the bodily upsets described above will come mental problems and conflicts caused through stress, sudden irrational outbursts and so on. Physical changes cause upset; but by the same token emotional strain causes physical symptoms, to anyone, whether male or female. It's a chicken and egg situation!

Whether the 5 of Batons is physically based in bodily changes, or emotionally based, individuals will 'not be themselves' and may appear to be acting 'out of character' to their loved ones. Sometimes it is as if their personality has suddenly changed. One man came to me believing his marriage was over because his wife was acting so strangely towards him. The 5 of Batons came up next to the Queen of Swords reversed, suggesting that she might be suffering from some 'women's complaint' which she felt self conscious speaking to him about. After I'd explained the potential situation in some detail his face lit up. "You've made so much sense out of how she's been acting," he said. "And, you know, I was so worried about myself, and her not loving me any more, that I never considered that she might have a medical problem."

Puberty, teething, the male 'menopause' and pregnancy are all relevant here. These are all created by natural changes occurring within the body. They are not to be confused with drug or alcohol induced psychotic changes. However, the 5 of Batons does indicate the body dealing with, and expelling, the effects of any drug used for medical purposes or addiction e.g. recovery from an anaesthetic, kicking out 'poisons' when suffering from a virus, withdrawal from nicotine, and any subtle changes when recovering from an illness.

Such things as puberty are rarely observed in their entirety because they take place at a subtle level. Yet his parents know that Tom has just thrown a mega tantrum because his body is undergoing major changes, and that his personality (prakriti) is crystallising, and evolving from boy to man. He is beginning to think differently, act differently, and learn to come to terms with bodily hair growth and an awakening sexual awareness. Everything is different from his experiences up until this point, and as yet he hasn't learnt to control the sudden rush of hormones.

Mentally the 5 of Batons comes through from the causal level as circling thoughts and inner arguments. We experience this as confusion and thoughts which persist on going round and round in our heads. These thoughts will simply not leave us alone. Often this is felt very strongly after a quarrel. We leave the arena and take time to ponder the dispute, only to hear a voice inside our head saying "I wish I'd said this", or, "I should have said that". In such situations we can drain ourselves completely by spending many futile hours letting the argument go on, profitlessly, inside our head. Sometimes it is one dreadful thought which drags on, the unhappy occasion replaying like a record stuck in a groove; the bitter sentence repeating, the visual scene coming back time and time again. Here we have the sound of the ether caught up in rajasika tejas (vikshepa).

When this happens to us our minds become so congested that physical symptoms occur, such as excess mucus, sinus problems, headaches and colds. All illness starts in the causal and subtle realm, and the 5 of Batons is the key to understanding this. A few examples may be seen as follows:-

With the 9 of Batons reversed - physical weakness and mental exhaustion.
With the 8 of Swords - stagnation, often relating to circulatory problems and blood flow.
With the 5 of Swords - legal quarrels.
With the 4 of Coins - an improvement in health.

When the card is displayed in the 'mental level' the 5 of Batons is predominantly related to inner, mental arguments. Likewise, when at the 'physical level' it appertains to many of the symptoms outlined above.

When **reversed** the 5 of Batons becomes externalised and shows itself as bickering, disputes and conflicts. This is not the same, however, as the direct, punchy anger of the 3 of Swords, but an expression of the circling thoughts within one's head. It is where people go on and on, grinding over the same old points, along with petty quarrels and general day to day differences of opinion. Often it is the type of 'fight' which gets everyone nowhere.

On a more positive note the 5 reversed indicates friendly debate, although political debate is more inclined to come under the realm of the 5 of Swords.

Key Words

Physical changes
Psychological changes
Circling thoughts
Reversed
Bickering

Bach Flower Remedy

White Chestnut - for persistent unwanted thoughts.

Toni Allen
The System of Symbols ©

The 6 of Batons

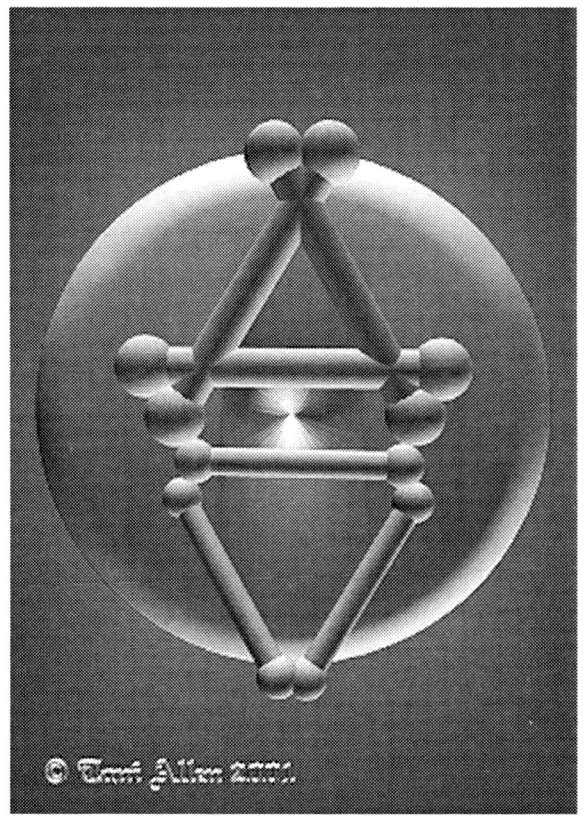

The 6 of Batons relates to fire at air.

Air, or the Pranas, keep all creatures going. The Pranas are vital energies; they make or keep us alive, discharge polluted air, regulate the digestive process, keep the body in balance and regulate involuntary movements in the body. Prana is the breath of life, vital energy and the capacity to desire and love.

As 6 and 4 interchange we also find ahamkara, the sense of solidarity and well-being about who we are.

Fire, or Tejas, influencing the pranas, gives a very active, vibrant sense of who we are and what we are doing. Prakriti at 3 is the embodiment of the three forces of Sattva, Rajas, and Tamas, and all these forces have to be felt by something which is conscious. When consciousness feels the force then ahamkara emerges.

Thus at the 6 of Batons we have a lovely sense of 'who we are'. We may well have struggled hard to arrive at this point hence it is often referred to as 'the victory card'. Related to the Lovers at 6 it also signifies that one's discrimination is pin sharp, and is therefore a good card to show clarity of mind. For one woman the card came up to signify the result of a court case with her former husband. She was needing to obtain a judgement to gain regular maintenance for herself and their young daughter. When I told her the 6 of Batons was the victory card she smiled wryly and said that she'd let me know the outcome. The day after the legal hearing she 'phoned to say that the judge had granted her maintenance, and that now her ex-husband was forced to pay. "I feel that it's a great victory," she said. "I can see my way clearly now. It's wonderful."

Due to the subtle interrelation between the numbers 6, 3 and 4, the 6 of Batons also represents two 3s working in harmony. The two individual natures at 3 work so well together that they merge into a new being. Thus we see the number 2 adding the bonding quality of water through its counterpart 8. There is also the connotation of someone else making us feel good about ourself.

The 6 of Batons may be interpreted as follows:-

The 6 of Batons often symbolises as near perfect a relationship as two people can have.

In such relationships the two individuals compliment one another. I shall start by talking about loving, male/female relationships; although exactly the same outlines stand equally for homosexual, or lesbian, couples. In general terms the King and Queen of Batons symbolise this couple. We are speaking of a natural order in the creation in which the man is the provider and the woman a homemaker; although once again, there are many variations on a theme depending on what comes naturally to any particular couple. It is the type of couple who like to do things for each other, and often don't feel as if their life is of any value unless they have someone else to do things for. When the 6 of Batons is seen in a reading it means that they have found someone who makes their life worthwhile.

Friendship is the most important issue here, and most especially the communication that takes place between them. Remember that air represents the mental faculties, and to find someone we can talk to in easy fashion, for hours on end, is a very rewarding experience. Great strength is added to a relationship with this card, as it often indicates that two people like each other and are friends before they fall in love. That may sound like a strange idea, but many people search for one high after another, constantly craving that wonderful buzz which the 2 of Cups gives us. Often I see readings in which a client has had several passionate relationships in the past, all of which have quickly burnt out. Now they have the 6 of Batons as the crux of a new relationship, and they find themselves amazed by the quality of friendship and trust with their new partner as the love steadily grows.

To some extent this card is akin to showing that the couple are soul mates. They do not necessarily have the same taste in clothes or decoration, or share the same opinions on everything; and yet they fit together like two halves of a circle. It is often their differences which make them so interesting to each other. This is because they are both allowing each other to be themselves within the relationship. This couple can also be very successful if they have a business together, as they work well as a team.

Outside marriage or other love relationships, the 6 of Batons speaks of any good working relationship or friendship. e.g. One's 'best friend', a business partner, or even the need to take a partner into an existing business. For a woman who is already in a steady relationship, and content, the 6 of Batons, when seen with regard to a man other than her husband, does not mean that she is about to dash off and have a wild affair. The card suggests that she has found a man she can talk to about many subjects and is the sort of man-friend she might ask advice of if anything was worrying her about her marriage. (the same, of course, would apply to a married man with a woman friend) Some people have a friend of the opposite sex simply to talk to, even when not married.

Reversed the 6 of Batons shows that the 'Perfect couple' are not getting on quite as well as they used to, due mainly to external circumstances rather than any 'falling out of love'.

The following example is a good indication of the different experiences between the 6 of Batons and the 2 of Cups, and the 6 of Batons reversed.

A young man, barely out of his teens came to see me. He had a long term girlfriend, whom he had known for years, and about a year before he came for the reading their relationship had flourished into sexual harmony as well as friendship. However, his 6 of Batons was reversed close to her Queen of Batons, and he had become unsure of the relationship since meeting another girl. This new girl was very sexy and intelligent but inclined to be rather bitchy. His King of Batons was reversed next to this new girl's Page of Swords, yet the 2 of Cups crossed them. He did not wish to hurt either of his young ladyfriends, but his strong sense of moral justice was driving him to choose between one or the other. When I suggested that his long term girlfriend was where his heart truly lay he admitted, "I feel this other girl's an experiment. She's very different, and not very faithful, always complaining, and tends to let me down at the last minute; yet she wants me to give up my other girlfriend."

This new girl had created a hiccup in his relationship. His youth demanded that he experience many aspects of life, and love, before settling down; and this tricky new character had offered him the opportunity to run his emotions to the limit and discover what jealousy, unfaithfulness, sexual compatibility and trust really meant. The cards suggested he run this new relationship to its limit and see what happened. Within a week he let me know that his new girlfriend had deliberately plotted to upset his long standing girlfriend and that consequently he had immediately disassociated from the new girl. "My girlfriend's put up with a lot," he said. "And yet she's still there. Isn't she wonderful. We've talked the whole matter through. At least we can talk to each other, and try and sort things out....nobody speaks with me at the same level that she does."

In business the 6 of Batons **reversed** indicates either the need for a business partner, or that a business partner is no longer so keen to be involved, depending upon surrounding cards.

Key Words

Compatibility/Best friend/Perfect partner/Business partner
Good communication/Victory
Reversed - A minor "hic-up" in an otherwise positive relationship
Possible failure/Need for a partner, or best friend.

Toni Allen
The System of Symbols ©

The 7 of Batons

The 7 of Batons relates to fire at fire.

This card is closely associated with the Chariot and all that it stands for. Tejas, the fire, light or glory which shines through the human being and makes up his stature, his light of knowledge, the heat which keep everything going.

Interrelated with the 3 of Batons, which gives inspiration and birth to the qualities of Tejas, the 7 acts in the physical realm, symbolising that actions planned at the 3 have now come to fruition, or are actively being undertaken.

The 7 of Batons is truly glorious and may be interpreted in practice as follows:-

For the individual it symbolises a deep knowledge and belief in oneself, which makes it possible to fully participate in the world. A great feeling of well being, coupled with a desire to act; plus knowledge of what it is that one wishes to achieve. It's a vital interest in life. Zest. This disposition is reliant on no other person or thing, money, status, or job, it comes entirely from within.

It depicts the questioner's deportment. Beauty is also apt, although I believe that charisma is a far more meaningful word. One can appear very scruffy through lack of finances, yet it is the way in which one carries oneself, the twinkle in the eye and the skip in the step, which make heads turn or friends stop to chat. The opposite, as indicated by the **reversed** card, shows that even the most beautiful person will not be attractive to others if they appear lifeless and dull, hang their head, or have lost their sparkle.

The apathy and resignation depicted by the **reversed** card is a type of depression, or more precisely, one of the facets of losing one's sense of self worth and unity with the absolute. It's as if the individual has given up; they no longer expect joy and sometimes they are so inwardly numb that they no longer experience pain. (We can see how this relates to the Star card at 17 with the concept of hope and hopelessness). In many readings for women I have seen it as that dragging feeling of 'I can't be bothered to put my make up on', or 'what's the point of getting dressed up to go out'. It's as if their inner fire of life has been extinguished and they can't find the energy to present themselves attractively any more.

I recall the 7 of Batons reversed coming up in one man's reading when I asked him to take a card to represent his wife. I gave a brief interpretation and he said unhappily, "She doesn't bother with herself any more. A mate came up to me the other day and actually said, 'Cor, your missus has let herself go, hasn't she?'" He looked very sad. "But she used to be such a smart woman. I mean, you can tell she's gone down hill when you mates start taking you aside and asking what's up." Although he was confused about what his wife might be experiencing emotionally to cause this turn about, he certainly saw the external result, and was deeply concerned.

On the path of life the 7 of Batons **upright** gives a sense of achievement, as if life is a high mountain which may be climbed, and we have reached the very top. It therefore holds an element of aggression in that we will hold the competition at bay, but by positive action, not by quarrels and aggression. We get where we are going through the qualities of our personality and innate abilities. However, with these qualities reversed we find a sense of 'things getting on top of us' and an idea that 'everybody is better than us', and feel it's an uphill battle to redress the balance.

Healthwise the 7 of Batons is incredibly healthy. When the card is **reversed**, however, there is more cause for concern. It comes under the realm of Tamasika Tejas, and is like a thick or hard covering which does not allow the individual's light to show, as when a lamp is shielded. Physically this may create symptoms of anaemia and tiredness. There is a resignation to one's fate and therefore to one's illness. The sufferer may believe that their condition is inherited, or 'runs in the family'; thus they believe that there is no way to be cured and consequently seek no aid to a remedy.

If a reading suggests that your client has given up hope for a cure then enquire as to whether they have sought any help from Complementary Therapies. Very often people simply do not know that alternatives exist. I keep contact numbers of practitioners whom I know for referral, and if I'm unable to recommend a particular type of practitioner, then I contact a friend of mine who has a network of associates that is of a far broader spectrum. Very often complementary medicine offers alleviation from symptoms which a general practitioner will only prescribe drugs to mask. Homeopathy, acupuncture and the Bach Flower Remedies are all easily accessible. As the 7 of Batons is strongly associated with fire energy which rules colour, I have found in practice that many people can be helped through colour therapy, such as Aura Soma, or even changing the colours which they wear.

Key Words

Self confidence/Charisma/Bright character
Reversed - Apathy/Resignation/Lack of interest in oneself

Bach Flower Remedy

Wild Rose – For resignation and apathy.

Toni Allen
The System of Symbols ©

The 8 of Batons

The 8 of Batons relates to fire at water.

The unmanifest, at 2, is the store house where all the multifarious forms of the creation lie stored before creation breaks out; they are absorbed in it when the creation is to be withdrawn.

In the realm of atomic or other structures, it is only the bonds, at 8, which keep matter together. It is called Sneha in Sanskrit. This Sneha is the bond between things and people. It is a sort of love which keeps them together.

In both cases the number 8 acts as the store which keeps all things together, and also as the bond which keeps them together on universal and individual levels.

At the 8 of Batons we are seeing the impression of fire working on these bonds, and therefore we find fire, or Tejas, which is systemised and organised. Tejas is the fire, light or glory, which shines through the human being and makes up his stature, his brilliance, and his light of knowledge.

We may interpret the 8 of Batons as follows:-

For an individual it is their ability to organise their energies. People with this card are usually found working in a job which suits them well; and within that position they are highly capable of being in charge, and commanding those below them in a highly positive and motivated way. There is no bossy-ness here, but much busy-ness. Often these people will appear to do little, yet without their clarity of mind, lesser mortals have nothing to revolve around. They are like the centre of a wheel. How often have we seen a successful small shop change hands, and although the new owner keeps on old staff, the business slowly fails? It was not the position of the shop, or necessarily the type of goods that made it prosperous, but the man who had formerly organised it. Of course, equally, the opposite happens, and a new owner can make a failing business profitable.

When next to a strong court card, such as the King or Queen of Coins, the 8 of Batons indicates that the questioner would do very well running their own business. If not their own, then definitely management. For some people this is the case, while others have surrounding cards showing frustration and despair because these powerful qualities have not found an outlet.

In one instance a female client had the 8 of Batons and the Queen of Coins covered by the 6 of Coins reversed and the 10 of Batons. This indicated that although she was more than capable, in fact excellent at her work, her boss used her. He requested that she did more hours for only a little more pay, and slowly sneaked in other people's workload onto her routine. "He asks me to do these things because I do them so well," she said proudly. "And I enjoy my work; but I do feel that he's taking advantage of me." He most certainly was. She was now left with the dilemma of whether to ask for an official post with more responsibility and an acknowledged higher wage, or to find a job elsewhere.

Since the fire, or Tejas, is controlled in the 8 of Batons, although it is an even number which are generally slow, this card is indicative of speed. All efficient activity runs smoothly, and therefore things get done quicker. Here there is no sudden rush followed by a lack of momentum;

or slow start and then a hasty finish. However, when the card is **reversed** all of these are suggested.

In physics water and fire don't mix, unless the fire is that of electricity, and then the water acts as a conductor and rapidly spreads the energy. Here is the brilliance of Tejas shown as a blinding flash of lightning. Although a simple interpretation, this comes up regularly for men, showing that they work as electricians or associated engineering. It also symbolises any electrics, such as those found in a house or car. So, if the question is "Are there any hidden problems with the house I intend buying?" and the 8 of Batons shows itself, then you know to advise your client to have the electrical wiring checked out before they purchase.

As bonds deal with emotions and essentially love, the 8 of Batons symbolises the beauty and motivation of love. It depicts a very natural love between two people, but does not have the same element of lust and expectation as the 3 of Batons. The 8 of Batons is controlled.

Control is a key word for this card. When upright the individual feels in control, they are orchestrating everything that unexpectedly comes up through the realm of 2 and the unmanifest. However, when **reversed**, the bondage of water stifles the fire, the unknown and unexpected overwhelm, and the individual loses control. Often clients use the phrase "I feel out of control in this situation, and usually I control my own life". It is generally outside influences that have set this course of events in motion. i.e. Problems at home affecting one's ability to work efficiently.

These phases of feeling 'out of control' are usually temporary because the client has a personality that is usually able to feel in control under adverse conditions. People who are less in control, or organised, would not generally have this card, unless it is taken reversed as a character card, or is situated close to other cards which show that they are always scatter brained, and disorganised. Often it highlights their need to be more in control and less flighty.

Key Words

Control/**reversed** out of control
Organised
Electricity
Management

Love

Bach Flower Remedy

Elm - People with this card often have great things to do with their lives, and are very capable. Elm will help strengthen them, especially, if the card appears reversed.

Vervain - for the reversed side of the card and individuals who are inclined to tackle too many jobs at once.

Toni Allen
The System of Symbols ©

The 9 of Batons

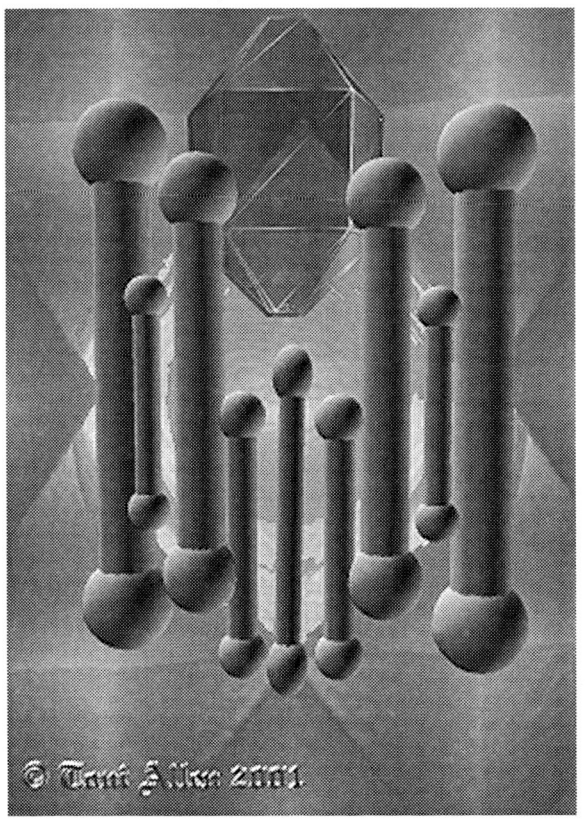

The 9 of Batons relates to fire at earth.

Fire, or Tejas, sits at the number 7, and reflects the qualities of prakriti, (Nature) at number 3.

The number 9 sits at earth (pritiwi), which is the perfect medium to reflect all five qualities of the physical world. It has smell and crystalline form of its own, the taste and bond of water, heat and form of fire, touch of air, and the sound of ether. In earth all sensations are possible.

The 9 of Batons manifests in several ways:-

To the individual it is the crystallisation of one's specific nature. One's nature is finely tuned and therefore everything is accomplished with ease. Even the little jobs one might generally avoid get done easily. As the number 9 reflects at the number 1 we have the qualities of both the

Magician and the Ace of Batons at work. A magical person who gets many things done in a bright and cheerful way. All of the bright ideas within the Ace become manifest.

When the 9 of Batons comes up in a reading we can see that the questioner has strength of character and inner warmth. Very often this is accompanied by a strong, robust body, and a healthy immune system. However, the placing of the card within the spread is very important, because this within itself is an ideal, and very few people live an ideal all of the time without some form of conflicting circumstance. I have seen examples such as the 9 of Batons in the line of the 'mind', while the 4 of Swords sits in the line representing the physical level. In such cases illness and hospitalisation have strengthened the individual's character, yet left their body weak. Without the infirmity their strength of character would not have crystallised, because in the process they found qualities within themselves which they did not previously know existed. i.e. patience, tolerance, compassion, tenacity.

When the 9 of Batons sits at the physical level in a reading it also holds the connotation of defence. Self-protection, but not aggression. Here we find strains of the Hermit. Due to the abundant qualities of Tejas at the 9 of Batons, others, who are not so adept at controlling or manifesting their own specific gifts of nature, will seek to covet qualities they do not possess when they see it manifesting in someone else. Therefore, although the 9 of Batons is in itself a very beneficial card, it has the power to invoke envy, jealousy, desire and anger in others less fortunate. Self-mastery means that we can accomplish many things specific to our own nature. For some it is not their path to master these specific talents, and yet they still hanker after these fruits whether physical, emotional or spiritual. Therefore this card also symbolises the need for psychic self-defence.

I recall a reading I did for a woman who was on the spiritual path. In her initial layout she had the 9 of Batons crossed by the 2 of Batons at the centre. Other cards suggested that she had done a lot of work on herself and was now authoritative within her field of past life regressions and spiritual healing. The 2 of Batons represented her teacher, whom she had studied with for many years. "She feels that I've surpassed her," said the woman. "She keeps putting me down and telling me not to do work without consulting her first. Then, if I have her sit in with a client it's as if she wants to take my energy away...but I can't give her my abilities." Her tutor had become like a sponge, wanting to claw back the woman's talents, as if she had given something of herself away by teaching her; and yet all she had truly done was guide her student towards her own inner light.

The 9 of Batons also symbolises the beauty on Earth. Crystal energy falls into this realm. Within the Earth's structure natural minerals have been heated to extreme temperatures and then cooled, creating the wonderful, often geometric shapes of the crystals. Thus the crystal is Tejas set in physical form for us to see and amaze at. Walk into any shop selling crystals, (you may include jewellery shops in this imagery) and you'll note that immediately their light shines out, uplifting the soul and bringing a gasp of awe. Many people now use crystals in various forms of therapy. The magic of number 7 is held in their multifarious forms, each crystal holding its light within a perfect construction; each mineral forming its own unique shape and structure. Although all crystals are manifested at 9 (earth) and hold the beauty and light of 7 (Tejas) it is possible to observe how each individual crystal vibrates with a different energy. Some have more of the quality of air, while others more water, fire or ether. An expert crystal therapist will note the crystals that an individual chooses, and from this be able to assess which energy vibrations they are in tune with, or which they lack and therefore require to assist with healing.

With the above it is vital to remember that the number 7 (Tejas) is very important. Tejas gives light, and with light we are able to see. Although ether is there we cannot see it. Air is there too, but we cannot see that either. Fire is the first element which we are able to witness with our eyes. We have light from the Sun, Moon, stars and lamp lights; and the earth reflects this light. The first visible manifestations are the Earth itself in the form of rocks, stones, mud, clay, minerals and crystals.

When the 9 of Batons is **reversed** in a reading it symbolises that the questioner has temporarily lost their way and that they are uncertain of their own abilities, and that they lack strength or courage. (Note the correlation between 9 and the 11 of the Strength card.) Surrounding cards may indicate a stronger personality holding them back, and all the while their own nature is weakened they cannot make the right progress for their soul's journey in this life time. I have often observed this for clients when one partner in a marriage (or permanent relationship) dominates the other.

There are various underlying reasons behind this; including, brutality, fear of being left alone if the partner excels and 'becomes somebody', fear of being outshone, or simply a desire to crystallise the partner at the age and proficiency at which they fell in love with them. The dominated individual, as represented by the reversed 9 of Batons, will still function, and efficiently, but procrastinate, nearly to the point of stand still at times, and often spend much of their time doing many, many things, all of which are irrelevant to their soul's true purpose. The little things get done and the large game plan gets left behind.

On the material plane the reversed card may depict any physical weakness, however it does not generally arise from apathy but a physical debility, i.e. a weakened muscle or bone. There is also the connotation of not being as strong as one used to be, which may arise from age, overwork etc. It also includes what I call 'brain fag' a sort of mental exhaustion, as if one's fire is all burnt out, and one's get up and go has got up and gone. It is not the same hopelessness as at the 7 of Batons reversed, because the 9 of Batons person still has a genuine desire for life, and is often frustrated if ill health holds up their progress. They want to get better, but sometimes so passionately that they burn themselves out because they refuse to give in and rest.

Key Words

Strength
Strong body/immune system
Self-defence/psychic self-defence
Crystals/Crystal Healer
Reversed
Mental weakness/tired body/weak immune system
Tiredness causes through the dominance of another

Bach Flower Remedy

Hornbeam – for mental fatigue

Toni Allen
The System of Symbols ©

The 10 of Batons

The 10 of Batons relates to fire at 1 with 0.

At 10 the same self which is 1 stands with the unmanifest Prakriti by its side. The 1 at number 10 embodies the nine manifestations within it. The creation starts with 1 and at 10 it again stands as 1 with all the nine manifestations.

As you will already have learnt from your study of the Major Cards, and other material, the number 10 symbolises us standing at the end, or beginning of a cycle. We can either go back through 9, 8, 7, 6, 5, 4, 3, 2, to reach 1 and unity, or we can go forward to the 1 of the next cycle. Depending upon what has occurred on our journey to the number 10 we either go back along a karmic path, go forward, having made new karma, or go forward having dealt with some of our karma.

The Batons relate to fire, and to Prakriti.

Toni Allen
The System of Symbols ©

The question which arises at the 10 of Batons is have we developed our own nature? Or have we succumbed to inbred, or karmic conceptions, of what we are supposed to do with our lives?

Let me relate a story to you. Ten people were going across the country to another land, and they had to cross a river. The river was shallow, but the currents swift. They managed to cross the river, and after reaching the other shore they wanted to make sure that no one had drowned. Each of them lined the others up and found the total of only nine; for none of them would count himself. They were sorry and disturbed. A holy man was passing along the bank and seeing them so miserable asked the reason for their worries. They explained their story. The holy man saw their difficulty, and foolishness, so he asked all of them to line up. With his stick he hit one and separated him from the others. The next one he hit twice, and then separated him. Likewise he continued until he hit the tenth man ten times and declared them ten and assured them that none were lost.

In Vedantic literature this traditional story is told to illustrate that the tenth is yourself.

It's a story which is so pertinent to the 10 of Batons. How often have we forgotten about ourselves...in more ways than one? How often have we placed everyone's dinner on the table, sat down and then realised that we've left ours in the kitchen! How often have we fussed and cared for family members during a time of grief or crisis, only to long for some compassion ourselves at the end of the day because we too are having a hard time?

How often have we sacrificed? Men tend to sacrifice the type of work they would really enjoy doing, and keep the job they already have, so that they can continue to support their family. Women often sacrifice career to raise a family. Many people sacrifice time, energy, and love. In the physical world we all have needs, and yet we sacrifice these needs as if our own desires are unholy, or unacceptable, or unnecessary.

In the spiritual world we all have karma to fulfil. We all have things which we, as unique individuals, require to act out in order to learn and grow. Whether these things are 'good', or 'bad' is irrelevant...we still need to experience them.

The 10 of Batons symbolises our personal energy, or nature, absorbed and used by others, which thus inhibits our own progress. In readings it shows

Toni Allen
The System of Symbols ©

itself as feeling burdened and often used by others. There is no space left for our own unique work in this lifetime, which leaves us feeling tired and worn out. A common complaint of people who have the 10 of Batons predominant in a reading is their inability to say 'No'.

Everybody has their own inner sixth sense of what they ought to be doing, and it is when they reach a state of mental and physical exhaustion that they realise something has to change. I have seen the 10 of batons in the following situations, but there are far too many to recount every possibility.

It came up on one occasion for a middle-aged woman whose daughter had just had a baby, which was her first grandchild. She had offered her daughter some baby-sitting and help, so that she and her husband could still go out occasionally and maintain a social life. "I've done my child rearing," the woman said despondently. "I had started a part time course at college, but I've just given it up, I haven't got the energy. My daughter brings the little one over all the time. I love the baby dearly but now I never get a clear day. During the week she wants to pop out shopping on her own...and takes hours over it, and at the weekends she comes up with her husband as a family...and I cook a Sunday lunch." The woman did not know how to tell her daughter that she did not want to look after her granddaughter so frequently. She did not wish to be thought selfish. "But I have my own life to lead, why can't she see that?"

In other readings I have often seen the 10 of Batons for people who do lots of things for lots of people. They baby sit their friends' children, they run their friends around in their car and they have their friends over for coffee when they themselves wanted to get on with some study or relaxation. Their energy is dumped on and absorbed by others. Everyone's demands become a burden...and yet they still don't know how to say, "Sorry, I'm busy right now."

Sometimes it's the family who create the burden. Some people become the mainstay of a family even if they are not the matriarchal or patriarchal figure. They run around after mum, dad, brother, and sister, sorting out their messes one by one, or simply being there for them at the drop of a hat. Yes, but these sound like wonderful people, I hear you comment. Indeed they are, but not to themselves. Some people use their time continually helping others in order to run away from what they really need to be getting on with. It also means that the people they help do not take on their own responsibilities and that they in turn do not fulfil their lives. Some people continually help others because they simply don't know how to take their own energy back by saying 'No'. Others are so busy doing other peoples work in life that they don't even realise that they have their own path, or special goals to achieve.

Sometimes life itself deals someone a blow and they suddenly find they have no time for themselves, as in cases where a husband or wife is abruptly hospitalised, or infirmed. These people come to me at a point where the burden feels too great and they are so worn out that they don't know what to do. Often when I suggest that they ask a relative to help out, or pay for some care, they believe it is wrong to ask for help, or selfish to want one night out a week away from it all to refresh their spirit. And yet once they have sought the help and taken just a few hours out each week for themselves they feel so much stronger and revitalised. On her second visit one female client, who was single-handedly nursing her elderly mother at home, said to me, "My neighbour comes in one night a week now and I go to an art class. When I get home we have coffee together and chat about what I've painted. It really is so refreshing and makes me feel alive again. She comes in during the week sometimes too, but not often, and I don't take advantage...after all I don't want her being burdened by me...do I!" This client had worked through her 10 of Batons and **reversed** the card in her second reading.

The 10 of batons is also common in the spreads of business people. They take on all of the responsibility for the running of a company or department, and never delegate responsibility to others.   This means that they get tired and worn out, and that others who wish to grow and mature within the framework of the business are not given a chance to cultivate their own potential. In this instance everyone gets bogged down and frustrated.

With the 10 of Batons the energy of 1 (Ace of batons) stands with the unmanifest Prakriti by its side.   Thus we see that our nature has more to learn about what is unmanifest within us. Some people feel that they have spent life time after life time doing for others and never achieving expression of their true talents. Their light has never shone through. It is only by the recognition of this fact that they can do anything to change their karmic pattern.

Toni Allen
The System of Symbols ©

There are two types of 10 of Batons people. Those for whom it is the above described karmic pattern, and those for whom it is a temporary circumstance brought about by a specific situation. Surrounding cards will give key indications as to which it may be. i.e. next to the 3 of Coins reversed suggests someone with a weak and subservient nature, thus it may be karmic. Next to the King of Coins suggests someone with a clear sense of who they are, who has taken on too much responsibility at work; a situation which can be easily remedied with reorganisation.

This, perhaps, is why the 10 of Batons **reversed** is such a wonderful card. It depicts a time of unburdening the self, of throwing off restrictions and taking back one's own unique power. It is also a time of giving back responsibility to others.

When one's own energy is released the feeling is of freedom and expansion. The following are just a few examples of the 10 of Batons reversed as seen in practice.

For one woman it came up to represent the first time she stood up to her husband and said 'No'. "No" she was not going to run around after his mother when she finished work, and then return home and cook his tea, and then do the ironing and lay out his fresh clothes for the morning. "I feel wonderful," she said. "I feel as if I've been his unpaid slave for so long now. He didn't take it too well, but at least he's realised that his mother is his responsibility, and that if she needs help that he'll have to put in a little more effort himself."

For one young man it came up to show that at last he had had words with his boss about the excessive workload he had been given. "Slowly I've been given everyone else's dirty little jobs to do," he explained. "But I spoke to him the other day and he's agreed to employ a part time office junior to take up some of the work load. It means that I can now get on with the job I'm paid to do."

In several cases I have seen the 10 reversed where up until this point the client has been nursing an elderly relative who has recently passed away. Most people describe it as a sudden release from a burden. Be warned, this does not mean that every time the card arises for someone who is a carer that his or her charge will depart this physical plane. As described above, some people release themselves by getting help, or placing an elderly or sick relative within a nursing home.

Key Words

Carrying responsibility for other
Burdened.
Failing to achieve one's purpose in life through doing too many things for others
A need to say 'No'.
Reversed
Saying "No"
Delegating
Making more time for oneself

Bach Flower Remedy

Oak – Oak types tend to be incredible plodders and never complain, even when overworked.

Toni Allen
The System of Symbols ©

The Ace of Cups

Cups relate to the element water and therefore to the number 8.

On a Marseille pack the Ace of Cups generally has a very Gothic style and is reminiscent of a baptism font. Many traditional churches have fonts with a very similar design and structure, and here we find a strong connection between the Cup and the vessel that holds the Holy Water, with which the infant will be anointed to bless him, or her, into the faith. The Christening ceremony, and likewise a baptism ceremony, joins the individual and the church. A deep union is forged, and a lasting bond created. Thus we come to witness the bonding quality of water used symbolically, especially in Christian ritual. Even those who later decide not to follow the faith, when asked which religion they follow, often initially answer "I was Christened into the Church of England", or something similar. It's as if they need to acknowledge their early bonding with the church.

Christianity is steeped in symbolism connected with water. Water represents bonds and attachment, and above all else the love which keeps people together. Christ's teaching is filled with actions of love and healing, his entire purpose to spread the art of compassion and understanding, and raise people's consciousness. Not only have we been left much in the scriptures attributed to water, but also in the continuing myths, especially those which appertain to the Cup itself as the Holy Grail.

The Holy Grail is probably the most famous Cup in history. Legend states that this was the cup used by Christ during the Last Supper. Later Joseph of Aramethea caught Christ's blood in it while he hung on the cross. Then he is said to have brought the Grail to Glastonbury, and it became the object of the quest for King Arthur's Knights.

Christ sacrificed himself so that mankind's sins could be forgiven. Thus the cup, and therefore the Grail, which held His life's blood, first symbolically at the Last Supper, and then in fact at the Crucifixion, has come to represent love and forgiveness. Here, however, we do not find the cup filled with water, but with wine. Wine symbolises fertility and abundance, as it is made from lush grapes that hang in large bunches. When the wine is transformed into blood it symbolises the life force itself, and it is the heart that pumps the blood around the body. Therefore we find the Cup associated with all of these attributes.

The story of the quest for the Holy Grail goes on to portray the Grail in a further light. This exert is taken from "King Arthur and his Knights of the Round Table", by Roger Lancelyn Green.

"Then Naciens the Divine Hermit came and took the Grail in his hands and after he had prayed, he brought it to Galahad and said:

'Holy Knight of God, I who have been the Priest of the Grail these many years give the Holy Grail into your hands that all things may be fulfilled. Now, Sir Galahad, my trust is ended, let me depart in peace. For I, many years ago, sinned deeply against the good Joseph of Arimethea who brought these wonders into Britain. And when he died this penance was laid on me: that I should live beyond the span of mortal man to be the Priest of the Grail until the coming of Sir Galahad the Good.'"

Here we find associations with the bonding qualities of water, and the connotation of a karmic debt to be paid. Naciens speaks of his sin;

Toni Allen
The System of Symbols ©

and his penance binds him to wait for Sir Galahad. Likewise we also find purity as Galahad was said to be without sin, and consequently the only knight able to find the Grail.

The Ace of Cups holds all of the meanings mentioned above and during a reading we may interpret it as follows:-

When upright the card suggests love, kindness and abundance. It is not a card of being in love, but a card depicting one's ability to love, and be open hearted and warm spirited towards others. Many things happen in our lives which threaten to block the flow of our love and compassion, and often I have seen the Ace of Cups come up for people who have been through extremely testing times, and yet still have the capacity to forgive and experience joy.

When the Ace of Cups is **reversed** we find the opposite. Throughout the Tarot we find the Cups illustrating the need to refresh and balance the emotions. At 14 with Temperance we see the figure pouring the water from one cup to another and back again. While at 17 with the Star Card we see the woman emptying out the cups into a stream. The Cup, or heart, cannot stay full of stagnant water, as it blocks the flow of the life force. If we stay bonded to old feelings, thoughts and ideas we become listless and dull, and there is no room for new emotional experiences. Part of the Vedic teaching is the art of non attachment. To act and yet leave no residue. To not become attached to the result of one's work or other activities. Thus the heart is left clear, and samskara is not built up. When we hold on, we are creating samskara, which will re-emerge in later life times and bind us to the same desires and motivations. Thus when the Ace of Cups is shown **reversed** during a reading we can see that the questioner is holding on to old attachments which are no longer fulfilling. These create limitations and inhibitions, as well as continued pain and suffering. Below are a few examples of how I have seen the Ace of Cups **reversed** portrayed in practice:-

1) Inability to love again after the break up of a relationship. This is due to the questioner still loving the ex-partner, or that they feel they will never love again, or that they feel they do not want to love again. Many people feel that to close down the heart's emotions is safer than re-experiencing the pain of rejection and suffering.

2) Lack of joy due to having been through many traumatic experiences.

3) An immediate reaction to bereavement. Often, in time, the questioner is able to realign him or herself.

4) Stuck in negative emotional experiences from childhood, especially where the family were not 'cuddly' and did not show affection easily.

Healers often talk about the heart centre, or maybe the Solar Plexus, being blocked, and this is exactly what the reversed Ace of Cups signifies. In physical terms it can represent lack of joy, and in some cases problems with the blood, as the heart is the centre for distributing the blood around the body. Anaemia is one possibility. Numbness, lack of feeling, and a sense of not belonging to the world and its pleasures can also occur.

Key Words

Love
Joy
Pleasure
Happiness
Open Hearted
Reversed
Broken Hearted
Hard Hearted
Inability to experience love
Pain and suffering through attachments to people or things we love
Inhibitions in experiencing love e.g. timidity, shyness

Bach Flower Remedy

Holly - For those who experience an absence of love, from both within and outside themselves.
Star of Bethlehem – For those whose lack of joy is due to trauma and shock.

Toni Allen
The System of Symbols ©

The 2 of Cups

The 2 of Cups relates to water at the unmanifest.

Number 2 is the state of the undifferentiated or unmanifest and, on the other scale, it comes under the realm of water. The unmanifest is the bank, or store room, where all things and forms lie hidden, and manifest when the time calls.

Water creates bonds. It is only the bonds which keep matter together. It is called Sneha in Sanskrit. The Sneha is the bond between things and people. It is a sort of love which keeps them together.

With the 2 of cups we have a cross resonance due to water sitting at 8. It is very much like the Ace of Cups being "doubled up". Hence it is the card of "falling in love". It is attraction. The water creates a bond between us and the other person and an instant recognition takes place. Because this feeling comes from the unmanifest, which sits at the causal level, often it is very hard to understand what the attraction is all about, especially when it happens suddenly. It's the stuff movies are made of. Eyes meet across a crowded room, senses prickle and something shifts inside us. There's a sense of compulsion. We have to know this person, move closer, speak with them. The first bond of love is established.

The 2 of Cups, however, is not always as simple, or as romantic as this; although often it can be. A sudden bonding can take place in many situations. We may even have known the person for a while, and then one day we see them and it feels different, as if something has come from deep within our unconscious and whispered, "I love this person".

It is not only the love link between man and woman which is represented here. I recall a woman questioner who came to me with concerns over her fourth pregnancy. With three children already she wondered if she had enough love to encompass another child. After the 3 of Batons, indicating the birth, the 2 of Cups was turned, showing an instant, unconscious bonding with the child. She doubted my prediction. Some weeks after the baby was born she telephoned to say that, quite against what she had believed possible before, she now found that she loved her new daughter dearly. "My love just flowed out to her," she said laughing. "I couldn't stop myself."

For some it is a karmic attraction. Old bonds rekindle and "fate" calls them towards each other. Often the Justice card (number 8) is close by when this is the case indicating that the couple were connected in a previous incarnation. People have multifarious views and preconceptions on "destiny" and karma. For some it's a straightforward. "I don't know why I love him (her)". "I never thought I'd meet someone", is also a common scenario, along with "Why did I have to fall in love with him (her) now, when the time just isn't right and I have all these problems." With these "fated" attractions it can either be a blissful reunion of two "old flames", or an apparently cruel twist that one ever became involved with the person in the first place. Some people talk of "karmic debt" and truly believe that they are with their partner due to some debt or re-alignment of power that requires working on in this lifetime. I have one client who stays with her partner for the sole purpose of working through personal karmic ties with him; even though the "love" went out of the relationship a long time ago, the bond is still very strong.

If what appears to be a karmic relationship proves difficult, and many questions arise concerning, "Why am I in this relationship?" "Why's this happening to me?" and so on, then it may be an appropriate time for the questioner to go for a far life regression to add insight to the situation.

As the 2 relates to duality and water to bonds, then the 2 of Cups can also be that very strong feeling that we have "met our other half" or discovered our soul mate.

The 2 of Cups speaks of unconditional love and indicates that the questioner is unable to stop loving that person regardless of how they are being treated. This is true as long as the bonds remain, and therefore for some it can also be "blind love", because in their present situation they are totally unable to switch off their feelings.

Loving someone does not, of course, always mean that love is returned. The position and placement of the card within the spread will shed light on this. e.g. If the 2 of Cups appears in the line of "the mind" are there any cards at the "physical level" to indicate reciprocation?

Surrounding cards will also show what form of love a person is attracted to. With variations there are basically two type of "falling in love". There is the passionate, lustful, possessive, sparks flying type; and alternatively the deep compatibility which grows from a true friendship, and companionship into love. The latter does not mean that the couple did not initially "fall in love", purely that their relationship is based on being friends first. With the passionate type of love, cards such as the 3 of Batons and the 3 of Swords will indicate lust and jealousy; physical attraction and sex also playing a major role. Friendship love is consolidated by the 6 of Batons; and these couples often start off liking the other's personality, yet may find themself unsure as to how physically attractive they find the body on offer. "I thought he was a wonderful man, but I've always gone for the slim, athletic types. Short and plump is drastically different", is a characteristic comment. These relationships are based on deep emotions, not flash in the pan infatuation. However, neither of these are to be decried, as both are important parts of an individual's development.

The 2 of Cups can also mean desire, as in any "I want" situation, whether towards clothes, food, property etc. Close to cards indicating work it shows that the questioner loves their job, while next to cards of opportunity it means that it's an attractive proposition.

Toni Allen
The System of Symbols ©

One student drew the 2 of Cups as her "card for the day" while studying with me; and when I suggested that she had fallen in love she flatly denied it. Not only was she one of my 'older' students, but her daughter was also in the same class! A happily married woman...we thought. And so she was. We went through the notes she had made for the day when she had drawn the 2 of Cups. Suddenly her eyes lit up as she spoke about a painting she'd seen in an art gallery. She laughed. "I was deeply attracted to it," she said "I wanted to bring it home, it was just so wonderful....it moved my spirit"

Remember:- the 2 of Cups as a single card depicts the initial stage of falling in love, or instant attraction. By itself it does not symbolise any ongoing relationship with the object of one's desire. Therefore the surrounding cards must always be read carefully to establish the circumstances, and whether or not a more permanent relationship will grow out of the attraction. The student in my earlier example loved the painting, but was unable to form a permanent relationship by hanging it on her own wall.

The 2 of Cups **reversed** can be interpreted as literally the opposite of all the above:-
Falling out of love/ finding something, or someone unattractive/ refusing to love/ disliking the attention of someone/ broken hearted and so on.

One male client who had the 2 of Cups reversed had recently embarked on a whirlwind romance. Initially he had had the 2 of Cups upright, but within weeks of them meeting they had started to share a house together, and suddenly everything changed. "She made some very strange phone calls," he said. "And she had a particularly telling scar on her body which suggested that she'd had a child by caesarean. When I questioned her she refused to give me a straight answer. I felt I could no longer trust her, and yes, without total honesty I fell out of love." The strong bond he had initially felt was completely destroyed through this situation and he even said that not only did he no longer love her, but also that he now found her physically unattractive."

Key words

Attraction/Falling in love/Bonding/Soul mate
Reversed - Dislike/No longer attracted to someone or something

Toni Allen
The System of Symbols ©

The 3 of Cups

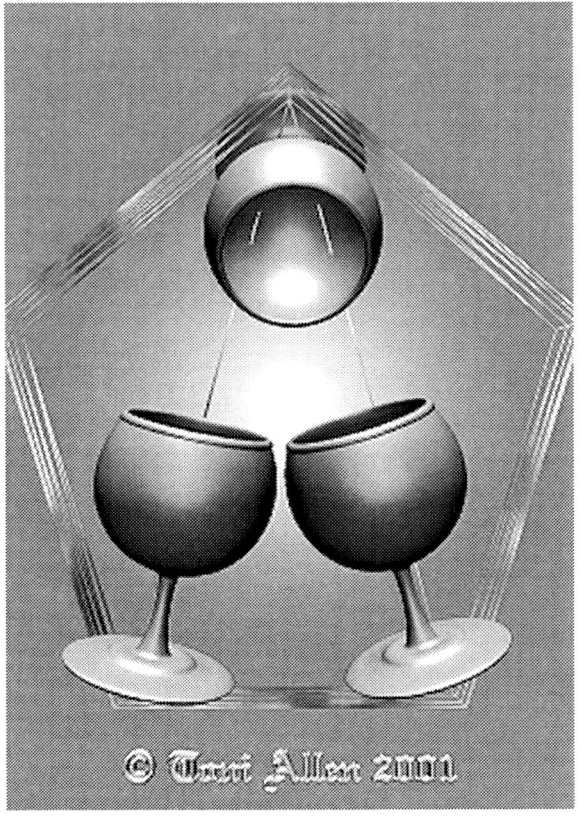

The 3 of Cups relates to water at nature (prakriti)

Prakriti, or nature, sits at the number 3, while its reflection is the number 7, which relates to Tejas, or fire.

Water stands for the bonds which keep people together. When the Cups of water sit at the number 3 of nature, it generally represents marriage....the natural course of events when two people wish to commit their union to a formal, or religious bonding. The Christian marriage ceremony recognises this by usually having words along the lines of "let these two who have been bound together....". I am by no means an expert in all forms of marriage ceremony, but I think that we can all recognise that two people go through a ceremony of some form or another when they wish to say to each other that they are, from that point on, bound for life in a love union.

When upright in a reading the 3 of Cups therefore means marriage, or the desire to marry.

Before I go further it is important to acknowledge that as times move on, and cultures change, that our interpretations for the cards must come into line with the age in which we live. From experience alone I have come to see that when the 3 of Cups is upright it often means that the couple are married, and have some document to say so, while when the card is **reversed** it means that they live together as common law man and wife, but are equally committed to each other. I have also see the **upright** card signify couples who consider each other a life partner, even though they do not co-habit, or have any formal marriage certificate. Thus judgement of the card must only be made by considering surrounding cards.

The 3 of Cups is a very simple card to interpret, but a few examples may add clarity as to how it appears in readings.

When placed somewhere within the initial spread of the reading, surrounding cards will show whether the marriage/long term relationship has problems, or is the mainstay of the questioner's life.

For example:- next to the Page of Cups reversed possible infidelity, or disloyalty, from one partner or the other.

Next to the 5 of Batons disputes, or arguments within the relationship, but not necessarily directly caused by the couple. For example, friction at work is causing irritability at home.

It is only with a full understanding of all the cards that an accurate picture can be formed.

When the 3 of Cups is placed further ahead in the future it can refer to the individual's desire to marry and have a family at some time. It is not uncommon for me to see young females, who currently have no regular boyfriend in their life, genuinely desire to get married and have a family. Sometimes they feel that they will never find the right person, and the 3 of Cups shows their "wish" somewhere in the future, when they hope to find fulfilment.

If the questioner is already married (or living as common law man and wife) the 3 of Cups in the future may refer to their partner giving support during hard times, or their desire to start a family and make the bonds between them stronger.

Occasionally the card reversed shows "hiccups" in the marriage, but nothing very serious. It is the type of difficulty experienced by the having of children and describes the newly formed 'young family', getting used to the demands that the new bonds between husband, wife and child create.

As yet I have never seen the 3 of Cups as at all malevolent. It is usually a positive card, although it does have its quirks. I have seen it on numerous occasions when two people are having an affair. Generally it is a female questioner and the reading has already established that she is having an affair with a married man. Suddenly the 3 of Cups will appear in answer to some question or another, showing that the man now feels that she is his new wife, and that the bond between them is far stronger than between himself and his official wife.

The 3 of Cups does not place any kind of restriction on the two individuals within the relationship. There is no barrier, or censure, to race, colour, or sexuality. I have seen it equally in the reading of a homosexual as his 'wish' card for a committed relationship, as I have for heterosexual couples. We all search for our helpmeet in life, that one special person who will be bound to us for life, whatever our preferences.

Key words

Marriage/living together
The desire for marriage
A relationship in which two people are strongly committed
Reversed
Minor difficulties within established relationships.

Toni Allen
The System of Symbols ©

The 4 of Cups

The 4 of Cups relates to water at Ahamkara or the feeling of "I".

Ahamkara:- Self-will, the ego mask, the principle in man which makes him feel separate from others.

As water relates to bonding, while its counterpart 2 relates to duality; at the 4 of Cups the feelings of separation of Ahamkara are heightened, and the soul potential for unity is disturbed, thus creating emotional isolation.

It is by no means the same mental anguish as the 4 of Swords, but is experienced as an emotional detachment or rejection, either of others or from others.

Water creates bonds. At the 2 of Cups we find the initial bonds of attraction, while at the 4 of Cups the flow of energy from one to another has been turned inwards, creating self-love, or a need for self protection.

Toni Allen
The System of Symbols ©

There are several distinct types of interpretation for the 4 of Cups depending upon surrounding cards.

In relationships it is indicative of boredom or rejection. Where marital problems can be seen in a reading the 4 of Cups will symbolise the coldness of one partner to another. It is that strange, icy feeling when you put your arms around someone else and feel nothing coming back from them; no warmth, no love, no emotion. It's as if the other person has switched off and we are left feeling rejected. In a reading one must analyse why the person is acting cold, or distant. e.g. the Queen of Swords might indicate a woman cutting herself off from people for sexual, mental or emotional reasons; the 10 of Batons indicates overwork and not having time for any pleasures in life; while the King of Swords might suggest a very austere, Victorian outlook to life, in which cuddles and closeness are not an acceptable part of every day life.

You will have to assess from surrounding cards whether the questioner is the one in need of emotional support, or the one refusing to give it. Very often the 4 depicts a relationship in which neither partner is prepared to offer the cup of love any more because they fear that it will not be filled by the other. Rejection plays a large part; and with rejection all kinds of emotional games take place, such as "if I think you're going to reject me then I'll reject you first, so that I don't get hurt." Love, in the true sense of the word, is unconditional. We love our children and our parents, even if we don't like them! With the 4 of Cups conditions and limits are placed upon the giving of love to another; and therefore if people do not act, or react, as expected, or wished, then a refusal to reciprocate automatically falls into place.

Selfishness, greed and an over demanding nature can all come under the 4 of Cups. Water creates bonds, and bonds create limitation; coupled with a strong sense of "I Am" the individual nature turns inwards. In severe cases it depicts neurosis. In a small child the repeated phrase is "nobody loves me" and for an adult we find the "needy child", who can easily feel rejected and snubbed as soon as they don't get exactly what they want.

In some readings it is apparent that the 4 of Cups has come about through a logical chain of events, e.g. in a situation where one falls in love with someone who is married. The desire for emotional and physical contact is very strong, and yet these feelings are deliberately stifled due to moral or social reasons.

Our first association is with the physical body, and this sits at the number 4, with the feeling of "I AM". The 4 of Cups therefore is also associated with one's physical emotional needs; the simple human need for a cuddle. Many clients refer to either their partner shunning them when they try to cuddle, or that they themselves are turning way. "I can't bear him to touch me" is a common phrase. It is not, however, to be automatically associated with sex. Desire for cuddles and comfort, a feeling of warmth or reassurance, is not the same as feelings of sexuality.

When the 4 of Cups is close to such cards as The Empress, or 3 of Batons reversed it indicates that the questioner is still very much in need of physical and emotional comfort; and that if they are not receiving it from an expected source that they will ultimately seek fulfilment elsewhere, for example, in a new relationship....or even in chocolate!

The theme of boredom and unfulfillment can also be associated with work situations. Quite simply the questioner is fed up with their job and needs to either find a more testing occupation or revitalise their enthusiasm for their present employment.

Reversed the card symbolises the initial steps taken to break away from the bonds of limitation and an attempt to experience new emotions. I saw this clearly for a man whose wife had left him for someone else. The 4 of Cups, along with other cards, signified her return and his ability to hold out his arms and to love her once again, even after all of the hurt and heartbreak. At the time of the reading he was adamant that, should she return, he would be totally unable to show her any affection considering what she had done to him. However, some months later he returned for another reading, saying that she was back and that he loved her more than ever.

The first steps to re-establishing emotional communication can be very awkward and fraught with highly charged feelings; yet, as the man above proved, it is possible, even in the most damaged relationships. I recall one client who had not seen her estranged mother for many years. Currently her mother was ill in hospital and the 4 of Cups reversed showed a reunion. On her next visit the client described how she had gone to her mother's bedside, held hands and that they had both slowly wept without saying a word. Her meeting with her mother had encompassed the physical side with the hand-holding* and the watery emotional side with the tears. (* Note 4s relationship to 6, which is the realm of air, the instrument for which is the hands)

Reversed the 4 of Cups can be a very tearful card. The bottled up emotions are released. However, closely observe the surrounding cards to gauge whether the questioner is being constantly tearful in private, because this again indicates an inability to express one's emotions within a relationship. e.g next to the 4 of Swords (isolation)

For some clients the urge to be touched is so acute that a positive expression of this fundamental yet powerful need is to go for massage or aromatherapy. Many clients have reported back that by going for massage they have managed to nurture themselves in a very positive manner by gratifying the bodies need for physical contact of a non sexual nature.

Key words

Feelings of rejection. Either being rejected or rejecting.
Lack of cuddles and comfort.
"Poor me"
Boredom.
Reversed
The initial stage of accepting love and comfort again.
Massage

Bach Flower Remedy

Chicory – For those times when in need of **constant** comfort – the needy child.

Toni Allen
The System of Symbols ©

The 5 of Cups

The 5 of Cups relates to water at ether (Akasha)

    Water creates the bonds; while ether carries sound, and stands as a bridge which joins the sensual world to the mental and causal realms.

    With the 5 of Cups we find the bonds of water holding the impressions coming into the ether from the mental and causal level; or those which are travelling back to unity from the sensual world.

    It may be a somewhat old fashioned phrase, but "feel the vibes" is exactly what the 5 of Cups is referring to. Atmosphere is a key word.

    The bonds of water trap consciousness in various ways, and one of the most easily recognisable is when it occurs in the fabric of a building, or place. Depending upon the original input we experience different sensations. If we take two highly different atmospheres, such as that found within the walls of a church (or any other religious temple) and that found within a dungeon, we can quickly recognise the two qualities simply by the inner response we experience. Any building which is constantly used for prayer or other religious activity has a very fine and satvic quality about it. The walls become impregnated by a high consciousness and generally the feeling we experience on stepping inside is one of peace. * By comparison the dungeon emits feelings of anger, frustration, danger, violence, hopelessness and death. When entering a dungeon in an old castle, even though it was last used many years previously, we are still able to sense a cold, creepy sensation and come away feeling oppressed. Dungeons are generally filled with Tamas.

* I feel I must note here the comments of one client who, when I put this scenario to her in relation to certain sensations she was experiencing in connection with her house, stated emphatically that she hated the atmosphere in churches and they made her feel uncomfortable and sick. This led on to us discussing various factors around her possible past incarnations in religious orders, and how she was replaying a similar role of master/devotee with her current husband. In both cases it was subservience she was trying to break away from, and currently to stop seeing her husband as an absolute authority in her life.

This, to me, was a prime lesson in atmospheres affecting different people in varying ways, for all sorts of reasons. There is no right or wrong to any sensation. However, those which do not fit the "norm", such as this example of satva making someone feel uncomfortable, do require further investigation.

These atmospheres can be almost physical in nature, and some individuals are so sensitive that any form of constant bombardment of a negative nature can lower their resistance to illness.

During a reading the most common way of seeing the 5 of Cups is as a bad atmosphere in the home, or work environment. Mostly it refers to the home because generally the questioner is more highly attached and has stronger bonds to it. Any couple going through a stressful period in their relationship might experience this. The atmosphere feels fine until the other half returns from work. It's as if he or she brings the atmosphere with them.

In some cases this is precisely what happens. Someone comes home, we call out "hello", but there's no response. Goose pimples ripple up our spine. We're so certain we heard them come in; and now we know it's going to be one of 'those' times again. We literally 'pick up' what the other person is emitting. Every situation and atmosphere has its root cause. Here are a few common examples.

1) The other person has been for a job interview and been turned down...again.

2) They've been to the pub and so violence or verbal abuse is anticipated....which needs only one wrong word to spark it off.

3) Proper communication broke down weeks ago and now the other person won't say anything other than mundane platitudes, even though everyone is bursting to have a row and clear the air.

In many cases the 5 of Cups indicates a marital breakdown in which the atmosphere has become so strained that the questioner knows that neither party can continue to live like it. Always look closely at surrounding cards to see what pressures might be causing the atmosphere. e.g. Long term unemployment or the strain of drug abuse or alcoholism in the home. When looking at the home we must always take into account the affect children have within it. The husband and wife may be in total harmony, yet find it difficult to live in ease with a screaming baby or a confused teenager. Likewise consider the possibility that others may bring the atmosphere with them when visiting.

As always there are many ways of looking in and around the meaning of a card depending upon the surrounding cards, or the question posed.

Trapped sound, or trapped consciousness, can also refer to 'a haunting'. The atmosphere left by a deceased partner is the 5 of Cups; and so is that creepy feeling that 'someone is there.' With departed loved ones an individual's reaction can swing from 'I feel my husband is so close, even though he's gone. It's such a comfort,' to 'I can't sleep, I wish he'd let me go.'

If the 5 of Cups comes up next to cards relating to a newly purchased home it may be that strange, or unpleasant things occurred there which left the atmosphere. Some people don't mind a haunted house, while others can become deeply disturbed. The haunting can relate to sensing anger or violence committed by the previous occupants, feeling uncomfortable in a room in which someone has died, or actually seeing a spirit.

One man who came to see me always had the 5 of Cups depicting

Toni Allen
The System of Symbols ©

his home. Ever since he had bought the house he had sensed a strange atmosphere. In time every relationship he had within that home broke down, starting off by his wife leaving him. I saw him over a period of some three years, starting initially shortly after his wife's departure. Two girlfriends came and went and then he decided to rent the house out. Every couple who rented the house split up, resulting in him constantly having to find new tenants. He then started to feel guilty and decided that he couldn't keep "doing" this to people. "That house is jinxed I tell you", he said one day. "I've had mediums in there trying to sort it out, a priest, you name it....but it's still the same." The last I heard of him he had decided to return to live in the house himself....on his own!

The 5 of Cups also symbolises the psychic "gateway" used by mediums to contact the spirit world.

What I write next is in no way intended to upset or devalue any mediums or psychics, who do highly valued work when contacting spirits, or souls, of the deceased. The popular film "ghost", starring Patrick Swayze in the lead role, illustrates the point I want to make. In the film the dead man's spirit is trapped between here and the after-life because he still wishes to protect and help his girlfriend. With the aid of a medium he achieves this and is then free to 'pass on'. The 5 of Cups refers to these 'trapped souls' whom mediums contact. Something emotional has bound their souls to the physical plane and holds them in the etheric level, making it difficult and painful for them to cross the bridge into the causal level from which they will journey on to be reborn. Interestingly people often see ghosts of young people killed in motor accidents. It's as if they didn't finish their lives, and resist moving on. In one television documentary a particular crash in which four teenagers were killed was discussed at length. Many people had had 'sightings', and not only on the anniversary of the crash. Interestingly only three of the youngsters were ever recognised. The fourth girl was never 'sighted', in some twenty years. I often wonder if she was the only one who passed on.

The 5 of Cups illustrates how sensitive an individual is to these atmospheres, and will therefore show psychic abilities. Workwise it is the card of the medium, psychic and healer. People with this card strongly placed next to the Queen or King of Cups, the Ace of Coins and especially the Page of Cups, will have the ability to intuitively sense what aches, pains and ailments someone else is suffering from. It also shows great awareness of being in touch with the causal realm, the space from which great artists, musicians, inventors and all creative individuals gain their 'inspiration' by crossing the bridge to search for what they find attractive.

On another level the 5 of Cups refers to the unseen link between people who have separated. Newly divorced couples, parents whose children have grown up and left home, or the partner left behind after a bereavement, may all experience the invisible ties which bind them to the other person. For some people it is experienced as an invisible tie between themselves and an estranged partner, which makes them feel that the other person still retains some power or control over them. When these feelings become so overwhelming as to affect the individuals day to day affairs the therapy Tie Cutting can aid in releasing the bonds and assimilating the relevance of such a deep bond.

I have also seen the 5 of Cups depict that someone is under psychic attack from someone else when the person is actually "sending" negative manifestations from the etheric level. To the person under attack and "receiving" the result can be anything from feeling 'haunted' to seeing spirits in a house that was previously clear. Most of these "sendings" are of a negative nature. However, when the "sending" is positive we hardly notice because the effect is one of upliftment and joy, which we usually term "absent healing".

The 5 of Cups **reversed** shows either a stronger attachment to atmospheres or spirits; or a breaking of these invisible ties. Surrounding cards will indicate the emphasis.

Key words

Atmospheres/Spirits, ghosts and hauntings/The invisible tie which binds two people/Psychics, healers etc.
The psychic 'gateway' used by mediums etc.
Reversed
Beginning to break the ties that bind.

Bach Flower Remedy

Walnut – gives protection against oversensitivity to certain ideas, atmospheres and influences.

Toni Allen
The System of Symbols ©

The 6 of Cups

The 6 of Cups relates to water at air.

Water creates bonds and air regulates the forces of nature.

The Pranas (air) are vital energies; they make or keep the body alive, discharge polluted air, regulate the digestive process, keep the body in balance and also regulate involuntary movements in the body. Everything is held by air.

Thus with the 6 of Cups we can see how the bonds of water have created ties so strong that the Pranas are stifled, thus making our physical bodies sluggish and trapping our minds and emotions in the past. When the 6 of Cups is at play in our lives we often find ourselves more interested in events which took place in the past, and therefore a feeling of nostalgia takes over, and we become increasingly disinterested in our present circumstances. Yesterday was always better or our last job more satisfying than the current one; while directly after moving house homesickness sets in.

I often refer to the 6 of Cups as a cleansing process.

In a state of consciousness the card symbolises standing in the present and looking at the past, present and future; then making any decisions based on what we have learnt from our observations before moving on.

By relating the 6 of Cups to the Lovers, which sits at number 6, we can see that with this Major Card we are shown the dilemma of the individual having to choose between following his (or her) habitual actions or a new type of action. It may be physical, mental or emotional change which needs to take place to release the bonds created by samskara.* Making such changes in attitude inevitably brings with it fear and anxiety, and it is only when one overrides these that any progress can be made. The 6 of Cups symbolises the process by which we analyse these emotional ties in order to bring about a constructive change. Sometimes we only achieve an apparently minor alteration in our pattern of life, but this is not to be criticised. Samskara is built up over many life times and we cannot, and must not, expect to over vault such deep rooted traits all at once.

In practice the 6 of Cups is interpreted as follows; again much depends upon surrounding cards.

Very few people come for a reading looking for a truly esoteric interpretation of their life, therefore much of what is written in the paragraphs above might well slide over their head or simply confuse the issue if we plunge in with a complex scenario about previous incarnations. It is wiser to start by speaking about mundane activities and let the more subtle side of the card show itself as the questioner relates to certain factors in their present life.

A good example of this was a male client I saw. He had separated from his wife about a year previously. It was the second time he had come to me and consequently we fell into an easy rapport. Although he claimed that he was over the initial impact of his separation and moving forward in his life, the 6 of Cups came up surrounded by cards suggesting a continuing strong emotional link with his wife and a constant repetition of old behaviour patterns. (The Devil, The Pope reversed, the Ace of Swords reversed, plus others. All suggested lack of trust, lies and communication problems) My client failed to see any connection between his wife and his current emotional outlook. I pressed on by taking more cards for future relationships. The 6 of Batons suggested a new companion who was very compatible, but it was literally surrounded by the 3 and 7 of Swords reversed, the 9 of Swords, the Knight of Swords reversed and the Hermit reversed. A veritable battle field! I mentioned two words, jealousy and violence. The key was found. Slowly he admitted that he had such a severe problem with jealousy that another man only had to say "hello" to a woman he was with and that, especially if he had been drinking, he was likely to lash out with his fists.

Although my client had initially failed to recognise the 6 of Cups, which is perhaps a more subtle card, he readily accepted the physical attributes of the Sword cards. During further discussion he admitted that he felt that factors in his childhood had first created his jealousy, and that his wife's affair, which led to their separation, had sent his emotions back to the past. He was so connected emotionally with past hurts that he could not imagine himself acting any differently. He was standing at the pivot point of the 6 of Cups, being present, while emotionally referring back to the past, and therefore finding himself unable to shake of the repeat behavioural pattern. Consequently he was reticent about future relationships. I recommended the Bach remedy Holly to help move him away from his constant feelings of jealousy and Honeysuckle to help bring him into the present.

On another level the 6 of Cups shows that the questioner may be moving house, or have the desire to move. When we move from one property to another we go through a very natural cleansing process. Everything is pulled out of cupboards and drawers to be packed ready for transportation, and in the process we stir up many memories. Age old garments are rediscovered lurking at the back of the wardrobe reminding us how we dressed in more youthful days, while trinkets bestowed by once loved, but now rarely thought of friends, are unearthed to tug at guilt, joy and sorrow. The list is endless. Each item holds a memory. Each brings with it the choice of whether to hang onto it for a few more years, stuffed inelegantly into the back of another cupboard or chuck it out. Maybe we will utilise it, or maybe, we will throw it away and sever the bond.

If the questioner is unable to sell their home, yet would like to move, the 6 of Cups indicates redecoration and enlivening the atmosphere where they live in various ways. If space is one of their motives for wanting to move then building an extension may take place. It is all about creating the correct space for our needs.

If the questioner does not intend to move then the card indicates this process of outward and inward cleansing going on for some other reason. Very often the 6 of Cups presents itself after a marital break up, indicating that the partner who is to stay in the marital home wishes to cleanse themself of the other's influence, break the bonds and create something of their own. Redecoration, spring cleaning and sorting out hoarded possessions is pertinent. Again, a client may be going through these physical motions and yet not realise the underlying emotional process which is taking place. With each old love letter they throw on the fire a stagnant bond is partly destroyed, while a change of colour scheme allows their own sense of what is modern, and "here and now" to lead them more positively into the future.

When a recent bereavement has taken place the questioner may well be doing the diametrically opposite process and refuse to change anything which the loved one used, created or preferred. How the person smelt becomes important and any type of house cleaning might destroy the presence created by the stale aroma of their after-shave or perfume. To stand still for a while in such a situation is a very natural part of the grieving process. Each individual reacts differently, and no one should ever be made to feel that his or her way of coping is wrong. However, if surrounding cards indicate that the questioner has been living in this deep rooted nostalgia for many months, or even years, then to interpret the card as a suggestion that the time has come to start considering appropriate change to the environment, can help to bring about a positive transformation for the questioner.

If the card is relating to an elderly, or ill person, then nostalgia is strongly indicated. The individual's desire to live in the past coupled with a strong belief that yesterday was better than today can inhibit healing, or, especially in the case of a much older person, indicate the onset of senile dementia where the mind wanders through the corridors of the past, and present circumstances hold no interest. I have seen classic examples of this where the questioner has had to make a hard decision to place an elderly relative in an old folks home. The 6 of Cups comes up to indicate that since the move away from their own home the relative has faded and lost all interest in the present.

To someone living away from home the 6 of Cups symbolises homesickness. To a teenager it indicates that it's an appropriate time to throw off the bonds of childhood and move out of home. Many youngsters come for guidance prior to taking their A levels, and the 6 of Cups very often appears after the Ace of Coins, indicating that after passing their exams that they will move away from home, either to work or take up further education. Whatever the circumstances leading up to the move the 6 of Cups reveals the initial feelings of homesickness, and a desire to cling to the emotional safety of a situation in which life's basic needs were provided for.

In connection with work and hobbies the 6 of Cups indicates collectors of antiques and memorabilia. Next to the 10 of Coins I have seen it for a woman whose work was investigating clients' past lineage and collating family trees. It also indicates historians and interior designers.

Perhaps the most pertinent example I have seen for a collector was with a young man in his mid twenties. Close to the beginning of the reading he had the 3 of Coins indicating study and craftsmanship, the 6 of Cups and then the 9 of Swords. I asked him if he could relate to the image of "craftsmanship, nostalgia, dwelling on the past and many swords relating to death." He burst out laughing. His main preoccupation in life, outside work, was collecting Samurai swords of exquisite craftsmanship. Many of these had been used in battle and would have struck a death blow. Partly he had come for the reading to see if he might be able to add a particular sword to his collection, but he also wanted to discuss his deep affinity with these swords and their history. He said it was as if he knew them. When I suggested that he had probably been a Samurai warrior in a previous incarnation he leapt on the idea, and admitted that this was a feeling he had held since childhood, yet could discuss with practically no one for fear of being thought mad.

In many respects this young man was possessed by the past. He had understood the use and ritual of these swords long before ever having read about them, and was now gathering them to him, in great abundance, in an attempt to get closer to a time in which he had felt very happy. I suggested that he might like to go for a far life regression to assist with the thoughts and feelings that overwhelmed him at times. He took this idea positively, acknowledging that to dwell on the past in such a fanatical way was inhibiting his ability to function wholeheartedly in the present and establish meaningful relationships.

The **reversed** card indicates a desire to go back to the past, and often the questioner with the reversed card is less able to see their own situation and need for change. It can also indicate the inability to move forward to a new home. e.g. their current house is on the market, but they have had no offers, and cannot move until it is sold.

Key words

Nostalgia
Living in the past
Childhood memories
Moving house
Decorating/spring cleaning
Homesickness
Reversed
Inability to move forward, even though one might want to.

Bach Flower Remedy

Honeysuckle – For all of the above, as well as any slowing down of the vital forces.

Toni Allen
The System of Symbols ©

The 7 of Cups

The 7 of Cups relates to water at fire.

Cups relate to water and the unmanifest. Mankind is most often bound up in a state of duality and separation; but when an individual becomes conscious of the "I" or Atman, he (or she) is able to stand back and observe the universe. Generally this profound experience goes undetected, or unrecognised. With the 7 of Cups it is manifest and made known through the realm of fire. Illumination, or enlightenment, takes place, giving rise to dreams and visions. That which is hidden in the unmanifest realm of The High Priestess comes to light.

Fire gives brightness, vision and colour.

During a reading surrounding cards will indicate the level at which the questioner is dealing with the world.

Toni Allen
The System of Symbols ©

The 7 of Cups can be interpreted as follows:-

When the questioner is depicted by one of the Cup Court Cards then they are very often actively participating in healing or other psychic activities. The 7 of Cups indicates that their 'power', or insight, will come through dreams and visions.

Some people ask which type of psychic work they would be best suited to, while others are consciously seeking a healer to aid with a specific problem. There is such a variety of healing systems available, and with so many combinations of cards it is difficult to draw hard and fast rules as to what they all refer to. Trust your own intuition. These are a few of my own observations as to the visionary potential of the 7 of Cups when placed next to various cards.

Next to the 6 of Cups...past life therapist/predictive dreams.

Next to the 5 of Cups or The Pope...mediums and those able to 'cross over to the other side'

Next to the Page of Cups...hands on healer/including gifted nurses.

Next to the 9 of Batons....crystal healer.

Tarot readers come under various card combinations depending on whether or not they are using the spirit world as a link. However, it is only the 7 of Cups which shows an ability to visualise relationships between symbols.

Astrologers may be depicted as 'intuitive' or 'scientific', and the 7 of Cups alone symbolises the more intuitive type. Generally if the questioner would benefit from astrological guidance, or is best suited to its study, then the Star Card is seen.

A fine example of the strength of the 7 of Cups was shown to me through a reading I gave to a woman who came to me for guidance on her chosen path as a medium and clairvoyant. She felt that she had "lost the gift" and was struggling between giving up or plodding on. She was depicted by the Queen of Cups, which indicated that she was already in possession of strong healing abilities. The Queen was crossed by the 7 of Cups with the Pope reversed in 'the mind' and the 2 of Batons at the 'physical' level. It became clear that although she experienced incredibly clear visions and prophetic dreams for her clients, that as yet she had not experienced clairaudience. She never heard voices, but thought that she should because her 'psychic tutor' received her messages through the spoken word, and hence she was expected to do the same.

Consequently my female client had blocked all channels through the etheric level (the Pope reversed), especially that associated with clairaudience, because of the dominance (2 of Batons) from her tutor. The reading went on to question, not her own psychic abilities, but whether it was time to release herself from her oppressive relationship with her tutor, and allow her natural talents and strength, as depicted by the 7 of Cups, to flow outwards. This she went on to do. Several months later she reported back to me that although she still did not experience clairaudience that by feeling less dominated by her tutor she had found inner contentment and pride in her own unique capabilities.

If the 7 of Cups is positioned close to the 3 of Batons or 3 of Coins, then the questioner is artistic. With the 3 of Batons the questioner's talents will lean towards fine art and design. e.g. designing knitwear, cake decoration, hairdressing, interior design. Surrounding cards will highlight whether these talents are used solely as a hobby or applied in their career. All creativity is of value and some people fail to recognise the artistic flair put into making panto costumes for the school, creating a cheerful well laid out home, or other "mundane" pursuits. These people deny all artistic ability and fail to see that they have a deep intuition when it comes to colour, shape and form.

Coupled with the 3 of Coins the 7 of Cups shows a more mathematical, geometrical application of visions and dreams. Men often have this combination when their work involves architecture, using blueprints, building or painting and decorating.

The 7 of Cups with either of these two cards and the Pope, or another 'sound' card shows a predisposition towards music, again either for work or pleasure.

In very general terms, and especially when shown in the line of 'the mind', the 7 of Cups symbolises daydreams. The emotional bonds created by water are made manifest as illusions by the Tejas. All of us at some time or another get lost in dreaming about our new love, wishing we had a wonderful new home or exciting holiday. There is nothing wrong with a little idle daydreaming as a form of temporary escapism, but for prolonged periods it can have damaging effects. Absentmindedness, confusion, fainting, poor memory and physical weakness can all evolve from a lack of interest in the present and a desire to 'run away' into fantasies. Continued daydreaming may culminate in a total blocking of vital energies and result in visual or auditory problems as a consequence of the individual becoming more attuned to the inside world than the outside.

Daydreaming can also hinder the healing process when one is unwell. When a person is 'there' and not 'here' then the body struggles on its own with no connection to everyday stimulus and vitality that can aid the healing process. A modern form of day dreaming is excessive watching of television.

The 7 of Cups by itself can be a very ungrounded card. Take for example the artist who doesn't paint, or the writer who has a day job and finds no time to write. What happens to all of their picture making energy? In extreme cases eccentricity and delusions take over, and then these circumstances create a sort of 'Walter Mitty' character. On the other hand many great artists are described as 'mad'. Is this simply because they dared to let their minds travel into realms that lesser mortals could not connect with?

Illusions, and hallucinations also come about through the use of drugs. Some prescribed medication creates a soporific effect and the patient finds themselves less able to cope with everyday affairs. However, others choose to use hallucinogenics specifically for the purpose of 'tapping in' to otherwise inaccessible realms. The questioner is likely to have the 7 accompanied by the 9 of Swords if this is the case; although please remember to use extreme caution in broaching the subject of drug abuse with a client, as, due to the nature of certain substances they may feel threatened.

The 7 of Cups **reversed** shows that 'dreams' are coming true and that the fire energy of the 7 is creating substance of our desires. In old books the 7 of Cups was always called "the wish fulfilment card", or "a sign of good luck". In practice I have found this to be more true of the card reversed than upright.

For one female client the 7 **reversed** came up as her card for the past and the line of the present suggested that she had a very happy marriage. It appeared that her dream man had come along and her wishes were fulfilled. "Oh yes," she agreed. "When I was little I wanted to marry a millionaire. As a young woman I went to Monaco for a holiday and there I met him. He is wealthy and wonderful and so far we have had fifteen delightful years together."

For another client the truth was a little more sobering. Many times he came to me for readings asking when he might meet his "dream" woman. Oh yes she was there, in his future, depicted by the 7 of cups **reversed** and the Queen of Coins. Then one day he came to me in panic. The first card taken was the 7 **reversed** and he recognised it immediately. "My dream has come true," he admitted. "I have found her, only now I am not so sure if I want the responsibility of a regular relationship and all it entails. I wished and wished for this and now I must look closely at the things I desire so passionately, because once I have them they are not as satisfying as one might have thought."

Key words

Healing ability
Artistic ability
Dreams
Illumination or illusion
The ability to create strong pictures in one's mind.   Colour is important.
Reversed
"The wish fulfilment card"
Dreams coming to fruition.

Bach Flower Remedy

Clematis – for those who have a lack of interest in the present and are inattentive- often very dreamy.

Toni Allen
The System of Symbols ©

The 8 of Cups

The 8 of Cups relates to water at water.

Number 8 is the state of the undifferentiated or unmanifest and, on the other scale, it comes under the realm of water. The unmanifest is the store room where all things and forms lie hidden, and manifest when the time comes. Thus the cycle of creation and dissolution is started and merged in this state which is under the realm of number 8.

The number 8 represents water which represents bonds.

It is only the bonds which keep matter together. It is called Sneha in Sanskrit. This Sneha is the bond between things and people. It is a sort of love which keeps them together.

With the 8 of Cups we find both forces of water working simultaneously. It is a card of warmth and love, comfort and ease, yet the contradiction set up here is that when things become too comfortable people set up a desire to "make something happen", to break away from the bonds which tie them. Everything has become too predictable, and something deep within tells us it is time to rekindle some kind of passion in our life before we stagnate completely. The unmanifest is literally what it says; that which has not been made manifest...the unknown.

In a reading the 8 of Cups can be interpreted as follows:-

A simple interpretation for the 8 of Cups is that the questioner wants to 'chase rainbows'. They feel that there is something much better over there than here. Usually the questioner is leaving, or wanting to leave, a place of either emotional or physical security. Outsiders can only see the external veneer of any situation. They often fail to realise that a comfortable home and a new car are very attractive wrappings for a dull relationship; hence family and friends generally try to entice the questioner to stay with words such as "now what on earth do you want to give all this up for?"

If you refer back to the Moon card, which sits at number 18, you will note that the dogs symbolise gossip, chatter and externally made fears. These 'dogs' are the people who turn up in the 8 of Cups to try and put the questioner off what they would really like to do, and create doubt and timidity.

When the card is drawn to indicate a person it shows that they are ambitious, yet prone to shyness, and easily led back into 'comfortable' situations rather than following their bliss.

The 8 of Cups may symbolise an actual departure, a desire to depart, or a move within a set environment; depending upon surrounding cards.

This card came up in the reading of a young woman who had recently finished her A levels and accepted a place at university, many miles from her parental home. The 8 of Cups showed her desire to let go of the "apron strings" and set off on a wonderful adventure through life. However, her mother was depicted as the Queen of Coins, and the 2 of Batons was close by, showing that her parent was trying to put her off going so far away. The girl was shy by nature, but the Fool came up in the future to show that she would stick to the idea of being a "free spirit" and go, regardless of her mother thinking that "she knew best".

In many cases the 8 of Cups depicts a husband or wife who desires more excitement, or challenge, in their life than their partner, and is therefore thinking of leaving the marital home. These people admit that there is very little wrong with the marriage, it has simply become dull and lifeless. With women in this situation they have often spent their life up until this point as a housewife, brought up children and held some type of non-vocational job. The children grow up and suddenly the mother realises how mundane her life has become and how very little she has achieved for herself.

When close to the Knight of Cups the 8 of Cups indicates foreign travel or a desire to live abroad. I saw this clearly for one woman. In her reading the World was in the future, and the 6 of Cups well placed to indicate a move of home. Her husband, the King of Batons, was reversed and crossed by the 3 of Coins. Other cards depicting study and struggle surrounded him and it became apparent that she was eager to emigrate. However, in this instance her and her husband were intending to leave the country as a couple, but everything was delayed while he worked hard to gain extra qualifications before they could depart. Ironically the friend who sat in on the reading with her looked at me and asked in an incredibly puzzled tone, "But I don't understand why she wants to go and live abroad, they've got everything they need here." The friend's obvious affection for her companion threatened to trap her and sway her opinion, even to the point of trying to make me change my mind about what I could 'see' in the reading so that her friend might be persuaded to stay.

Any journey depicted by the 8 of Cups is a voyage of self discovery, whether the individual leaves the place of comfort permanently, or only temporarily. Each of us has within us a deep knowledge that 'something' out there is right for us. That is, if we haven't already found it. The right job, the right partner, the right path in life. Those of us who haven't found it, and don't yet know what that 'something' is that we're searching for, acknowledge the lack in our lives by experiencing feelings of apathy, and discontent. The journey may appear to be 'out there', but in reality the physical form is purely a tool towards discovering more about oneself.

When positively placed in a reading the 8 of Cups symbolises progress. It shows that a deeper meaning has been found in the pursuit of some inner vision, and the rainbow must be chased, even if it overturns established routine, ritual, and relationships.

When coupled with various cards we can see what type of situation a person is moving away from, or desires to leave.

With the 8 of swords, the individual feels trapped or confined in a stagnant relationship, or situation of emotional torment.

With the 7 of Coins reversed, the place of work, or type of work, offers no further opportunities. This is a combination that often leads people to suddenly give up their job without having secured another position.

With the 4 of Swords, a desire to leave a place of illness or confinement. A possible indication of recovery from ill health.

The 8 of Cups **reversed** indicates that although the desire is there to leave a situation that the questioner is in fact going no-where. Often a husband or wife asks "Will I leave my partner?" and the 8 of Cups reversed states an emphatic "no". Sometimes it can be that the questioner does not have the strength to do it, even though it would be a positive move. Again surrounding cards will indicate what is holding the individual back.

One client, whom I saw regularly, always had the 8 of Cups reversed in her readings. She was in a constant dilemma about whether or not to leave her husband, and was trying hard to lead her own life, following activities that interested her, even though he disapproved. During one session the 8 came up next to the Pope reversed and I asked her who had been advising her to stay with him. She had already told me that she regularly went for far life regressions and on this occasion she informed me that her therapist had told her that she must stay with him as she owed him a karmic debt. I asked her if she thought that after thirty years of marriage that the karmic debt might already be paid. "Yes, I suppose it is," she replied. "Then why stay?" I asked. She shrugged. "I don't know. I suppose it's because I've been told that I owe him. I know that I've been bound up with him in many other life times, and I'm frightened of not paying off the debt this time round and having to come back and live with him again."

Whether her therapist was right or not is anybody's guess, but I do know that my client still lives with the same dilemma, intimidated by her husband and frightened to tread her own path for fear of retribution. Only now the therapist has laid something extra on her, a deep guilt that she may not be "playing out her karma" if she leaves him. In the Moon card the dogs drive us back into the stagnant water. The 8 of Cups guides us to test the waters of the unknown and expand our consciousness through life's rich tapestry. When reversed it invites us to re-live the same scenario over and over again.

Key Words

Chasing rainbows.
Leaving a situation of security in order to follow one's bliss.
Going where our heart leads us.
Making a positive move.
Reversed
Wanting to leave a person or situation, but staying due to fear, lack of finances or being persuaded by others.

Bach Flower Remedy

Larch - In case we feel we might fail, even when we are capable.
Cerato - So that we might trust our inner voice and thus take the leap into the unknown.
Walnut - To help break the ties with those who might wish to influence us to stay.

Toni Allen
The System of Symbols ©

The 9 of Cups

With the 9 of Cups we find water at earth.

Water sits at the numbers 8 and 2, while earth sits at the numbers 9 and 1.

The number 9 represents the complete fulfilment of creation, where physical phenomena have matured in full glory. Earth is the perfect medium to reflect all five qualities of the physical world. It has smell and crystalline form of its own, the taste and bond of water, heat and form of fire, touch of air and the sound of ether.

Water (Jala) has taste and bond of its own, heat and form of fire, touch of air and the sound of ether.

Number 8's reflection at 2 is the state of the undifferentiated or unmanifest. The cycle of creation and dissolution is thus started and merged under the realm of number 8. The bonds of water hold all things together. It is called Sneha in Sanskrit. Sneha is the bond between things and people.

With the 9 of Cups we experience the glorious perfection of this bonding process at both a physical and spiritual level. When upright the card represents physical pleasures and when **reversed** the spiritual level is emphasised. The 9 of Cups therefore symbolises a sense of well-being based upon our bonds with other people or things.

When interpreting the 9 of Cups we find the following:-

A common interpretation in a reading is that the questioner has a found a fulfilling relationship in which they feel totally at one with the other person. This often brings about an euphoric sense of well being. It is not to be confused with the unknown and expectant quality of the 2 of Cups; the 9 of Cups relationship is based on a crystallisation process, when the relationship has taken shape and form, and both parties know what the association entails.

The happiness found in the 9 of Cups is not based upon material well being, but a sense of belonging. Two people may not have much in life, yet are completely content and fulfilled when in each other's company. The bond between the two people is all that is necessary.

The bond created does not have to be between two people who are 'in love' with each other. Often during a reading the 9 of Cups symbolises the sense of well-being which the questioner has found through other means. The most important alternative to relationships is the bond that some people find between themselves and their faith. They find themselves fulfilled through their creator. On many occasions I have seen what would appear to be incongruous layouts where the 9 of Cups is involved. e.g. The 9 of Cups at the 'mental' level and the 9 of Swords at the 'physical' level. This reading symbolised that while "all Hell" was breaking loose in the questioner's life through death, loss of financial security etc., that their innermost faith and union with the absolute (God) had raised them above a total absorption in their pain, and given them the capacity to ride out the storm with love in their heart, even at those times when it would appear that others wished to harm them. This, of course, stands for people of any religious persuasion.

If the two 9's were on the opposite levels in a reading then the interpretation would be reversed. With the 9 of Cups at the 'physical' level and the 9 of Swords at the 'mental' level it would indicate that the questioner is putting on a show of inner harmony while their mind was wracked with pain, fear, grief, and so on.

Surrounding cards will add information as to the source of the questioner's inner contentment, e.g.

With the 4 of Coins, financial security.
With the 6 of Cups, a move to a better location.
With the 3 of Batons, inspired work of a creative nature.

When the 9 of Cups is found **reversed** in a reading we have the same bonding, yet at a more intense level. It symbolises an extreme of pleasure. Often the 3 of Batons refers to the sexual act, but the 9 of Cups reversed symbolises the perfect orgasm, that moment of total bliss where two people merge as one physical entity and experience a union which goes far beyond mind and body. The French describe it as "La petite morte", the "little death". We fleetingly die as two people to be reborn as one. Our duality and separateness momentarily leave us. This type of "peak experience" can also be achieved through meditation, or prayer, where the individual relinquishes him or herself and experiences the total unity of creation.

Physical matter changes its properties when its crystalline structure is dissolved in water. The taste and bond of water, when held too long at earth causes fermentation and decay. A simple example of this is rotting apples left fallen under the tree in heavy rain. If, once the rain has stopped, you go down and stand under the tree you will notice the pungent smell of the apples where they have started to ferment. A positive application for this process is the fermentation used in the production of alcohol. Some animals, especially dear, employ this process by eating large quantities of apples and letting them ferment in their stomachs. They then stagger around as drunk as lords!

Thus the 9 of Cups reversed symbolises indulgence in alcohol; but not to drown one's sorrows, simply to take the edge off reality by dropping the niceties of social boundaries. Alcohol, taken in moderation, helps us to feel closer to others by removing inhibitions. We are more able to bond with others once our ego identities have been sufficiently released. For this reason the 9 of cups reversed symbolises a party or happy social occasion. It represents specifically weddings, birthdays and all celebrations; even without the use of alcohol.

A male client asked when he would get the opportunity to speak with someone about an important issue, in which differences needed to be resolved. So far no time had appeared right for broaching certain subjects. The 9 of Cups reversed came up along with the 10 of Coins, symbolising a happy, family occasion, based upon the bonding of family inheritance. I suggested that this was a family wedding, and this would be the right time to speak with the person in question. At the time my client thoroughly disagreed with my interpretation. He was adamant that no member of his family had any intention of getting married, and his only sister was the sole candidate. His was the only wedding anniversary coming up, and as he and his wife were separated he had no intention of celebrating it. He preferred to view the cards as celebrating Christmas, which at that period was nearly nine months away, and yet currently he had no intention of celebrating it with his extended family. However, he could not envisage the person he wished to speak with being invited to any family celebrations.

Two weeks after the reading he knocked on my door, desperate to speak with me. "I had to come and see you in person," he said. "My sister told me this morning that she's getting married in three months time, which tallies exactly with your prediction. What's more she's invited the very person I want to speak to!" His later report was that the wedding had offered the ideal opportunity to speak openly with his estranged friend over a couple of drinks, and that their differences had been resolved.

At all times the distinction between the 9 of Cups and the 9 of swords must be noted where alcohol is indicated. The 9 of Cups symbolises the use of alcohol to break down inhibiting barriers so that we can feel closer to others, whereas the 9 of swords indicates the use of any mind altering drug to blot out mental anguish and torment. The latter is generally a very lonely process and does not encompass the same social interaction and desire for union. A person who is absolutely inebriated is completely unable to relate to anyone. Conversely a person who is tipsy is able to flirt more openly, become more tactile with those he or she wishes to become close to and is generally more gregarious. The stimulation offered by the 9 of Cups is euphoric, while that of the 9 of Swords is depressive and isolated.

Key Words

Euphoria
Sociability
A sense of belonging
Reversed
Moderate drinking.
Celebrations/Parties

Toni Allen
The System of Symbols ©

The 10 of Cups

The 10 of Cups relates to water at the end of one cycle and the beginning of another.

The Cups relate to water, which is bonds, and on the other scale, the unmanifest. The number 10 represents 1, the absolute, and 0, the circle which all nine numbers sit on; thus the number 10 holds all the nine manifestations within it as 9 is the limit of numbers. At 10 we therefore find everything which is within the absolute and everything which is within the free spirit.

The free spirit either makes new karma, or deals with the old. At number 10 there are two options; to go back along the circle through 9, 8, 7 etc. and deal with unfinished karmic issues; or, to go forward towards 1, as certain karmic issues have been dealt with. On the latter path, new karmic issues will present themselves, but having dealt with one issue our attitudes and behavioural patterns will be different. The number 10 therefore represents either the need to work further on old issues, or to make fresh beginnings from a strong standpoint of self-knowledge.

When we put these elements together in the 10 of Cups we find a large picture of emotional bonds, either needing to be dealt with, or having been dealt with. The absolute and free spirit stand as an observer over these bonds. In general terms the upright card shows positive bonds and the reversed card negative bonds.

When interpreting the 10 of Cups we may find the following:-

Most commonly the 10 of Cups symbolises the emotional ties we have with our family. It is a very positive card and shows how the family bond gives many people purpose and contentment in life. For many men the family, which they have created, as opposed to the hierarchical family from which they have come, gives them a reason to get up and go to work in the morning, to buy a property and set up home. More often than not the 10 of Cups indicates that a couple have children, and again, simple as it may sound, many men find self-worth and contentment by providing for their family, plus great joy at coming home to their wife and family. In readings for women it indicates that home-life makes them happy. For whichever sex it provides a loving environment to go out from and return to.

Sometimes the 10 of Cups indicates that the questioners' family is the main-stay of their life, and that they have a loving relationship, which supports them through their times of trouble. Often the card is seen like this when it pops up out of nowhere, sitting in the middle of a rather dour reading like a fresh oasis of nourishment. When I point out to the client that they have a strong, supportive family, their eyes light up, and I hear comments such as "Oh yes, I couldn't get through this without them", or "I know my family will always be there for me."

Perhaps the strongest, and most important, interpretation for the 10 of Cups is the inner contentment that the individual possesses. It indicates that they have an unwavering faith in themselves, and that they are able to rise above adversity. Sometimes this is coupled with a deep religious (belief system) disposition, and inner knowledge that they are not the body, or the mind, which is so easily broken, but the spirit which dwells within the physical form. In this context the water is relating to the unmanifest, and the absolute and free spirit at 10 are observing the hidden truths which the High Priestess has to offer.

When seen in the 'future' in a reading the 10 of Cups shows that despite whatever problems the questioner is currently going through that they will, once again, be able to experience happiness and peace of mind. For some people this simple assertion for the future gives them great hope. The 10 of Cups is always full of love and whether that love is provided by a warm, caring family, or one's own inner feelings of self worth, it means that the questioner is not lonely, whether alone or not. When feeling warm and cuddly inside, strength abounds and we can achieve anything.

For some people the 'family' referred to may be their church, faith, or any other group that they consider to be a part of through emotional ties, as opposed to business or professional affiliations.

The only time when the 10 of Cups has any hint of sadness in it is when **reversed.** This usually depicts a happy outcome, but tinged with sadness, as if the individual has been through many trials and losses, and overcome obstacles to obtain a state of happiness. This shows that the questioner is still, in some way or other, bound up in the past, and has many sad memories, even though they have now reached a state of inner contentment. One can forgive or let go, yet one need not forget people, places and experiences that have helped make them who they are today.

Key Words

Contentment
Inner contentment
Family
Happiness
Reversed
Renewed contentment after turmoil or struggle

Toni Allen
The System of Symbols ©

The Ace of Coins

The Ace of Coins relates to earth at the absolute.

Earth is where physical form has matured in full glory, while the absolute at number 1 signifies the start of creation. Thus with the Ace of Coins we find a card which symbolises both the beginning and the end. Throughout our journey of the Tarot I have been referring to the circle which the numbers sit on. I have explained how this circle represents the number 0, and how 0 is the great unmanifest consciousness from which everything is created and to which everything returns. Thus we can see that with the circular symbol of the coin we have an image which represents the beginning, the end, and everything else.

The symbol most closely representing the same universal truth as the Coin is the Ouroboros. The dragon, or serpent, coiling round in a circle to bite its own tail. It represents infinity, the beginning eating the end, in a form that never ends. Some schools of thought say that the serpent is a symbol of evil itself, while others say that it is the serpent from the Garden of Eden, who beguiled Eve into eating from the Tree of Knowledge of Good and Evil. With the latter we find the concept that the human condition is bound up, self perpetuated by the knowledge it gained from the fruit. This is the continuous cycle of man, to go round and round, constantly searching for answers, looking for a way out of the repeat cycle of birth and death and rebirth. Yet we are all one. It is our knowledge of good and evil which gives us the notion of duality and binds us to this earthly plane.

With the Ace of Coins we find all of these ideas and more. The Coins symbolises the Earth and all things created from the earth. It is both the seed and the fully mature tree, the pen and paper and the completed manuscript, the initial effort and the end result.

Personally I see the Coin cards as symbols of wisdom and wealth. We have all been given a human body in which to experience the creation in all its glory. In order to gain knowledge and wisdom we require a physical body, so that we can learn through the senses the body endows us with, as well as the spirit. Our purpose on Earth is to attain self-realisation, and in order to achieve this we need to dispel duality and reach unity. Most of our learning on this journey arises through life's lessons, and the body is our vehicle. Without it we cannot experience touch, smell, sight or taste. At times when the true nature of the self is clouded through pain, grief and upset, something like a warm hug, the sight of a beautiful bird in flight, or the smell and taste of a favourite food can make us feel better. The earth provides us with everything we need. Food to sustain us, light to see by, warmth, shelter and other people to be our companions.

All of the above provide the stage on which the self can gain wisdom. Fundamentally there are two types of wisdom and knowledge; that which is gained from life and that which is learnt second hand through watching others, books or other media. Wisdom from life experiences includes intrinsic knowledge that we are born with and have carried over from previous lives. Thus we find those who from an early age are naturally gifted in one field or another. In this life time the talent comes to the fore and they are given the opportunity to crystallise the gift and make right use of it. Everyone has inherent skills, and once recognised they often choose to go on a course of study so that they can progress their learning. Even natural healers and psychics with an inborn gift seek out a master, or school of learning in which they can channel their skills and insight.

We can see how wisdom is acquired. To many it simply means going to school and then on to higher education in order to gain qualifications. Why do they do this? In order to say, "I'm an expert in maths"? Or in order to achieve a good position in life and command a higher wage. For some it is the love of the subject itself, while for others the learning is only directed towards the pay packet at the end of the day. Thus we find that wisdom and wealth are inextricably involved with one another. The more we know about a particular subject, the better our skill, the more an employer is willing to pay us. And if we're really high on the knowledge and wisdom stakes then we rise to the lofty heights of being in charge and employing others. Sometimes we even find people who pursue a particular subject out of love for it alone and have the world thrust glory and money on them because they are exceptional. An example here would be the young man who works in the bank and plays his guitar in a band in the evenings. One day a record producer goes along to hear him play, because there's a rumour about the young man's brilliant guitar work. Bingo! The young man is given a recording contract, which makes him a fortune.

In a reading the Ace of Coins has many connotations. It represents the act of learning, the desire to gain knowledge, and also the certificate itself, which in this day and age is so important to many people, because it shows that they have achieved a certain level of understanding and competence. With their piece of paper their knowledge can be well rewarded. The Ace also represents any type of documents that hold important information. I have seen the card come up in the "future" for clients due to take exams, showing that they will pass, and then had feedback to say that they have. (Remind the client that they have to keep on working at the same pace otherwise they might be inclined to stop studying...after all, they've been told they will pass!) I have also seen the card come up for people in legal battles indicating that they will receive further documents which will add to their knowledge of the case.

The Ace of Coins also shows very simply that an individual knows what to do in a certain situation. They have deep understanding of themselves and their own specific gifts as well as limitations. Often their "knowing" comes from their higher self.

The Ace of Coins also depicts one's feeling of self worth. Do we value ourself? Or do we feel worthless? Many people equate self worth with their qualifications, how much money they earn, what type of house they live in and their family. However there are other things, which have less material worth, but a far greater personal worth. Courage, compassion, understanding, loyalty, and love are all qualities which we learn about throughout life and which we can come to own and value ourselves through. Often people believe that that are worthless because they do not own many possessions, or earn a lot of money, and yet their families love them dearly and they are viewed by others as strong and noble. We all have positive qualities and the Ace of Coins in a reading helps direct our attention to our strengths, whatever they might be. Some old books on the Tarot say that if the Ace of Coins is turned up during a reading that it outweighs all negative cards in the spread. It shows that the questioner can overcome their problems through wisdom and knowledge. In general I have found this interpretation to be well substantiated, and have often seen individuals in the most difficult dilemmas come through shining when they have the card.

When the Ace of Coins is **reversed** it shows that the questioner is struggling with their sense of self worth, wisdom or wealth. Financially the card by itself seldom indicates any drastic financial downfall, but emotionally it can show feelings of loss of faith in one's self. It can also show the individual struggling with their own values, or having difficulty coming up with a solution to a problem. As ever surrounding cards need to be taken into account, but on its own the Ace reversed is never without a hint of happiness. All changes, or re- evaluation of our ideas, values and wealth are there to teach us more, and can therefore only bring about more wisdom.

Key Words

Wisdom
Wealth
Self worth
Certificates

Documents
Intrinsic knowledge brought through from previous lives.
Reversed
Lack of self worth
Changes in what we value
The need to study and gain wisdom
Changes to our finances

Toni Allen
The System of Symbols ©

The 2 of Coins

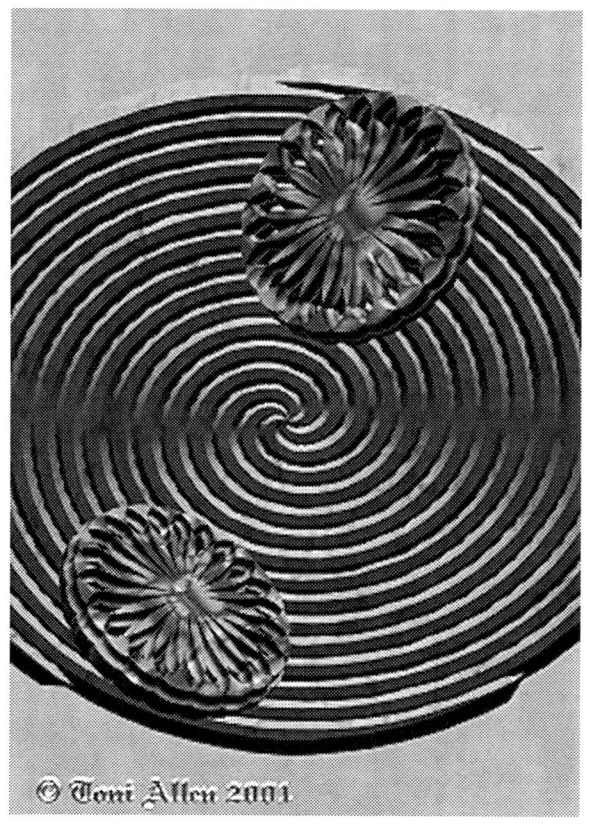

The 2 of Coins relates to earth at duality, or the unmanifest.

All the multifarious forms of the universe lie stored in the unmanifest before creation breaks out, and are also absorbed in it when the creation is to be withdrawn. When we add the physical quality of earth to this equation we can see that something is waiting to come into creation and take on one of the qualities held within earth.

Number 2 is the representation of the duality of the I and the non-I. It is the stage where 1 stands as the consciousness looking around. Whatever comes into view forms another unit which is the unmanifest prakriti.

Linking these facets together we discover how the 2 of Coins symbolises a dilemma of 'what to do'. It represents the vacillation between 'this' and 'that'. Something needs to be done about a situation, yet at the 2 of Coins we are bound up in indecision. * What should we make happen next? If we do 'this' then we create that outcome from the unmanifest's storehouse, and if we do 'that' then we will make something quite different manifest. Once we take action, which will not come about until the number 3, the dilemma will go. Hence the 2 of Coins within itself is a card of no action, while the predicament remains.

* Note that as 2 and 8 are interchangeable we also find the bonds of water effecting the situation. "I am attached to this or that idea, and therefore am unsure about doing this or that."

Do not confuse the 2 of Coins as having the same potent discrimination as symbolised by the Lovers Card. The Lovers Card speaks of the faculty of discrimination itself, and one's ability to make the correct choice of path in life, whereas the 2 of Coins is more concerned with whether or not one is able to be decisive about the little choices we all need to make every day. Such issues as "should I wear this or that?", "I'll do this, no I won't, I'll do that". It's the card of the eternal ditherer, or at least a phase of eternal dithering, in which nothing is achieved. Sometimes it does reflect much larger issues in life, such as "I'll leave my partner, no I won't, I'll stay"; but even then other cards will generally show that the questioners entire decision making process has become disorientated.

If we relate the 2 of Coins to the Hanged Man at 12, and the High Priestess at 2 we can understand a little more of why these decisions are so hard to make. The Hanged Man, by the very fact that he is suspended between two posts, speaks of 'waiting to see what will happen next', while the High Priestess always speaks of 'the great unknown'. Thus at the 2 of Coins we do not have enough information on which to base our decision. Our inability to connect the personality with the higher self blocks our guidance from the greater source. True inner wisdom is lost. We might just as well flip a coin and act on whatever 'fate' chooses for us. At this point it's interesting to note that many people come for a reading when the influence of the 2 of Coins is prevalent in their lives; and showing itself within the central line of the first 5 cards. These people are genuinely confused and have come for a reading in the hope of reconnecting with a higher part of themselves. The process of the reading helps them to sift through their mental debris and aids them in making their own decision.

Remember also that as the Coins represent wisdom, which is often gained through experience, that the 2 of Coins may depict someone coming up against a situation which is entirely new to them, and therefore they have no personal experiences to draw upon.

In a reading the interpretation for the 2 of Coins is as variable as the amount of cards one can place next to it! Its very nature creates these abundant alternatives. The following are guide-lines:-

When speaking of the questioner's personality structure it shows a deep rooted indecisiveness. Generally the problem will be ingrained from childhood, and the Lovers card often comes up close by to highlight this.

It is said in Vedic philosophy that at the age of sixteen we are given a new faculty of discrimination, and apparently this comes about naturally with puberty. When I was first introduced to this concept I was as sceptical as you are at the moment. The only real idea in our culture that I could associate this with is that in this country we acknowledge sixteen as being in some way special by calling it the 'age of consent'. At sixteen a young adult is recognised as knowing their own mind, and therefore able to choose whether or not to have sex as a consenting adult. Perhaps I had found some truth in this philosophical concept? However, a year or so after first hearing about this new faculty of discrimination I was still pondering the theory. As often happens I was given an opportunity to find out about it with some first hand experience. Within the space of a month I had three teenage clients between the ages of sixteen and seventeen. As a matter of professional policy I never take a client under sixteen, unless accompanied by a parent, as I believe they still come under parental guidance, and are far too open and vulnerable to have a reading on their own. Hence these three youngsters just happened to be my three youngest clients to date at that time. Every one of them had the same fundamental problem. Every one of them had suddenly found that they were invited to make their own decisions in life, and did not know whether the choices they were making were right for themselves or not.

Perhaps society had projected the 'discrimination faculty' onto them when they reached the 'age of consent'; or perhaps it was the other way round. However, all three of them spoke openly with me about feeling different, and finding they had additional things going on in their heads than before they reached sixteen, and were finding they now had a new responsibility to themselves.

So what happens with this faculty of discrimination? Who guides us on using this new tool? Generally it is parents. However, when the 2 of Coins is strong in a reading, and there are authority cards depicting parents or teachers close by, it shows that around the age of sixteen the questioner was not allowed to 'grow up' by testing their own discriminatory faculties within the safety of the family. There are many variations on this theme. One is that the young adult was constantly told what to do, and therefore once they left home, had no 'voice' ordering them around. They found they had no yardstick by which to lead an individual life. Consequently they were left uncertain as to whether or not any action they were choosing was correct, either for themselves or socially or morally. This type tend to either stay pinned to the families apron strings, choose a dominant partner to make decisions for them, or make many mistakes before they sort themselves out. Alternatively we find people whose parents 'cut the apron strings' of advice once the questioner had reached 'maturity' at around sixteen, and thus left their offspring to flounder. These parents might have said such things as, "it's your life, you must make your own decisions now", or "I don't want to interfere", even when the questioner was turning to them for guidance.

The permutations for scenarios on the above are innumerable. Each client will have their own individual dilemma. Placing blame and fault finding are non productive, and although a certain amount of ground will need to be covered to discover the root of the problem, finding ways in which the questioner can take positive steps to overcome their indecisiveness within their current situation is the most beneficial way forward.

The 2 of Coins does not always speak of a fixed psychological pattern, and depending upon surrounding cards it can symbolise an immediate predicament. The questioner may have a very difficult choice to make between what they know will be two equally distressing outcomes. e.g. the woman knows that her husband will attempt suicide again if she leaves the marital home, yet is desperately unhappy in the relationship. If she goes there is his threat hanging over her, and the affect it will have on the children, yet if she stays she sacrifices her life to utter misery, and affects the children in a different way. Which does she choose?

Such traumatic circumstances make it difficult to see which is the best thing to do for everyone's long term happiness; and this may make

Toni Allen
The System of Symbols ©

the questioner feel, and act, in a very unstable manner.

As with any number 2 all of this occurs on the inside, and is therefore more difficult to detect by others. For this reason the 2 of Coins also indicates an ability to smile through troubles, even though one's inner being is in utter turmoil. Until we have reached a decision our inner waters are anything but calm and stable. Take a moment to think on how many times a friend has said, "I feel so much better now that I've made a decision about what to do". They may not even have done anything about their decision yet, but the act of deciding has released them from bondage.

When in a state of indecision a questioner may let time pass to see what transpires in a situation. The Hanged Man would indicate this. Often they let others make their move first, or events take their course, so that then they will have that magical piece of information which until then has been missing; and on this they base their decision. However, in real terms this can push a situation to its limits and have severe repercussions, especially if the questioner is the very person whom everyone else is waiting to make the all important first move.

I saw a pertinent example of this with a businessman. He came to me in a state of great anxiety. The 2 of Coins crossing the 10 of Coins as the first central cards told me that he was having a dilemma regarding property and business. The card in the 'mind' was the 4 of Coins reversed, indicating that he was holding on tight, and the 5 of Coins at the 'physical' level indicated his change of financial circumstances. The Page of Cups in the 'past' showed the years of loyalty and service his staff had given him. How could he possibly choose who should be laid off? If he did lay them off then where would he ever find such a good team again? Some of the 'old boys' had been trained by his father (relevant to the 10 of Coins, family business) and yet if he held on to all of his staff then nobody would have a job. He had already procrastinated for several months, cut wages and dithered around his dilemma whilst searching for new routes out of the predicament.

The cards showed him the way forward by pointing out a building he possessed which, if put to alternative use, could add a new dimension to his trade and create employment. It was already an idea he had toyed with. This was the missing information needed to make up his mind, confirmation that his crazy idea was right. The Justice card rested poignantly on the new project showing it to be a fair and just way out of his mire. The Page of Coins symbolised it was a final gamble. The last I heard from him was that his building had become a club and several amazed craftsmen had turned their hands to pulling pints...just until his other business climbed out of the recession!

Dithering, lack of concentration and instability may all come to the fore and create physical symptoms. These might show themselves in extreme fluctuations in mood, e.g. Crying and laughing. Happiness and depression. Physically the body will alternate between activity and apathy, hunger and loss of appetite, constipation and diarrhoea. The 2 of Coins will also depict travel sickness and morning sickness.

Reversed the 2 of Coins indicates that the questioner may be choosing not to look at the many alternative ways in which a situation may transpire through their actions. Alternatively it may be the first indication that the questioner has, at last, made up their mind about a long term issue. However, in general, the card is more heavily influenced by surrounding cards rather than whether or not it is reversed.

Key Words

Indecision
Vacillation
Lack of discrimination
Dithering
Reversed
No idea what alternatives there might be

Bach Flower Remedy

Scleranthus – For those who are swayed between two possibilities.

Toni Allen
The System of Symbols ©

The 3 of Coins

The 3 of Coins relates to earth at fire.

The 3 of Coins holds all of the qualities of 9, Earth, where physical phenomena have matured in full glory, 1, Atman, the absolute, 3, Prakriti, where nature unfolds itself and 7, Fire, which gives us energy and ability to perform practical works.

The 3 of Coins symbolises activities based on knowledge and natural talents. Exact crafts are indicated, such as masonry, architecture and boat building. All of these activities require plans and precision. Inspiration may come from the artistry of the 3 of Batons, but practical application comes from the 3 of Coins. It is the art of making something out of the physical materials that the earth provides. Ceramics and sculpture are also included here.

In an ideal world the 3 of Batons and the 3 of Coins work hand in hand....then one achieves perfection. In practice, however, the individual very often lacks one or the other.

Two apt examples are two very different men who came to me for readings. Both had the 3 of Coins prominently placed. One was a builder. When I suggested that he was an excellent craftsman he grinned and showed me a document from his wallet stating that he was a member of The Guild of Master Craftsmen. His trade was based on construction and renovation; and in his spare time he was 'doing up' a Victorian property to its former glory. However, he had no intention of starting to build a house form scratch. The other man I saw as someone who worked with plans, was well financed and highly artistic, but not so good at practical skills. He was an architect, revolutionary in his designs and progressive in outlook to the point of incorporating solar energy in major buildings; yet hopeless in the manual art of building.

The 3 of coins on its own, although a card of exactitude, also speaks of natural talent. However, this type of talent does not have the same showy flair as that of the 3 of Batons. Here the talent is latent, plodding, and has to be worked on through study and practice. Therefore the card also symbolises a course of study and practice, which suits the individual. Someone may have a yearning towards a particular subject, yet require a tutor to 'unlock' their own innate wisdom on the topic. Once started this type often feels that they already knew much about the subject.

In this respect it is also the card of working under a master, and although it may sound a little old fashioned apprenticeship is a very appropriate word. These days this takes many forms e.g. going to university or other places of study, a job training/work placement scheme, joining up with the forces, or studying under a spiritual master.

Surrounding cards will influence the type of training, and if followed by the Ace of Coins then exams will more than likely be passed and certificates gained.

Tejas (fire) is light, and with the 3 of Coins we have Sattvika Tejas, the light of knowledge, which comes through the absolute (1) and manifests at earth (9). A good tutor passes on their knowledge to us, willingly. When this is **reversed** we have Tamasika Tejas, the fire of lamp light etc, which one finds on earth. In practice this manifests as the type of tutor who engages in deceitful, or unsavoury activities. They steal student's ideas, take advantage of facilities, meanwhile teaching very little and are prone to criticise the less able. Thus the 3 of Coins also depicts the 'master' whom one studies under and surrounding cards will show the quality of the master.

When the 3 of coins refers to personal relationships we find that if the card is upright one is able to be an equal partner to another, command respect and is masterful in the wisdom of when to give and take from others. However, when the card is **reversed** one's willingness to have someone as a master is turned into a weak willed subservience to another. It is like being under someone else's thumb; the proverbial doormat.

Reversed the card indicates that for many years an individual has been a 'good' girl or boy, and done everything an apparently wiser and more knowledgeable person has directed. Fear is not immediately indicated, simply an inability to stand up for oneself. Often this stems from a childhood in which parents were predominantly strong characters and therefore to gain approval for their actions the child became a "people pleaser" rather than following their own wisdom on a matter. In many cases it is also karmic. There is much to suggest that in previous incarnations these 'doormats' were involved in religious orders or other activities, such as slavery, in which they were forced to follow the discipline of another person, or organisation's, greater authority and wisdom. Over many lifetimes of subservience their self will has been severely damaged.

In husband/wife relationships this type of subservience comes up directly as one partner constantly 'walking over' the other and telling them what to do, or making every personal decision for them.

This is not to be confused with the same unconscious, mental pressure, as the unseen force of the 2 of Batons. The 3 of Coins presents itself as a much more overt force in the individual's life. 3 of Coins types will generally do anything for a quiet life, and I saw this for one young woman who was swayed by her mother. Her wedding was arranged, but the 3 of Coins reversed was crossed by the Queen of Coins. The Sun reversed followed. I suggested that her mother was making all of the wedding plans, including choosing some items or activities which she did not want. "It is Mum's day as well," she said, "But I don't want to start a row over the roses she's chosen for the bridesmaids."   It was an apparently simple matter, but the young woman had set her heart on carnations for the bouquets, the first flowers her fiancé had given her. In discussion she accepted that she always did what others wanted, and found it difficult to stand up to people she genuinely respected, like her mother.

This young woman's subservience would not go away simply by telling her mother to change the flowers. Persistently standing up for herself was going to be the only way to change life times of servitude, otherwise she would find it difficult to achieve her own aims and goals in life.

For many people this subservience comes up as being 'people pleasers'. The 3 of Coins symbolises the crystallisation in physical form of our nature, or personality. It therefore describes how we manifest our nature to others. If, when we are young, our parents, or other carers, do not approve of our behaviour then they tell us so, or shun us, or refuse to feed us until we are 'good', and so on. To gain approval we bend our unique personality out of shape. Sometimes it is necessary to do this, because as a fragile infant survival is our only aim. If we demand and do not get, then we find it more beneficial to be quiet and stay alive. As adults this distortion of our true nature continues the same routine. We become frightened to demand what we need from friends, or loved ones, unconsciously believing that if we do then once again we will be rejected.

Many people act out this theme with their partner and end up constantly letting them choose which film they go and see, what type of food they eat, where they buy a house, and so on. Some people experience much larger pressures, such as pleasing the cultural system into which they have been born. Even in these supposedly "modern times" I have seen many woman of various ethnic origins who suffer from enormous family repression if they do not conform and become little else in life than a "good wife" or "good daughter".

The 3 of Coins upright also speaks of natural wisdom, especially in the handling of finances, so it's a card of good business sense. It can also mean that a person is born into money, and for this reason it sometimes refers to the nobility; although this tends to be a much older interpretation, as many people these days have worked for their money and not inherited it solely through class breeding. Because of these connotations with nobility I have also seen the card refer to individuals who do noble work, such as charitable fund raising, or concerning themselves with natural issues such as saving the planet and its animal inhabitants.

It is interesting to note that as the 3 of Coins refers to craftsmen, especially those working in natural substances such as stone masonry, that it also symbolises the Freemasons. On several occasions I have seen it distinctly refer to members of the order, either specifically referring to my client, or in response to a direct question. For example, one client wanted to set up a particular property for business, but kept finding himself thwarted. He asked "Is this situation being influenced by the Masons?" He took just one card for an answer, and drew the 3 of Coins. I explained the card's connection with builders and masons. He smiled and responded, "That's a good enough answer for me."

Key Words

Craftsmanship
Apprenticeship/tuition/finding a master
Nobility or noble action
Sound business ability
Freemason
Equality
Reversed
Weak willed/doormat/people pleaser/subservient

Bach Flower Remedy

Centaury - For those who are servile instead of being a willing helper. The positive side of Centaury is one who serves wisely and quietly.
Cerato – For those who distrust their own convictions. The positive side of Cerato is one who holds much wisdom and intuition.

Toni Allen
The System of Symbols ©

The 4 of Coins

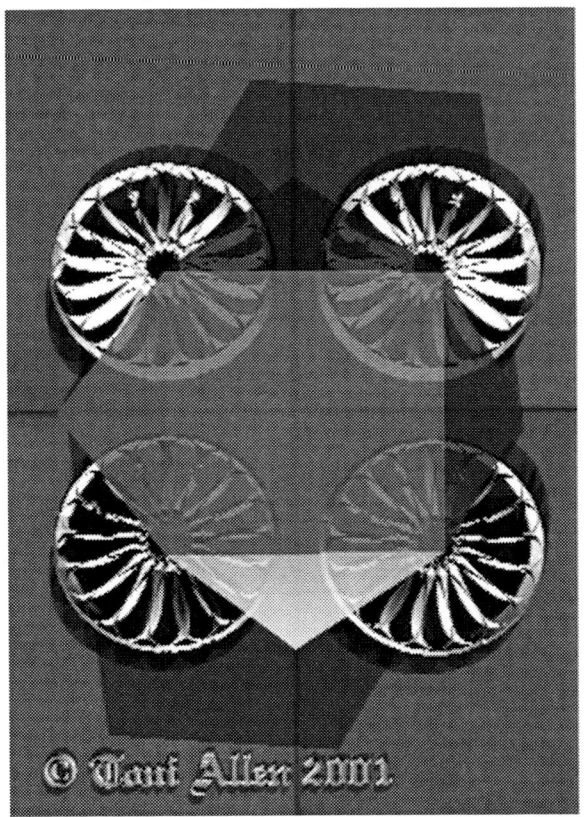

The 4 of Coins relates to earth at Ahamkara, or 'I Am'.

In earth all sensations are possible. The element earth is glorious because it is only through earth that all things of the world are created. It is the end of one cycle (9), where the absolute (1) stands as the beginning on the other side; thus it is the base of all physical phenomena on one side, and the basis of all phenomena from the other.

At the 4 of Coins the Ahamakara experiences these qualities through the feeling of 'I'.

Thus the symbolism of the 4 of Coins is all things which we experience at a physical level, both within ourselves and outside ourselves in the world around us.

As the Coins symbolise wisdom the card signifies an individual who knows themself well.

Therefore, at a personal level the 4 of Coins symbolises excellent health. The Ahamkara interrelated with the air (Pranas) at 6, bestows a great feeling of well being. The body is in total balance. We can relate to this via the Temperance card at 14. As the individual has a strong understanding of who they are, they are in tune with their body, to the point of knowing how to feed and regulate its activity to maintain harmony and realising what is out of balance should they become unwell. Knowledge eradicates fear, and this helps regulate the life giving force of the pranas. Due to this the 4 of Coins is rarely seen in connection with bad health, but if it does come up then it shows that the client's inner wisdom has helped them to control hopelessness, sorrows, fear etc., which all inhibit the healing process.

In many respects the 4 of Coins is the card that most represents the personality itself. If you refer back to the numerology associated with the Emperor at number 4 you will see that Ahamkara is the feeling of "I am". Personality is the feeling of "I am", plus whatever helps sustain the ego by giving it a veneer of safety. A security blanket. The self is the perfection within, which cannot be touched by anything, while the ego is the self-made mask; which, as we see with the symbolism of the Tower at 16, is false and easily broken down. We all attach many things to our personal "I am" to make us feel better, both in company and in private. Sit for a moment and reflect on a few themes that you associate with your personal feeling of "I am".

Here are just a few common examples:-
"I am" successful in my job.
"I am" wealthy.
"I am" a wife/husband.
"I am" loved.
"I am" a teacher/banker/writer/lawyer, healer etc.
The list is endless. All of these add to our feeling of uniqueness and make us believe that we are what we have or do.

When we place the opposite associations to these "I Ams", we can see how negative beliefs can also affect us.
"I am" unsuccessful in my job.
"I am" poor.
"I am" nobody's husband/wife.
"I am" unloved.

Toni Allen
The System of Symbols ©

"I am" unemployed.

These statements will all evoke different reactions from you. For example, you may feel sad to know that some people have an ego mask which believes that they are unloved. On the other hand you may have no empathy at all with someone who's ego mask believes that they are unsuccessful in their job, your reaction may be that they should work harder or change their line of work.

In the world we all generally like to project ourselves as popular, likeable, successful and loveable. The 4 of Coins shows us putting on our best front to the world, no matter what is happening at an inner, unseen, emotional level. It's like saying to the world "I am" okay, regardless. However, as seen with the opposite examples above, none of these traits are eternal, each can be reversed or changed, sometimes in a matter of seconds. The unloved person can find love, and the rich person can become poor. Due to the human desire for things to stay fixed and unchangeable, especially that which we regard as good or positive, the 4 of Coins also symbolises holding on to what we have and protecting ourselves from outside influences which might wish to take away what we have.

In a reading the 4 of Coins may show itself as follows:-
Generally the 4 of Coins will represent the client and their "okayness" about themself. Surrounding cards will be very important as they will highlight whether the client truly does feel okay or if this is a public persona. e.g. 4 of Coins at the 'physical' level and 9 of Swords in the line of the 'mind'.

People who have the 4 of Coins strongly placed in a reading are generally capable of amassing money or possessions; whether by work or marriage. If the individual is working then it shows a position of responsibility, or authority, and a keen use of the Coins faculty of wisdom.

Interpreted at the level of family and home life the 4 of Coins depicts security, prosperity and comfort. This in itself, however, does not necessarily make a married couple happy. I have seen this card many, many times in readings where a couple's relationship is breaking down. Typically the husband is not cruel, or brutal; so the wife does not feel in imminent danger and see any need to run to safety. The husband works hard to provide the necessities of life, plus enough luxuries, such as holidays, nice cars, good home and so on to make life extremely pleasant.

Toni Allen
The System of Symbols ©

Children are not immediately implied by the 4 of Coins, so there is not necessarily a young family to keep the woman tied to the man. Their home life is physically sheltered, secure, and difficult to replace overnight. Whether seen from the woman's point of view or the man's, neither party want to leave the stability offered by the 4 of Coins, even if they no longer love each other. Divorce is not only emotionally draining but can also financially crippling. Both parties realise that a separation could cost them a lot in terms of what they have built up over the years. Thus they choose to stay together in order to perpetuate their financial stability.

With regard to separations the 4 of Coins can also show that one party wants to leave the other, and the card represents everything which is to be divided. It also relates to our opposites mentioned earlier, in that for a woman to say "I am" so-and-so's wife, may give her a meaning in life and a great feeling of self worth. To suddenly have this pulled away overnight may well leave her feeling as if she is a nobody, because she had previously evolved her ego identity around the security of being that person's wife, and once threatened with no longer having that role, she finds that she has failed to make herself secure within herself. This, of course, works equally for a man being so-and-so's husband; and then he may wonder why he has been working hard and securing all of these possessions around him only for someone else to take them away.

For the business man the 4 of Coins is always extremely positive. In one reading I saw this card well placed in 'the future' for a man whose business was going through great financial difficulties. When he came to see me he felt as if all was lost and yet somehow kept struggling through with the help of his wife; shown by the 5 of Coins crossed by the Queen of Coins. He ran a tea shop in a holiday resort, and with one bad season followed by a smaller winter trade finances were looking grim. The 10 of Batons reversed next to the Page of Coins showed that he could take a risk and 'off load' something that he no longer needed in order to gain extra capital. The 4 of Coins followed his 'gamble' showing that the extra funds acquired would re-establish his business. At the time of the reading he could not imagine what it was that he could 'off load', but agreed to keep an open mind to the suggestion.

Many months later he returned and told me that he had rented out the top floor of the tea room to a woman who made and sold craftwork. This, he said, not only provided an income, but also cut his overheads, made the tea rooms easier to run, and attracted customers. "We also display some of her craftwork," he said. "It gives a wonderful fresh feel to the place, and people just love it."

Reversed the 4 of Coins symbolises greed and excessive "holding on " to material objects, or emotions. For some people it is holding on to the job which they have, even though they don't enjoy it, purely because the money is good and they have acquired a certain standard of living which they do not wish to risk in order to find a more enjoyable occupation. For others it is wishing to acquire more and more possessions e.g. avaricious business men, collectors who hoard too many of their favourite artefacts, or women who crave more and more jewellery.

We can all hold on to many things, including false ideas about ourselves. Some people hold onto the feeling of being 'unloved', even when they are dearly loved by someone. Others hold onto the idea that they have to do it all, because no one else is as capable; thus they refuse to delegate and become tight and rigid in their ways of doings things. There are as many individual 'holding ons' as there are people in the world. If this appears to be the crux of your client's problem then it is worth taking cards to explore from where the idea initially arose so that healing work may be initiated.

Healthwise the reversed card indicates over protection. Sometimes people feel that they must be well, and that to become ill is weak. Such people do not wish to let go, or be seen as vulnerable. This creates tension, stiffness and constipation.

Key Words

"I am" plus/Prosperity/Security/Stability
Reversed
Holding on too tight to many things
Holding on to a false ego identity
Fear of letting other's get close

Bach Flower Remedy

Rock Water - when the card is reversed...for those who are too hard on themselves.

Toni Allen
The System of Symbols ©

The 5 of Coins

The 5 of Coins relates to earth at ether.

When the causal and subtle world is transformed into the coarse world, then it is done through the ether, which connects both. It is like a transformer which changes one type of energy into another. It is a bridge which connects the two worlds. The physical aspect of ether is sound.

In earth all sensations are possible:- The sound of ether, the touch of air, heat and light of fire, the taste and bond of water, and the smell and crystalline form of its own. Earth is the glorious end of one cycle, where the absolute stands as the glorious beginning of another.

When we have finished a piece of work, of any description, we are happy to let it pass on, and for things to change. We are content when something is completed. It gives us a sense of achievement. This is seen in the 10 of Coins, which then becomes the Ace of Coins on the next cycle. However, when things change right in the middle of a project, or before we are ready to move on, then we become distressed, disorientated and often discouraged. This is what happens at the 5 of Coins. An apparently enforced change in physical circumstances happens when we would least choose it. Something unexpected comes through from the causal level and sets up a new vibration within material circumstances that we have come to rely upon.

All physical, or more precisely worldly, changes, whether 'good' or 'bad' are depicted here, so the interpretations are many. I emphasise the word worldly, because bodily changes are more generally depicted by the 5 of Batons. At earth all things are possible; and the Coins within itself depict wisdom and wealth...that which we have strived for. In most people's lives they strive for the physical comfort of the wealth which Coins can buy, and therefore changes in financial circumstances are often shown.

In a reading the 5 of Coins may be interpreted as follows:-

One of the most important aspects of the card is seen within partnerships or relationships, whether a marriage or friendship. Marriage vows include "For richer, for poorer, in sickness and in health", a loyalty which many people stand by, even in close friendships. Therefore the card represents a partner, or close friend, who is there through thick and thin, willingly standing by your side, regardless of what life throws in your direction. It is a true friendship because it is not based on money, or any attribute you may have to give other than yourself.

For one woman, whose live in boyfriend had recently left her, the 5 of Coins showed her distress at no longer having his support. It depicted both his friendship and the sudden change in physical circumstances his leaving her had created. He had helped her with many practical matters, and without him 'holding her hand through life' she felt as if she was drifting and quite incapable of coping on her own, even though she was a very intelligent woman. Most of us need to know that someone is there to offer a shoulder to lean on, perhaps someone who knows our history and personal circumstances.

Conversely, on other occasions, the card has shown a questioner's desire for such a special person; someone they can 'phone up at three o'clock in the morning during a time of personal crisis, or simply be there for them when problems arise. With continued readings one client had a personal breakthrough concerning the 5 of Coins. She realised that many of her problems within her most recent relationship stemmed from her partner's lack of willingness to be there for her on an unconditional basis. She recognised that he always placed various conditions on whether or not he would support her emotionally and she ultimately equated that this was the same pattern as had existed with her parents. All she wanted was for her partner to listen and offer a few words of wisdom, yet he was unable to offer them freely.

We all have our own unique game plan in life, and deep within us we feel that we are gradually travelling from point A to point B. We take exams and seek out appropriate jobs, hopefully with prospects and good wages. We form relationships and maybe have children; then buy homes with our good wages and build families or businesses, believing that we have sound prospects and time in life for work and recreation. Suddenly something happens, something unique to our life plan changes, a fundamental part of the structure is pulled from underneath us and we discover that we've lost our way. We're left drifting without a paddle. Whatever happens the key issue is that we did not consciously choose it, and are therefore totally unprepared.

Such examples are:-

Circumstances where, as with the woman mentioned earlier, our partner chooses to leave us, and it is not a joint or mutual decision.

We lose our job.

Our partner dies.

Our house burns down.

It is these struggles which hold people together. Close friends gather round the bereaved partner and offer support. Couples cling together and help each other through after the loss of a job. There is someone to lean on. Most often we take these people who offer support for granted and their quiet sagacity is not recognised until after the crisis is over.

Sometimes it is the struggle which keeps people together, or has even created the bond between them in the first place; and once the adversities are over, they find they no longer need each other. Usually two people have the same problem, or have experienced similar upsets in the past, which creates the link between them. They share the same knowledge and wisdom. They "know" what that situation is like. One man had the 5 of Coins showing that he had split up with his girlfriend. They had met each other shortly after separating from their respective marital partners. Over the months they had supported each other through the strains of divorce proceedings, and learnt a lot from witnessing the opposite sexes point of view. They stayed together for a few months after their divorces were finalised, but then found they had little else in common. "It's a mutual break up," he said. "It's strange. It might sound as though we used each other, but we didn't. We did need each other...and now, well, we just don't anymore."

In many readings I have seen the 5 of Coins interpret as loss of income. The card tends to come up when a business is struggling and on the brink of collapse, bringing with it a feeling of destitution. The 5 in itself does not mean that all is lost, because it sits at a pivot point, and life could therefore swing one way or the other. Cards taken for the 'future' will express how things will go, but remember that part of the process of a reading is to highlight how the questioner's personal karma is unfolding and that they are always in control, and therefore can do something to change any possible outcome.

Here are a few examples of the 5 of Coins followed by a card in the 'future':-

6 of Coins...balance of payments will stabilise.

10 of Batons...much running around after other people with little reward, showing that something needs to be off loaded.

Page of Swords...look to surrounding cards, as trickery and deceit are involved, which is possibly why the business has lost cash flow.

Page of Coins...assets can be sold to increase funds. Risks need to be taken.

Less specifically the 5 of Coins shows that the questioner has been through many changes and is continuing to do so. Often in this type of reading more than one minor 5 card will be turned up, emphasising the many levels of change. One young woman had three 5s, Coins, Batons and Cups, indicating that through her loss of business and income, her relationship with her live in boyfriend was suffering as he could not earn enough to keep them both. This set up a bad atmosphere in the home (5 of Cups), which created quarrels and tension (5 of Batons). Due to these factors he had threatened to leave her on many occasions recently, and this in turn was making her suffer severe pre-menstrual tension. (5 of Batons)

"We used to be so happy", she said. "Now even that has changed." These many factors added together were making her feel increasingly lost and confused.

Related to the Major Cards at number 5, the Pope and the Devil, we can note that the Pope shows these changes are dealt with wisely, while the Devil indicates that the changes are karmic. However, sometimes this karma is not personal. Hundreds of businesses close down during a nation wide recession, and during these times one can see that it is the karma of the nation which is influencing the individual.

When **reversed** the 5 of Coins is more likely to indicate that the questioner has no special friend to help them, although in other readings I have seen it as a more auspicious card, indicating the sudden introduction of such a person into their life. In all readings surrounding cards influence each other, and I believe that with the 5 of Coins these will imply more than whether the card is reversed or upright.

Key Words

Sudden changes in circumstance.
A special 'someone' in our life who helps us through thick and thin.
Friendships based on similar circumstances. Thus the other person fully understands how the other feels and what we they going through. Once the difficulties are over the friends tend to drift apart.

Reversed
The need for a special someone to lean on.

Toni Allen
The System of Symbols ©

The 6 of Coins

The 6 of Coins relates to earth at air.

Earth is the basis of all physical expansion and it provides everything where the multifarious forms and creatures find their abode. In earth all sensations are possible.

Air makes or keeps us alive, discharges polluted air, regulates the digestive process, keeps the body in balance and also regulates involuntary movements in the body. Thus when the earth of Coins and air and coupled together we find a symbol of balance and regulation in physical matters.

In practice the 6 of Coins will interpret as follows: -

As Coins relate to wealth and wisdom it shows that in matters of wealth, wisdom is used, and vice versa. The simplest interpretation is therefore balanced finances. The questioner's income is enough to cover outgoing commitments such as bills, mortgage/rent, food, heating etc., yet allows for a few luxuries in life. Within itself the 6 of Coins is not a card of great prosperity, but it shows good money management, and therefore there are some pleasures in life such as holidays, good clothing, and outings. This does not mean that the questioner never has debts. Credit companies are there for sensible people to use sensibly, and the 6 of Coins depicts a capability to repay loans which are within the questioner's means. If cards in a reading show that money has been mismanaged, and the 6 of Coins comes up in the 'future' then it shows that the questioner is capable of using their wisdom to sort matters out.

The 6 of Coins relates very much to the rhythm of our own breath. We breath in and then we breath out. When life is in balance on a physical level we breath easily. When life is out of balance we do the opposite and even use phrases such as "holding my breath until it was sorted", "felt I couldn't breath", "there was no room to breath", or "took my breath away".

Money is a form of life energy which we can all relate to. We work, and then we get paid. We use our wisdom to make money and this gives us a feeling of self worth. Physically accumulating money, which then gives us the advantage of being able to buy whatever we wish within those means, is the basis for many people's lives. Within the process there is the quality of fair pay, and fair play. If we have skills we expect to be paid for them accordingly, and often we work hard studying in order to acquire new skills so that we can be paid a higher wage, and thus achieve more and enhance our lives. The 6 of Coins does not, therefore, only talk about money, it also talks about being treated fairly, both within the work place and within relationships.

For one woman the 6 of Coins came up to represent one of the qualities within her relationship with her boyfriend. She was prosperous whereas he was not; and yet he insisted on paying for at least half of their nights out and treating her to small things whenever possible. "I could easily afford to pay for everything," she said. "But he won't let me. He pays for his rent and so on, personal stuff like cigarettes and clothes, then takes me out whenever he can. We have a lovely time and he never takes advantage of my money. Other men I've known have often made me feel like a meal ticket, yet this man makes me feel very special, as if I am important and not just my bank balance."

The complete opposite is symbolised by the **reversed** card. Here the balance is lost. Very often it means that the questioner has been ripped off, or had advantage taken of them.

Here are a few examples of the reversed 6 of Coins:-

1) A young woman worked hard for her boss, but he kept her on a low wage, making her feel cheated and misused.

2) A husband gave his wife a small amount of housekeeping and made her beg for necessities such as shoes for the children, sanitary protection, and heating in the kitchen. He classed these as 'luxuries' and said that he gained no personal advantage for himself when paying for them. On the point of the kitchen he apparently classed it as 'her' room as he never used it, and yet she stood in it for hours making his meals!

3) A woman found that her ex boyfriend, who had lived with her in her own house for several years, was suing her for half the property. "He never paid a penny towards the mortgage," she said. We used to go half and half on the food; but he never put money towards the bills, such as heating, because he classed it as my house. Now he's gone back to his ex-wife, and I feel that he's deliberately cheated me. Deliberately lived with me so that he can walk away with the money from half of my house."

4) A man found that he had been 'ripped off' by a confidence trickster.

5) Some years previously a man had put time and labour into helping his brother and his wife do up their kitchen and build an extension. Now he was asking them for some help to decorate his living room and they had refused. "After all I've done," he said bitterly. "I spent months round their place. I didn't help them just to get a return, but now I feel used. All I asked was for a few hours over a weekend, and they won't even come and hold the ladder for me."

The last example brings us to the more subtle side of the 6 of Coins. We don't always anticipate payment for our labours, sometimes the exchange is merely of energy. We would like a return in the form of a favour of some kind or another. When the card is up the **right** way it symbolises give and take, a willingness to exchange energy with someone else in order to keep the world running smoothly. For various reasons we are all more capable of doing certain things than other people; perhaps because we are tall, or strong, or small; educated in a particular field or have a special interest. When the card is **reversed** the energy one naturally gives out during any activity is being abused. Here the 6 of

Coins can be related to the 3 of Coins and you will need to judge whether the questioner is willingly doing an activity for love, or as an unwilling slave.

On rare occasions the 6 of Coins upright depicts beneficiaries who are willing to give money without expecting a return. For example:- a sponsor or grant agency. However, one is usually required to live up to the other's expectations and produce the work involved. e.g. the sponsor will not pay up if one doesn't run the race.

I have also seen the card, when placed in the 'future' during a reading depict a visit to the bank manager to ask for a loan. When upright the answer is positive and the loan is sanctioned because one is able to meet repayments. However, when **reversed** it suggests that the questioner is over stretching themselves and their proposition will not be met favourably, or that the interest rate at the particular company they are visiting is too high and that they can find something better.

Key Words

Balanced finances
Give and take
Exchange of energy through time or favours
Sponsors and loans

Reversed
Taking advantage of someone or being taken advantage of.
Putting a lot of effort in for little or no reward
Being underpaid in connection with one's skills and abilities.

Toni Allen
The System of Symbols ©

The 7 of Coins

The 7 of Coins relates to earth at Fire or Tejas.

Tejas is the fire, light or the glory which shines through the human being and makes up his stature, his brilliance, his lights of knowledge and the heat which keeps everything moving. On the other side of our circle number 7 falls at 3 and Prakriti, nature. This Prakriti is the matrix which sets up the direction of the creation in a general way and the conduct or behaviour of the individual in a special way.

Coupled with the qualities of earth, where physical phenomena have matured in full glory, we find a card symbolising an individual who uses their talents and skill to make money…and enjoys themself!

The 7 of Coins depicts the questioner's career. Whatever work they have chosen to do they get a buzz out of it. The work suits their nature so consequently they are able to shine and earn a reasonable wage. However, even though it's their ideal they still have to work hard. The 7 of Coins is not a card of riches or easy money. Every penny made is worked for.

In a reading the 7 of Coins can show several aspects depending upon surrounding cards.
After the Ace of Coins it often indicates that qualifications have been gained and that the questioner will find appropriate employment in which they can utilise their skills and start to build their career. Remember that Major Card number 7 is the Chariot and we can see how at the earth of Coins the individual is able to bring these qualities of knowing their direction in life and self knowledge into the physical realm and gain advancement for themself.

For those who are already in a stable career it shows daily routine and the continued effort required to maintain one's position.

Next to the Emperor it suggests that the questioner is in charge at work, or that they might be promoted to management.

Next to the Lovers that the questioner has decisions to make regarding their career.

When the 7 of Coins is **reversed** we find the opposite. People who draw this card work because they need the money and not because they enjoy the job they're in. For some people this aspect of life becomes a total drudgery, while for others a kind of apathy sets in and they cease expecting anything else from life. Here the earth puts out the fire, and the individual's personal tejas ceases to shine.

One client who drew the 7 of Coins reversed was in her early thirties, recently divorced and now a single mother. She took a job that was well paid in order to support her family. "The work's okay", she said. "The people I work with are good to me, and we have a laugh, but the work isn't taking me anywhere. There's no advancement." Meanwhile she didn't really know what to do with her life. "My career was mother," she said. "But I can't stay at home full time now. I need to be a good mother by providing more for my children than any state benefit would. That's my real job, looking after the kids. The work I get paid for is just a means to an end."

For one older man the reversed card was drawn in connection with his high flying job. "I can't leave now," he said. "I'd lose out on my pension benefits. But I don't enjoy the work anymore. Technology has changed my position so much. I don't get the same level of personal contact with others that I used to, and that's not me, I like being with humans rather than computers. It's driving me nuts, but at least I've kept up with the times and stayed in employment, unlike some of my contemporaries."

This man's story illustrates how something he had once loved and enjoyed had been radically changed by current trends. Initially he had chosen his work because he loved it and it gave him a positive sense of self worth. Sadly this scenario is becoming frequently more common and many individuals are finding that their chosen career no longer exists. For many the only option is to retrain. However, they must first go and seek out, once again, that something special which fires them with enthusiasm.

For one client the 7 of Coins came up **reversed** even though she was a real career girl and claimed to love her job in computers. "Is it really what you want to do with your life?" I asked her. "I want to make money," she said. "And computers are where the money's at. I always wanted to become a vet, but the qualifications took so long to get that it would have been years before I could be out in the work place earning my living. I'm buying my own flat now and I've taken on this new job. Computers are my career." After this initial consultation I saw her several times, and with each visit she looked more and more drawn and tired, the long journey commuting to London each day gradually taking its toll. I could see her personal tejas ebbing away. In every reading she had the 7 of Coins **reversed**. She admitted to hating her new job, but said that she stayed because she couldn't have less than a year in one company on her C.V. "It looks bad," she said. "Employers don't like it." The last time I saw her she said that she was going to sell her flat and move up to London and stay with a colleague. "I'll lose money on the flat, of course," she said. "But it'll be better for my health, maybe I won't be so tired." I asked why she was persisting with a career which undoubtedly gave her no joy. "The money's good," she said, and we left it like that.

The irony in this woman's life was that she pursued the career for the money alone. Meanwhile her health suffered and she lost much of the money she had earnt by deciding to sell her flat. The physical, earthy side of life, had become a burden to her, and her own brilliance had been lost in the process.

Toni Allen
The System of Symbols ©

To follow one's bliss is, perhaps, one of the most difficult challenges in life. Parents, teachers and the world try to shape and guide us along the path it best prefers. Some people find their path and then struggle to step outside the conformities which life puts upon us all and do their own thing. One client who had the 7 of Coins upright had chosen his life's work as a complementary therapist, but was failing to make enough money to make ends meet. "I'm going to jack it all in," he declared. "I'll go and get a job serving in a shop or something." The rest of the spread suggested that an alternative solution would present itself to him, but he wasn't having any of that. "I shall never practice again," he asserted. "I've had enough." The next time he came to see me he told me that he had been offered a part time job in complementary therapy clinic. "I can practice my art," he said joyfully. "And get a set wage." "I thought you were going to give it all up," I said. He smiled wryly. "You knew I'd never do that," he said. "I live and breathe my therapy. To not practice would be like putting the lights out. My last reading said there'd be an alternative, and I've found it."

The 7 of Coins does not necessarily represent bad health in itself, but as we have seen the reversed card can indicate tiredness, apathy and listlessness due to lack of joy in one's working life.

One's working life does not necessarily represent a paid job. For some their vocation is to be a wife or husband, to be a homemaker or to be a mother. It is what the individual fills the bulk of their time with and enjoys the most.

Key Words

Enjoying one's work/Career/The correct work and steady income
Reversed - Working just for the money/Not in a career
Failing to find one's true vocation/Having to work at something that one no longer enjoys

Bach Flower Remedy

Wild Oat – Of assistance in selecting a career and finding one's true path in life.
Wild Rose – For those who are resigned to their lot and have lost their ambition and purpose in life.

Toni Allen
The System of Symbols ©

The 8 of Coins

The 8 of Coins relates to Earth at Water.

    The element of water is the element of bond. Due to bonds all the shapes of the universe have their existence. Number 8 acts as the store which keeps all things together, and also as the bonds which keeps them together on universal and individual levels. Bonds also create limitation. The whole universe of forms is thus distributed in different types of limits.

    We have seen that at Earth all of the elements come together and physical phenomena matures in full glory.

    With the 7 of Coins we saw the action of doing the work, and finding bliss in the correct work for oneself. At the 8 of Coins we find the boundaries within which we are required to work, and also the things which we actually create while at work. Not many people like the word limitation or limits. It makes us think of restriction, or in some way a lack of abundance. Yet the entire universe is made up of limits and boundaries. Without these boundaries, bonds and limits nothing can be achieved.

Each task, activity or object to be created has its own specific set of boundaries. At Coins and Earth we use our wisdom and knowledge in order to make the most of these limits and produce the best work possible. The sculptor needs to know the rudiments of their materials, the computer operator needs to know how the machine functions and the gardener needs to know which plants will grow in what type of soil and the conditions required. And so it is within each profession, or daily task. When we understand these limits we are able to draw on our wisdom and create the most magnificent sculpture, the most advanced computer programme or the most glorious garden which provides us with beauty, fruit and vegetables, and a sanctuary for the animals who share our planet. When individuals do their work well and come up with something new and innovative we say that it is "ground breaking" or "destroying old boundaries". The knowledge for these activities has always been within the human race, it's only that once in a while someone with a more innate knowledge and wisdom understands the bonds which mankind has lived by until that point and uses that knowledge to go further.

Bonds create everything in the physical world and without them we would have no tea cups, chairs, tables, shops, clothes, people, and so on and so forth. Everything created of matter has bonds. Every day we work by these rules. Consequently if we work well within the perameters of our job then our work is recognised as being good and we are praised and admired. Thus the 8 of Coins is the card of "Good reputation". Reputation makes or breaks a man. It can offer promotion, higher earnings and esteem within one's community. While a "bad reputation", the **reversed** 8 of Coins, brings with it loss of earnings, lack of prospects and often a group of socially unacceptable associates.

I have observed the following points during readings.
Often the card is frequently associated with builders or other craftsmen due to the physical quality of what is being produced. When upright next to the Emperor or 4 of Coins the person being indicated is often a self-employed builder with a good reputation. I recall a time when I saw the card **reversed** for a woman whose husband was a builder. When I

Toni Allen
The System of Symbols ©

suggested that his reputation was under threat she said that at that time they were being sued by a couple who were not happy with the repairs done to their roof. "My husband was so stupid," she said. "He had so much work on that he sub contracted that job. The cowboys he got to do the roof bodged it up and when he said that he would rectify it for the couple they refused, and started legal proceedings instead. His entire reputation's now at stake."

One woman who worked for a large company asked whether she might be promoted at work and drew the 8 of Coins. When I suggested that she was efficient and had a good reputation she shrugged and said that she did her job well, nothing more. The next time she came for a reading she said that she had gained her promotion. "They liked my politeness, attitude and ability to work within a team," she said with a smile. "Who'd have guessed that such simple things go to making one popular at work." What this woman did not recognise was that the bonds she worked well within were her team. The team created her limitation, in that she was not expected to be personally outstanding, merely an efficient cog within the whole scheme of things, which she did with consideration and regard for others.

There are many ways of gaining a good reputation.

Artists display their paintings, someone buys one and puts it in their home. A friend calls round, sees the painting, likes it and asks where they got it. Thus the artist gains a commission or sells another piece. In some cases people buy the artists work purely because they have a reputation, and the general public believe that it must therefore be good, or beautiful, or valuable, or something which will accrue in value.

Thus we can see that getting a name for oneself goes a long way in many types of work. "Where did you get your hair done," we ask. "Which printer did your business cards?" "Who did you go to for a Tarot reading?"

Showing off our goods, or skill, to maximum potential is another way of gaining business or promotion. The idea is to use the watery bonds to attract someone to what we produce. We want them to desire and fall in love with what we have to offer. If in retail we dress our shop window with the newest and most fashionable goods. In the office we ensure that our work is neatly typed, well spelt and not covered in coffee stains. Every kind of work has its own unique way of being presented.

Everything from self promotion to advertising falls within the realm of the 8 of Coins.

When the card is **reversed** we find the opposite. People are displeased or unattracted to our work. However, it is not always our work which people do not like. With the upright card it is something unique about us which people are drawn towards when we sell ourselves without any tangible product, such as when teaching. Likewise, when the card is reversed, we find people acting with caution or circumspection in their dealings with us.

One female client was having difficulties within her relationship and had recently split up with her boyfriend for the umpteenth time. She drew two cards to find out more about his character and motivations. The King of Batons was turned next to the 8 of Coins reversed. When I suggested that he had a bit of a bad reputation, especially in connection with his sexual conquests, she nodded sagely. "That's why we've split up," she said. "He's a lovely guy, but so flirtatious, and everybody gossips about who he's slept with. Even if he gave up sleeping around I still think people would think that he is, because of his reputation."

Key Words

Good reputation
Self promotion/advertising
Promotion at work through ability and skill
Mastering materials we work with
Reversed
Bad reputation
For young businesses or new enterprises a need to gain a reputation.

Toni Allen
The System of Symbols ©

The 9 of Coins

The 9 of Coins relates to Earth at Earth.

Earth is the basis of all physical expansion and it provides everything where the multifarious forms and creatures find their abode. It is also the glorious end of one cycle, where the absolute stands as the glorious beginning on the other side. The element Earth is glorious because it is only through earth that all things of the world are created.

With the 9 of Coins we find Earth working at Earth. Thus it is a card of abundance. There is no struggle within this card, even though we find the cyclical action of beginnings and endings. A wise man knows when to let go, even of something which to others might appear to be abundant. Without letting go there is no room for the new and fresh, no

Toni Allen
The System of Symbols ©

space in which to create something different and thus gain divergent experiences in order to progress ourselves and work through our karma.

Earthly abundance gives us a feeling of security, a safe base from which to go out and do our daily work and return to in the evening. Although the card can represent either an abundance of wisdom or wealth, in general terms it is a very rare person who comes for a reading and is looking only to their spiritual life. I have found that these types have often already gained substantial material wellbeing, either through hard work or inheritance, and this then enables them to concentrate entirely on their spiritual path without any worries or concerns about their physical needs being met. Most people have human dilemmas, and reach a point in life of the 9 of Coins through their own endeavours, and are concentrated on physical comforts and money in the bank to see them through a rainy day or retirement.

The 9 of Coins can therefore represent property or money in the bank. However, it also indicates places where we feel safe, go to for safety, or visit in order to regain our abundance.

During readings I have seen these indications through the following examples.

Often the card symbolises a place of convalescence, such as a rest home. This is not the same as a hospital. (4 of Swords.) It is a place where we go to relax, have our needs met without any struggle on our part such as having to do the washing up or cleaning, and regain our strength. Mostly in hospitals one is ill, while in a rest home we may have been ill, but require continued rest in order to recuperate fully and quickly. I saw this clearly for one man whose wife had just undergone a major operation. "We've been considering a very nice little place on the coast," he explained. "I think the rest for a couple of weeks will do her good, but she keeps saying I'm fussing. This reading's clinched it, she's going, and that's that."

While currently working at a health farm doing lectures on Tarot and offering personal readings to clients I have seen this card many, many times. Clients go to the health farm to dip out of life, recover from stress, and generally have others do everything for them…just for a few days.

For teenagers and young adults living at home I have seen the card as two distinct possibilities. One is that they do not feel very safe and secure within their home environment and therefore go and visit a best

Toni Allen
The System of Symbols ©

friend whose family makes them feel welcome and wanted. The other is that their home represents security, and therefore they feel safe about exploring the world outside it. With the latter this can encompass teenagers who go away to study, but know that they will always be welcome home again. For one parent I saw the card with respect to her daughter, indicating that she had reached a new level of understanding concerning her mother's role and that regardless of what happened that her mother would always be there for her.

For one young woman, who had recently married, the 9 of Coins symbolised her running home to her parents at the first sign of trouble. "I did," the woman admitted, "But I'm back with my husband now. At home with Mum and Dad everything's done for me, like paying the bills and getting the shopping. I've never been in a position before where if I don't do some of these things that nobody else will do them for me." The cards indicated that she and her husband needed time in which to build their resources and establish their own sense of abundance, and also discover what was of value and importance in their new life as a couple.

One client particularly came for a reading in order to see what the cards had to say regarding whether or not it was appropriate to place her elderly mother in an old folks home. She immediately drew the 9 of Coins which suggested that the specific home she had in mind was safe and well run, especially when she drew the Page of Cups next to it, showing good service and caring staff. However, had she drawn the 9 **reversed** the opposite would have been noted, and this is how it was for one couple who came to me when they were highly distressed as to how their elderly relative was being treated in a nursing home. "They don't clean the rooms," the man said, "And you know how smelly old folk can get." "And the food's appalling," his wife added. "Just because they're old doesn't mean they can't taste anything." All of their comments about the nursing home highlighted how the relatives physical needs were not being met, and how the senses, which are all experienced through the physical body, were being assaulted or not considered.

With the **reversed** 9 of Coins we find a temporary lack of abundance. I say temporary because the 9 of Coins is never destitute. People who draw this card never go without completely. One woman drew the card shortly after her and her husband had moved to a new house. "It's a much higher mortgage," she said. "And even though we can afford it, and we discussed finances before we made the decision, I wasn't fully prepared, or hadn't fully understood, what we might need to go without at other levels in order to maintain the payments." Overall she was finding it a sharp lesson in what she did, or did not, value. Such as not being able to go out so much, or buy so many new clothes. She missed these luxuries, and said that she now wondered if their old house had really been adequate, because she missed the more affluent life style that went with it.

To some people the 9 of Coins reversed symbolises a place which is not safe or does not support their needs. I have seen the reversed card drawn by married women with a husband who works hard and brings in a good wage. Yet the home is too far from other people and they feel left out of the community, or their husband's long hours make them feel vulnerable being at home on their own in an isolated area.

Key Words

Abundance
Rest home
Nursing home
Place of safety
For young adults away from home, when they know they can return home and always be welcome.

Reversed
Temporary lack of abundance
Unsafe place
A place which does not support one's needs.

Toni Allen
The System of Symbols ©

The 10 of Coins

The 10 of Coins relates to Earth at the end of one cycle and the beginning of another.

0 is the unmanifest, full of potential, while the realm of Earth represents the beginning and the end. We therefore find a card which encompasses birth, death, and all things which have brought us to who we are and where we are today. This is in relation to our wisdom, wealth and physical body.

The 10 of Coins therefore symbolises the following: -
The hierarchical family, from which we come. This includes both natural and adoptive families.

Toni Allen
The System of Symbols ©

Family wisdom – both in terms of how intelligent our parents are and skills they naturally pass on.
Family karma – as opposed to our own personal karma, although of course, the two are inextricably linked.
Hereditary illnesses which have been passed down through the generations, or a propensity to such illnesses.
Genetics. This includes family features and physical deformities.
Inheritance. This includes money to be inherited, or money one leaves as inheritance. It also covers what an individual inherits from their family by way of morals, attitudes, class, upbringing, social graces and so on.
Elders – One's parents or grandparents, or becoming an elder through the death of an elder
Solid establishment of family:- often seen as the birth of grandchildren.

All of the above are of a cyclical nature. The end of one brings with it the beginning of another. Situations and circumstances, knowledge and wisdom, are passed on from one generation to the next. Financially we might leave our money and property to our children, and if they use the resources wisely then they in turn will be able to leave these things to their children. Family karma in the form of habits, traits and foibles carry through from one generation to the next, that is, until someone sees the fault and working through themself seeks to change the patterning. Knowledge is passed down too. When we are young we might admire our grandparents for their wisdom acquired over many years, they seem to know so much more about life than we do. We get older and in time become the grandparents, taking on the role of the wise elder and advisor to the young. Whatever our circumstances, and whether we come from a conventional background, single parent family or other family unit, we still carry with us the subtle substance of our forefathers.

Many types of complementary therapy take into account one's family medical history before a condition is diagnosed and treated. Great consideration is given as to the illnesses which one's parents, grandparents and even great grand parents suffered from. Often we are unable to trace our history back very far, but the practitioner will listen to see if our forefathers suffered from TB or gout, and so on. Some complementary therapies believe it is passed in the blood, others in the pranas, the breath of life we were given from our parents at the time of birth. The rhythm of their lives becomes the rhythm of our own, and in consequence the

Toni Allen
The System of Symbols ©

illnesses they suffered are hidden within our physical bodies as a susceptibility to certain types of disease.

In practice I have seen the 10 of Coins as all of the above and the following examples illustrate some of my points.

One female client came to me at a time when she was very confused about her direction in life. She was happily married, had two school age children and worked part time to earn some pocket money. However, her husband had a very well paid job and so she did not need to work as all of her physical needs were met with comfort. "I need to do something different," she said, "But don't really know what." I asked her to take two cards and she drew the 10 of Coins crossed by the 2 of Batons. It appeared that her parents had shaped her along very traditional family lines, and she admitted to working part time, as this is what her mother had done before her and her grandmother before that. "I don't want to be a sponger," she said proudly. "Women in my family don't just sit back and expect the man to do it all." The female members of her family's predisposition to work had been drummed into her as an unconscious patterning from an early age. Consequently as soon as her children were both at school she had taken the first available job. This type of work, however, in no way fulfilled her full potential, or gave her any sense of achievement; except the wage packet at the end of the month. The cards were suggesting that only by letting go of the idea that she would be a "sponger" if she stopped working would things ever change. She needed to take time out to discover what she might truly like to do. Over a period of several years she managed to gain good qualifications and became the first woman in her family to have a full time career.

When one woman came for a reading she was concerned about her boyfriend. She took two cards to represent him and drew the 6 of Cups and the 10 of Coins. The cards suggested that he was in some way living in the past and wishing to go back in time to how his parents had lived, maybe to relive happy memories of childhood. To my astonishment the woman confirmed this totally. He had recently bought the house in which his parents had lived for many years and in which he had been born. He was doing it up, not by changing to modern refurbishment, but by ripping out all of the new fixtures and fittings and taking everything back to how it had been when he was a child. This obsessive behaviour was the root cause of my client's concern for him.

Toni Allen
The System of Symbols ©

When the 10 of Coins is drawn for questions connected to work there are various alternatives depending upon surrounding cards. The card can symbolise that the questioner is following the family's traditional occupation, or continuing in a family business. If the questioner is self employed it can suggest that the family runs the business and that the questioner does not, therefore, have absolute control. This also implies that apart from having a head of the family, such as father or grandfather, who takes more control, that there may also be other family power issues manipulating the running of the business. I have seen the latter in the form of my client being a younger brother or sister, and therefore being dominated by an elder who feels that they should have more say in the way things are run. I have also seen conflict arise when a family member is adopted, and that although they have been given equal shares in the company, the blood relations have sought to pressurise them into selling up, or simply made life unbearable once the elders have left the business or died.

In connection with work I have also seen the 10 of Coins associated with those who look after other people's long term finances in the form of insurance, life policies, or solicitors handling inheritances. When one client drew some cards to find more out about his wife's attitude towards their family the 10 of Coins was drawn. Next to the Queen of Batons reversed and the 3 of Coins a certain element of coldness was indicated, as well as an over emphasis on her children being important only as a way of continuing the blood line. Her work, money, and providing material goods rather than affection were also highlighted. Manipulating money was undoubtedly her mode of expression. "Absolutely," my client responded. "She works as an accountant. How much the children will be left as an inheritance is far more important to her than whether or not she attends their birthday parties."

Another important side of the 10 of Coins is how it inter-relates to the 4 of Batons, a subject I have mentioned in the earlier chapter on the 4. We all originate from some form of family unit, whatever structure it might take. Often we radically dismiss the morals and ideas encompassed within our family, and rebel as a teenager or young adult. Sometimes marriage encourages us to break the family cycle and we seek to create a lifestyle and home life that is far removed from our roots. However, as time passes, we often find ourselves apparently swinging round full circle

Toni Allen
The System of Symbols ©

and bumping into our parents as ourselves. Suddenly their attitudes have become our own and we find ourselves remarking on how we never understood why they used to tell us to do this or that, and now we have come to a more mature and knowledgeable outlook as to why certain perameters need to be abided by. Some people take this phase of understanding in their stride and settle down to a similar type of middle and old age as their parents did, while others yet again rebel and often end up destroying much of what they have already created, due to a total abhorrence of the idea of repeating their parents patterns, or taking on their attitudes.

Neither side of the story is right or wrong, and during a reading it is the card reader's art to judge whether an individual is unconsciously repeating family karmic patterns, or whether it is their path in life to consolidate something of value which the family has been working towards. e.g. Someone who originates from a comfortable middle class background finds that by their early forties they have achieved the same status as their parents. They can either sell up and travel the world with the attitude of "I'm not going to be like them"; stay where they are and be comfortable, or say to themself "My parents got this far, but I can take it further." Each of these alternatives is correct for different people with different family issues. Surrounding cards will indicate whether the individual is resolving family karma or merely continuing the cycle.

When the 10 of Coins is **reversed** the only notable difference is that the family in question tend to be more fixed and dogmatic and less inclined to consciously choose change and expansion of ideas. This can raise issues such as prejudice if a family member wishes to marry outside their own colour, race or religion; as well as lack of acceptance if a family member wishes to better themselves, or even take a job which the family consider "beneath them". In many cases the family will ostracise any family member who steps outside their own tight boundaries, and maybe even never speak to them again or cut them out of inherited family money. One client who had the 10 of Coins reversed, found after his father's death, that although his father had always said that he was not prejudice, that a few weeks after he had married a Vietnamese woman, that his father had changed his will and completely cut them out of any inheritance.

Key Words

The hierarchical family
Family wisdom
Family karma
Hereditary illnesses
Genetics.
Inheritance.
Elders
Solid establishment of family
People who work with investments.
Reversed
Narrow minded family values
Inability to accept changes within the family.

Toni Allen
The System of Symbols ©

Court Cards

All writers and theorists on the Tarot have to some degree manipulated the Court Cards to fit their own system of interpretation. In all there are sixteen Court Cards, and yet a very common practice is to attribute the Kings, Queens and Pages to some acceptable, recognisable concept, such as the twelve signs of the zodiac, or the twelve apostles. Meanwhile the Knights can go a begging, as if they're an interference, rather than some part of the whole. In all, much time, effort and strategy is spent on "fitting" the Court Cards around one preferred theory, which at times gives the impression of a size sixteen trying to squeeze those few extra inches into a size twelve; certain bits pop out, and demand attention.

Another widespread habit is for the occultist to endeavour to better his predecessors system and re-align the Knights or Pages, maybe even rename them. Crowley achieves this by creating a Prince and Princess for each suit, and does away with the Pages altogether. In addition Crowley places each Prince in a chariot, thus likening them to Knights, yet maintains Knights on horseback intact. To some students this creates a lot of confusion and consternation between the "rights" and "wrongs" of certain packs. Many students find Crowley's pack, and those of his copyists, delightful to use for their colour and symbolism, yet flounder around, not knowing what to do with the glut of Court Cards on display.

If one looks at the history of both playing cards and Tarot cards, two histories which are inevitably linked, we find that throughout certain periods, especially in Spanish playing cards, that there has been no male Page at all, but a female Page, or Sota; a custom which persists in some regional designs. Traditionally in English playing cards we have Jack, King and Queen, while on the whole Spanish cards have King, Knight and Page; the female Page appearing to co-represent the Queen. Throughout history these combinations have remained reasonably stable for playing cards, while Tarot cards have nearly always had, King, Queen, Knight and Page. Crowley, Waite and other members of the Golden Dawn studied the history of Tarot and its associated playing cards as part of their esoteric teaching, so it is no surprise to find these exponents and their later followers, squeezing in as many Court Cards as possible from the various packs they studied. Although Waite has a traditional assembly of Court

Cards he claimed to have "rectified" the Tarot and its numbering system, while Crowley adds the Prince and Princess, echoing the concept of a female Page.

In truth there is no "right" or "wrong" way of how many, or which Court Cards, merely alternative ways of seeing the same thing. Like any long-term concept, the Tarot goes through changes according to the time, place and culture in which it is used. It is entirely up to the individual as to which design and assortment of Court Cards they prefer. However, it is always wise to remember that as much as one may like a particular pack due to its inspirational designs and glorious colour, there is little point in continuing to work with a pack if the Court Card interpretations fall flat in a mish-mash of vagueness. I have seen many worthy students struggle, and then gloss over the interpretation of the Court Cards during practice readings, rather than admit that they have not grasped the meaning of them in the pack with which they have chosen to work.

There is no doubt in my mind that Crowley set the precedence for the extra Court Cards, and there is also no doubt that he knew what he was talking about. But do we? I feel that we do not, unless we are one the stalwart few who have studied his works extensively to the last degree, and made it our life times work to follow exclusively in his foot steps. My hat off to all of you out there! I fear that the rest of us mere mortals will continue to see his Court Cards as beautiful designs, and never attain full grasp of them. I also fear that many copyists will continue to add Prince and Princess', write a few brief words on each in their accompanying booklet, or book, and fail to convey any clue as to how, or why, they reached such a meaning, leaving the student with a one off interpretation, with little or no room for expansion.

I dare say that what I write next will come under criticism, as, no doubt, you will jump up and down exclaiming, "but this is her system!" It is indeed.

So, what, or who, are the Court Cards?

I work on the premise that the Court Cards are exactly that: cards depicting members of the King's court. During a reading these people will depict real people in the questioner's life and not Queen Elizabeth 11 and her courtiers. However, they will show the rank and disposition of either the questioner or people in their life.

Before concentrating on individual interpretations it is a good idea to grasp who these Court Cards are in relation to each other. The simplest way is to visualise a medieval court.

The King and/or Queen rule. They either rule together or alone depending on whether or not they have a partner.

The Knight serves the King and Queen. Often the Knight goes into battle for the King and Queen, whether in reality or at the hustings in a jousting match. The Knight also goes on quests of enlightenment, such as for the Holy Grail. The Knight always wears the King or Queen's colours and swears his allegiance. He is generally of noble birth and high in rank.

The Page serves the Knight. His main role is to ensure that the Knight's accoutrements are ready for battle. The Page also serves the King and Queen. He fetches and carries for them, knows his place, and learns from his masters. The Page is also of noble birth, but the youngest of the courtiers.

My teaching methods come from the stand-point of a traditional Marseille Tarot Pack, with the Court Cards outlined above. If you have chosen, and prefer to use a pack which includes Princes, Princess or any other court cards then simply fit them into the above scheme of things. Consider such points as their age, rank and status. Princes and Princesses are also of noble birth, but lack the authority and judgement of a King or Queen. In some respects they are very similar to a Page, but if your pack has gone the whole hog and includes a Page as well then I would judge that the Page is younger. Likewise, if your pack lacks a Queen but has a Princess then it may be appropriate to up rank her.

The art of placing these figures in the context of real people is slightly more complex, because each Court card can represent an individual at any age, or phase of their life. Every human being is made up of a myriad of subtle parts that go to make the whole personality, some inherent, some manifested due to a certain set of circumstances at a particular time. Often these parts, or sub personalities as some people refer to them, are contradictory to what appears to be the individual's most prominent persona. Remember that the persona-lity is simply a mask, and that behind the facade each individual has their own samskara and karma to relate and react to. At times, in order to deal with specific situations, it is vital that we grow and change; which means that at times we apparently act out of character with what others have come to know us as.

To choose or not to choose?

Some Tarot readers practice the system of taking a Court Card at the beginning of a reading to represent the questioner. This choice is coming from what the reader intuitively perceives of the questioner, and many people go home from their reading feeling bright in the fact that they have been seen positively as the Queen of Coins or King of Batons. I prefer to let the cards flow and allow my clients own unconscious mind to pick out appropriate images to represent themself and others during the natural course of the reading. I feel that this is by far a more appropriate system, because if the client is feeling crabby and bitter then the Queen of Swords will show her face. Not once have I had a client come to me, having previously had a reading elsewhere, and say "Oh look, the Queen of Swords, that was the card chosen to represent me during my last reading."....yet every other Queen has been chosen! I feel that there is a lesson to be understood here. Simply that an honest interpretation of the Queen of Swords as a kick off point for a reading, in which the reader has **not** chosen the card themself, is probably the fastest way to make a client feel insulted enough to leave immediately, or at least never return. It may be the truth about the client, but when chosen by someone else it psychologically becomes "his or her opinion" and "Not me." Conversely, when chosen intuitively by the client it becomes "guidance" or "a higher source" which intrinsically knows and understands one's pain.

The Essence of the Court Cards

The Page

The Page symbolises all of the following:-
The new person emerging after a time of personal rebirth.
The child within us/play
A learning process
A time of service to others

Toni Allen
The System of Symbols ©

A child or youngster within one's life.
The Page is the young energy of the suit, and can depict either a male or female person.

Each time we go through a phase of inner death and consequently rebirth we are shown in the cards as a Page. Sometimes we "die" as the King or Queen of one suit and are reborn as the Page of another, indicating that we have finished a phase of giving one type of energy within us priority, and are starting to concentrate on another. e.g. Dying as the Queen of Coins (business woman) and being reborn as the Page of Cups (caring and nurturing), perhaps after the birth of a child. Other times we are still "alive" as the King or Queen of one suit and the Page of another suit will symbolise us learning to balance ourselves by drawing into play an energy which we had previously ignored or not given enough emphasis to. e.g. King of coins (rational business man, fixed in logic) and the Page of Batons (allowing oneself to make mistakes while taking a more intuitive approach).

The Page as the child within us symbolises that part of ourselves that we have not yet learnt to fully use or understand. It has, perhaps, lain dormant for many years, either through our own neglect or through repression by others.

As a learning process the Page symbolises both discovering the use of latent talents and also the process of study and learning required to pass exams and other examinations.

When appearing as a card of service to others the reader needs to use their intuition and judgement to gauge whether the Page is depicting true service or forced subservience.

The Knight

The Knight is always depicted on horseback. By his very nature he is swift and alert, regardless of which suit it is. Again the Knight can depict either a male or female person.

The Knight serves the King and Queen. In consequence he is a messenger, fighter, traveller and any intermediary between the crystallised consciousness depicted by the King and Queen and the youthful Page.

The Knight does depict a person, or character type, but more importantly he carries the essence of the suit from one situation to the next, yet never gets off his horse, and consequently does not appear to participate for long periods. His manner is quick and fleeting. He can therefore inspire, direct, challenge, avoid, flee, communicate, love, destroy or disappear from the scene without damage to himself.

The knight is that part of us which we send into the fray. How often have we found a confrontation by telephone easier to handle than a face to face discussion? Or, after a broken relationship, found it easier to be romantic while on holiday; when there is less chance of commitment or the drudge of daily life spoiling the buzz? Or found an inner strength we never knew we had in the heat of the moment? All of these activities, which may often surprise us, are the Knight at work, bringing to us the quality of a particular suit, when most needed; defending us, protecting us and offering wisdom.

The King and Queen

In general terms the Queen represents a female questioner or a woman in the questioner's life, and the King a male questioner or a man in the questioner's life. However, there are many masculine women types and feminine male types, for many reasons; therefore each sex may be symbolised during a reading by a card of the opposite sex.

There are many instances, but here are a couple of simple examples. A woman may be depicted by a King when she is the main breadwinner. A man may depicted by a Queen when he is studying spiritual work.

Please do not get these "sex changes" confused with concepts of homosexuality, lesbianism, trans-sexualism or any other gender changes/preferences within the individual, whether physical, mental or emotional. Indications of all the above do come up during a reading, but specific cards, where they are placed and all surrounding cards are taken into account. It is very rare for just one card to emphasise an individual's sexual preference. Some further examples to aid your judgement on the matter will be expanded upon within the section for each suit.

The Queen

The Queen is the feminine quality of the suit in crystallised form. She depicts the mature woman.

The King

The King is the masculine quality of the suit in crystallised form. He depicts a mature man.

The Court Cards within a reading

Any Court Card that comes up during a reading will indicate either the questioner or someone within their life.

Many Court Cards suggests either a large family or a large circle of friends and acquaintances. This often means that the questioner is tied up with dealing with these personalities on a physical, demanding level, or that they are influenced by them to a point where they are not allowed to be themself and make their own decisions. A typical example is a woman with a large group of female friends who all want to rule her life and tell her what to do.

The positioning of the Court Cards within the spread is very important. Appearing on the line of the physical level means exactly that, that these characters are physically around and either helping or hindering the questioner. When appearing on the line of the mental level the Court Cards indicate people who emotionally influence the questioner. They are on the questioner's mind a lot, or maybe "in their head" as a bad memory or even on a spiritual plain as a departed loved one whom they feel is still around.

Another important positioning aspect is when the questioner has one court card on the physical level and a contradictory one on the mental level. e.g. Queen of Batons at the physical and Queen of Swords on the mental, which would indicate a public mask of joviality while inside they are feeling tense and lonely.

Toni Allen
The System of Symbols ©

The Sword Court Cards

The Page of Swords

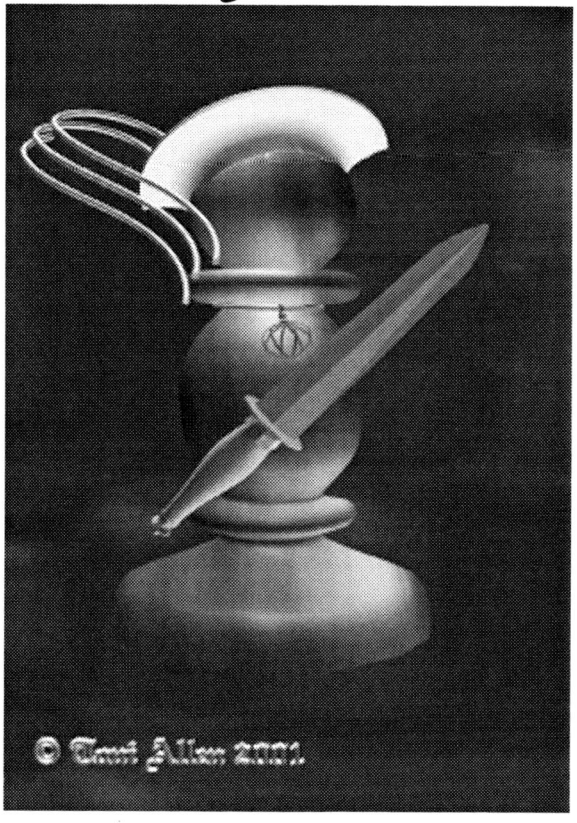

The Page of Swords is probably one of the most interesting and complex of all the Court cards. An entire book could probably be devoted to him alone!

The Page of Swords is the youthful part of air. Air relates to the mental realm. Thus the Page symbolises how we learn to use our mind and the process by which we come to a decision, or conclusion, on the matter in hand. The Page is continuously practising with different ways of thinking. Due to the non-crystallised form of air which he represents the Page can change direction easily...and when we are talking about thought patterns, ideas and even belief systems, this makes him a veritable mental gymnast. He is alert, quick witted, hard to fathom and apparently devious and dishonest. The latter two because he can so easily say one thing one minute and the complete opposite the next, while appearing to be equally sincere about both.

Air is also the realm that holds our personal samskara in the form of latent mental images and thoughts locked in from past incarnations.

The Page of Swords is often given a bad press, but the interpretation of how an individual uses the mental agility of the Page of Swords will depend upon surrounding cards. As always everything needs to be considered within the context of the whole.

In one context the Page of swords is the archetypal teenager. Many a mother has come to me in great distress due to the upheaval created by their teenage son or daughter going through a typical Page of Swords phase. This might include anything from stealing, swearing, drug taking, excessive alcohol intake, arguing, and a profound lack of respect for parental control or compromise. All teenagers go through some form of rebellion, but in general it is those with a marked inner conflict who show up as the Page of Swords. This conflict is not directed solely at the parents, even though all outward signs suggest that this is the case. They are in disharmony within themselves, discontent and miserable and often lacking direction, regardless of how much support is being offered. Not yet having found the best ways in which to utilise their talents, or occupy their busy minds, they experiment with mind-bending experiences such as drug taking or alcohol abuse. Sometimes drink and drugs do not play a part. These teenagers have rarely set their hearts on a vocation, and, as the saying goes "The Devil makes work for idle hands", and consequently mental energy which could be placed on study is utilised to try and outwit and outsmart everybody around them. Life becomes a game to them, manoeuvre versus counter manoeuvre, which results in domestic flare-ups and disputes. (Note that some artists depict the Page of Swords on a chess board e.g. Balbi)

Here it is important to remember that discrimination (buddhi) is awakened at the age of sixteen. (see The Lovers). Suddenly the child is no longer a child and they must learn through their own mistakes. Decisions do not comes easily when we have never had to make them on our own before.

Toni Allen
The System of Symbols ©

Sometimes this type of teenager's lack of direction may arise from unresolved personal experiences, which have created mental blocks and trauma. On a few occasions I have seen the card represent a much younger child, but in these instances there have generally been specific circumstances contributing to what the parent often describes as "bad behaviour" e.g. known cases of abuse, specific learning difficulties, hyperactivity, divorce, or bereavement.

By experience alone I have learnt that when depicting the fixed personality (as opposed to a phase of change) of someone over twenty-six, this card illustrates that the person has not grown up and still prefers to play mind games rather than knuckle under to the harsher realities of life. In some cases these people continue habits acquired in youth and become hardened drinkers or drug takers, very often their personality completely transforming when under these influences. Their partners describe them as "Jekyll and Hyde", sinister and "werewolf like"; some alter ego taking over after a few beers or their latest blast of coke.

Whether good or bad, these individuals have the ability to put on a different hat for every occasion. They are social chameleons. They easily fit in with the Lords and Ladies at Ascot one day, beer swilling pals the next and sit as chairman of the board the day after; always charming one minute to get what they want, and hostile once they have taken what they sought. Women come to me and say, "He was fine while we were out at his friends, and when we got home he just lashed out at me, shouting that my dress was wrong for the occasion and that I'd let him down." Under these circumstances the Page of Swords type can become physically dangerous. The dress being wrong is totally in his head, a mental illusion. He could have mentioned that it was inappropriate before they left, but he enjoys the mind games too much; and when pushed to the extreme it won't only be verbal abuse that he lashes out with.

Another attribute of the adult Page of Swords is that they can often have such an unsure image of their own self worth and where they belong in life that they can be very showy people. They adorn themselves with glitz and glamour, enjoying the fine art of "dressing up". When taken to an extreme their uncertain self image and ability to change their way of thinking, coupled with the desire to dress up comes out as cross dressing. I emphasise that on the rare occasions when the card is seen in the light of transvestism that it has nothing to do with homosexuality; more that they are showing the world one image and taking on a very different one in private.

I have also seen the card represent homosexuals of both gender, especially when they are still "in the closet" and not letting their sexual preferences be commonly known. For one young man the Page was in the past coupled with the World Card. It literally depicted him "coming out" and letting the world know that he was gay.

In complete contradiction there is the positive side of the card which portrays an adult who has to stay alert in their work. I have seen this for prison wardens, private investigators, and others who work in mentally exacting, devious, or covert operations as part of their job. I once did a reading for a man at a fete. The Page of Swords depicted his working life and he admitted that he had to stay mentally on his toes for fear of, quite literally, being stabbed in the back. The surrounding cards showed that he worked abroad and that there was a military connection. The traditional interpretation of "spy" sprang to mind, and his only reply was a smile and a comment about me being good at my job. He undoubtedly needed all of the wily Page of Swords mental elasticity to stay alive. He paid me, and when I looked up he had gone, having disappeared into the crowd so quickly it was as if he'd never been there.

Not everyone depicted as the Page of Swords is fixed in this state. For some it is a learning phase. I saw this for one woman. She was locked in a miserable marriage and in consequence found herself more mentally alert and "on guard" than ever before. Her concentration was pin sharp and she felt that some part of her mind had been awoken by the stress of the situation. Suddenly she was learning to think more for herself and yet at the same time frightened by this new faculty she had acquired.

Above all the Page of Swords symbolises that the individual is having difficulty dealing with their personal samskara, or, that they are actively endeavouring to deal with it.

No card is ever all "bad" and it is up to the reader to judge what is happening with this character within the context of the reading. Let me round of with an example.

In the reading the questioner's eighteen year old son was depicted as the Page of Swords. He had, it appeared, gone completely off the rails. This included, amongst other things; driving her car while drunk, hitting the proverbial lamp-post and then having the audacity to telephone and ask her to send a taxi to pick him up in case the police appeared on the scene. He then moved his girlfriend in to live with them without so much as mentioning it beforehand to his mother and went on to smash up several windows in the house. The questioner was beside herself with frustration and felt completely powerless, especially as he had more recently threatened to hit her.

Several cards were drawn to see what could be done. Rather than showing that this awful sounding youth should be locked up and the key thrown away, the cards outlined that he was going through a personal breakdown due to a bereavement. It transpired that her son's "bad behaviour" had started soon after she had split up with her boyfriend, who had lived with the family for some three years. Her husband had died eight years previously and she admitted that her son had never outwardly grieved for his father, but withdrawn inside himself. It appeared that her boyfriend's departure from their life had triggered off all of his deep sense of loss, rejection and suffering which he had bottled up after his father's death. Consequently the Page of Swords not only symbolised his present behavioural pattern, but also the latent pattern of behaviour he had stored up due to his earlier unresolved emotional experience.

Reversed

When reversed the Page of swords shows a marked change in that he is liable to be more sinister and far less able to change for the better. A character to be very wary of.

Key Words

Mental gymnast
Changeable character
Manipulative
Prone to drinking/drug taking
Likes dressing up/flamboyant/transvestite
Needs to be "on guard"
Secretive
The "spy"
Sometimes depicts homosexuality.

Toni Allen
The System of Symbols ©

The Knight of Swords

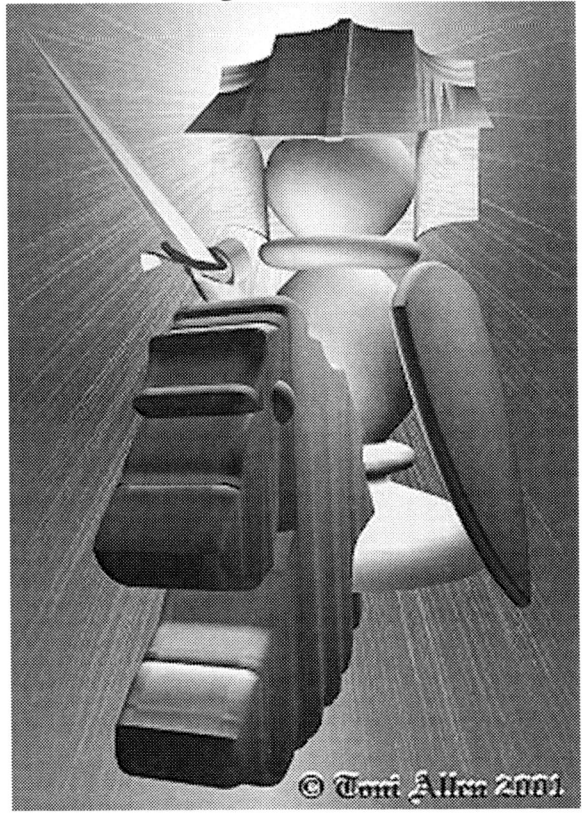

The knight of Swords symbolises mental movement. An active thrust forward for a desired cause. He is the archetypal knight in shining armour. Tenacity, courage, fortitude, resilience, determination and plain bloody mindedness all come within the realm of this knight.

The Knight of Swords is that part within us all which fights for the truth. He holds the sword of duality in his hand, the same symbol held up by the Justice card, only the knight thrusts it forward, holds it high as if riding into battle. He is that part of us which demands truth regardless of how difficult the circumstances are....and he will not let go until he finds it.

There are some people who fall within this type, although more often the card represents the bringing in, or use, of this particular quality when need arises.

Toni Allen
The System of Symbols ©

One example of this was a reading I did for a woman who was shown as the Queen of Cups which was characteristic of her feminine qualities. The woman worked in a large department store selling women's clothing and said that she was happy in her chosen career, enjoying the femininity of her work and finding great pleasure in assisting women choose their evening finery. Her home life held nothing exceptional. Then the Knight of Swords appeared in relation to her work. When I suggested that she was "fighting for a cause" and capable of "getting up on her high horse" over a particular situation at work that aggravated her she looked perplexed. She said that she had just applied to become department manageress, but felt that this might take her away from dealing directly with customers, a side of the work she loved. However, when I said that her desire to become manageress had nothing to do with more pay and the promotion, but something to do with injustices that she felt she could only be dealt with more efficiently from a higher position, she readily agreed.

"The top management are cutting hours, and so nearly everyone is becoming part time," she said, "This means that very few people now have adequate security...pensions, benefits...its all being taken away...it's a con." She went on to say that she had confronted various people about the situation and intended taking the matter further due to the social injustices she could see taking place. In fact she was very well versed in all of the political, legal and social aspects of the situation. In this instance the Knight of Swords highlighted the fact that it was something she felt very strongly about and felt she had to challenge for her own peace of mind, even if it meant giving up a side of her work she really enjoyed.

The Knight of Swords can also symbolise the individual who is striving to "get somewhere" in life, pitting themself against life as if it's a challenge rather than an adventure.

This is also true of the "seeker on the path", who "does" their meditation or fasting as an ordeal rather than a subtle process of change. There is no laid back letting it happen with this card, intensity rules the day. We all, in our various ways, come up against and deal with karmic influences, but when we go into Knight of Swords mode our determination to get at the truth of a situation can often overshadow intuition and answers subtly coming through from beyond the ether.

As a character this is the person who dedicates all of their time to fighting social, political or judicial injustices. A pen and paper warrior who seeks to change various man made laws for the good of the people. This would include followers of Green Peace etc., who fight for the rights of everything which lives on this planet, but in an active, non violent manner.

Reversed

This Knight when reversed shows that the fight has gone out of someone. Generally they have been in the mental battlefield for far too long and they simply do not have the mental capacity to continue. They have given up. Often I see this with individuals who are currently in litigation over family matters, or property.

Key Words

Mental fighter
Tenacity
Intensity
Fighting for a cause
Courage

Toni Allen
The System of Symbols ©

The Queen of Swords

This is the Queen of air, and therefore a Queen who is steeped in mental activity. In an ideal world she might well symbolise a woman with perfect discrimination, using her sword with a razor sharp edge of judgement. Yet the world we live in is far from ideal, and although these illustrations start off as mere pictures on paper, when transcribed into the real world and fleshed out with human characteristics, we find that the Queen of Swords is bitter and resentful; a living embodiment of the reversed Justice Card.

Again there are many alternatives for the Queen of Swords. Like the other Court Cards in this suit she is suffering while in the process of dealing with her personal samskara. Personally I find two distinct options for the card, either a woman who is temporarily acting like the Queen of Swords through adverse circumstances, or the woman who is fixed as a personality type. Both have very similar characteristics.

Toni Allen
The System of Symbols ©

We all have Samskara and Karma, and the purpose of being alive is to learn from life's lessons and thus perfect our being. Life is but an illusion, Maya, and the ego but a mask of duality. The self within is perfect and cannot be damaged or hurt in any way what so ever. When we identify strongly with the body, or the ego, and forget our higher self; then life becomes painful and the world of illusion around us a fearful reality. The mind is the part of us which holds onto the illusion, keeping it locked in with thoughts and memories. If we fail to let go of these by using discrimination to clear a path through the ether to the higher self, then we suffer the possibility of creating more personal samskara.

The Queen of Swords stands at this cross roads of life, filled with pain and distress, often knowing that how she presently feels and acts is not her true self.

Traditional interpretations call the Queen of Swords "The widowed, divorced or separated woman." I have found all of these to be true.

The widowed woman may at one time have been a Queen of Batons type, someone who often lives through and for someone else and enjoys the companionship a partner brings. Consequently bereavement leaves a large gap in her life. Loneliness, grief, isolation; and then, whilst in this weakened state, she has to take control of an array of household necessities which have been thrust upon her, such as finding money for the mortgage, paying the bills and general household maintenance. All these things her husband used to manage, but quite abruptly she is independent, and suddenly vulnerable to the crooks and con men who see her as an easy target once there is no man to protect her. For some people this is a temporary phase of adjustment, in which they learn to come to terms with their loneliness and find new ways of thinking in order to reach out to the world once again. For others it becomes a fixed state and breeds resentment, anger and a struggle to maintain control.

The divorced or separated woman is very similar. Both this type and the former may feel enraged that their partner has left them alone, but the divorced or separated type has someone to lash out at, so they may appear more active in their anger and retributions.

The Queen of Swords may feel lonely even when in a crowd of people, while conversely the feeling of lacking power inclines them to want to control everyone around them with an iron rule, making them unpopular and therefore creating further separateness. Often she is seen as the archetypal "wicked mother in law" who controls her children through mind games and threats of removing her love or an inheritance. I have seen this on many occasions where the husband is seen as a "Mummy's boy", still pandering to his mother's every whim after the death of the father. He is not permitted to take his place as head of the family, the matriarchal figure still clinging on to power through family funds, maybe even to the point of trying to split him away from his family so that he will move back with her and take away her loneliness.

Not all women who live by themselves are the Queen of Swords. Many women enjoy the freedom of independence. It is those who prefer companionship and yet suddenly have bereavement or divorce thrust upon them who become embittered because it is not their choice to live alone and manage their daily affairs.

Another side to the Queen of Swords is female health problems. Our thoughts are very influential over our bodies. When we feel happy our health is good and when we are sad our resistance to disease lowers. In this respect the Queen of Swords depicts a woman having difficulty with her femininity and the female processes of the body. e.g. Has had a hysterectomy, menstrual cycle is out of balance, suffers with P.M.T., or hormonal changes after childbirth. There is also the possibility that the feminine side has shut down and that the woman either is not having sex due to not being in a relationship, or that, although still in a relationship, she feels estranged from her partner and therefore they are not having a sexual relationship.

In one reading my female client was depicted as the Queen of Swords. Her marriage was on the rocks and she felt very lonely and brittle around her husband. They had stopped having sex several months before and in consequence she felt that the marriage was over. We continued the reading and then she was symbolised by the Queen of Batons, and beside her the King of Batons. It became obvious that she had already embarked upon an affair, this new man making her feel alive and vibrant. "Much more myself", she commented, and yet she continued to display all of the attributes of the Queen of Swords when in her husband's company.

The Queen of Swords is a complex character, and surrounding cards will aid in assessing why someone is feeling like this and whether the type is fixed or temporary.

All of the above sounds rather daunting, as if there is no positive side to the character at all. Once I saw the card representing my client and in fact I had done readings for her husband as well, and she always came up as the Queen of Swords even though they were well suited and content together. In this instance it was positive. She worked as a local councillor, and her discrimination was often called into play over difficult decision making. The card depicted her occupation and the tough line she was required to take, rather than her overall personality.

Reversed

When reversed the Queen of Swords indicates a fixed state and less likelihood of change. On occasion it has also indicated the sudden loss which initiates the feelings of loneliness and isolation.

Key Words

Divorced/widowed/separated woman
Lonely
Bitter
Spiteful
Isolated
Sexual problems
Female problems

Toni Allen
The System of Symbols ©

King of Swords

The King of Swords is the King of air. His mental patterns are fixed, either in stubbornness, or controlled manipulation.

With the King whatever situation he is in he feels he must win at all costs, so he uses his discrimination accordingly, always going down the path where his ego will come out on top.

In a fixed state he can be stubborn and ruthless. It's as if he has his own private book of the law and anyone who disagrees with him is wrong, or maybe even mad for daring to have such different thought processes. As he always believes that he is right he will argue that black is white and white is black...if that is the point of view he first put forward. There is no backing down for this man.

Another clever trick up his sleeve is to steal your standpoint and claim it as his own. Let me expand with an example. One day you argue with him and, for simplicities sake let's say that you've argued that grass is green, while he claims it is brown. He will not shift and therefore you give up, exasperated. The following day he breezes in and states that grass is green. "That's what I said yesterday," you exclaim. He says, "So you're saying that grass is green?" "Yes", you reply. "Well I'm so glad you can see reason and agree with me at last," he says. At this point you will probably continue hitting your head against a brick wall by muttering such comments as "I said that all along", to which he will claim that you never did. And so it goes on. There is no winning against this man.

In business this man is tough, and not always to be trusted, the card **reversed** showing a higher degree of dishonesty. He has incredible stamina, not through any robust physical strength, but a mental doggedness which keeps him going regardless. For this reason he makes a strong business adversary, and a difficult man to work for as he demands the same high level of commitment from every one else around him. He lives off stress, and enjoys mathematical, computer or financial work.

Due to his rigid state of mind the King of Swords can become very inflexible within his body. This may manifest as arthritis, mobility problems, stiff shoulders or general stress.

Again one has to distinguish between the subtle differences of the type who lives off stress and challenge, and the more ruthless argumentative type; or even whether the subject is out of balance and that stress is affecting them adversely.

Occupations indicated by the King of Swords are strongly connected to the sword, either as justice, or as the blade itself. For these reasons he depicts judges, barristers or solicitors, and the surgeon. When **reversed** the card suggests that the legal man is corrupt or that the surgeon is incompetent. Interestingly I have found individuals who participate in martial arts or sword fighting as a hobby to be more highly represented by the Page of Swords due to his flexibility and agility than by the King, even if they are masters in their field. However I have found that acupuncturists, who use needles to heal, are represented by the King as they are following a highly specialised set of rules and come closer to the surgeon due to their knowledge of anatomy and physiology. Their needles can also be viewed as tiny swords.

Key Words

Ruthless
Strong willed
Always has to be right
Able to turn your argument against you
Stiff/rigid
Stress
Mathematician, Computer orientated work, Legal profession, Surgeon
Reversed
Someone who corrupts the law
Tendency to shout in order to command authority
Extremely argumentative
Bully

Toni Allen
The System of Symbols ©

The Baton Court Cards

The Page of Batons

The Page of Batons is the youth of fire, or nature.

Of all the Pages this one is most likely to represent the questioner's child.

The Batons energy is that of our true nature, and in this youthful state we endeavour to find out who we truly are. Often the card will come up for an adult who is going through a phase of change, maybe from marriage to divorce, or at a period when children have grown up, or started school, and it's time to find oneself again. Many changes bring new beginnings, and with them a phase of reassessing who we are. For this reason the Page of Batons is often seen as a card of rebirth.

For many people, of either sex, divorce brings with it a sense of freedom, and an ability to once again be oneself. In many instances the marriage has been a struggle during its breakdown and in consequence one has lost the knack of having fun and simply "being". Finding out once again what we really enjoy for ourselves, as opposed to what our partner had persuaded us to like, or become a part of, is a difficult task. I liken this Page to a toddler learning to walk. We bravely take a fresh step forward, give way at the knees and fall, but resiliently stand up again, determined to let go of life's props and become an independent person in our own right. We find the ability to laugh at our mistakes, learn from a succession of quick lessons and ultimately go it alone. Only when **reversed** does the card show us thrashing and screaming on the floor, demanding attention from all around in the vain hope that they might guide us to an understanding of what our true nature holds.

Our true nature can be buried, lost, forgotten, manipulated or forsaken in many ways. Perhaps one of the most common scenarios in a reading is when the Page of Batons is seen close to the 2 of Batons. Here we find an individual's nature dominated by someone else's, and consequently lost. The earliest form of domination comes through our parents or guardian, and even though we mature, many of these initial ideas and concepts about ourselves stay with us as blocks and barriers for life. It is not uncommon to find in a reading that failed relationships stem from earlier programming by parents. Such affirmations as "You're useless, worthless, unlovable" etc., resound within us and we therefore anticipate defeat before we even start. Very often a relationship breaking up acts as a catalyst for age old buried feelings of inadequacy to rise to the surface. It is then that the individual dons the persona of the Page of Batons and embarks on the exciting journey towards finding their true nature.

Sometimes this journey includes fire energy activities such as the search for appropriate artistic and other creative pursuits. Sometimes it is testing everything we have never tried before, a bit of this and a bit of that, so that when something feels right we can pursue it; because if we don't try we will never discover whether something suits us or not. This may even include changing the colours we wear, as we adapt our style and appearance to accommodate the new us. Sometimes it is a bursting out of passion and lust for life; after all, everything is so much more fun when we follow our true path.

The Page can also symbolise the awakening of intuitive faculties, especially if the questioner is following a spiritual path.

Key Words

Learning to find one's true nature
Dealing with blocks which have covered the true nature
Having fun
The child
Intuitive individual

Toni Allen
The System of Symbols ©

Knight of Batons

Batons rule fire, or tejas, the light which illuminates each one of us.

The Knight of Batons carries this energy to us, which manifests in the form of inspiration. It is our personal light of knowledge; and here I use the word knowing, not in the sense of something learnt from a book, but a deeper sense of knowing from within the psyche. Often the Knight represents a flash of insight into a situation or a communication from our higher self, so that we know the right course of action.

For many people, especially those following a spiritual path the Knight comes up to symbolise their connection with the causal realm, a tuning into a higher knowledge beyond themselves. However, when the card is **reversed** it shows that this side of themselves is switched off, or not working properly. I saw this for one woman, who although already a practising spiritual healer, had chosen to join a local healing group. The "elders" within the group had forbidden her to practice her healing art until they had deemed she was ready. In consequence her Knight of Batons was reversed and she felt that she would never be able to reconnect to her inner voice again. She had come for a reading because she felt suspicious about the correctness of the group she had joined, and did not feel it was benefiting her. Rather than supporting her in the use of her wonderful gift, in a very short space of time, they had managed to damage her confidence and trust in it.

Another interpretation for the Knight of Batons is communications, in fact any type of communication as long as it is not one person standing in front of another. In today's world this goes beyond the old fashioned interpretation of "the letter" and now includes; telephone calls, faxes, e.mails, mobile phone text messages and even telepathy. In a reading the card often shows that the questioner is waiting for an important communication, which will shed led on, or help resolve, a difficult situation. When **reversed** it symbolises that the communication is delayed or will not arrive.

For some people the card indicates that they need to phone someone and that their call will be well received, while for others it means that they need to sit down and speak heart to heart to someone they love, and need to communicate beyond the physical.

Key Words

Inspiration
Personal insight
Messages on any other level than face to face

Toni Allen
The System of Symbols ©

King and Queen of Batons

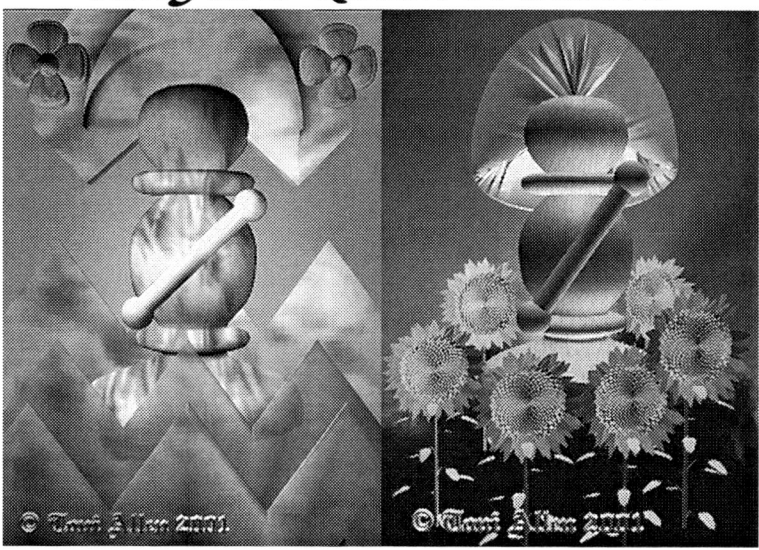

Fire, or Tejas rule Batons from the number 7 and from the number 3 they are ruled by Prakriti, or nature.

I have linked the King and Queen in one section because they symbolically epitomise the perfection of one's nature. There are no set rules as to what an individual's nature should be. Animals, on the other hand, live by their nature alone and therefore cannot reach self realisation in this life time because they lack discrimination. For example, it is within the cat's nature to hunt birds, and however well trained our domesticated feline is it will not discriminate between the sparrow in the hedge outside and little Tweety-Pie in the cage, should he be given half an opportunity to catch either. Our treasured puss will not think twice and say "Oh dear, I had better not catch Tweety, because someone will get upset." If hungry he merely thinks "Dinner!" and goes for it.

Like the cat, all humans have their own specific nature. However, unlike the cat, humans have the faculty of discrimination and human parents sometimes use this with a heavy hand when it comes to their own offspring. Intellectual parents often wish for their children to become intellectuals, regardless of the child's inborn creative talents. "Art gets you no-where," they say, and insist that you study science and mathematics. The child's true nature becomes misshapen or hidden and, for many, it takes a life time of self discovery to ascertain what went wrong and when.

The examples of parental influence on the child's individual nature are endless and exhaustive, here are just a few suggestions:-

The crying child will not be attended to until it is "good", and quiet. This may result in a feeling that one cannot ask for what one needs in life.

"You do not deserve...", "No-one will love you if you act like that", "You are not allowed", "Who do you think you are....?" and "You'll be punished if you do that again" are all potentially nature destroying patterns of speech found in parents. No parent is all good, and no parent is all bad. Life is full of contradictions and each and every individual has parents whom in some way, moulded whom they are today.

There is also the influence of teachers, other family members and additional authoritarian figures to take into account.

There is also the family karma to consider and social and economic background.

An example of family karma is the wealthy family who, for generations, have been brought up to act "properly". The children have always been taught to only speak when spoken to, not to exhibit emotions in public, especially the boys, and if male to aspire to university and if female to aspire for a "good match". Conversely a male child from a poor family may aspire to university, and be intelligent enough, but be deemed "getting above his station" because he wishes to rise above the class into which he was born.

Some of this may sound a little old fashioned, but it applies heavily to older clients. Today it continues, and younger clients almost have the reverse problems. Females especially are "expected" to do well and follow a career, and often thought worthless or "wasted" if they wish to settle down and have a family.

So how does all of this apply to our King and Queen of Batons?

The Queen of Batons is a woman being true to her nature, and the **King of Batons** is a man being true to his nature.

In general terms the cards apply to the individual's home and personal life rather than working life, although it suggests that they are happy within their work, whether it is intellectual, financial or emotional. Specifically for employment the card describes people who work with nature, such as farmers, gardeners, or those concerned with environmental issues. It also indicates an individual's inherent talent such as a "natural" ability to paint, write, sing, or play a musical instrument. Whether this talent is utilised to create a career will be illustrated by surrounding cards. Sporty types also come under this realm.

This King and Queen are happy, joyous people because they have discovered the pleasure of being themselves. In partnership both like to share their time and talents with their partner, and are not stuck to the routine of conventional living, such as the woman washes up and the man mends the car. If this is what suits them, then fine, but if he's an excellent cook and she's great with a spanner, then it will come easily to them to flaunt social expectations and simply do their own thing. The one downfall of both King and Queen is their gregariousness; and for this reason alone they often seek companionship and partnership for the sake of it. Isolation and hours of solitude do not come easily to them unless they know they have someone to share their experiences with at the end of the day. When in relationship they function incredibly well, however, without it they often feel that life has no purpose because there is no-one special to do, or achieve things for. Lack of someone special in their lives, or even a best friend, can turn these Court Cards upside down.

When reversed the Queen indicates a burning desire for the woman to become herself, especially within relationship. Some woman, due to earlier conditioning and suppression of their true nature, believe that they are not allowed to express themselves creatively in relationships. In consequence they choose a spouse who criticises their personal forms of self expression, their partner's reaction thus confirming the earlier impression set upon them and making them fearful of becoming themself. A common example is the man wishing to dominate how the woman dresses, especially once they are married, or have a family. This places the woman back in the role of being a child and "not allowed" to choose her own clothing. Disobedience might result in lack of love, and for women with a family to look after rejection consequently becomes a much more far reaching circumstance.

The Queen of Batons **reversed** in a reading always indicates that the questioner realises that she is out of balance and recognises that she desires change and the strength to become more the type of person she realises she is underneath.

The King of Batons reversed has very similar problems to the Queen. Often he is unable to express himself naturally in relationships, and sometimes this is not only emotional but also encompasses the sexual, physical side of the relationship. He may find it difficult to cry in front of his partner, or admit that he is unfulfilled in his work. Having been brought up with the concept that he is the main breadwinner he may find it impossible to change career to something more fulfilling, yet less well paid. His dominant parental phrases may be "You're a failure", or "A man has commitments", thus his lifelong striving to be a success in the working world his parents chose to push him into him.

Both the King and Queen **reversed** tend to have no sex life. This can be for a number of reasons such as simply no longer fancying their partner or having no one to share their bed with. However, in both cases a sex life is usually desired and surrounding cards will indicate the source of the problem and how it might be resolved.

The chapters on the 2 of Batons and The Lovers offer further reading and information on how the personality and true nature can be influenced by those around us.

Key Words

Living life by one's true nature.
Creative flair.
Love of nature.
When reversed true nature is suppressed
Sexual desires denied expression

Toni Allen
The System of Symbols ©

The Cup Court Cards

The Page of Cups

The Page of Cups relates to the youthful quality of Water.

    Water is the bond between things and people, a sort of love which keeps them together. Thus the Page of Cups symbolises faithfulness and loyalty. The young child trusts in its parents without question, the magic bond between them acting like a golden thread of warmth and reassurance. As we grow older the same deep bonds take place between ourselves and our friends and partners. In times of crisis one particular friend will often show themselves more willing, or able, to help, and then the bonds grow stronger between us. Favours are returned, and over the years we come to know and recognise that person as someone we can rely on, even if we don't see them for long periods of time. This is the Page of Cups within us all, a true friend and a faithful lover.

When those bonds are broken, or for one reason or another become over stretched, or inhibiting, then the Page of Cups is **reversed**. This is a sign of disloyalty, untrustworthiness or unfaithfulness. It is not uncommon to see the Page of Cups representing infidelity on the part of the client or their partner. The card usually shows itself when the party who is having the reading has been unfaithful, or knows about their partner's lack of faithfulness. More often than not sexual unfaithfulness is illustrated between man and wife, rather than a verbal, or other, disloyalty. Inevitably this type of situation sets up a deep lack of trust and, depending upon surrounding cards, the Page reversed can suggest past damage and hurt created by the pain of finding a partner has slept with someone else. Consequently it is very hard for the individual to let go of this hurt and allow others to get close and create those special bonds needed to form the basis of a lasting relationship. The card therefore also symbolises lack of trust.

For some people these impressions stem back to feeling deserted by their parents. A common example is when someone has been sent away to boarding school. The Page of Cups **reversed** also illustrated a point with a client whose father had died when he was very young, and then his mother committed suicide in his teenage years. This left him with a deep distrust of any type of "permanent" relationship. "Everyone I loves leaves me," he claimed. "There's no point in getting too attached".

Disloyalty and breaking of bonds can arise from many other situations. Friends let us down, or don't appear to have time for us. In more acute cases we hear that they have back stabbed us through bad words, or deliberately set about discrediting us with colleagues or family. Life is structured through the bonds which keep all people and things together and unconsciously we rely on these bonds for our very existence.

There are several occupations symbolised by the Page of Cups. Nurses especially due to their special bond with their patient, but moreover all caring professions such as those working with the mentally ill or elderly. Although perhaps a little old fashioned now butlers, valets and other personal servants would also be indicated, because they are expected to be loyal and trustworthy. It also includes all those who aspire towards using their psychic ability as a vocation. Generally, with the Page, we find a person in the stages of learning the psychic arts, although frequently they are naturally gifted in seeing clearly the bonds of attachment between the past, present and future. The Page then grows up into either the King or Queen of Cups who is a master in psychic arts.

Key Words

Faithful
Trustworthy
Loyalty
Caring professions
Aspiring psychic

Reversed

Unfaithful
Untrustworthy
Disloyal
Difficulty in establishing meaningful relationships

Toni Allen
The System of Symbols ©

Knight of Cups

The Knight of Cups is a multi-faceted and fascinating Court Card. He represents the moving part of water and symbolises emotions brought, or awakened within us, by other people.

Water is associated with attachments and bonds. A highly logical part of us all repeatedly tells us, and re-evaluates the fact that we are free spirits and people of choice. Only there are times in our lives when things happen which appear to be outside our personal realm of choice. "I didn't choose....." is a very common phrase. These times of apparent fate, or destiny, arise from our personal samskara and karma unfolding. We are all **bound** by latent behavioural patterns from previous incarnations, and although we rarely recognise these, life itself triggers them all of the time. The Knight of Cups symbolises those times when these unseen patterns are aroused by an individual who enters our life, and due to the impact that person makes on us, a hidden part of ourselves is suddenly awakened, often with dramatic consequences.

"I didn't choose to fall in love with him/her", is the comment made by many people when they find themselves attracted to someone who, for one reason or another, is deemed unsuitable or unavailable. Love is blind, and when old bonds of attachment gallop into our lives via the Knight of Cups we appear fated to fall in love with the wrong person. There are many forms of karmic connection between people and the scenarios they play out are often painful due to these previous bondings. E.g. A woman falls in love with someone else's husband, and they recognise some deep impression between themselves, as if they are soul mates. Perhaps they were lovers in a previous life? Or a woman finds herself going out with a man who continuously hits her, and yet cannot break away. Perhaps they enacted the same theme in a previous life and did not manage to resolve matters then either?

As in all situations, surrounding cards will give hints on the type of bonds between the individuals.

Some karma is positive and some negative. We all possess latent talents carried over from previous lives and often they lay dormant until someone, as represented by the Knight of Cups, awakens them in us. Love is one talent we may have hidden deep within ourselves, and a lover coming into our life is one aspect of this card; yet there is also the love we have for other things. I have seen many clients who have a typical Knight of Cups in their life. The person comes and goes, bringing with them a terrific sense of passion and awareness for the client's talents. Writing, painting, spiritual awareness, money making.....in fact, anything. Inspiration is the key word here. Without the connection with the individual represented by Knight of Cups the client undermines their own passion in a particular subject, believing maybe that they are not worthy or good enough. When the Knight of Cups sees their efforts they fire them with enthusiasm. "I've always been attracted to writing," said one woman. "And then I showed this friend a short story I wrote years ago. She encouraged me to write more. I don't see her very often, and when she's not there I feel she's wound me up and left me to survive on my own. There's no support except when she's around. And yet those times when she is show me how much I love the process of creative writing."

Not being there is another aspect of the Knight of Cups. He comes

Toni Allen
The System of Symbols ©

and goes like a will o the wisp, creating deep bonds and then disappearing. He is the lover who fails to guarantee when they will return, or the married man or woman who can only been seen here and there around other commitments. He is also the archetypal traveller, and as such also depicts the long distance love affair, where one partner has travel as part of their job, or lives over seas. For this reason he can also symbolise a foreigner, or simply a person who loves to travel.

Another, perhaps more obscure, interpretation for the Knight of Cups is the person we are destined to fall in love with, and yet we are unaware of them, even though they are close by. Every time we come close to meeting them we move away, or simply do not recognise who they are. Often people ask me about future relationships and if one is shown in the reading they then, quite naturally, ask if they already know this person. If the Knight of Cups turns up then the answer is yes. Frequently the questioner has been in a difficult relationship, or just broken away from a long term commitment, or has other upsets in their life which have made it difficult for them to be open and ready to accept a fresh relationship. When the time is right they will recognise the love attachment who has been in their sphere of life for quite some time.

I saw this for one man and the cards also suggested that the woman he would fall in love with worked for him. "I know all of my employees," he said "And quite frankly none of them appeal to me." About four months later he made an appointment to see me with his new girlfriend. "She's worked for me for about three years," he sighed. "It wasn't until we had to work late one night and I took her for dinner because we were both starving that I really got to know her. She was there all the time, yet I never saw her."

Another client had a similar story. She had been seeing me for some time and the Knight of Cups always came up for future relationship. When she met the man she later married she found that for years she had been in the same places, and social scene, yet never met him. "It's so uncanny," she said. "Friends had mentioned him to me and yet we'd never met. Then I found out that he's friends with other friends of mine! And we'd been to the same private viewing of an artist we both know, and there were only about twenty people there....I never noticed him....Can you believe it, it's as if we've been following each other around for years until it was the right time for us to meet."

When **reversed** the card symbolises that these emotional bonds are not coming towards us. E.g. Our lover is not travelling to see us. Our inspirational friend has not called for a long time, and we therefore feel lost. It is not an appropriate time to go "looking for love". Nothing "turns us on" any more.

Key Words

A karmic meeting between two people
Travellers/foreigners
Lack of commitment from a lover
A deep feeling of destiny or fate
Reversed
Lack of attachment
Emotional drifting

Toni Allen
The System of Symbols ©

The Queen of Cups

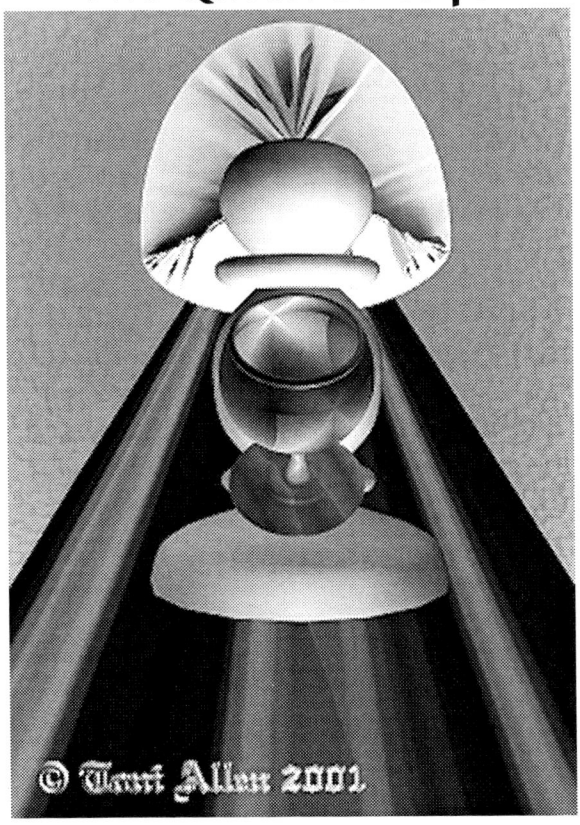

The Queen of Cups represents the feminine side of the bonds symbolised by water.

' 'The Queen of Cups is, perhaps above all else, the archetypal mother figure. On one side of our circle water sits at the number 8. The watery side of the Queen of Cups as mother is easy to recognise. We speak of early bonding between the mother and her child, and recognise that the womb from which we are all born is fluid; a safe haven from the outside world and a place that lures us back in times of trouble. We all seek out the comfort of the womb in various ways, such as rolling ourselves up in a warm protective duvet when we feel ill, or soaking in a warm relaxing bath with the lights dimmed low. In this respect the Queen of Cups represents a woman who nurtures and protects us, loves and cares for her children, and is there to give us a healing cuddle regardless of how old we are.

On the other side of the circle water sits at number 2 and is the state of the undifferentiated or unmanifest. All of the multifarious forms of the Universe lie stored in the unmanifest before the creation breaks out, so again we find the symbol of the mother, the female creator whose waters break and she gives birth to the human child. We also have the symbol of Mother Nature here, the unseen force which gives life to all creation.

As a mother figure the Queen of Cups is dedicated to caring for children and family. Sometimes she is a nurse, but more often her emotional bonds are linked to those closest to her. She is loving, kind and gentle, a giver rather than a taker and the **reversed** side of the card shows someone who is weak and giving to a fault without due consideration for themself.

The Queen of Cups is also the clairvoyant or "seer". This is due to her ability to link in to the unmanifest realm while simultaneously being able to assess the bonds that her client has with people, places and events that have manifested as karma. Remember that the negative side of the bonds of water is bondage, and this is the tie that binds us to repeat cycles of activity and inter action with specific souls. It is interesting to note that the traditional art of scrying is carried out using a water filled dish, in which the clairvoyant sees images which are then interpreted or relayed directly to the questioner. The same principle is used in crystal ball gazing, only the clear crystal replaces the water.

Mediums who apparently see ghosts, or spirit entities, as they might like to refer to them these days, are also represented by the Queen of Cups. Any soul that has not released itself, or been released, from the physical plane is in a state of bondage, and the Queen is able to sense or see these spirits.

Any human being, male or female, is able at some level or another to tune in to these vibrations. If the questioner is not on a spiritual path and therefore using these abilities in their work, or caring and mothering, then they are likely to be going through a phase of being highly sensitive to their surroundings and atmospheres within their environment. If the questioner is also represented by another Court Card, then the Queen of Cups suggests that they are feeling very emotional or, if the card is **reversed**, over sensitive and maybe tearful and overwhelmed by many emotions.

In a man's reading the Queen of Cups may simply suggest his wife, partner or mother; any woman that he loves and cares for. Sometimes it suggests a new love interest, or that his partner is reliable and caring, even if he is going through a tough patch. A review of surrounding cards will help in placing the importance of the woman to him. One thing to keep in mind here is that although the man may love this woman, he may not necessarily be having a sexual relationship with her; for here we are talking about the emotional side of love relationships, not the physical.

Key Words

Mother/Mother figure
Caring woman
Psychic/Clairvoyant/Medium
Sensitivity
The woman a man loves
When **reversed** we find over sensitivity and tearfulness, damaged or blocked emotions and a propensity to feel rather than think.

Toni Allen
The System of Symbols ©

The King of Cups

The king of Cups symbolises the masculine aspect of water.

With many men water's quality of bonding, as exhibited by showing emotion or affection, does not sit easily on their shoulders and is often viewed as a sign of weakness. The King of Cups is by no means a weak man, although he is sensitive and caring, and able to express his emotions; which in the eyes of some men represents vulnerability and feebleness.

I recall an incident several years ago when inadvertently I called at a friend's house at an inopportune moment. A friend of her husband's had been killed in a tragic accident and the husband and a male friend had just returned from the funeral. Both were sitting in the kitchen drinking coffee and reminiscing about what a good fellow the dead man had been. Rather than seeing me as an intrusion my friend asked me to stay, as she was finding the men's sorrow a little difficult to deal with on her own. The men's banter continued and we sat and listened intently to stories of both courage and playfulness. Suddenly the husband's friend burst into tears and wailed, "Oh God, I'm going to miss him." From that point on he sat and sobbed quietly, tears of grief streaming down his face in an unstoppable torrent. After ten minutes or so the husband slapped him on the back with "Come on mate," type of comments and a drawn, embarrassed expression. The friend was totally unable to stop and continued to weep quietly, talking through his tears, completely unconcerned by his overt display of emotion.

The husband's friend came across to me as a typical King of Cups. He was in no way ashamed of an emotional display at such an appropriate time. Meanwhile the husband was deeply self-conscious of the high emotion. My friend took me aside and commented on how much she admired her husband's friend's deep feeling and courage in being able to show it.

Most boys are taught from an early age to "be a man" and "not to cry". So for a man to grow up full of compassion and open tenderness is a rare breed indeed. In a reading the King of Cups will depict a good father figure, who enjoys playing with his children and mucking in during the early years by changing nappies and allowing his partner quality "time out" from the daily chores. He's a good dad and loving partner, but unless the cards show another side to his nature during work, the King of Cups tends to be overly sensitive in the work place and consequently lacks the stamina to pursue a strong career unless he's managed well by someone else.

His powerful awareness makes him an excellent artist or interior designer, able to merge with the needs of the general public or personal client. I have also seen the King of Cups strongly placed for men who enjoy renovating and restoring buildings, because they possess a keen focus on the vibration of previous occupants who have left their substance on the building. Male nurses and men who practice any spiritual work are also seen here.

When the King of Cups is **reversed** he becomes picky and grumpy. He tends to act out a routine of "poor me" and "nobody loves me" making everyone's life around him a misery. If in a relationship he can make his partner feel responsible for his unhappiness and treat her like an unloving mother, or make numerous demands on her time and vitality; because when out of balance no-one can love him enough, regardless of how much effort they put in. He can be a very sour character. Often it is useful to explore this card further by taking extra cards to find out what previous experiences have stopped his positive emotion from freely flowing and are keeping him bound in his own stagnated arena.

Key Words

Loving father
Good husband/partner
Artistic/sensitive
Professions associated with caring/sensing what others need, perhaps in interior design etc.

Reversed

Sour and compulsively seeks attention.
Feels unloved due to early trauma that has left him stuck in negative bonds.
Controlling

Toni Allen
The System of Symbols ©

The Coin Court Cards

The Page of Coins

The Page of Coins is the youth of wisdom or wealth, and comes under the realm of earth and the absolute.

As with all of the youthful Page cards the Page of Coins is learning to use the faculty at his disposal.

When we acquire new wisdom in the recognised form of certificates and qualifications we are then presented with the dilemma of where to utilise our talents. Do we wish to go on to further our education and use this wisdom to gain a place within higher study? Have we reached the highest goal we have set ourself and now it's a question of which type of career to make best use of this qualification? Then, if it's a matter of getting the best job with our certificated wisdom, how about how much it pays? Acquiring wisdom can lead to acquiring wealth, and, in matters of education one generally leads to the other.

All of this comes under the realm of the Page of Coins. He represents any of us when we have these decisions to make. Earth is his ruler, and the physical world and the substance which makes it liveable are his domain. To many of us this simply means money; the acquiring of it and the uses of it. Having enough money makes us feel safe and secure because it provides for our basic physical needs in the form of housing, heating, and food. Learning the art of wise use of money, and other physical resources, is something we all practice over and over again.

Some people only feel secure, and have a sense of oneness within themself, if they have enough money in the bank. Others do not care so much about the accumulation of wealth, but place their interest in wisdom and security in knowing who they are. The Page displays this conflict and the dilemma of whether we sacrifice wealth for the pursuit of higher wisdom or vice versa.

For some people the Page of Coins symbolises that they have reached a stage in their life where they have to decide what to do with certain resources available to them. Having a very beautiful diamond necklace worth thousands of pounds is a wonderful treasure to possess; but what is its worth, stuck away in a bank vault, when one's business needs cash flow? Does one sell the necklace to sustain the business? Or keep the treasure and let the business go under? In every day life there are many variations on this theme, such as the need to sell family heir looms, or often, when a couple move in together, the need to sell one of their properties. Should one do this, or should one do that?

The less positive side of the financial dilemma is where the individual constantly takes risks with finances and specifically the Page of Coins can represent the hardened gambler. Someone who constantly makes uneducated decisions regarding money, everyone from the man who throws his wages into a fruit machine, to the businessman who goes through a phase of bad financial control and chances losing everything.

When the Page of Coins comes up during a reading on the subject of marital breakdown the client is in a quandary about whether they will be financially self supportive should they decide to leave their partner. This card comes up for many women, who have already decided that their relationship is loveless, or completely beyond rekindling, but are trapped financially. Often they have children to support and cannot see themselves able to provide such a high standard of living on state benefit or a single wage. Whether to leave their partner or not is no longer an emotional decision, but a practical, financial one, based solely on physical security and the financial needs of all concerned.

Due to the Page of Coins connection with both Earth and the Absolute it can also represent a time of looking at who we are and where we are going in life. When we become out of balance and lose our inner sense of being, and trust in our own inner wisdom, then health problems often result and with this Page the warning signals come in a physical loss of balance. Dizziness, loss of spatial awareness, and depressive mood swings due to chronic indecision can all overwhelm us when we are in a negative Page of Coins phase.

When the card is upright it shows that decisions need to be made and when **reversed** it indicates that although one realises that things need to change one's wisdom has failed and there appears to be no positive way to change the situation. Sometimes the reversed Page also highlights the individual's need to take a chance and stop playing by safe bets in life. Wisdom does not grow by continually repeating the same patterns.

Key Words

Learning to use wisdom or wealth
The gambler
Body physically out of balance

Bach Remedy

Scleranthus – for those swayed between two possibilities, and physically for lack of balance.

Toni Allen
The System of Symbols ©

The Knight of Coins

Numerically the Coins are aligned with the Earth at 9 and unity at 1. At number 1 we find the Magician, the perfect embodiment of man with his full potential laid out before him. At 9 we have the Hermit, the seeker on the path, his inner light symbolically lighting his way with his lamp. We are all unique individuals, each with our own karma and personal samskara to deal with in this life time. We all express ourselves in multifarious ways and come in a variety of shapes and sizes. To find full expression of our unique selves we have been gifted with a physical body and consciousness. Through air we are given intellect, through fire brightness and beauty, through water the ability to bond with others and through earth our physical form. Thus the Knight of Coins depicts us on our life's journey of self discovery.

How many times have we heard people say "I don't know where

my life's taking me" or "I don't feel that this is the right course of action" or "I've lost my way". Alternatively we might hear them say, "I just know that this is right for me", or "I now feel that my priorities have changed and this is the way forward" or "My circumstances have changed and I have to make a go of what life presents to me, even though it's not of my choosing". All of these comments can be related to the Knight of Coins.

We are all born into our own particular set of circumstances and from there on our life unfolds. In adult life we continuously make conscious decisions which we believe will fulfil us, while unconsciously our karma plays out. It's all a journey of self discovery. But like any journey we need a travel plan, or at least an idea of where we're headed. If you pick up some balls of wool and knitting needles you can knit quite happily for hours, enjoying the practice and shape of different stitches, textures and colours. At the end of the day you may have a very interesting piece, but not necessarily an item of any use. Once in a while this is fine, but eventually the nature desires some feeling of accomplishment or worth from its labours. So, we then create a pattern and decide that our efforts will go into making a sweater or tea cosy. We have just as much fun, but at the end of it an article of some functional use is created. Pleased with our efforts we start another item, maybe a little more complex this time, and so on, until we reach perfection.

Life is the same. With no journey plan, or pattern, we drift aimlessly around, making the same mistakes or continuously ending up with what appear to be practice pieces with no results. The Knight of Coins upright symbolises those times when we are assured in our life plan and know where we are going and what we are striving to achieve. When **reversed** the card depicts us lost and floundering, unsure of where we are going, or even if we are on the right path.

The Knight of Coins covers every life situation in which we instinctively *know* whether proceeding with, or going into a particular situation, is right or wrong for us.
Here are just a few examples:-

When referring to career, or job, upright the Knight shows it is the right job, and reversed that we will not achieve our full potential.

When relationship difficulties arise the Knight **reversed** shows that we are unable to continue with something which does not allow us scope to fully express ourself, while upright it shows that our wisdom can aid us in resolving conflicts. Sometimes the questioner will be surprised to find the Knight upright, suggesting that they stay within the relationship, when all they want to do is walk away from a partner. In these circumstances the cards will be symbolising that there is further karma to resolve and that the questioner has more to learn from the given situation. Often the client will return some months later and express how certain "stuff" has been cleared and they now feel more positive about leaving and that there is less residue between them and their partner. At this time the Knight will also come out upright to show that leaving is now the correct path for them.

The Knight will also show whether a course of study is correct for the questioner.

In general terms the **reversed** Knight of Coins will show the questioner's general dilemma in being unfulfilled by their life circumstances. It is then the art of the Tarot reader to have the client take cards for the specific question of, "What is making you feel lost, and how do you rectify it?" Whatever the specifics the Knight of Coins reversed in a reading always shows that the questioner has lost a sense of value, and self worth, in their life. Things change. Career girls decide they would like to have a family, but find it difficult to express this, while highflying businessmen suddenly want to "drop out" and dip out of the rat race. What was once good and fulfilling is no more. Likewise people leave us, or tragedies take them away. That which we had based our lives on is no longer there to give us purpose or a reason to live. In these circumstances the Knight of Coins teaches us that value and self worth comes from more than money, or being valued through another. Courage, fortitude, resilience, independence, and living through deep suffering are all traits which crystallise our being, whether we like it or not.

Key Words

Being on the right path in life/Knowing which way to go in life
A good decision
Reversed - The wrong path for us
Lack of game plan in life/drifting
Suddenly being knocked off our path through unforeseeable circumstances

Toni Allen
The System of Symbols ©

Queen of Coins

The Queen of Coins is the Queen of Earth. Due to the quality of earth, which, sits at number 9 and has smell and crystalline form of its own, the taste and bond of water, heat and form of fire, touch of air and sound of ether; this Queen holds knowledge and understanding of the qualities held by all of the other Court Cards. For this reason she is often seen as a wise woman whom others take their problems to. She is a good listener and non-judgmental in attitude, and has the ability to stay grounded within herself and, although not necessarily unmoved, is definitely unruffled and not shocked by whatever someone might have to impart.

This is the wisdom side of the coins. As well as being a good counsellor, she may also depict the keen student, or someone who has studied hard and has a string of qualifications under their belt.

The wisdom and wealth side of the coins unite to form the

"perfect" or idealised business woman. This female uses her wisdom to create her own wealth and is often self-employed, in high management, or a position which involves self sufficiency and personal decision making. All manifestation takes place at earth and this creates a multi-talented individual.

It also produces a feminine type which is highly, and occasionally overly, concentrated on physical appearance. Making oneself presentable in a modern cut throat world of business is essential, but the Queen of Coins has the desire to carry it all one step more and, with some individuals, this can be taken to the point of having to buy a dress with the right label to display how much one is worth, or wear clothes of distinction which overwhelm the personality underneath rather than enhance it. This desire for wealth and opulence can spread into the home and the Queen of Coins will always display her wealth through either an abundance of items or a select few which are unquestionably worth a lot of money.

The Queen of Coins will always save a little harder to buy exactly what she wants rather than make do, although she is also a great one for a bargain, after all, the more she saves the more she can buy!

The dual nature of the Queen of Coins reflects the overall dual nature of mankind in the physical creation. She is either wise and generous with her time and wisdom, or prone to thriftiness with her money and resources. When **reversed** this queen has the ability to be downright mean, stubborn and unforgiving. The hoarder, the miser and the seeker on the path who believes that she is right, or that it is her wisdom alone and no-one else's, can all be seen in the reversed card.

Due to the coins sitting at the realm of earth the Queen of Coins can also depict a woman overly concerned with her physical body, not only through the clothes she wears but in its shape and size as well. Thus when the card is **reversed** and there is an over protective holding on to the physical creation the queen can depict a susceptibility to put on weight and over eating.

The earthiness of this queen can also show a fixed nature and a certain immobility in the concept of who we are. Through experience I have seen many variations on this theme. e.g. :- When going through divorce or separation the Queen of Coins will be reversed if the woman is endeavouring to come out of the situation financially secure; yet surrounding cards may suggest that she is wanting more than her due. On the other hand another woman going through a similar set of circumstances may also be depicted as this Queen, and yet upright, the card will show that she is secure in who she is within herself and is willing to go with the flow and change accordingly. Others may feel completely broken, and come up reversed, not through greed, but because all that they have known and recognised as extensions of themselves within the physical world are being taken away, or changed, and this has left them feeling vulnerable and destitute. In all circumstances surrounding cards will need to be carefully observed to assess how a particular situation is affecting the individuals wisdom or wealth.

Key Words

The Queen of wisdom and/or wealth.
Good adviser.
Business woman/career woman
Highly qualified, or taking qualifications
Positive sense of self identity
Enjoys displaying wealth through clothing/home decor/personal style important

Reversed
Meanness
Propensity to be overweight
Greedy
Poor self image or over the top display with clothes (often caused through feelings of inferiority)

Toni Allen
The System of Symbols ©

King of Coins

In many respects the King of Coins is very similar to the Queen, only the male version.

Here we find the archetypal businessman, someone who spends their whole life in business for the sole purpose of creating wealth and security. Banking, commerce, stock broking, and management are all indicated here. Some people work because their job is their vocation, a certain something which inspires and enlivens them. The King of Coin's inspiration is money, and it doesn't matter through what method he makes it. The King of Batons type might well be dedicated to art because if he never painted again it would make him feel hollow. Not so with the King of Coins type. This man will eagerly sell the art work for a profit, manage the artist because he feels a profit coming on, or organise exhibitions and sales of work. Yes, he makes money, and a reputation for himself, but

Toni Allen
The System of Symbols ©

hardly ever produces anything tangible. In fact, through years of experience I have found the King of Coins to be all of the above, or in management, or self employed. The most popular material expression of this man's abilities has often been shown to be in the building trade, where he runs his own team and creates strong "earthy" constructions.

As a workaholic the King of Coins stands streets ahead in his ability to clear a profit through his own wisdom and ingenuity. He constantly strives to be a "somebody" and measures his status, as illustrated to the world, by his family, home, life style and over all achievement. This having been done he can then sit back at the weekend and find himself content with who he is in the grand scheme of things. But what kind of a family man, or husband, does this make him? In some respects it makes him a little cool and aloof. Physical needs are attended to first and then he will mete out words of wisdom and direction. Sensual pleasures will be important to him, although sometimes food and the preparation, or indulgence in it may override sexual needs. After all putting on a spread for guests or business associates gains recognition in the world. Meanwhile activity in the bedroom, unless to prove prowess through the procreation of children, may be offered by way of gratitude or, when the card is **reversed**, for self gratification alone.

Like the Queen of Coins **reversed** the King of Coins can depict the same meanness and stubbornness. Meanness is not a very pleasant trait in anyone, but in a man the quality often has far wider consequences than in a woman. A mean man will not provide time, effort or money for his families needs. I have often seen the King of Coins reversed symbolise a family man of substantial resources. The house is perfect, the children go to private schools and from an outsiders point of view he is a good provider. His wife and family, however, experience a vastly different picture. They know only the man who leaves early for the office and comes home late, or stays away over night. He puts food on the table, but has no time for "soppiness" by way of cuddles. Often he has been brought up to "be a man" and the only yard stick he was given as a child is that to achieve in the world will gain love and acceptance. Thus, by the same token, he offers his children congratulations for gaining good exam results, but has little time to spare on their problems; while his wife is praised for an excellent dinner party and charming outfit, but not encouraged to be herself, or achieve in her own right. After all, it may detract from him, or mean that she has less time to attend to his needs. I have seen several examples of situations in which the wives of such men have rebelled during mid life, when he is at the peak of his career, and she has suddenly turned "hippy" or "arty", and started serving up macro biotic food to his business associates, or started bunking off to adult education to paint or sculpt.

Again the variations on these themes are exhaustive. Upright the card shows that the man feels good about himself and is physically successful, while **reversed** it depicts a time of crisis in which he holds rigidly onto what he believes he knows about himself. **Reversed** he can be shut down and difficult to get close to emotionally. It can also depict an individual overburdened by work, or overwhelmed by the responsibility of it all.

A couple of interesting examples stick in my mind for the King of Coins. During the beginning of one reading a young man had the King of Coins surrounded by other Coin cards. When I explained that I saw him surrounded by money and the quick exchange and making of it he chuckled. He leaned forwards toward me and said softly, "I work as a croupier in a casino. I'm surrounded by money all day..." He then laughed. "Pity it isn't all mine, eh!" Another young man was a student of mine. At the time I ran a small evening class and as part of the instruction I asked all of the students to take the Court Cards, shuffle them, and then fan them out face down. Without being able to see the pictures they then intuitively chose a card to represent themselves. The young man chose the King of Coins. At the time he was very "alternative" and into his spiritual path. When I suggested that his life path was to be a businessman creating lots of wealth and using money efficiently, he shrugged it off, and simply said that that wasn't for him. When the group sessions finished I didn't see him again. However, several years later another member of the group bumped into him, and she phoned to pass on a message. "He's working in insurance!" she exclaimed. "Short hair cut, snazzy suit and super car! Very prosperous...and very content. He asked me to tell you he's very happy as the King of Coins...and that you were right...it just took him a while longer to find out what he was about."

Key Words

Business man
Responsible
High achiever
Emphasis on home life style as a sign of prosperity
Reversed
Meanness
Stubbornness
Lack of warmth
Excessive self control
Control of others for self-protection/or aggrandisement

Bach Remedy

Elm.....especially when the card is reversed, as it helps with the sudden feeling of being overwhelmed, even though the individual is usually highly capable.

Toni Allen
The System of Symbols ©

So, who gets on with who?

When I teach students on a one to one basis I first run through the Court Card characters pretty much as I've laid out so far. Then I take all of the Court Cards and lay them face up and play what I call the "Marriage Game". Many a student has smirked and paired them of in Kings and Queens of their own suit. Easy isn't it? Or is it? I give them a moment to think and then ask "Will the King and Queen of Swords really stay married, or be happy together, for very long?" "I shouldn't think so," they reply. "Then why marry them off?" I ask.

Now the fun starts. It may sound like a silly game, but when practised it gives invaluable insight into the possibilities arising during a reading. Another trick is to think of people you know, or have met, who are typical of each Court Card. Flesh them out a bit. If Auntie Flo is a lovely Queen of Cups type then keep her in mind as you place her next to a King. If your best friend is going through a divorce then maybe she's the Queen of Swords....and what about Fred, hasn't he just been made a manager? How about the King of Coins for him?

The following are brief examples and by no means an exhaustive repertoire. Play the game yourself, or with a friend, and make notes on your comments and insights. You'll be amazed at the wealth of ideas and information that springs up and offers invaluable knowledge when put into practice during a proper reading.

Queen of Coins and King of Cups

She is going to be strong and business like. She likes abundance and good things in life. He is sensitive and caring. He'll make a wonderful father, but she might have to give up a prosperous career in order to produce children for him. Is he able to provide enough income while she does this? Maybe not, unless he's got his own private fortune tucked away. Even without children she'll be the dominant one. She may appear a little hard to him. If he's creative then she may view his work as whimsical and not a "proper job", unless she takes on the role of being his manager or agent; and then the world's their oyster....She'll make his efforts make money, and keep him organised.

Queen of Swords and King of Swords

Both too bossy, embittered, rigid and wounded to get on well together. Their sex life might start off intense but end up being criticised by one another, which would lead to a lack of relaxation and pleasure.

Page of Swords and any Queen

At first he may appear interesting, outrageous and incorrigible. A passion to be tamed. He's a loveable rogue, and generally very sexy....but I have yet to see anyone happily married, or in long term relationship, to this chap...it simply doesn't last. He's too slippery, diverse and dishonest to be stable in a relationship. If the couple are still together then she is probably a battered wife, or too frightened to leave him.

The Page of Swords can also represent a female and in those instances it is simply the other way around, with the King character being the long suffering partner. She just might meet her match in the King of Swords....but it's not a happy union.

The King and Queen of Batons

By far the happiest couple in the pack! Both are fun loving and joyful. They are content with who they are and therefore able to give their partner space to be who they are. Both enjoy doing things for each other and for other people. They usually have a great sex life too!

There are many more permutations of Kings and Queens, Pages and Knights, Kings and Pages. Play the game. Try them out. Have fun!

Toni Allen
The System of Symbols ©

The End

The end is but a beginning, and just like our friend the ouroboros, the serpent biting its own tail, we come to learn that all endings are but a renewal.

I hope that you have enjoyed my insights and that in the never ending cycle of birth, death and rebirth that you will meditate on the images and words offered, and carry the inspiration forward with your own intuition and creativity.

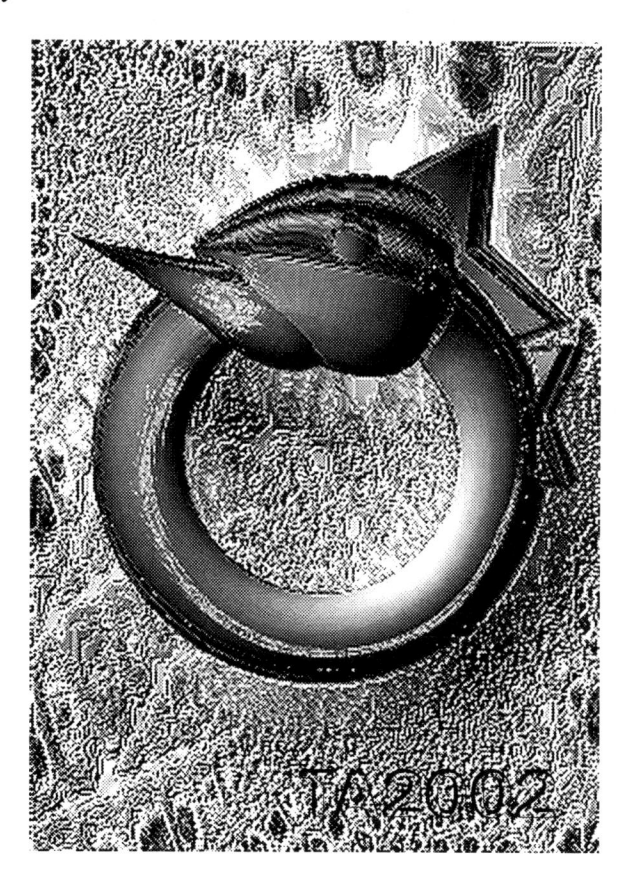

Toni Allen
The System of Symbols ©

Toni Allen has been a tarot reader since 1980 and an astrologer since 1990. She has lectured on the symbolism and use of the tarot at many venues in the UK, as well as teaching at adult education and to private students. During many of her talks she offers hands on demonstrations so that members of the audience can witness the power of the cards for themselves and take home their own personal message. She has an international clientele, built up over the years due to the accuracy of her readings.

Toni Allen perfected her unique system of symbols over 20 years ago and has been teaching it ever since. Using a system based on vedic numerology and symbolism she moves away from pictorial tarot and invites students to learn a new way of seeing the cards.

Owing to popular demand she now reveals her secrets. Her system demystifies minor card interpretation, offering fresh insight for accomplished readers and an easy to comprehend guide for beginners. The rational system outlined depends on nothing except the numbers and elements referred to in the minor cards, therefore leaving the student free from any confusion or constraint that reliance upon pictorial pips can bring.

The text encourages personal exploration while at the same time offering spiritual enlightenment by revealing how the tarot is a symbolic and numerical reflection of life and the universe. With true understanding of the essence of each card and why it interprets as it does the student is more able to connect with their own intuitive abilities and therefore gain confidence, regardless of previous experience.

All 78 cards are described in both their symbolic terms and equated with modern day interpretations and many real life examples offering an holistic approach. Many of the cards are associated with Bach Flower Remedies to add an effective healing tool.

Throughout The System of Symbols is illustrated with black and white images of Toni's own tarot designs, all of which can be viewed in colour at www.tarotastrology.co.uk or www.toniallen.co.uk